Jo Com
Co

THE DISINHERITED FAMILY

ELEANOR RATHBONE

THE DISINHERITED FAMILY

*With an Introductory Essay
by Suzie Fleming*

FALLING WALL PRESS

First published in 1924
Third edition 1927
This edition first published by Falling Wall Press in 1986

Printed in Great Britain by Billing & Sons Ltd., Worcester
Cover printed by Doveton Press Ltd., Bristol
Cover design by John Morton

ISBN 0 905046 14 5 (cased)
ISBN 0 905046 13 7 (paperback)

The text of *The Disinherited Family* used here is that of the third
edition, as republished in 1949 by George Allen & Unwin Ltd.
in an edition entitled *Family Allowances*.

Falling Wall Press Ltd.
75 West Street, Old Market, Bristol BS2 0BX, England

CONTENTS

INTRODUCTION
ELEANOR RATHBONE:
SPOKESWOMAN FOR A MOVEMENT
by Suzie Fleming

THE
DISINHERITED FAMILY

Part One
THE PRESENT ECONOMIC STATUS OF
THE FAMILY

Illustrations

Plates between pages 120 and 121

NOTE TO 'ELEANOR RATHBONE: SPOKESWOMAN FOR A MOVEMENT'

Because Eleanor Rathbone and the movement which won Family Allowances have been so hidden since the 1940s, I felt that introducing them had to be the priority; this was not the place for a detailed critical analysis of Eleanor Rathbone's writing, nor to draw detailed comparisons between the movements for State payments to women of the 1940s and 1980s. Today's movement, built on the one which went before, is inevitably broader in its demands, seeking payment not only for the work that mothers do, but for all the two-thirds of the world's work that the United Nations estimates is being done by women.

S.F.
January 1984

ELEANOR RATHBONE:
SPOKESWOMAN FOR A MOVEMENT
by Suzie Fleming

ALL IN A LIFETIME

Eleanor Rathbone was born in Liverpool in 1872, into a wealthy non-conformist family which already had a distinguished reputation for campaigning radicalism. Her great great grandfather, a Liverpool shipowner, had been one of the founding members of the Liverpool Anti Slave Trade Society, her grandfather was listed by the Tory Government as a subversive for his Reform views, and her father, the first Rathbone to enter Parliament (as a Liberal MP), was responsible for the introduction of district nursing, whereby for the first time nurses went into the homes of people too poor to pay for medical help.

But it was Eleanor Rathbone who made Rathbone a household name. She was among the most famous of the suffragette leaders; she was the most politically independent of the women MPs elected to Parliament in the wake of women's suffrage; and above all she was for over thirty years the leading spokeswoman of the movement for financial independence for women. Her greatest achievement was the success of the campaign for Family Allowances, the first universal State payment to mothers, which she led.

Eleanor Rathbone first made her name in the suffragette movement in the years before World War I. By 1919, when Millicent Garrett Fawcett retired as President of the National Union of Women's Suffrage Societies (NUWSS) — the largest of the suffragette organizations — it was Eleanor Rathbone who was elected to succeed her. The significance of that election is difficult to recapture now because the size and scope of the suffragette movement has been so misrepresented in popular histories, but this was a mass women's movement on a scale which has not been seen in Britain since. Demonstrations of hundreds of thousands of women were commonplace, not only in London but in Lancashire and Yorkshire; women of all classes underwent forced feeding and even death in prison for the cause; and there were hundreds of local suffragette groups, the majority of whom were represented by the NUWSS.

The suffragettes campaigned for the vote as a means to the end of greater social and economic freedom for women, so that most of them were also involved in the myriad campaigns which were the backbone and fuel of the women's suffrage movement. Eleanor Rathbone was no exception. In the years before World War I she spoke all over Lancashire and Cheshire for the NUWSS, was President of Liverpool Women's Industrial Council, Honorary Secretary of the Victoria Women's Settlement, organizer of the Domestic Workers Insurance Society and a founder of Liverpool University's School of Social Science, where she also lectured. In 1909 she became the first woman member of Liverpool City Council, elected as an Independent because she put women's priorities above party politics, and never joined any of the political parties. She had also already achieved a national reputation as a campaigning social worker and social investigator with the publication of two major reports: *How the Casual Labourer Lives*, about dock workers and their dependants, and *The Condition of Widows under the Poor Law in Liverpool*, which was written as evidence for the campaign for State payments to widows, of which she was a leading member.

From the first, Eleanor Rathbone saw the campaigns for women's rights and for financial independence as inseparable. Since 1904 she had been arguing not only for equal pay but for payments to mothers, and in 1917 she founded the Family Endowment Committee, whose report, *Equal Pay and the Family*, made detailed recommendations for a State endowment of motherhood. In 1924 *The Disinherited Family* was published, setting out a wide-ranging and authoritative case for financial independence for mothers and maintenance allowances for children, to be paid to every mother. This book was to become a classic in her lifetime, and provided the theoretical base for what became known as the Family Allowance Campaign. And from 1929 she carried the case into the House of Commons with her election as an Independent MP.

For the next twenty years her name was linked with the campaign for Family Allowances, and the introduction of Family Allowances as a State payment to mothers undoubtedly owed more to Eleanor Rathbone than to any other individual. Throughout the 1920s and 1930s, she worked to mobilize support from women and men outside as well as inside Parliament. Her political reputation was such that even in 1926, a moment of great bitterness against the upper class, she was invited to address not only numerous women's meetings but also miners' union meetings all over the North of England.

But it is important to add that Eleanor Rathbone's activities were not confined to Britain. As well as attending a variety of international conferences to argue the case for Family Allowances, she was deeply

committed to the view that women's needs were in general the same
internationally whatever their race or nation. In 1932 she visited
India to see for herself the condition of Indian women's lives, and to
find what Indian women wanted from independence; in 1934 she went
to Palestine to inform herself firsthand on the situation there, particularly as it related to Palestinian and Jewish women; in 1937 she was in
Barcelona to see for herself what the Spanish Republic had achieved,
and in Yugoslavia, Romania and Czechoslovakia to assess the threat of
a Nazi takeover, and strengthen the case against Appeasement. By the
late 1930s and early 1940s, she was as likely to be quoted in the press
for her outspoken opposition to the racist immigration laws (by which
Jewish refugees from Nazi Europe were either being refused entry to
Britain or interned on arrival) as for her vocal and continuous pressure
on the Government to introduce Family Allowances.[1]

In campaigning for State payment for mothers, she based herself on
what she believed to be a mass movement for financial independence
for women, and on her own personal experience of financial independence and the freedom it had allowed her — the freedom not to have
to live with a man for financial support (from 1919 she shared her
household with a woman); the freedom to be in politics as an
independent because she had the financial means to pay for her own
election campaigns; the freedom to determine her own life as far as
was possible within the constraints which operated for women. It was
to her credit that she wanted every woman to have a right to that
freedom, and that she identified so closely with women whose situation
was in many respects so different from hers.

The introduction of Family Allowances in 1945 was widely regarded
as the most radical of all the post-war Welfare State legislation. It
provided for a redistribution of wealth in women's favour more substantial than any single piece of legislation before or since. As such,
Family Allowances represented 'the beginning of a movement destined
to make more difference to the status of women and the welfare of
children than anything that has happened in the world since the
beginning of Christianity.' (D.F. p.280.)

Putting Unpaid Work on the Agenda
Eleanor Rathbone was already in her fifties when she wrote *The
Disinherited Family*, and in it she distilled the ideas and lessons of
long years of campaigning. While books alone don't change the world,
this one was peculiarly successful in driving home the claims that
women had been making to a share in the wealth they help to produce,
by making their case in a form that legislators and policy-makers would

find difficult to deny. Beveridge, whose report of 1942 laid the basis for the post-war Welfare State legislation in Britain, wrote in 1948:

The campaign for family allowances . . . received its greatest impetus in the publication twenty-four years ago of *The Disinherited Family* . . . In all the legislation of recent years . . . the greatest break with old tradition under the influence of a new idea is represented by the Family Allowances Act . . . What [Eleanor Rathbone] had done was by any standard amazing.[2]

And he added:

The Disinherited Family is to be read and read again, not just for what it has accomplished but as an inexhaustible source of ideas as to what remains to be done.[3]

The book is an analysis of various alternative strategies for 'family policy' — that is, it examines the State's financial relationship to the family, and to women and children in particular. Its fundamental contribution is to place 'the family' and women's work in the home in an economic context, to show that bearing and raising children is not simply a private undertaking but a socially and economically necessary job, and to argue that the women who do this work and the children they produce are entitled to a share of the economic wealth of society in their own right.

Since the 1960s, when movements of single mothers on both sides of the Atlantic demonstrated outside Welfare offices to demand that the State recognize the value of their work in the home,[4] the value of domestic work to the economy has re-emerged as a political issue. Taking the lead from single mothers, other housewives have increasingly been voicing publicly what they have always discussed in private — that their work should be recognized, quantified, valued, and ultimately paid.[5] In the early 1970s an international Wages for Housework Campaign was launched demanding a State wage for housework, based on the women's liberation movement, and the mass movements of mothers, single and married, which were evident in the public political arena. (In Britain, for the first time since the 1940s, mothers were mobilizing on the issue of Family Allowances. [See p.94 below.]) Since that time, the discussion of women's unpaid work has escalated — by 1980 the United Nations had produced figures estimating that women do two-thirds of the world's work, receive only 10 per cent of world income and own less than 1 per cent of world assets.[6]

Governments and political parties are now increasingly aware that the movement for financial independence for the women who have been doing that unpaid work has to be reckoned with. In Britain in 1975, Barbara Castle, Social Services Secretary and former member of the Parliamentary Select Committee which had felt the impact of the

Family Allowance Campaign of 1972-3 (see p.94 below), said in introducing the Labour Government's new 'Child Benefit' Bill:

It is appropriate that this measure should be put before Parliament in International Women's Year . . . It may be premature to talk of giving the wife and mother her own wage, but she certainly needs control of her own budget if the family is to be fed and clothed.[7]

In 1979 the Liberal Party's National Conference passed a resolution calling for a State salary to be paid to mothers or fathers (depending on who was looking after the children).[8] In 1982 the National Conference of Labour Women was examining proposals for a 'home responsibility payment',

. . . a taxable benefit paid to those with the care of children or infirm relatives, whether or not both parents were in paid employment.[9]

In the United States in 1977, the first national women's conference in over one hundred years, which was attended by 40,000 women, passed a resolution calling for welfare to be called a wage:

. . . and just as with other workers, homemakers receiving income transfer payments should be afforded the dignity of having that payment called a wage, not welfare.[10]

Since that time, discussions of a 'Displaced Homemakers Act', proposing that grants be made available to help divorced and widowed women over forty who have provided 'unpaid household services' for a number of years;[11] proposals for a Social Security wage for housework, whereby women's pension rights would include credits for the years spent working in the home;[12] provisions for an unwaged wife to have legal entitlement to half her husband's income;[13] and over four hundred other bills intended to provide financial and practical help for housewives have been before US Congress.[14] In 1978, the US President's Special Assistant on Women's Affairs stated publicly that 'the central issue for women is economic, and that the nub is payment to housewives'.[15] And in Canada, the Advisory Council on the Status of Women has produced a document evaluating the pros and cons of some form of State payment to women for their work in the home.[16]

A similar phenomenon of an international movement for financial recognition for women's work in the home and an international response was the context for Eleanor Rathbone's work. But in the 1980s that movement is even more widely international, for now the weight of Third World women's needs is adding a new dimension and urgency to the issue, and making clear just how universal is both women's unpaid work and their insistence on payment. At the 1980 United Nations Mid-Decade Conference on Women, Paragraph 103 of the World Conference Programme of Action called on member nations of the UN to:

Redefine, where appropriate, the term 'worker' in accordance with the ILO standard definition of labour force participation, in order that the contribution of unpaid work that women do in the farms, at home and in other fields can be recognized and reflected in the gross national product.[17]

And the UN International Labour Office's Bulletin *Women at Work* not only consistently documents the unpaid work of women in the Third World, the East and the West, but has commented in a recent editorial:

Most women are permanently working, but not permanently employed in the workforce. It is this difference between work and employment which is a major issue today ...

Women are food-providers, education-givers and health-dispensers for the family and society. They manage a range of jobs involving food-growing, food-gathering and food-distributing. In education . . they evolve, design as well as deliver, the code of behaviour on life as teachers and mothers . . . In addition, women are weavers and makers of garments, cleaners and sweepers and furnishers of homes ...

If the distinction between market and non-market activities of women were to be abolished and economic value assigned to all work performed by them, there would be a number of important consequences . . . In the coming debate of the 1980s and beyond the vast human endeavour of women working will have to be taken into account.[18]

It is appropriate that it is at this moment of widespread international interest in women's unpaid work that *The Disinherited Family* is being republished. The 'disinherited family' which it describes is now visible in the Third World as well as the metropolis. Eleanor Rathbone traces the process by which, as a cash economy grows, the contribution made to the economy by the work of women and children becomes increasingly hidden, and women and children find themselves financially dependent on a man's wage; and she describes in great detail what the implications of this development are for women, children and men.

In confronting the contradiction of an economic system which on the one hand assumes that wages are related in some way to labour, and on the other lays down that the wage paid to a man should also support a wife and children, Eleanor Rathbone lays bare the poverty and dependence of women and children which are the inevitable result. The inexorable logic of her case for direct provision for women and children, including the relationship between that provision and the achievement of equal pay for waged work, was never seriously refuted, even by those who disagreed profoundly with her specific proposals.

These questions are crucial today when the payments and services women won with the creation of the Welfare State are under attack; and when the premise that men need a 'family wage' is again being used to justify lower wages for women as against men, and for men getting

priority for jobs in the context of high unemployment.[19] So, too, with
the appearance of a flood of studies dealing with women's unpaid work
in the home,[20] the republication of this book is particularly important
because it goes beyond their frame of reference to confront not only the
existence of that unpaid work — which they are finally recognizing, docu-
menting and computing — but the question of who should pay for it.

Recent histories of the introduction of Family Allowances have
played down both Eleanor Rathbone's contribution to that legislation
and the legislation's significance for women, at the very moment when
women are once again mobilizing for State payments to mothers.[21] To
present the introduction of Family Allowances as something other than
a women's victory is to deprive women of their history at the very
moment when it could be strengthening their claims. It seemed vital
therefore that a brief account of that history should be published
alongside this book. In addition, that a book written nearly sixty years
ago should be immediately relevant today is a tribute not only to its
author, but to the massive women's movement which produced and
shaped her. I have therefore tried below not only to give Eleanor
Rathbone her due, but to describe something of that movement. I
begin by describing some of the influences on Eleanor Rathbone in the
years before she wrote *The Disinherited Family*, and then trace the
continuity of the movement for financial independence for women
through the 1930s and 40s. This provides the context for the campaigning which resulted in the achievement of State payments to
mothers in 1945.

A NEW HOPE AND PURPOSE

The period between Eleanor Rathbone's adolescence and 1924, when
The Disinherited Family was first published, was one of great social
upheaval. These were years during which hundreds of thousands of
people went on demonstrations and mass strikes, ended only by the
outbreak of World War I in 1914; they were years which saw the
blossoming of the women's movement. Eleanor Rathbone was part of
this ferment and was shaped by it:

. . . she was, in the middle 'nineties, a fierce feminist. A dozen years later, nearly
all active-minded young women were feminists and their feminism was expressed
by adherence to the women's suffrage movement. Eleanor was a suffragist —
talked suffrage, in fact, with an ardour approaching importunity — at a time when
the public was scarcely awake to it as a practical political issue.[22]

She was sixteen years old when news of the Bryant and May match girls
strike appeared in the newspapers in 1888, seventeen when the London
dockers marched through the centre of London with wives, mothers

and girlfriends, carrying 'stinking onions, old fish-heads, and indescribable pieces of meat stuck on spikes, to show the city magnates what the dockers had to live on.'[23] When the Manningham Mill girls went on strike in the early 1890s, and when laundresses in London demonstrated with railway workers in Hyde Park in their attempt to form a union, Eleanor Rathbone was starting university.

Contemporary observers noticed the

... stir and murmur among women. Overworked mothers and wives, young girls too and older women who were unmarried, and living by their own labour, at factory or workshop, wakened as from sleep and began to conceive new hope and purpose.[24]

This 'new hope and purpose' was typical not only of working class women, but also of the middle class women active from the 1880s onwards. Eleanor Rathbone's was the first generation to reap the benefits of the feminist agitation of the mid-nineteenth century for financial independence for women of their class. Women had fought for the right to a university education and access to professional jobs (and therefore an independent income) to escape from the claustrophobia of the Victorian family they had grown up in as daughters, and which awaited them as wives. They knew only too well, from their own experience, how little value was placed on women's time in the home, and were desperate to break out through the professional channels they were forcing open.

Florence Nightingale's *Cassandra*, written in 1852 when she was thirty-two and completed on her return from the Crimea, gives a vivid impression of the conditions of life of the wives and daughters of 'society men'. Her account, which is obviously autobiographical, makes clear that middle and upper class women were forced to submit to a daily routine which was making them mentally and physically ill.

A married woman was heard to wish that she could break a limb that she might have a little time to herself. Many take advantage of the fear of 'infection' to do the same ... Women never have an half-hour in all their lives (excepting before or after anybody is up in the house) that they can call their own, without fear of offending or of hurting someone.

... time is the most valuable of all things. If they had come every morning and afternoon and robbed us of half-a-crown we should have had redress from the police. But it is laid down, that our time is of no value. If you offer a morning visit to a professional man, and say, 'I will just stay an hour with you, if you will allow me, till so and so comes back to fetch me'; it costs him the earnings of an hour, and therefore he has a right to complain. But women have no right, because it is *only* their time.'[25]

The passionate anger of women like Florence Nightingale was the motive force in opening up some of the professions to women. They wanted a life of their own, and fought for the right to higher education which would give them the authority to enter the already existing professions, and to bless with the name of professionalism — and a wage — the charitable 'voluntary' work into which more and more of their creative energies were being channelled. In the 1870s the universities were opened to women for the first time, and in 1886 were empowered to give women degrees. At the same time the Married Women's Property Act of 1882 meant that married women could keep their own earnings. Women were insisting on earning their own money for the work they did outside the home both because, as Florence Nightingale so clearly pointed out, they knew their time would have no value until it was paid for, and because they needed that financial independence. As single women they wanted to live away from home (as the upper and middle class professional women increasingly did by the early twentieth century), and if they did marry, women needed the money to be able to lead their own lives and to survive a divorce if their husbands so disapproved of their new independence that they made their lives intolerable.[26]

The charitable work that had once been expected of these women as part of their household duties was transformed into a source of independent income as women turned nursing, visiting the sick and other 'good works' into paid jobs. The first army of social investigators who went into the homes of the poor, gathering data and finding out how the poor actually lived, was primarily a women's army. Some of them became famous for their work, which provided the detailed background to the welfare legislation that they helped to put on the statute books. Beatrice Webb's *My Apprenticeship* records something of their experience, but there were hundreds of women like her, including Eleanor Rathbone, who worked as a social worker in Liverpool from 1897. They used their experience working for bodies like the Charitable Organisation Societies to press for social legislation. They took part in the University Settlement projects which sprang up in the working class areas of many of the big cities, and provided an education for the women and men of the upper middle classes into how the 'other (much larger) half' lived. They were the generation of women who took on the jobs opening up with the expansion of State and local government: they worked as sanitary inspectors, factory inspectors and district nurses. And they stood for office on School Boards, Boards of Poor Law Guardians and local councils.

In organizing to rid themselves of the unpaid philanthropic work which was expected of middle class women as part of their duties, these women first of all socialized that housework — and then increasingly forced the State to pay for it. This thrust by middle class women perfectly complemented demands from working class women for the State to bear a larger share of the cost of reproduction of the workforce, so that the need of women of different sectors to off-load their unpaid housework provided an impetus for the creation of the 'Welfare State'. This meeting of needs also meant that middle class and working class women for the first time found themselves working together side by side, campaigning for women's representation on local bodies like the Poor Law Guardians[27] and then sitting on these bodies. This fight for representation on local government and welfare boards was an integral part of the fight not only for a 'Welfare State' but for representation in Parliament through the vote. In this fight middle class women naturally looked to working class women as allies, since without their support there was no chance of victory. And that need for allies in turn forced a new awareness of the priorities of working class women.[28]

Working Class Priorities

One major working class priority was for cash to be available to women who were destitute, since working class women were always only one step away from starvation. In particular, mothers who found themselves destitute either through desertion or widowhood, or because their husbands were unemployed, had to have access to financial support from the State. In 1913 the Poor Law still provided the only source of State support for widows, unsupported mothers and the families of most unemployed men[29] – those people who today would be eligible for State support through Supplementary Benefits (welfare). The history of the Poor Law, and its gradual transformation through National Assistance to Supplementary Benefit, is a crucial backdrop to the fight for women's right to economic independence, and it is therefore no accident that pressure for reform in the administration of the Poor Law should have been a central part of Eleanor Rathbone's feminist political activity in the years before World War I; nor that other leading suffragettes had their own history of involvement with Poor Law reform. Emmeline Pankhurst, for example,

> . . . began her public political career by standing for the School Board and marching with the unemployed to the Poor Law Office where they demanded the right to work. She was active on the Board of Guardians, which administered poor relief, and she campaigned for better conditions for people in the workhouse.[30]

The basic principles of the 'New Poor Law' of 1834, which was still in operation at the beginning of the twentieth century, are those that underpin the modern welfare system which is its direct descendant. The overriding principle was that State assistance should be linked to deterrence, so that there should be more hardship involved in getting money from the State directly than in getting a paid job (however low the wages) or in getting money from an individual man (however unpleasant the working conditions in the home — including the level of domestic violence). Then, as now, the intention was to 'encourage' women to search for a job, or to accept financial dependence on a man, whatever the terms, rather than look to the State for financial support. And where the families of unemployed men were concerned, deterrence 'encouraged' men or women to accept any wages rather than apply for poor relief, and so keep down the general level of wages in the area.

But at the same time there was always the contradictory need to make sure that adults and children did not starve and ruin their health to the point where they would no longer be fit for work. Ultimately it was the bargaining power of the claimant which determined the relative importance given to the provision of help or the insistence on deterrence, so that the extent to which the punitive aspects of the Poor Law could be enforced (in particular, the provision whereby no cash payments would be made, and help given only to those who entered an institution, the Workhouse) was always variable.[31] In addition, there was a great deal of flexibility in the administration of the Poor Law, because all its provisions were recommendations rather than law, since poor relief was financed out of local rates and administered locally. 'Boards of Guardians' elected by local ratepayers set policy for the area.

By the early twentieth century, payment of 'out' relief, i.e. relief paid to people living outside the Workhouse in their own homes, was considerable. There was a growing conflict in the minds of the Poor Law Guardians between their anxiety to maintain 'deterrence' and their awareness of the hardships faced by the women and men applying for relief, a conflict heightened by both the militancy of the unemployed and the arrival of working class members on to the Boards of Guardians with the abolition of property qualifications for these elections in 1894.

A number of these working class Guardians were women, who were anxious to get elected in part because the majority of the Poor Law claimants were women (single mothers, deserted wives, widows and old age pensioners claiming in their own right, as well as wives of men who claimed). Once elected these Guardians battled away to improve the workings of the Poor Law, transforming the day-to-day provision of relief while politicians were still debating whether the Poor Law and its punitive provisions should be abolished, and enabling women to get some money for themselves by ensuring that in most parts of the country 'out relief' was paid more widely, and with fewer sanctions and intrusions by the Poor Law officials.[32]

In Bolton, Lancashire, a 'Bolton Association for the return of Women as Poor Law Guardians' was formed in 1897, working closely with the local Women's Co-operative Guild.[33] Selina Cooper, a former cotton mill worker and a mother, and Harriette Beanland, stood together as Labour candidates for the Bolton Board of Guardians in 1904,[34] and their election address explains their interest in standing:

... as the bulk of the recipients of *Poor Law Relief* are of the *Labouring Classes*, we are of the opinion that it is to the best interest of the *Poor* to be directly represented by people who can *realise* their *sufferings* and *privations* to the full extent. We would also remind you that a large number of applicants for relief are *women* and *children*, and from past experience, we have no hesitation in saying, that it is almost imperative that *women* should be on the *Board* in order to administer acts and receive confidence that could not be extended to men in the same capacity ...[35]

Mrs Bury, another Lancashire women who sat as a Poor Law Guardian, recalled:

... before women sat on our Board all girls with sad histories had to come alone before a large body of men. Now, after I had pleaded with the Board and got a resolution passed, the women Guardians and matrons dealt with the cases in a separate room.[36]

Middle class mothers who sat as Poor Law Guardians were also drawn to sympathize with applicants for relief. We know of Mrs Pankhurst's involvement with claimants because her daughter Sylvia recorded it.[37] But there were many other Poor Law Guardians and other women doing social work whose sympathies were channelled in the same way, both as a result of the militancy of the poor and because their direct contact with working class women brought a new understanding of how working class women had to live.

The impact of their contact with working class women was reflected in the views and writings of the social workers and social investigators who formed the lower rungs of the State apparatus, including Eleanor Rathbone. In 1913, her *Report on the Conditions of Widows under the Poor Law in Liverpool*[38] appeared, the result of fifteen years' experience working with some of the poorest families in Liverpool, and a major contribution to the campaign for widows' benefits. (See D.F. pp.207-8 and 375.) In this report, Eleanor Rathbone's understanding of a woman's situation, and the sophistication of her arguments in favour of financial recognition for the work done by mothers, are both firmly grounded in her first-hand experience of the lives of the widows she had met. But her style is that of a campaigner and not simply a social investigator, and her case not only the humanitarian plea that women needed the money, but also that women had earned it. She advocated a State scheme of widows' pensions, on the same principle as the non-contributory Old Age Pension introduced in 1908 for the over-seventies, at the same time pointing out that 'pension' is an inappropriate word in this context:

It should . . . be recognised that a widow who is doing her duty by her young children . . . is not a pensioner upon the bounty of the State, but is earning the money which she draws from it by services just as valuable to the community as those of a dock labourer, or a plumber, or a soldier, perhaps even not much less valuable than those of the Relieving Officer or Poor Law Guardian who now browbeats or patronizes her.[39]

In making the case for the social importance and financial value of the work of child-rearing, Eleanor Rathbone was grounding her arguments for financial recognition for mothers in the importance of their product to the State. In 1913 this was a telling consideration for any Government, because the falling birth rate had threatened the supply of labourers for the economy and made the survival and welfare of babies and children a new priority.

THE FALLING BIRTH RATE
Since labour power is the most crucial element in the production of profit, securing an adequate and appropriate supply of 'citizens' and workers has always been a major factor in State planning. From the slave trade which transported millions of people to other continents to work for the colonial economy, to the Enclosure Acts and Highland Clearances which forced people off the land and created a massive pool of labour power which had no option but to sell itself for wages, to the international population planning of today, the first question for governments and industry has always been how many people of what type are needed or not needed where.[40]

From the 1870s onwards, the birth rate in Britain was falling, and at the same time Britain's imperial supremacy was threatened by the growing industrial imperialist nations of Germany and the United States. The question of guaranteeing the supply of labour power, in terms of both the 'quality' and quantity of present and future workers, could no longer be left only to 'natural replacement' and immigration. A rapidly falling birth rate meant there was no guarantee that the supply would match the demand for new workers.

The falling birth rate therefore caused a huge shift in State thinking and planning. Infant and child health became matters for public concern, as the State had a new interest in their survival; the health and welfare of adult workers carried a new weight because health and strength could not be damaged beyond repair by poverty if labour power was in short supply; the welfare of mothers, without whom there would be no future citizens and workers, had ultimately to be considered. In other words, the falling birth rate was a major factor in the development of the Welfare State in Britain, *and was the terrain on which Eleanor Rathbone fought for Family Allowances*. It is important therefore to look at what lay behind it, in order to see why and how women were having fewer children — because there can be little doubt that it was *women* who brought the birth rate down as a result of their own conscious actions. It was women's active participation in history through their decision to bear fewer children which laid down the basis for the creation of the Welfare State.

The Move to the Cities
In 1851 only half the population of England and Wales lived in urban districts. Fifty years later the proportion of the population living in towns had grown to 77 per cent, and was still growing. At the same time, it was unmistakable that the birth rate was falling fastest in precisely those urban areas. The massive migration from countryside to town revealed by these figures is still going on in most of the world, but for people born and raised in a town or city in a metropolitan country it is hard to conceive what the change means for the millions of people who have experienced it, and in particular what it has meant for women. In late nineteenth-century England, in a pattern which has been repeated the world over, the exodus from the countryside was led by young people, always the most mobile in any society, and of those, women were in the majority. In 1911, domestic service was still the largest source of employment in England.[41] Young women went to the towns to earn their keep when the family could no longer afford to keep them at home, and in the big cities there was a surplus of women over men.

Something of what these changes must have meant for women in nineteenth-century England can be gauged from the experience of women who have faced them more recently, not only from Third World women who have spoken of their experience of migration to new countries,[42] but from the experience of women who have left their homes and families in rural areas to move to cities in the same country.[43] The move from the countryside means first of all that young people are freed from the restraints and tradition imposed by parents, grandparents, uncles and aunts. Women have talked of the family expectations and duties in a rural society, where the need for children to help work the land combines with traditional assumptions about women's place in society to ensure that they marry young and have many children. The move to the city means a new independence for women, which is reflected in new expectations.

The burgeoning demands and strength of the working class movement — to which women were integral — and the falling birth rate both expressed these expectations. When women married, they refused to give birth to a child every year, as the most effective way to reduce the burden of work and increased poverty that resulted from each new birth, and as a protest against the current conditions of motherhood. In other words, *women as producers of labour power went on strike.*

The support and encouragement of workmates must have been crucial to the success of that strike. Young full-time housewives, crowded together in the forced intimacy of the tenements and terraced houses of the urban slums, had their workmates right next door to back them up. This description from the US of women immigrants to the city in the middle of this century gives us some idea of how this support may have worked.

In the neighborhood some women will get very close to others. These women in a court or a street will help each other out if they need help and make the time of day go faster. They talk of things they would not dream of talking to their husbands about, even if their husbands would listen . . . The women discuss all the things that affect their lives — whether or not to have children and how many to have, how to save money on clothes, housewares and food, which stores have lower prices, the best method of birth control, sex problems, going to work. In the discussions many things are resolved. Women get new attitudes as a result of hearing other women talk . . .[44]

That this community amongst women was also a feature of early twentieth-century Britain is confirmed by Eleanor Rathbone's impressions, recorded in her *Report on the Condition of Widows in Liverpool:*

In so close a community there are many and varied sources of help . . . One unfailing source is that of neighbours and friends. They know the circumstances of the family as no outsider can hope to know them and time after time come to the rescue, helping with food and shelter, clothing, attendance as the case may require.[45]

She also points out in *The Disinherited Family* (see p.195):

New ideas are passed from one woman to another in confidential talk . . . A striking instance of this is seen in the history of birth control . . . The women like Brer Rabbit 'kep' on sayin' nuffin' about it in public.

Where urban jobs were available to women after marriage as well as before, as in the Lancashire mill towns, and financial necessity dictated that women take them,[46] the birth rate fell fastest of all. Mothers were naturally divided about whether or not having a job was a good thing

— because on the one hand they valued the financial independence it brought them, and on the other resented the 'double day' of mill work and housework, as well as having to leave babies from only a few days old.[47] But there could be no doubt about one of the ways women used the increased social power that money gave them. They used their economic independence to insist on smaller families. Among Lancashire women textile workers, earning the highest wages available to working class women, the birth rate was lower than in any social class except that of 'skilled professionals and businessmen [sic]',[48] where women were also unusually independent financially both before and after marriage. As Eleanor Rathbone notes (see D.F. p.322 ff.) it was the most independent women who were in the lead in the birth strike. Women's relative economic independence was inseparable from their ability to go on a 'birth strike', since a birth strike depended on having the power to ensure that husbands agreed to co-operate, (especially as 'contraception' usually amounted to abstinence [see pp. 25-6 below]).

Losing Money

One element in women's attitude to family size was that what each new child meant to the family economy had changed; for now each new child would mean the woman was made more dependent on the father. In rural societies, a child represents not only a new person to care for and feed, but also an economic asset. And in the first period of the industrial revolution, young children's input into the family economy continued as they went into the factories from a very young age or else helped with industrial work in the home. But from the mid-nineteenth century onwards, protective legislation progressively excluded children — and mothers — from paid work outside the home. And from the 1870s onwards the introduction of compulsory schooling put an end to much of the work children did in and around the home. Mothers complained bitterly to the new Board of Education:

I now write a few lines to you to ask you if my daughters can leave school because we cannot find them in clothes and feed and keep a home for them any longer without there help there Father his 60 years of age and he goes 4 miles every morning and 4 miles back that makes 8 miles a day and then if it is fine all the week so he can work on the farm he gets 14s but if it his wet he cannot work on the farm he his paid for the days he does work so his earning never amounts to more than 10s a week and very often under 10s in the winter months so what can we do if there should be any illness not a farthing to keep ourselves with . . . 4s rent for the house 4 children to keep in food and clothes to provide . . . it relly cannot be it his impossible . . . and this cruel law of a school board it his too bad we cannot do it because the climate his not warme enough for them to go without clothes.[49]

Demands for maintenance allowances for schoolchildren were a feature of the programmes of all the radical parties in the late nineteenth and early twentieth centuries, with some success.[50] And in 1911 when schoolchildren in many parts of the country went on strike, they demanded shorter hours, less discipline, and wages.[51]

Children's increased financial dependence accentuated the mother's dependence on a man's wage. In addition, urban living meant both that before marriage many young women had a job with a cash income, and that they were usually forced to give up that cash income on becoming mothers. In most parts of the country, only a small percentage of urban married women went out to work after having children, and though women took in washing, sewing and more 'industrial' home-work (from matchbox-making to chain-making),[52] having children meant for most women the end of their own wage, and the independence that went with it.[53]

Then as now, young women who had a wage of their own valued the freedom between school and marriage that this money gave them. And naturally, women with this new-found freedom viewed the pros and cons of marriage in a new way.[54] Whereas in 1871 over one-third of women were married by the age of twenty to twenty-four, by 1911 fewer than a quarter were.[55] Women held on to their independence for longer before 'settling down', and also used late marriage as a major way of limiting the numbers of children they would have.

Once married, birth control was still primarily a question of abstinence. Although some contraceptives were available, and some were even advertised in the popular press, not only were they often inefficient, but their cost and the complications of using them put them way beyond the reach of most couples:

By the 1880s sponges, soluble pessaries, rubber diaphragms and syringes were sold by chemists, but success was not guaranteed unless two methods were combined. Spermicidal solutions for use with sponges or syringes had to be mixed by the woman herself, using quinine and other ingredients in a process resembling a chemical experiment. One recipe for contraceptive powder, for instance, involved mixing 35 parts of powdered starch, 15 of boric acid, 10 of gum arabic, 2½ of tannic acid and 2½ of citric acid. Successful female contraception required time, space, perseverance and above all, money. The minimum outlay required was 5/- to 6/- . . . the sheath, the cheapest mechanical method . . . could be bought for 6d per dozen, though 3/- per dozen was the usual price. Since even skilled workers could expect to earn only 30/- per week, and one third of families existed below the poverty line on less than 21/- per week, it is evident that sheaths, even at the lowest prices were for many an unattainable luxury.[56]

It is clear that the fall in the birth rate was not brought about primarily by a spread of mechanical methods of contraception, when the expense and inconvenience of the contraceptives available are taken into account. Nor could it have been brought about primarily by an increase in abortions, although the incidence of abortion was very high. The evidence from women who wrote about their experiences to birth control campaigner Marie Stopes is that withdrawal or complete abstinence were widely used,[57] and that behind the women's 'birth-strike' was a sex strike of huge proportions.

Sex and Politics

It is now more generally accepted that the falling working class birth rate was not the result of a new 'enlightenment' filtering down to the working class from the middle class in the form of birth control education[58] — which is the view that was once the currency amongst historians. That working class people made their own decisions and their own history in this respect is now being increasingly acknowledged. But it is important to note that at the beginning of the twentieth century it was widely recognized in the women's movement that the falling birth rate was something that women had brought about — that it was a conscious action and an index of women's revolt against the burdens of motherhood in a society which made no direct provision for mothers and children. (See p.29 below.)

In many cases, refusing to have more children meant insisting on complete abstinence from sex for years on end. The letters to Marie Stopes from both women and men are full of references to the tensions and rows which resulted from this kind of sexual self-repression. They make clear both that women were the instigators of the birth strike, and that the hardships involved were considerable.

. . . I am terrified at the thought anytime he comes near me and it causes unpleasant scenes in the Home.

I cannot always refuse my husband as it only means living a cat and dog life for both of us.

My husband . . . has refrained from any relation whatever since that time, but lately he is beginning to fret under the strain, being the average strong, healthy working man, and although there is no word of reproach, the fits of irritableness and bad temper, are getting worse and more often, and I feel sure will end in a separation soon if nothing can be done.[59]

That millions of women and men were forced to abstain from sex in order not to have children is a historical fact of major importance. Sexual history cannot be separated from economic and political history — not only because people's sex lives are framed by their economic and social relations, but because people's anger at being denied sex has economic and political consequences.

Just because men going on strike for more money do not actually say that one of the reasons for their strike is to be able to afford sex, either with wives or prostitutes, does not mean that this is not an important factor. And just because women do not often talk (as they do in their letters to Marie Stopes) about sexual frustration as an additional burden, and about an increase in the work of running the home because bad tempers are one result, does not mean these matters can be ignored. For women, too, this sexual frustration is an additional fuel to militancy; both because they have to deal with their own sexual repression and the limitations on their own possibilities that such repression represents,[60] and because they have to manage with men who are bad tempered and even violent.

Much of this violence was expressed in the home. But to the degree that women were able to assert their own needs, and to the degree that men felt sympathy for their wives and did not blame them for the poverty which dominated family life,[61] this violence also exploded onto the streets, contributing to both the male working class militancy and the massive women's movement which so terrified the Government.[62] Men organized to get more money from their employers and from the Government (for example in the form of unemployment pay) as the most obvious way of dealing with the crisis in the home — the crisis of poverty, overwork, hunger and sexual frustration.

The impact of women's organizing on men's militancy, through not only the sex strike, but also their close awareness of what men's wages would actually buy, was an important aspect of the women's movement. Women have always been of key importance in every strike or pay demand by men, because it is women who have to keep the family going on the money the man brings home; and as Eleanor Rathbone notes (see D.F. p.191), women by nagging men made their own 'contribution to the growing forces of social discontent' in prompting men to take action. More recently, the significance of this 'nagging', in preventing men's real wages from being undermined by rising prices, has been analysed in more detail:

... that pressure which women place on men is *a defence of the wage, not an attack*. Precisely because women are the slaves of wage slaves, men divide the wage between themselves and the general family expense. If women did not make demands, the general family standard of living could drop to absorb the inflation.[63]

But from the early years of the twentieth century, women were also organizing massively in their own name in the suffragette movement — organizing in a way that has been widely acknowledged, albeit in somewhat limited terms.

Militant Action

Reducing the suffragette movement to a fight for the vote, as most accounts do, has obscured that women wanted the vote not as an abstract right but, as Rathbone makes clear (see for example D.F. p.376), because they hoped the vote would give them more power over government decisions, would be a lever in getting the many things they needed and were demanding.

The Disinherited Family refers to many of the demands women were making: for more money in men's pay packets on which so many women were dependent; for free school meals and better housing conditions; for improved maternity benefits and a free maternity service to improve the conditions of childbirth; for contraception and family allowances; for widows' pensions and custody rights; for higher wages for women's work outside the home and the endowment of motherhood. It was all these demands (and the organizing for them) which made the suffragette movement — with its political militancy and massive women's demonstrations. In Sylvia Pankhurst's account of the suffragette movement she records numerous demonstrations, for example:

. . . textile mill hands, mothers and wage workers demonstrated with Mrs Pankhurst in a torch-light procession to Hunslet Moor (near Leeds) where 100,000 assembled.[64]

The main centres of the suffragette movement were those areas where women already had access to independent money — Lancashire and Yorkshire, where the textile industry provided waged work for working class women both before and after marriage, and London, where the newly independent professional women and office workers were concentrated, and where in the East End an unusually high proportion of working class women had a wage of their own after marriage as well as before.[65] This relative financial independence was crucial to the ability of women to campaign for their civil rights — yet, as far as I know, this connection has not been made in accounts of the suffragette movement.

With the dramatic increase in women's militancy signalled by the suffragette movement, the Government came under twofold pressure. For now it was confronted by a women's movement in which overt political militancy matched the more covert women's strike going on in millions of homes.

Eleanor Rathbone describes the subterranean women's revolt in this book:

. . . there are . . . a very large and growing number [of women] . . . who are either consciously or subconsciously in revolt. These find their most articulate expression through the membership of such bodies as the Women's Co-operative

Guild . . . But their numbers far transcend such membership; for the habit of joining societies and attending meetings is comparatively new among women and is limited by the circumstances of their lives. Those who are most encumbered by children and household cares have not the time for it, and those who are poorest or unhappiest have not the clothes or the spirits for it. Hence most of those who do attend are the older women whose children are at school or at work. But what the younger women are thinking can be gauged by one significant fact, the decline of the birth-rate. (D.F. p.192.)

And she was not alone in seeing the falling birth rate as a measure of women's militancy against the conditions of their lives. In her introduction to the book *Maternity*, published in 1915,[66] Margaret Llewelyn Davies, Secretary of the Women's Co-operative Guild (see p.35 below), makes the same point: 'There is a kind of strike against large families.'[67] And in Germany in 1913, the Social Democratic Party was organizing meetings 'Against the Birth Strike' ('Gegen der Geburtstreik') at which eminent speakers like Rosa Luxemburg and Clara Zetkin tried to persuade the working class women in their audience to have more children.[68]

Eugenics and Motherhood

The issues raised by the birth strike were frequently couched in terms of a widespread debate about eugenics[69] and the future of 'the race'. This meant discussing not only the question of ensuring an adequate supply of workers, but the 'quality' of that supply; and among the most racist eugenists were not only imperialists and employers but socialists. Sidney Webb of the Fabian Socialists was concerned that the fall in the English birth rate would mean that the 'vacuum' would be filled by 'freely-breeding alien immigrants' so that the country would 'gradually' fall to the Irish and the Jews', and therefore viewed the value of English manhood and womanhood in a new light.

The most valuable of the year's crop, as it is the most costly, is not the wheat harvest or the lambing, but the year's quota of adolescent young men and women enlisted in the productive service of the community.[70]

Even revolutionary socialists had their own brand of eugenics. They called on women to breed to provide fighters for the proletarian armies, paralleling the imperialists' call for fighters for the imperial armies. Here is an eyewitness account of a meeting organized by the revolutionary 'Social Democratic Party' in Germany:

I came to attend a meeting *against* the limitation of offspring; it soon proved to be a meeting very decidedly *for* the limitation of offspring, for every speaker who spoke in favour of the artificial prevention of conception, or undesired pregnancies, was greeted with vociferous, long-lasting applause while those who tried to persuade the people that a small number of children is no proletarian weapon, and would not improve their lot, were so hissed that they had difficulty in going on . . . the feeling was that though the Clara Zetkins and Rosa

Luxemburgs and all other literal and figurative old maids, could talk and scold until doomsday, the diminishing birth-rate will go on diminishing still further until such a time when the people will feel that by bringing a child into the world they are not increasing the sum total of human misery, ill-health and wretchedness.

What particularly amused me − and pained me − in the anti-limitationists was the ease and equanimity with which they advised the poor women to keep on bearing children. The woman herself was not taken into consideration as if she was not a human being, but a machine. What are her sufferings, her labour pains, her inability to read, to attend meetings, to have a taste of life? What does she amount to? The proletariat needs fighters. Go on, females, and breed . . .[71]

In fact, on all sides political 'leaders' wanted to use mothers as breeding machines, to produce fodder either for the 'imperial' or 'industrial' army, or for the 'proletarian', working class army.[72] And according to their particular point of view, they were concerned either that mothers high up the social scale breed more than other mothers, or that mothers low down the social scale breed most. In either case their disregard for the actual circumstances, needs and views of the mothers themselves was almost total.

What Eleanor Rathbone thought of the eugenists is clear in *The Disinherited Family* (see for example pp.312-3), where she clearly characterizes those eugenists concerned at the falling birth rate as being politically motivated by the ambition that the Anglo-Saxon race should dominate the world. (They want more children simply 'as colonists and as future defenders . . . as "cannon fodder".') She also identifies those concerned that the population might be too *large* as politically motivated − by the fear that the working class is taking too big a share of the nation's produce. (The 'working class seems to them like a headstrong boy, conscious of its strength, insistent in its appetites . . .') But in the atmosphere that the widespread eugenics debate engendered, women generally used the terminology of eugenics to put their case, and Rathbone was no exception. Working class mothers, whose letters appeared in the Women's Co-operative Guild book *Maternity*, for example, threatened that unless the Government did something for mothers 'race suicide' was inevitable − that is, they would refuse to have any children, even if it meant the end of the race. Referring to both her own and other mothers' sufferings, and their aspirations for a better standard of living, one mother writes:

Race suicide, if you will, is the policy of the mothers of the future. Who shall blame us?[73]

Her threat is well borne out by the numerous accounts in the book of the desperate attempts made by mothers to cut down on the numbers of children born.

In *The Disinherited Family* and elsewhere, Eleanor Rathbone argued the case for family endowment in the context of the influence of eugenics. She had to address herself to the various objections eugenists might have to family endowment, because their influence could not be ignored. Would family endowment increase or decrease the birth rate? Would it increase the birth rate of the 'wrong' sort of mother or decrease the birth rate of the 'right' sort? Pointing to the fact that the group with the highest birth rate was the poorest section of the population, and that eugenists were generally dismayed at this fact, Rathbone argued in the 1920s that family endowment would not increase but decrease their birth rate. For example, she told the Eugenics Society in 1924:

. . . there is a strong revolt among all sections of women who have leisure to think and sufficient independence of mind to plan for themselves, against the excessive physical strain placed on them by too frequent child-bearing. Family Endowment, by relieving women from their present complete dependence on the good will as well as the ability of their husbands to support them, would make them better able to regulate their own destinies in this respect.[74]

In *The Disinherited Family*, she ends the section on population, which deals with the objections of eugenists to family endowment, on a similar note. Turning the eugenists' arguments on their heads, she points out that the mothers who can best teach a future generation the qualities the eugenists most value for the Anglo-Saxon race are not the docile women admired by the anti-feminists, but precisely those women whose militancy has made the feminist movement. (See D.F. p.323.)

Elsewhere in her writing she was more explicit about the relationship between financial independence and birth control, making clear that a woman's ability to control her own birth rate begins with her having not only the determination but the means to restrain her husband in the bedroom. She pointed out that it is precisely because this is a financial question that women with the least money have been the least able to bring down their own birth rate, and argued that even a limited Family Endowment paid towards the cost of children only, would mean for the mother that

Even where the husband's habits were worst and his claims most unreasonable, the little measure of relief from her complete dependence on him which the payment of the allowance would ensure her might do something to raise her crushed spirit *and enable her to protect herself.*[75]

Eleanor Rathbone used the eugenics debate to press the case for family endowment, and trimmed her speeches and writings to the needs of the moment and to her audience. She has recently come under attack for her supposed support for eugenics (see p.53 and note 163), but although there are examples in her writing of contempt for the very poor (for example, D.F. pp.318-9), her view was clearly that any 'bad habits' were the result of environment rather than genes. Writing of the relationship between bad housing conditions and a high birth rate, she summarizes:

Families that are herded together like animals tend to become like animals – to lose hope, and ambition, and self-control. Lack of privacy and sufficient bedding increases the difficulty in practising either contraception or continence. (D.F. p.319)

But she also concludes:

Does it not all point irresistibly to the conclusion that direct provision paid to the mother would raise the standard of life of the poorer wage-earners and that an orderly and self-respecting living is the best cure for indiscriminate and dysgenic breeding? (D.F. p.321)

In other words, although she characterizes the poorest parents as 'unfit' (D.F. p.319), she attributes this to financial circumstances and blames the circumstances rather than the parents.

Anyone who believes that providing more money for 'unfit' parents will make them 'fit' cannot seriously be characterized as a supporter of eugenics. And Eleanor Rathbone's outstanding record as a campaigner against the racist immigration laws and for immigrants' rights, her championing of the rights of Black women in the Third World[76] and her campaign for the poorest of mothers to have the money they needed must ultimately be the proof of which side she was on.

Certainly she was convinced that money in mothers' hands was essential if women were to have the right to self-determination and control over their own fertility; and that women would use this money to limit family size or have children they otherwise could not afford according to the needs of the individual woman. (Amongst other things, she was convinced that financial independence for mothers was the key to ending rape in the home [see D.F. p.197].) At those moments when the eugenists wanted the birth rate to fall, she was therefore able to argue that family endowments were essential. When they wanted the birth rate to rise, she argued that family endowment would also make that possible. When they wanted the birth rate amongst the poorest women to fall, family endowment was the answer. When they wanted the middle class birth rate to rise, family endowment was again the solution. She knew that all of these were true precisely because some women would use the money to have children, and others would use the money not to have children. Either way, the fact that eugenists and others were concerned about the birth rate could clearly be used to women's advantage. And whenever State planners and politicians alighted on the importance of motherhood to replenish the population, Eleanor Rathbone was happy to use to the full the advantage that the birth strike provided.

WINNING WELFARE FROM THE STATE

In 1899, recruitment for the army to fight the Boer War revealed that the 'British race' was 'in decline'. Not only was the birth rate falling, but one in three of the men who volunteered for the army was found to be physically unfit. It was not news to mothers who had been powerless to prevent the illnesses of poverty that their sons were sickly and unfit. But now in the wake of the Boer War the poor health of young men had become a matter of 'national' concern. One result of this new concern was that mothers were subjected to a barrage of advice on how to look after their children. Books, pamphlets, articles and speeches were published by the hundred on how working class mothers had to be better educated for the job. And do-gooders invaded their homes with leaflets and admonitions. Women health visitors were appointed by many local authorities and told to:

. . . visit from house to house in such localities as the medical officer of health shall direct: to carry with them disinfectant powder and use it where required . . . to give hints to mothers on the feeding and clothing of their children, and use their influence to induce them to send their children regularly to school . . . to urge, on all possible occasions, the importance of cleanliness, thrift and temperance.[77]

Their useless intrusions were of course heartily resented, but they had the power to be more than a nuisance. Medical Officers, Sanitary Inspectors, Health Visitors and all the varieties of social workers appointed by the expanding local governments could ruin a mother's life. The Children's Act of 1908 gave them increasing powers to take into care children of mothers they considered 'unfit', so beginning a long tradition of professionals deciding who is or is not a 'fit' mother.[78] And even when the measures imposed were not as drastic as taking children away, they could be cruel enough in the name of 'health':

I should like to know how much more spite you intend to put upon my child, for it is nothing else. First you send the Sanitary Inspector and I have my home taken away, then my husband has to get rid of his few rabbits and chickens, and now you cut the few hairs my girl was just beginning to get so nice . . . I know she had no need to have her hair cut off as it was washed with soft soap last night. The child is thoroughly heart broken.[79]

But of course, as Eleanor Rathbone makes clear in this book (see for example D.F. pp.177-8), the reason that mothers living in poverty were unable to care for their children as they wanted to was not that they were 'unfit' or lacking in education, but that they lacked the means.[80] Advice about cleanliness and hygiene was all very well, but with the nearest cold water supply six flights of steps away, with only one sauce-pan, no stove but only a fire for cooking and to heat the water, with six or eight people sleeping in one room, and with a water closet in the yard, it is no wonder that conditions of cleanliness and hygiene were inadequate. Advice to mothers about breast-feeding was all very well if they were strong and well enough nourished, but what if the mother had no milk? Admonitions to keep the window open for 'fresh air' (often from a stinking yard) were impossible to follow if mothers lacked the clothes to keep the children warm during the day, and the bedclothes to cover them at night.[81] As Eleanor Rathbone points out repeatedly, the wonder was that working class mothers managed as well as they did.

Reports on the conditions in which mothers and children were actually living, compiled by sympathetic women social workers and campaigners, began to filter through to the authorities from the early twentieth century onwards. It was one of the major achievements of the women's movement that middle class professional women put their skills to use in this way. And as the infant mortality and child health statistics showed little sign of improvement, the authorities were gradually forced to recognize that what was needed was not simply advice but practical help either in the form of social and welfare services or as cash payments.

Working Women Organize

Women campaigned for social services, welfare provisions and cash payments in a variety of ways, in campaigns which went on alongside the campaign for a greater say in decision-making through the vote. They argued the case that mothers and children should receive recognition, in both cash and kind, for the fact that their well-being was a vital asset to the economy.[82]

The overlap in personnel between different organizations and the way in which the same women are found campaigning on a number of fronts reflect the reality that all these apparently 'separate' issues are connected, so that Eleanor Rathbone, in being active in all these aspects of the women's movement,[83] was by no means unique. The lives of other women activists who were her contemporaries tell the same story of membership of numerous organizations and the interweaving between the various campaigns.[84]

The campaigns for practical help for mothers and babies countered the view that mothers 'ought to do better' with publicity about the actual situation of working mothers, deputations of working mothers to government offices, demonstrations, letters to the press, and pressure on local authorities to fund the charitable welfare schemes that were being set up to help mothers. An example of their success is that charitable 'schools for mothers' set up from 1906 onwards to provide not only 'education' but, more practically, free or cheap meals for the mothers who attended, were gradually funded by local authorities, and became 'infant welfare centres' and mother and baby clinics.[85]

The first cash payments to mothers won from the Government were through the 1911 National Insurance Act, which provided for a maternity benefit for the wives of men in work. This was a major victory, which was confirmed when, after further pressure, this benefit was made the legal property of the mother (1913) following intensive campaigning by women's organizations, in particular the Women's Co-operative Guild.[86] The difference that provisions of this kind made to the well-being of mothers and babies is reflected in the dramatic fall in infant death rate – from 163 per thousand in 1899 to 95 per thousand in 1912 – and in women's own accounts, although it is significant that the maternal death rate remained high.[87]

The provision of maternity benefits and practical help for mothers were major victories for women. In 1915 *Maternity*, a collection of *Letters from Working Women* (that is, mothers, most of whom were working full-time in the home)[88] was published as part of the Women's Co-operative Guild campaign for higher maternity benefits, maternity and infant welfare centres, free meals for mothers, home help services, pure milk depots and a host of detailed demands for State aid for mothers. The letters provided unquestionable evidence of women's need for all these provisions and of women's determination to establish that as mothers they were entitled to a share of the national resources:

I nearly lost my life. I was in labour from 1 o'clock in the morning until 7.5 at night. Then the doctor used instruments. He stated I had worked too hard, and not rested sufficiently . . . Two years after I had a miscarriage . . . I then had to lie in bed a whole month. I kept a small girl, and used to do my own ironing and knead my bread in bed unknown to the doctor . . . I feel sure that if I had had a maternity benefit then to help me, I should not be suffering now inwardly . . . The mother, when funds are low, goes without much food, pleading headache, etc. so as to try and blind her husband. I think an expectant mother should rest at least half an hour every day, and especially towards the last should have no heavy work to do, such as washing and ironing . . . The child is an asset to the nation, and the mother the backbone. Therefore, I think the nation should help to feed and keep that mother, and so help to strengthen the nation by her giving birth to strong boys and girls . . . I only hope that . . . it is the mothers that are getting the benefit of the maternity benefit, and not the husband, and . . . the landlord.[89]

The Women's Co-operative Guild which was responsible for this and other campaigns to benefit mothers was described by contemporaries as 'the greatest working women's organization of modern times'.[90] It was made up of housewives (67,000 of them by the early 1930s) who came together in the Guild to be part of the 'Housewives International' – as the International Co-operative Women's Guild described itself.

... the Guild ... has always acted as the Housewives International, to formulate
and synthesize the needs, demands and objectives of the housewife in a comprehensive programme.[91]

Although some trade unions had more women members, for example
in the textile trade, none of them, not even the women's trade unions
founded in the 1890s, campaigned for the millions of women who were
either full-time at home or doing part-time jobs in addition, either as
sweated 'home-workers' or as 'half-timers' outside.[92] The Guild
membership was drawn from these women and it campaigned to give
housewives a voice in politics.

Many of the Guild's members testified to the difference it had made
to their lives, for example in *Life As We Have Known It* by Co-operative
Working Women, which was published in 1931 with an introduction by
Virginia Woolf. She describes the importance of the organization in
that introduction:

The minds of working women were humming and their imaginations were awake.
But how were they to realise their ideals? How were they to express their
needs? . . . It was the Guild . . . that drew to itself all that restless wishing and
dreaming. It was the Guild that made a central meeting place where formed and
solidified all that was else so scattered and incoherent. The Guild . . . gave them
in the first place the rarest of all possessions — a room where they could sit down
and think remote from boiling saucepans and crying children; and then that
room became not merely a sitting-room and a meeting place, but a workshop
where, laying their heads together, they could remodel their houses, could remodel their lives, could beat out this reform and that.[93]

Other organizations campaigned for similar provisions to those demanded by the Guild, and organized on the same principles of representing housewives and mothers. Sylvia Pankhurst's East London
Federation of Suffragettes campaigned throughout World War I for
free milk for nursing mothers and babies, free meals, and creche
facilities, as well as for jobs at better pay for East End women. They set
up a Woman's Hall which dispensed milk, eggs, barley for babies'
barley water, Glaxo and rice,[94] and had doctors there and at other
mother and child welfare centres to give free medical advice. They had
a 'Babies House' nursery for children from two months to five years
for mothers going out to work; set up cost-price restaurants with two-
course meals for 2d a head; and ran co-operative boot, toy and garment
making factories to provide employment at decent wages. At the same
time, they campaigned successfully for financial support from the
Local Government Board for their welfare work,[95] and for the Government to regulate wages so that women taking over 'men's jobs' in the
war industries would get equal pay.

Both the East London Federation of Suffragettes and the Women's
Co-operative Guild used the occasion of World War I in particular to

press the demands of working class mothers, arguing that since losses on the battlefield underlined the importance of motherhood and child-rearing, the Government must do something to help.[96]

Organizations with a more middle class membership also took up the demands of housewives and mothers. The Fabian Women's Group, comprised primarily of middle class women who were members of the various socialist groups and the Independent Labour Party, campaigned for those organizations to represent the needs of 'working women', and published pamphlets and tracts in their own right to impress public opinion. In 1913 they published their first book, *Round About a Pound a Week*, a study of how 'working mothers' (i.e. mothers full-time at home) managed on a budget of a pound a week, which was the standard of living of the average working class household.[97] They set out to prove that

. . . the cause of infant mortality was not that mothers were ignorant or degenerate, but that they had too little money to provide for their own and their families' essential needs; that they lacked decent housing, domestic equipment, adequate food and clothing, and any facilities or opportunities for recreation.[98]

Their book provided evidence which was used to the full by campaigners, including Eleanor Rathbone. (See for example D.F. pp.170-2.)

The Fabian women became convinced that the key to an improvement in women's situation lay not only in the vote but in economic independence for mothers. Their pamphlet on *The Economic Foundations of the Women's Movement* says of middle class professional women:

Most women . . . can only continue to preserve that economic independence, so keenly appreciated and won by such fierce struggles, on condition of compulsory celibacy and, what to many women is far worse, compulsory childlessness. Against this state of things a revolt is beginning which so far is barely articulate, but which is bound to make itself heard in public before long. What women . . . want, is not this forced alternative between activity in the human world and control of their own economic position on the one hand and marriage and children on the other, *but both* . . . Least of all does she desire to sink back into a state of economic dependence.[99]

At the same time it recognizes that

What the woman of the proletariat feels as her grievance is that her work is too long and too monotonous, the burden laid upon her too heavy.[100]

It concludes that for both classes of women the 'endowment of motherhood' by the State is essential:

No act of citizenship is more fundamental than the act of bringing into the world and protecting in his helpless infancy a new citizen, and therefore the most reasonable solution to the problem . . . is that women during the period when these activities must absorb their whole energies should be supported by a State endowment . . . a system of which we have already made a beginning in old age pensions on the one hand, and maintenance scholarships [for schoolchildren] on the other. Among the most honoured and respected of all those endowed by the State should be the women who are rendering to it the greatest possible service, that, namely, of ushering into the world its future citizens.[101]

THE ENDOWMENT OF MOTHERHOOD

The demand for a cash payment for mothers from the State, referred to as 'The Endowment of Motherhood', 'Family Endowment', 'Family Allowances' or 'Mothers' Pensions', was first voiced at the end of the nineteenth century[102] and was widely supported by women of all classes. Mothers writing in the Guild's book on *Maternity*, for example, stressed that the maternity benefits already won had made a great difference to them, but that they needed substantial and *long-standing* cash payments from the State, and not just a short-term benefit. In fact the parallel was often drawn between old-age pensions and 'pensions' for working mothers — for at a time when pensions for people no longer working were being demanded and won, it seemed very possible that women in their homes could win a substantial pension from the State:

What is necessary for mothers is State aid for every child she gives birth to. If this is necessary for the aged, it is more so for the mother with the children [sic].[103]

I am firmly of opinion that if the State wants strong, healthy, useful citizens, they should provide the mothers in the homes with sufficient wages where the husband's wage is inadequate.[104]

It was a demand which looked eminently possible to achieve at a time when much more 'impossible' demands were being met. The introduction of unemployment benefits, in effect a State endowment for those who were *not* working, was a revolutionary concept which became a reality. Old-age pensions, paid initially on a non-contributory basis, were in effect State back-pay paid in recognition of years spent working for low or no wages. It is not surprising therefore that the term 'Mothers' Pensions' was used in a variety of ways to make the best use of the victory that pensions represented. 'Mothers' Pensions' was used to suggest a State payment for mothers who were working in the home and had a husband; who were widows or separated; or who no longer had children at home but had earned their right to a pension for life. One MP thought it necessary during a debate on 'Mothers' Pensions' in the House of Commons in 1923 to explain that in this context 'Mothers' Pensions' might be paid to widows only, or to 'mothers whose family breadwinner has become incapacitated', and not to all mothers:

We do not claim that there ought to be a pension in respect of every child born to every woman. This is not a plea that the woman should be endowed simply because she is a mother.[105]

This disclaimer is a reflection of the fact that demands for the endowment of motherhood or mothers' pensions were widespread, and that the pressure of the women's movement had put women's economic needs on the political agenda.

What women meant by endowment of motherhood, mothers' pensions, family endowment or allowances was often deliberately ambiguous. The main ambiguity centred on whether this was to be a subsistence allowance for children paid to the mother, or a payment for the mother's work, or both. In a way which is typical of this ambiguity, the working mother quoted opposite talks on the one hand of the mother getting a pension like the old-age pension, and on the other of State aid for every child. It was of course always easier to argue the case for the children, but women were also referring to their own independent needs when they did so. Even when the demand was for a children's allowance only, it was recognized among women that money for the children paid to the mother would in fact mean money for the mother. Whether or not they spelt out that they wanted the money not only to feed the children but also as mothers in their own right depended primarily on what women gauged their power to be, and therefore whether they felt they could openly make a claim for themselves.

The way Eleanor Rathbone deals with the question of motherhood endowment in this book is a classic example of this ambiguity. Overwhelmingly the arguments in the book centre on the situation of women. It is a book about women much more than it is about children — not only in terms of the proportion of space devoted to each, but in the detailed empathy with which she writes about the lives of women, in particular of those women forced into financial dependence on men. In the course of the book, she repeatedly makes the case for mothers to be paid an allowance in their own right, as well as a subsistence allowance for their children, for example:

In this country such proposals as have been tentatively made by reformers have generally started with the desire to acknowledge the services and establish the economic independence of the wife and mother, and the name by which they are known in popular phraseology is 'the endowment of motherhood'. It is clear that the hardships in the lot of the married mother and her aspirations after a securer and more honourable status, which have been described in Chapter III, would not be fully met by a form of provision which merely secured to the children the bare minimum necessary for their maintenance and left the mother completely dependent, as she is now, on the will as well as the ability of her husband to support her. (D.F. p.362.)

    . . . nothing can justify the subordination of one group of producers — the mothers — to the rest, and their deprivation of all share of their own in the wealth of a community which depends on them for its very existence. (D.F. p.345)

Yet when it comes to putting forward specific demands, she compromises on the question of payment for the mother's work. She suggests that perhaps a combination of direct provision for the mother and strengthening her claim on her husband's income might be the answer (D.F. p.362), although she has earlier written of the limitations of trying to split the husband's income (D.F. p.207); she suggests that family endowment should be a subsistence payment for children only, on the grounds that there would be less opposition to this more limited measure (D.F. p.363), although she makes the case that this would leave mothers economically dependent and vulnerable.

I have dealt below (see pp.56 and 67) with some of the reasons why by 1924 Eleanor Rathbone felt unable to come out as explicitly for payments to mothers in their own right (in addition to children's subsistence allowances) as she had done earlier (see D.F. p.258), even though *The Disinherited Family* undoubtedly makes the case for financial independence for mothers. She contradicts herself repeatedly in her uncertainty about what to demand in the political and economic climate of 1924 and a depression which 'has been the severest experienced in living memory' (D.F. p.175). On p.237, for example, she writes that a woman whose children are at school might not be doing enough work to justify payment of an allowance for her work on top of the children's allowance, though she points out on the very same page that 'the work of looking after a house, husband and two schoolchildren, without domestic help, is . . . amply enough to occupy one woman.' (D.F. p.363 footnote). Yet her uncertainty is not about economic independence for the mother. Rather, she makes eminently clear that the way *to make a start* towards State payments for mothers is to appeal on behalf of the children, both because the falling birth rate had established they were a national asset and because whereas men of all classes felt threatened by women's demand for economic independence, an appeal made on behalf of children could more easily command men's support.[106](See D.F. pp.340-5.)

The fact that all the 'Family Allowance' payments being proposed in Britain before 1945 were proposed as payments to the mother, whether or not they were payments for the children or payments for the mother as well reflected a widespread acknowledgement of the injustice of women working in the home for no remuneration and the fact that the case had already been widely made that mothers should receive some payment. Women's writings of the period often refer to the injustice of women's unpaid work in the home, even when they are not concerned with specific demands;[107] for example, Margaret Llewelyn Davies writes of '. . . the unpaid work of the working-woman at the stove, at scrubbing and cleaning, at the washtub . . .' in her introduction to *Maternity*, and comments:

. . . the wife is still the inferior in the family to the husband. She is first without economic independence, and the law *therefore* gives the man, whether he be good or bad, a terrible power over her.[108]

Elsewhere, Margaret Llewelyn Davies also argued the case for 'the National Endowment of mothers', suggesting in 1918 that 'a concentrated effort should be made to secure it without delay.'[109] The Fabian Women's Group characterized their main aim as

. . . to study the economic position of women and press their claim to equality with men in the personal economic independence to be secured by socialism.[110]

And while they say nothing here about unpaid housework or a wage for mothers, the study which was subsequently published as *Round About a Pound a Week* was initially called *The Mother's Allowance Scheme in Lambeth.*

A Wage for Mothers

Those who were explicitly in favour of an allowance for the mother as well as the child differed in what they were proposing. Some of the Fabian women, for example, were particularly anxious to emphasize that once the immediate duties of the pregnant and nursing mother were over, this State endowment should not continue. They saw motherhood endowment as a very temporary payment, in effect simply a briefly extended maternity benefit.[111]

But there were many other women who meant by 'State endowment of motherhood' a wage to be paid to all mothers working in the home. In 1917 a collection of essays was published, under the title *The Making of Women: Oxford Essays in Feminism*[112] which argued for special provision for women as mothers, and for financial independence for women at home, and makes clear that a debate on this issue was already in full swing. (See pp.51-2 below.) And the writings of women who were prominent figures of the 1920s to 40s are peppered with references to the demand for State payment to mothers, spelt out quite explicitly as deriving from the view that economic independence for women working full-time in the home was the key to economic independence for all women.

This view was in no way confined to Britain. In 1920 the American campaigner Crystal Eastman wrote:

What is the problem of women's freedom? It seems to me to be this: how to arrange the world so that women can be human beings, with a chance to exercise their infinitely varied gifts in infinitely varied ways, instead of being destined by the accident of their sex to one field of activity – housework and child-raising. The second, *if and when* they choose housework and child-raising, to have that occupation recognized by the world as work, requiring a definite economic reward and not merely entitling the performer to be dependent on some man.

This is not the whole of feminism of course, but it is enough to begin with. 'Oh! Don't begin with economics', my friends often protest, 'Woman does not live by bread alone. What she needs first of all is a free soul.' And I can agree that women will never be great until they achieve a certain emotional freedom, a strong healthy egotism, and some un-personal sources of joy – that in this inner sense we cannot make woman free by changing her economic status. What we can do, however, is to create conditions of outward freedom in which a free woman's soul can be born and grow. It is these outward conditions with which an organized feminist movement must concern itself.[113]

In Britain, the most famous woman writer of the inter-war period, Virginia Woolf, was no less forthright in her call for a State wage for mothers as the cornerstone of economic independence for women. In her famous anti-war essay *Three Guineas*, published in 1938, she appealed to professional women for their support in pressing for a wage for mothers, arguing that the professional woman

. . . must bind herself to press for a money wage for the unpaid worker in her own class – the daughters and sisters of educated men who, biographies have shown us, are now paid on the truck system, with food, lodging and a pittance of £40 a year. But above all she must press for a wage to be paid by the State legally to the mothers of educated men. The importance of this to our common fight is immeasurable.[114]

She also appealed to professional men, to whom the essay is apparently addressed, to support the demand in their own self-interest:

For if your wife were paid for her work, the work of bearing and bringing up children, a real wage, a money wage, so that it became an attractive profession instead of being as it is now an unpaid profession, an unpensioned profession . . . your own slavery would be lightened. No longer need you go to the office at nine-thirty and stay there till six. Work could be equally distributed. Patients could be sent to the patientless. Briefs to the briefless. Articles could be left unwritten. Culture would thus be stimulated. You could see the fruit trees flower in spring. You could share the prime of life with your children . . . If the State paid your wife a living wage for her work which, sacred though it is, can scarcely be called more sacred than that of the clergyman, yet as his work is paid without derogation so may hers be – if this step . . . were taken the old mill in which the professional man now grinds out his round, often so wearily, with so little pleasure to himself or profit to his profession, would be broken; the opportunity of freedom would be yours . . . But since three hundred millions or so have to be spent upon the arm-bearers, such expenditure is obviously, to use a convenient word supplied by the politicians, 'impracticable' and it is time to return to more feasible projects.[115]

The fact that a writer like Virginia Woolf, who did not see herself primarily as a political activist, should have been preoccupied with the question of financial independence for women suggests that there was a massive movement making these demands when she was writing. Financial independence is quite explicitly a major theme of her two most famous non-fiction essays – *A Room of One's Own*, first published in 1929, and *Three Guineas*, first published in 1938 – and she understood profoundly that without it women would never be free.[116]

As more women's writing from the 1920s, 30s and 40s is republished, the currency that these ideas had among women becomes more obvious, and the continuous line between the campaigns for the endowment of motherhood of the earlier part of the century and that of the late 1930s and early 1940s becomes apparent.[117] At the same time, the magnitude of what women were demanding is often disguised because the demands for the endowment of motherhood, or for 'family endowment' to be paid to the mother, are usually confused with Family Allowances as introduced in Britain in 1946. The Family Allowance Act of 1945, as the first universal payment to mothers by the State, was a major victory, but it was in no way all of what women were asking for.[118]

The demand that women were making was essentially for financial independence for mothers who had no money of their own, and for the period 1900-40 that amounted to a demand for State payment to the overwhelming majority of adult women. Figures from 1911 show that more than two-thirds of women over the age of fourteen had no waged employment,[119] and therefore had no income, or at best only a small income from part-time 'home' work done for cash. The one-third in waged employment would have been made up largely of young women working before marriage and motherhood. In other words, the proportion of mothers who were full-time at home would have been overwhelming. This is explained, amongst other things, by the fact that at the beginning of the twentieth century, a woman of twenty could expect to spend one-third of her remaining life either pregnant or nursing a baby under a year old,[120] and could expect to bring up five or six children. In other words, she would have a very full-time job at home. Although by the end of the 1940s the birth rate had fallen dramatically, shifting the burden of women's work (see p.77 below), it is important to remember that as late as 1931, only one married woman in eight had a job outside the home, and by 1939 the proportion had risen only to one in seven.[121] In these years then, the demand for a State endowment of motherhood amounted to a demand for the State to pay for the work which was most adult women's full-time job, and was the only demand which spoke directly to the economic dependence of millions of women.

It was in this context that, as we have seen, Eleanor Rathbone described even the most limited scheme of family endowment:

... the beginning of a movement destined to make more difference to the status of women and the welfare of children than anything that has happened in the world since the beginning of Christianity. (D.F. p.280)

And when Eleanor Rathbone and others used the phrase 'family endowment' rather than 'motherhood endowment', as a more neutral term which might more easily gather support from those in power, their critics were well aware that what they were in fact talking about was a very subversive demand indeed.[122] One critic wrote:

It will be obvious that, despite reasurring assertions to the contrary, Family Endowment, if introduced on any scale that would adequately give effect to its objects, would, for good or for evil, involve a violent revolution in the system whereby wages are at present determined. It is doubtless wise policy on the part of the advocates of a fundamental change to represent their panacea as an easily assimilated dose of tonic with which the patient is already familiar; but a wise patient should know what it is that is being prescribed . . .[123]

. . . Family Endowment . . . on its more rational and comprehensible side . . . is concerned with the relationship between the fertile woman and society at large; but unfortunately it trails off into the deeper depths of feminism . . . It sees in woman, by virtue of her motherhood, a person who is rendering service to the community at large, rearing children 'for the future of industry and of the State'.[124]

Woman is thus in her capacity as a mother the instrument whereby the existence of society is continued, yet she depends on a mere husband . . . In consequence there is a degradation in the status of women which, if unremedied, may render the grant of the franchise an empty dignity. At this point the more purely feminist argument enters, and finds in the dependence of women the teeming origin of many evils with ramifications in the remotest parts of our social life. 'Few of us realise', we are told . . . 'how constantly and subtly this half-conscious, but ever-present sense of the economic dependence of the woman upon the man corrodes her personality, checks her development, and stunts her mind . .[125]

Society, if it is to raise women to the height of their full stature and unstunt their minds, has to face the problem of substituting 'a system of more direct payment of the costs of its own renewal' . . . when, however, it is considered how these ideas conflict with the ordinarily accepted views of the relationship existing between the State and the family, it will become apparent that, . . . Family Endowment is not inaptly described as a 'very heavy charge of social dynamite.'[126]

Through the ebb and flow of this campaign to win economic independence for women working in the home, posed sometimes directly as endowment of motherhood, and sometimes indirectly as family endowment or family allowances, Eleanor Rathbone is a continuous presence, writer, organizer and public spokesperson. From 1917 onwards she concentrated her considerable energies on this campaign, as the experience of wartime Separation Allowances brought proof of the practical feasibility of the State endowment for motherhood she had always advocated.[127]

Separation Allowances: The First Step

In 1914, with the outbreak of World War I, the first extensive experiment in a State wage for housework had begun in Britain, with the payment of 'separation allowances' to the wives of servicemen. From March 1915, these allowances were paid direct to mothers through the Post Office, and paid every Monday one week in advance.[128] In March 1915, the rates for ordinary soldiers' wives were:

   12/6 paid in her own right to the wife;
   5/-   paid to her for the first child;
   3/6   paid to her for the second child;
   2/-   paid to her for the third and each subsequent child.[129]

The men contributed a total of 3/6 per week from their wages irrespective of the number of children they had, so that the allowances represented a substantial payment from the State over and above the deduction from the man's pay-packet.

A mother with two children was therefore receiving 21/- a week, with three children 23/- a week, and so on. And there was an additional allowance for some London mothers, presumably to take account of the higher cost of living in the capital.[130] While these amounts sound small today, set against the 'Round About a Pound a Week'[131] on which the average wife of a London working man in steady employment supported a family in 1913, they were a significant payment — even allowing for the rapid inflation of the war years.[132]

Once granted, they provided a springboard from which to demand more extensive payments. There was an immediate campaign to increase the amount paid as the mothers' allowance from 12/6 a week to £1, for the allowance to be paid to war widows, and to be continued even after the children were grown up.[133] The Women's Co-operative Guild wrote in December 1914:

the Government should consider £1 a week [for the wife] as a reasonable sum for women employed in the all-important work of the care of children and the home . . . it is not only the children's lives which must be considered. The mother's maintenance should be adequate for her lifetime, because she will have given the best years of her life to her work.[134]

These proposals were also supported by other women's organizations, the Workers War Emergency Committee representing trade unions and 'labour' organizations, MPs and even some local authorities.

Male trade unionists backed demands for an adequate widows' pension, including for childless widows, with the argument that a woman must get

. . . enough to live without working [sic] if she desired not to work; for otherwise she would be at the mercy of those who underpaid female labour.[135]

A sentiment which was backed up by the Editor of *The Nation*:

. . . if she has enough to live on, she may choose some other mode of life; if she becomes a wage earner, her independence may make her more particular about her terms. A correspondent wrote to *The Times* in alarm the other day to say that if all soldiers' widows were to have pensions that would keep them, the upper classes would soon find themselves short of servants.[136]

This same question of the independence a widow's pension would give women, and the implications for the choice over what jobs and wage they could accept or refuse, was debated in Parliament:

Mr. Asquith said the other day that if the childless [war] widows' pensions were raised beyond 7/6 a week she might compete unfairly with her sister in the industrial market. Mr Barnes took up this point with some vigour, urging that a higher pension would remove the widow altogether from such competition, and that a small pension always tends, as in the case of commissionaires, to depress wages.[137]

Meanwhile, at the suggestion of the Miner's Union, the National Workers' War Emergency Committee pressed that the allowance to soldiers' wives should not only be increased to £1 for the woman herself, but should be paid 'without any deductions from the pay of the person serving at the front.'[138] The same committee campaigned for an allowance of £1 a week to be paid to men who came back from the war injured or disabled and unable to work, *in addition* to any allowance paid to his wife. And women demanded the extension of the allowances to mothers who were dependent on sons fighting in the war, and to 'unmarried wives'. A conference held in Bradford of representatives of 'all political, religious, trade union, social, co-operative and women's organizations' agreed that

With the moral question they were not concerned; the argument was that economically these people should be no worse off [and that] unmarried mothers should be given the status of dependants.[139]

No Strings Attached
Alongside the demands for increased payments came demands that the payments should have no strings attached, and that women should receive them as a right and not a charity. In the first few months of the war, payment of the allowances was administered by charitable organizations, but massive pressure all over the country forced the Government to introduce direct and unconditional payments, paid through the Post Office (at that time the only government office with branches in every neighbourhood)[140] setting a precedent for the Family Allowance payments of 1946. A circular sent out by the Home Secretary in December 1914, calling for the supervision of women drawing allowances by the charities at that time administering them, and suggesting

that the police be called in to investigate any cases of child neglect, drunkenness or misuse of the money so that allowances could be stopped for 'unfit' mothers, was met with a barrage of criticism and opposition. The National Union of Women Workers wrote to the press:

> The Government in deciding to stop allowances in certain cases are adopting a principle which must be watched very closely, i.e. that employers of labour have a right to decide how their employees or their dependents shall spend their earnings. It may suit the Government to talk of grants and allowances, but our members, who are ordinary persons, prefer to speak of wages. They maintain that the State has no right to withold wages when they have been earned, and these so-called allowances have been earned in all conscience.[141]

Pressure built up from women and men all over the country, and strong words were used even in the Parliamentary debates:

> We have had enough of fussy people pestering the working classes; . . . we have had enough of the insufferable superiority of the voluntary societies.[142]

The Government was forced to climb down and withdraw the circular, smarting from the discovery that the days when working class people had to be grateful for 'charity' were over, and that this 'allowance' was perceived by working class women and men as a wage that had been earned, and therefore as a right.[143]

The quotations above from newspapers of 1914 give some indication of the level women's and men's militancy had reached by the beginning of World War I. The rebellions in Ireland, the suffragette movement, and the extensive — and often violent — waves of industrial strikes fuelled each other in their assault on the Government.[144] These three aspects of the working class movement were in practice connected to one another, not only in personnel, and in a general exchange of power which is always the result of different sectors of the working class challenging the State, but more particularly because the tactics of each sector of the movement were learnt from one another. The suffragette bombings and destruction of property had their precedent and parallels in the armed Irish rebellion which culminated in the Easter Rising of 1916; the mass strikes of the period, disconcertingly independent of the established trade unions, turned easily to riots and window breaking (a favourite tactic of the suffragettes);[145] the hunger strikes and forced feeding undergone by the suffragettes were repeated in Ireland;[146] and the mass meetings, demonstrations and Parliamentary lobbies organized by women were not only met by police charges and organized beatings by gangs of thugs, but were not averse to using physical violence on their own behalf. In a firsthand account of suffragette meetings in Glasgow, suffragette organizer Jessie Stephens made clear not only the extent to which women mobilized men to support them at public meetings, so that the meeting hall would be lined by dockers ready to deal with any violence from the opposition, but also the readiness with which women used violence in their own self-defence.[147]

In 1914, the Government, faced with a rebellion on all fronts, was relieved at the breathing space the war provided. At the same time, it did not feel confident of being able to persuade a population to fight, persuading mothers and wives, fathers and sons, to contribute to a 'war effort', without some concessions. The payment of Separation Allowances was intended as a palliative to women, to maintain at least the acquiescence in the war of soldiers' wives. But it became instead a massive precedent, which was immediately latched upon by campaigners as a 'great experiment' in the Endowment of Motherhood by the State.

As we shall see (pp.61-2 below), that precedent also found expression in the extension of unemployment pay to include additional payments for dependent wives and children, marking a major turning point in both the history of the unemployed and the campaign for family allowances.

Practical Experience

The introduction of Separation Allowances provided incontrovertible evidence of the possibility of achieving a State endowment of motherhood:

> In this great experiment of separation allowances, the State has led the way in recognising the claims of mothers and their children. Is it unreasonable to hope that the principle, once being universally introduced, may become established, and that something may evolve out of the present system which shall be both applicable and practised in normal times?[148]

So wrote one campaigner, in the Liverpool Women's Industrial Council's Report on *The Social Effects of the Separation Allowances: An Experiment in the Endowment of Motherhood.*

This 'experiment' in State payments to mothers and children marked a turning point in Eleanor Rathbone's campaigning. In 1914, when war broke out, she had been asked by Liverpool City Council to deal with the administration of immediate relief to the wives of servicemen. A relief fund was established very rapidly, and thousands of families provided with daily food. At the same time, Eleanor Rathbone began to organize the social service machinery necessary to handle the massive volume of Separation Allowance claims made inevitable by a huge service call-up. In the months which followed, she had firsthand experience of hearing from women who came to claim about the difficulties of their lives — women who were not only from the poorest section of the community, which she had already visited as a social worker, but from other sections of the working class. These women spelled out to her that even for women married to men who had been in regular work the Separation Allowances, for all their inadequacies, meant they had more money in their hands than they had ever known.

One result of that experience was the detailed knowledge of and empathy with the lives of working class women which so distinguishes Eleanor Rathbone's writing. (See for example D.F. pp.177-95.) Whatever detailed and reasoned arguments Eleanor Rathbone used over the years in campaigning for State allowances, it is in the passages where she describes the reality of women's lives that her writing is most alive and passionate. At the same time, her work administering Separation Allowances demonstrated to her not only that the machinery for State payments for mothers and children already existed, but that the payments had transformed the lives of the women and children who received them in precisely the ways she had anticipated.

ELEANOR RATHBONE AND 'NEW FEMINISM'

The end of World War I found Eleanor Rathbone established in her reputation not only in Liverpool, but in the national feminist movement. Since 1911 she had been a member of the national executive of the National Union of Women's Suffrage Societies (NUWSS), and in the Spring of 1919, she was elected as President. The NUWSS had branches all over the country, and was based on a large 'grass roots' following of both working class and middle class women. (For example, two of the most prominent campaigners of the working class suffragette movement in Lancashire, Selina Cooper and Ada Nield Chew, worked full-time for the NUWSS.)[149] In 1919, with the major battle for the vote over, the NUWSS changed its name to the National Union of Societies for Equal Citizenship (NUSEC), and in electing Eleanor Rathbone as President began to take sides in the debate already raging about the future direction of the women's movement.

By the end of World War I, the recognition that women had played a crucial part in the war effort was commonplace. Women had clearly kept 'the country' going, and their work both in the home and in the paid labour force was more visible than ever. It was not that women's paid employment was a new phenomenon. (As we have seen, in 1911 domestic service was the largest industry in Britain.) But with the arrival of women in 'men's jobs' — in engineering, munitions and transport for example — there was a new public awareness that women were 'capable' of work outside the home. At the same time the very obvious dependence on women as homemakers during a war, and the fact that so many women ran the home without a man to 'look after' (or rather oversee) them, highlighted women's skill in home management.

One major result of this new public acknowledgement of women's contribution to the economy was the vote. Women were in a stronger position then ever before to press their case, and in the revolutionary atmosphere of post-war Europe, where, amongst other things, women were leading rent strikes and the squatting movement, the Government was anxious to avoid a renewed confrontation over suffrage. Sylvia Pankhurst records:

Undoubtedly the large part taken by women during the War in all branches of social service had proved a tremendous argument for their enfranchisement. Yet the memory of the old militancy, and the certainty of its recurrence if the claims of women were set aside, was a much stronger factor in overcoming the reluctance of those who would again have postponed the settlement. The shock to the foundations of existing social institutions already reverberating from Russia across Europe, made many old opponents desire to enlist the new enthusiasm of women voters to stabilize the Parliamentary machine. Above all, the changed attitude of the large public of all classes towards the position of women, which had grown up in the great militant struggle, made impossible a further postponement of our enfranchisement.[150]

In 1919, women over thirty were enfranchised, and although the franchise had still to be extended to full adult suffrage, the major battle for votes for women was won. The immediate question for the women's organizations that had been built during the suffragist agitation was what were now the priorities for organizing? In order to answer that question, women were debating what feminism meant. Did it mean simply equality with men, or special provisions for women which recognized the differences in their lives from men's — beginning with the fact of motherhood?

Equality: On Whose Terms?

In 1917, Eleanor Rathbone had set up the first Family Endowment Committee, which in Spring 1918 published its report, *Equal Pay and the Family: A Proposal for the National Endowment of Motherhood.* (See D.F. p.258.) Also in 1917, her essay 'The Remuneration of Women's Services' was published,[151] making the case which underpins the title of the Family Endowment Committee's Report — that women will never achieve equal pay while a man's wage is supposed to support a family, and therefore that a State payment to mothers and equal pay for women working outside the home are two sides of one coin.

The significance of the response to women's entry into 'men's jobs' during the war had been neatly characterized by Maude Royden in

'The Future of the Women's Movement', published alongside Eleanor Rathbone's essay.[152]

A woman who bore a child or many children, ran a household, and brought up a family fit and virtuous, was still only an arrested man and a perpetual minor, but a woman who can clip tickets in a tramcar is recognised at once as a superwoman – in other words, a man.[153]

While women who were equal to men on men's terms had got some recognition, that recognition amounted to a put-down of the work women were already doing and the skills this work demanded.

Royden, Rathbone and the 'New Feminists' felt that in demanding simple equality with men, the women's movement would fall into a trap in which the specific work and needs of women as homemakers and mothers would continue to be ignored and undervalued. They therefore argued for specific recognition for women as mothers, in particular through cash allowances. On the other hand, the 'equal rights' advocates felt that any demands based on women's special needs would undercut their claim to equal rights with men, in particular, equality in employment. A fierce and often bitter debate between the two sides followed, splitting women who had campaigned together for years in the suffragette movement. Eleanor Rathbone and Millicent Garrett Fawcett (whom Eleanor Rathbone had succeeded as President of the NUWSS) found themselves in fierce opposition to one another. And so did the working class Lancashire suffragettes Selina Cooper and Ada Nield Chew.

Selina Cooper . . . was a strong believer in giving mothers a guaranteed weekly allowance of their own. She had worked closely with Eleanor Rathbone as a National Union [NUSEC] organizer in 1905, and now she joined her in the campaign for family allowances. 'She went speaking, all for nothing, just her expenses, all over Lancashire and Yorkshire', [her daughter] Mary Cooper recalled.[154]

Ada Nield Chew was one of those who strongly disapproved . . . If 'babies were cared for during the hours the mothers were at work by trained mothers in special baby homes . . . the Lancashire married women would lead the van in the intelligent progress of her sex and class.' Child allowances should be combated by all enlightened women . . . The children must be cared for, and women must care for them. But not by paying poor women to be mothers. Women must be financially independent of men. But not by paying poor women to be wives. Marriage and motherhood should not be for sale.[155]

It is quite clear from these debates that opponents of family endowment or children's allowances regarded them as synonymous with a State endowment for mothers, and in fact made no distinction between the two demands. In other words, they opposed Family Allowances precisely because they would be a State payment to mothers and a wage for the work women were doing in the home.

The following passage, from a recent account of the movement for Family Allowances,[156] sums up the case of Eleanor Rathbone and the 'New Feminists':

Under Rathbone's leadership, the NUSEC moved towards claiming a real equality for women, meaning that 'the whole structure and movement of society [should] reflect in proportionate degree their experiences, their needs and their aspirations.' It was argued that feminists should work for reforms which reflected the reality of women's interests, rather than those which aimed to make them equal to men on men's terms. Women should be able to choose a mode of employment which suited them best, whether in the home or outside it, and should receive fair recompense for it. Family allowances or endowment were the key to the policy which evolved out of the new feminist goal of real equality. Women might thereby be paid a wage for their valuable work in the home as well as receiving a cash allowance for each child . . .[157]

The disagreements between the New Feminists and some of their opponents were fought out in NUSEC:

The NUSEC as an organisation did not adopt family allowances as part of its official platform until 1925, and then in the face of severe opposition from feminists who favoured an individual rather than a collective solution to the problem of inequality . . . [who] believed that feminists should work for an end to all legal disabilities, [and] it would then be up to each woman to make use of the equal opportunities available.[158]

The equal rights feminists objected to Eleanor Rathbone's insistence that legal and professional equalities were not enough. Meanwhile, Eleanor Rathbone and the New Feminists insisted that for most women equality with men in a world shaped by men's priorities would not solve the problem:

It is after all a poor kind of equality which Mr Fox accorded to Mrs Stork when he invited her to partake on equal terms of refreshment served in a flat saucer specially adapted to the elastic contours of his own flexible tongue. And feminists awoke to the fact that from some aspects our whole social fabric, man-made through generations to suit masculine interests and glorify masculine standards, was in the nature of that incommodious saucer to which Mr Fox accorded Mrs Stork equal access.[159]

The New Feminists felt that, for most women, a fundamental shift in the definition of what constitutes work, and remuneration for work in the home, were the fundamental issues, along with State maintenance for children. Without these measures most women would continue to be financially dependent on men; and also, the reality of equal pay and equal employment outside the home would be impossible to achieve.[160]

Rewriting History

These issues are still being debated in the women's movement today, with the same strength of feeling they aroused in the 1920s and 30s. Now that women already receive Family Allowances there are few who would openly oppose them,[161] even if, as *The Times* put it on the first pay-day (6 August 1946),

With the Family Allowances Act the thin edge of Miss Rathbone's wedge has been well and truly hammered into our social system.

But those who feel passionately that a State wage for mothers would undermine women's access to equality with men are profoundly aware that Family Allowances paid to mothers are precisely a payment in recognition of women's work in the home, in other words, a wage for motherhood. They have therefore tended to distort the history of Family Allowances, and to play down or overlook the massiveness of the movement for State payments to mothers which Eleanor Rathbone spoke for. This tendency to hide the history and scale of mothers' demands for payments has taken a number of forms, but central to them all has been the divorce of the introduction of Family Allowances from the women's movement, either by writing Eleanor Rathbone and the women's campaign for Family Allowances out of history, or by disconnecting the fight for financial independence for mothers from the achievement of Family Allowances,[162] or by discrediting Eleanor Rathbone, for example by the suggestion that her prime motivation was eugenic.[163]

The final touch has been to suggest both that Eleanor Rathbone was more concerned about State control of fertility than women's control over their own lives, and that feminism was barely an issue in the achievement of Family Allowances:

. . . Concern with women's independence and equality was not of paramount importance in the [1940s Family Allowances] debates and talk about increasing the value placed on motherhood was not an end in itself but largely a means to other ends – a bigger population.

(See pp.89-91 below for quotations from some of these debates, which make nonsense of this statement.)

Eleanor Rathbone accepted that family allowance would put the State's hand 'on the tiller of maternity' and thought it right that the quality and quantity of the population should be controlled . . .[164]

Above the article in which these particular statements appeared was a large photograph of Eleanor Rathbone with the caption:

Eleanor Rathbone, leading spokeswoman for the campaign for family allowances, did not mind the State's hand 'on the tiller of maternity'.[165]

The 'quotation' which is actually about *society* having its hand on the tiller of maternity, is taken from *The Disinherited Family*:

When society has taken upon itself the direct maintenance of children, whether it does it through the State or through the machinery of industry, it will have its hand for the first time on the tiller of maternity. Without any fussy interference or prying inquisitiveness into the privacy of individual families . . . it can do something at least to control the quality and quantity of population by methods less wasteful and ruthless than those of starvation, war, pestilence and the struggle for survival. (D.F. p.324.)

The context which precedes this passage is a discussion of whether the introduction of Family Allowances will increase or decrease the birth rate, and deals with the birth rate from the point of view of what women want. In particular, it details why women will never return to having eight, twelve or fourteen children; but also makes clear that women have been forced to limit the number of children they have by the conditions presently attached to motherhood, i.e. 'the economic conditions of glorified serfdom' (see D.F. pp.321-3):

There is no doubt that what tends to deter the abler and more thoughtful women from child-bearing, or at least induces them to bring it to an end at an early age, is . . . the complete dependency it involves for themselves on the husband's wage and the consequent inferiority (in a community dominated as ours is by money values) of their status to his; all the public opinion in short that expresses itself in the sayings, 'a man should be master in his own house'; 'he who pays the piper should call the tune'. (D.F. p.322.)

. . . So long as the battle for the suffrage and for women's education hung in the balance we feminists were very careful what we said and in whose presence we spoke when treating of these matters. But now that those irrevocable gifts have been given, we can afford to speak our minds . . . the work that a woman does in her own home in bearing and rearing children is not only so much more important to society, but so much more skilled, varied and interesting than nine out of ten of the jobs done by working women, or for the matter of that by working men, that only crass bad management on the part of society has made it seem more distasteful than tending a loom or punching a tram ticket. Divorce maternity from the economic conditions of a glorified serfdom and there will be no danger that the majority of capable women will shirk their fair share of it. (D.F. p.323.)

To divorce the passage about 'the State' controlling maternity from this context in which it appears is of course to change its meaning. It is also to ignore the fact that Eleanor Rathbone was saying that, without family allowances, the birth rate is more ruthlessly controlled by poverty and starvation. While it may be true that Eleanor Rathbone endorses some form of population control, there is no doubt that she was primarily concerned to give women the power to determine their own birth rate (see pp.31-2 above) — in sharp contrast to those feminists who even today advocate population control in the Third World as a 'solution' to poverty and starvation.[166]

For those who are anxious to attack Eleanor Rathbone, there is no shortage of material in her writings which can be accurately quoted and used to discredit her. There is no need to quote her out of context or to attribute to her motives that were not hers. For example, she writes in The Disinherited Family (p.318) of the 'dregs' of the working class, and on p.365 suggests 'provisions for checking the marriage of the mentally deficient or diseased, by requiring a certificate of health on marriage.' For me, these, and her proposals to exclude single mothers from the benefits of child allowances and motherhood endowment (see D.F. p.360), are prime examples of where I would want to criticize her – along with her willingness to compromise on crucial issues, like that of whether mothers' subsistence should be included in Family Allowance payments. But in exposing these, for me Eleanor Rathbone's weaknesses, the question remains – which individual achieved more for women in this period? And who better represented the millions of women, inside the home and outside, who were mothers? In particular, it is significant that none of her opponents had any alternative proposals to deal with the dependence of mothers and children on a man's wage whose consequences Eleanor Rathbone so vividly describes.

Women First
As someone involved in the practical activity of achieving political change, Eleanor Rathbone trimmed her arguments and demands continually to fit the political realities of the moment. For example, while her motivation was always feminist, at times her style was not. But suggestions that she was more interested in the population rate than women, or even that she was more interested in the welfare of children than the welfare of their mothers,[167] are to my mind clearly contradicted not only by the assessment of contemporaries, who always understood that her interest in Family Allowances was as a means of endowing motherhood, but by the evidence of this book, written when she was in her fifties and at the height of her powers, in particular by the passion in her descriptions of the conditions of women's lives. This concern is not matched by either the nature or the extent of her descriptions of children's needs, population considerations, or any other subject. And it is striking that, whatever the subject in hand, the question of what women think, feel or do is forever cropping up. In my reading of *The Disinherited Family*, the overwhelming proportion of the book is about women, and however Eleanor Rathbone may have couched the specific demands, her motivations were unmistakably feminist. But now that the book is once more in print, the reader can make her/his own judgement.

In Eleanor Rathbone's campaigning, of which *The Disinherited Family* was a part, she was concerned always to be realistic, that is, to take account of the particular balance of power between the working class and the State, and between women and men, as she perceived it. In 1935 she summed up her campaigning standpoint as follows:

We knew when it was necessary to compromise. There is a school of reformers which despises compromise. Suppose they set their affections on the moon. Their way is to go on chanting, 'We want the moon, we *want* the moon, we want *the* MOON.'[168] The plan which experience taught us was to begin by declaring, 'We want the moon,' but when certain that was unobtainable, to say firmly, 'If you can't give us the moon, give us that particular star, that big one'; if that failed, 'At least let us have that little star, just near the horizon. You know you can reach that one.' And when we got it, from the vantage ground of that little star, we proceeded to grasp at those nearest it.[169]

In other words, when she changed her immediate demands, that did not mean that she had changed her objectives, only that she thought it un-realistic to ask for everything at once. Thus although for Eleanor Rath-bone the importance of Family Allowances was always as a stepping-stone to a State endowment for mothers, this was not always at the front of her arguments because she sometimes did not think it politic to mention all that she and other women wanted.

In the political climate of the 1920s and with the end of the suf-fragette campaign, many middle class women withdrew from political activity, or else concentrated on their own careers rather than on the needs of women generally. In 1921 Eleanor Rathbone observed:

Like every other political and social movement, we have depended and must necessarily depend, largely on women who have some money and leisure to spend on something besides the struggle for existence. Such women had mostly got all they wanted for themselves out of the women's movement when it gave them the vote, the right to stand for Parliament and local authorities, and to enter the learned professions. Consequently, many of them have either left the movement or are giving it rather a half-hearted and inactive allegiance. When they were working for the suffrage, they found it good propaganda to speak and write of the wrongs of the sweated woman worker, the unhappily married wife, and the Poor Law widow . . . But now these useful arguments have served their turn, and the pledge implied by their use seems to be forgotten.[170]

It was already evident to working class observers, even before the vote was won, that the alliance forged between middle and working class women in the suffragette movement might not last. One woman wrote of the first Labour Party Women's Conference of 1918:

. . . the middle class educated women were divided from working women not only by their class but by their dismissal of the need to improve the condition of women who were mothers . . .[171]

But with the achievement of the vote, these divisions deepened (see pp.49-52 above). One result was that the New Feminists found themselves battling, even in the organizations of the women's movement, for mothers to be represented; and it was not until 1925, and then only after concerted campaigning and some bitter argument, that even NUSEC, with Eleanor Rathbone as president, was persuaded to support Family Allowances.

In the face of opposition from many of the women of her class, Eleanor Rathbone felt a new kind of isolation. But she drew strength from her confidence in the subterranean women's movement (see D.F. pp.191-5) with which she was always in touch.

THE WOMEN'S MOVEMENT BETWEEN THE WARS

There is a myth that the women's movement died in 1914, with the outbreak of war, or at the latest in 1919 with the achievement of the principle of female suffrage. World War I and the end of the suffrage agitation did mean that a certain phase of the women's movement was over — not only had some women got all they wanted, but the demonstrations of tens of thousands of women which had characterized the pre-war period were a thing of the past. The movement now entered a new phase.

The recent experience of the women's movement of the 1960s to 80s provides a clue to what happened to the earlier movement. In the eyes of the media and public recorders of fact, the absence of demonstrations, street protests and large national events is prima-facie evidence of a movement's demise. In reality, in the 1980s nothing could be further from the truth. Women's groups of almost every kind now abound — from women opposing cruise missiles to prostitutes' organizations,[172] from mums' groups to women's studies. The movement has grown beyond all recognition, encompassing women of all backgrounds to a much greater degree than in the 1960s or early 1970s, and involved in every possible kind of activity. Whether or not there are mass demonstrations cannot be the only measure of a movement.[173] Rather it is a significant measure of the strength of today's movement that women in the 1980s assume rights which were being contested in the more publicly militant days of the late 1960s and early 1970s.[174]

The same kind of phenomenon seems to have been true in the 1920s. Women like Vera Brittain and Dora Russell, who were politically active as young women at that time,[175] assumed a freedom from parental control which was still hotly contested in 1905, assumed a degree of equality with men which the suffragettes had had to fight for, assumed a sexual frankness which was still taboo before World War I.[176] Both of them were already able to consider that the right to have children *and* a life of their own should be theirs, whereas for the majority of early militants the only alternative to being totally trapped by motherhood was not to have children. Women in the twenties grew up in a different world from the one their mothers had grown up in, and a crucial part of that world was a new level of power for women. They wore different clothes (one-tenth the weight of the Victorian dress of their grandmothers), cut their hair short, danced outrageous new dances like the shimmy. And they had a more openly defiant attitude. As well as the writing of the period, which vividly challenges the myth that women in the 1920s were conservative (Dora Russell writing in 1925 said it was a downright lie and 'insidious propaganda'),[177] there are plenty of indices of the strength of the women's movement in the 1920s, once your criteria are not membership of self-pronounced feminist organizations, or mass demonstrations of women making overtly 'feminist' demands.

One very good example is the explosion in membership of the Women's Co-operative Guild, which grew from 31,000 members in 1921 to a staggering 67,000 members in 1,400 branches by 1931. The influence of the Guild on individual women's lives (see p.36 above) as well as on legislation of the 1920s and 1930s cannot be overestimated. Women and men from working class backgrounds, who recall the inter-war period, refer time and again to the involvement of mothers and wives in the Guild, and testify to what the Guild meetings meant to the thousands of women who attended them. Women interviewed in the Rhondda Valley in the 1970s about their memories of the coal-mining community of the 20s described not only the drudgery of their mothers' lives as 'the slaves of slaves', but their mothers' determination to be treated with more respect by sons and husbands, and the degree to which membership of the Guild made that possible. One woman re-called her mother's weekly excursions to Women's Co-operative Guild meetings, and her comment 'I'm not as dull as I used to be.'[178] And in refusing the backbreaking physical housework of preparing nightly hot baths for the miners — husbands, sons and brothers — and washing pit clothing, these same women pressed the miners to demand amenities from the mine-owners which would reduce the women's working day.[179]

The legislative history of the 1920s tells its own story of women organizing. In 1919 the Sex Disqualification Removal Act removed the last legal disabilities faced by professional women. In the same year, the Maternity and Child Welfare Act provided Government funds for welfare clinics — a measure for which the Women's Co-operative Guild had campaigned over the years. In 1923 the Matrimonial Causes Act brought greater equality in grounds for divorce. 1925 saw a series of Parliamentary Acts which brought new protection for mothers, with the Guardianship of Infants Act giving mothers equal rights to guard-ianship of their children (who previously had 'belonged' to the father), the Summary Jurisdiction (Separation and Maintenance) Act and the Widows, Orphans and Old Age Contributory Pensions Act — all of them measures for which Eleanor Rathbone had personally campaigned, and which were also part of NUSEC's programme.

Improving Working Conditions

Of more immediate significance to most women than even these important legislative victories were the Government Housing Acts, beginning with the Rent Restrictions Act of 1915 (the result of rent strikes organized by women), which was followed by the Housing Acts of 1919, 1923 and 1924, and by various legislation providing Government subsidies for house building programmes and slum clearance in the 1930s. The massive housing programme of the period 1919-41 increased the housing stock of England and Wales to the point where there was, at least in theory, a housing surplus.[180] In the 1920s, most of these houses were built by local authorities, but there were Government subsidies for both local authority and private houses, which were built to new standards. They went to working class families, many of whom enjoyed running water and decent amenities for the first time — though even the council rents were beyond the means of families of the unemployed. The 1930s also saw a boom in home ownership for the working class, with relatively low-cost private housing and mortgages made available to wage-earners.

New housing standards, and a new awareness among architects that architecture should be about people[181] benefited women most of all, and it was widely recognized that housing was above all a women's issue. For all the ugliness and social dislocation that some of the new housing estates and flats brought, there was a world of difference between fetching water from a standpipe in a yard with open privvies, and being able to turn on a tap and flush a toilet of your own (even if the toilet was outside the back door); between cooking on an open fire and turning on a stove.

Although housing is often missing from 'women's issues' or women's victories, there were many women in the 1910s and 20s who were profoundly aware that housing was a feminist issue. Eleanor Rathbone was one of them. In this book she refers several times to the fact that the house is the woman's work place, and that the 'housing issue' is therefore the issue of housewives' working conditions. She even makes a direct link between housework not being paid and the inadequacy of domestic architecture, making clear that the waste of women's time due to bad planning results from no value being placed on their labour time. (See D.F. p.188.) She had made housing her special concern as a Liverpool City Councillor, and her maiden speech in the House of Commons in 1929 was in response to the Government's latest Housing Act. In pressing for rent rebates to be scaled according to the number of children in the family, so that the State in effect would pay towards the cost of housing for children, she helped to push through a clause in the 1929 Housing Act allowing councils to make rent rebates proportional to family size, and at the same time scored a victory for the principle of Family Allowances which she was quick to capitalize on.

The rent strikes and squatting of the 1920s and 30s were always organized by women, even though men often took much of the credit. It was women who paid (or refused to pay) the rent in most working class families and who confronted the rent collector. It was women who insisted that they and the children must have a roof over their heads even if officially there was no housing available, and who were thus the initiators of the squatting movement. It was women who both felt most acutely the impact of inadequate housing or high rents, and physically confronted authority when rents were withheld. It is no accident that Sylvia Pankhurst, organizing in London's East End before and during World War I, thought that the vote could be won by a massive rent strike. And no accident either that it is women pensioners who recall the rent strikes their mothers organized.

Women's part in the general working class militancy of the 1920s and 30s has been as hidden as their central role in every working class movement. During strikes, women had to keep the strike going by feeding a family on next to nothing. And when the unemployed organized, and met in kitchens and on street corners, women played a key part. They also did their own share of demonstrating and more formal organizing. The following is taken from a description of the aftermath of a demonstration of miners' wives in Mansfield. They had gone to picket the house of an advocate of a return to work during the 1926 miners' lockout:

The demonstration then started on its return: while on the road home the women were stopped by . . . the Clipstow miners' union official who told them to mind their own business as they could look after their own affairs constitutionally. Well, they got over him alright and proceeded home after doing a good day's work.[182]

During the 1926 General Strike, some of the Councils of Action which sprang up all over the country included housewives as members, while the unemployed 'Go to the Guardians' demonstrations of the 1920s, demanding relief outside the workhouse for all the unemployed, always included large numbers of women. That the formal unemployed organizations often continued the sectarian trade union tradition of excluding women from meetings or committees did not prevent women making their own demands heard. London women, for example, demonstrated in Whitehall demanding milk for expectant mothers, as well as equal relief for single women living at home, whose parents were expected to support them and who were being forced into street prostitution to survive.[183]

In times of high unemployment, as in the 1920s and 30s, there is a subtle shift in the balance of power between women and men. While women carry the extra burden of managing a home on relief or unemployment pay, and may suffer directly the violence of men's frustration with poverty and lack of jobs; at the same time, since the man is not the breadwinner, he is not the boss in the home and in the community to the same degree, and the contribution that women's work in the home makes to the family is more evident. In addition, for families with dependent children, the unemployment pay of the 1920s and 30s for the first time recognized the existence of women and children – as a result of the claim women had been making for recognition in every sphere.

Kitchen Politics and the Unemployed

In 1915 a special 'out of work donation' for unemployed ex-servicemen had been introduced which followed the precedent established with Separation Allowances by providing for the wives and children of servicemen on the dole. This meant that an unemployment benefit for the first time included allowances for the family. In 1918 this temporary 'out of work donation' had been extended to all workers covered by health insurance, and in the 1921 Unemployment Act the dependants' allowances established in the 'out of work donation' became an integral part of unemployment pay.[184] The payments were for a maximum of thirty-two weeks only, and the amounts were at first very small (5/- a week for the wife, and 1/- a week for each child), but the break with the principle of 'insurance' (since contributions were not made on this basis), and in particular, the acceptance by the State of financial responsibility for the wives and children of the unemployed in a measure which was outside the Poor Law, and financed directly by central government money, was a victory of major significance. As one historian noted:

The government, in this bill, conceded the whole principle of family allowances, though without admitting it. The precedent was more important than the scales.[185]

The interplay between the level of unemployment benefits achieved by the unemployed movement between the wars and the final introduction of Family Allowances is dealt with in more detail on p.84

below. *But the significance of the campaigning by women which resulted in unconditional State payments for mothers and children through the Separation Allowances during World War I, and its immediate impact in creating a precedent for unemployment pay, has never been recognized.* It was this precedent of 'dependants' allowances' which lay behind the new phenomenon by which families of men on the dole might receive as much or more than when the man was in waged work, an anomaly which was to lead inevitably to State dependants' allowances for the families of those in work.

Throughout the 1920s and 30s there were families who were better off when the man was unemployed and collecting benefits for the family as well as himself, than when the man was in work. A survey in Cardiff showed that 45 per cent of married men had received less money in wages in their last job than they were receiving in unemployment allowances.[186] In addition, where the wife often did not know what the man earned when he was in work, she knew exactly what his unemployment pay or relief amounted to, and therefore what she could claim.

The history of the 1930s, in particular, is often presented as unrelieved defeat for the unemployed, since evidence of those victories that there were, and of the resistance that women and young people in particular were putting up, is often ignored. For example, just as since the 1960s many young people have made clear that they would rather be on the dole than do many of the jobs that are being offered, so in the 1930s 'work-shy' youth were the dismay of some contemporary observers:

Many people, particularly the young married men, were better off on the dole than on the low wages which they could earn if employed – especially if work was intermittent . . . Many men out of work accepted their fate . . . To such men a spell of employment was a holiday . . . Some might join a WEA class, like the Durham miner who took a five-year course in English literature; others found a use for their leisure in reading, or in taking part in plays or joining in the other activities of a community house or unemployed men's club. Some went for long walks – a week's walking holiday on 3s 5d was the recollection of one; others played football . . . Some worked in an allotment, others kept poultry . . . Many found odd jobs . . . The young men had never known steady work and did not fret at the lack of it. They 'were undisciplined and carefree, the dingy butterflies of the back streets . . .' In Cardiff, 52 per cent of the unemployed youths interviewed visited the cinema once a week and almost half of these twice a week; in Liverpool and Glasgow as many as 80 per cent went to the cinema at least once a week. Others resorted to the many licensed clubs which existed in the cities, where billiards, gambling and raffles flourished . . . The 'disinherited youth' had grown up on the dole, after holding some blind alley job or serving a barren apprenticeship. Many had come to accept this existence in Liverpool . . . 30 per cent of the unemployed men aged 20 to 34 could be classed as work-shy . . . [187]

Photographs taken by Humphrey Spender of the 1936 Jarrow protest march[188] provide striking evidence that the spirit of defiance amongst unemployed youth evident today was a feature of the 1930s as well.[189] It is interesting that even these photographs have been desscribed as depressing,[190] in spite of the 'ocular proof ' they provide that the Jarrow march was far from the gloomy silent procession of so many descriptions. It is interesting too that the reality of the spirit of that march emerges not in the historians' accounts, but in these contemporary photographs by a particularly honest observer – and in the oral tradition. Alan Price's pop-song, derived from firsthand accounts alive in his own community, tells its own story of the Jarrow march, and of women's part in it:

> My name is Geordie Mackintyre
> And the bairns don't even have a fire
> So the wife says, 'Geordie go to London town
> And if they don't give us half a chance
> Don't even give us a second glance
> Then Geordie with my blessings burn them down.'
>
> Come on follow the Geordie boys
> They'll fill your heart with joy
> They're marching for their freedom now.
> Come on follow the Jarrow lads
> They make your heart feel glad
> They're singing now, yes now is the hour.
>
> My name is little Billy White
> And I know what's wrong and I know what's right
> And the wife says, 'Geordie, go to London town
> And if they don't give us a couple of bob
> Won't even give you a decent job
> Then Geordie with my blessings burn them down!'
>
> Come on follow the Geordie boys [etc. as in chorus above] [191]

The impression of women's involvement in the Jarrow march, in this case as instigators, is backed up by comments from Harry Henderson, who marched against unemployment in the 1930s and again in 1981:

Mr Henderson . . . said yesterday [1 May 1981] he was surprised that so few women would be marching the whole way. 'The Jarrow march was led by a woman, Ellen Wilkinson,' he said, 'and women are more vulnerable to unemployment than anyone else.'[192]

There were even women's contingents on some of the 1930s unemployment protest marches. For example, in 1932 a national demonstration against the means test included a women's contingent which had assembled in Burnley, Lancashire, for what was to be a three-week march, and included women from all the Northern industrial towns.[193]

Gains and Losses
The thirties was a decade of resistance and organizing as well as of defeat.

This was the decade of the depression, but it was also a high point of working class activity. Women from the Leeds clothing industry, for example, look back to the thirties as a time of great excitement – not only because as young women entering a trade and having money of their own they had a measure of independence which they enjoyed to the full, but because they led the employers quite a dance. One woman, Gertie Roche, in an interview about her life recorded in 1972, recalled the 1930s as a period of continuous conflict with management at Burton's clothing factory, the major employers in the Leeds rag trade.[194] She started work as soon as she left school at fourteen, in common with most of the other Leeds women of her generation:

I've been sent home a few times for insolence when I was young. I remember I put my hat on . . . before one o'clock and they sent me home.[195]

She was told not to come back, but her workmates threatened to strike if she were not allowed back next morning, and the forewoman backed down. 'There were always little strikes going on in Burton's before the [all out] 1936 strike.'[196] At the same time, she and others of her workmates were very conscious of the international climate which provided the framework to what was happening in Britain:

At that time the big campaigning issue was the Spanish Civil War . . . we collected tons of food for the Spanish refugees . . . And we were really involved in trying to get the refugees out of Spain . . . There was a fantastic amount of political activity . . . one continuous campaign . . . It was really wonderful to belong to it.[197]

Eleanor Rathbone was also inspired by events in Europe, and active in support of the Spanish Republicans, including vocally challenging the Government's non-intervention policy in Parliament. She visited Spain in April 1937 and wrote of her visit that it had been

. . . far more inspiring than depressing . . . In these days of defeatism, it is something to have seen a great city full of men and women who throughout a year of deprivation, terror and suffering have looked death in the face without losing their courage, their complete confidence in the victory of their cause, or even their high spirits.

. . . a great people – great at least in the qualities of courage and devotion to un-selfish ends . . . Think of them as I saw them . . . in Madrid and Valencia, men and women, young and old, without a trace of fear or dejection in their faces though bombs were crashing a few yards away and taking their daily toll of victims . . . building up a system of social services that would have been a credit to any nation at war . . .[198]

In some industries, there were more jobs for women than ever before. But there were also parts of the country where there were simply no jobs for women at all except in domestic service. In many industries that did employ women, a marriage bar was introduced – especially in office work — so that a woman who married lost her job automatically. Women fiercely resented being forced into financial dependence on a husband, and fought the marriage bar wherever they could, often hiding their marriage when they couldn't confront the restrictions outright.

Women's refusal of financial dependence and poverty was also, as ever, reflected in the population statistics. After a brief baby boom following World War I, the 1920s and 30s saw what was described as a 'collapse' in the birth rate, with an all-time low in 1933, and by the late 1930s babies were again high on the agenda of Government concern.[199] Women had put them there. The movements for financial independence and birth control, whose interrelationship Eleanor Rathbone describes so vividly in this book (see D.F. pp.192-5), were becoming more and more visible as she had predicted. Working class women increasingly had the power not only to impress upon their husbands that birth control was important, but to impress on a wide variety of campaigners that birth control should become a public political issue. In 1921, Marie Stopes' first birth control clinic had opened in London, and by 1925-26 clinics were opening in several towns outside London. From 1923 onwards the Women's Co-operative Guild campaigned for the Ministry of Health to allow birth control advice to be given in the maternity and child welfare clinics, and by 1934 was calling for the legalization of abortion — an idea which would have seemed quite outrageous twenty, or even ten years earlier, and testimony to how forcefully women asserted their own needs during the intervening years.

At the same time, large-scale unemployment, wage reductions in some industries, and the defeat of the 1926 General Strike, must be taken into account to understand what women considered they could win during the second half of the 1920s and the early 1930s. For example, some opponents of both birth control and State payments to mothers feared that in this climate the State might want to use these measures against women — birth control to solve unemployment by 'population management',[200] and State payments to mothers to keep women out of the job market, or to keep men's wages down.

In 1938, with the Tories firmly entrenched in government, Labour MP Ellen Wilkinson, who had been a great supporter of Family Allowances in the early 1920s,[201] feared that any Tory support for Family Allowances must mean that they would be misused, and argued against their introduction:

Now from that hard-shelled imperialist . . . Mr. Leopold Amery, comes the proposal for family allowances . . . [they] want to feed the existing and potential cannon fodder with the greatest economy . . . Pay the money for the upkeep of each child, don't give it [through wages] to the individual workmen, who may have a few or no children. In short, apply the Means Test to wages.[202]

In the same article, she clearly distinguishes between Eleanor Rathbone and the 'Amery type':

Eleanor Rathbone MP, a well-known feminist, a great fighter for democracy and not in any sense a 'female Amery', has led the movement for family allowances for years. As a feminist I have a certain sympathy . . . Miss Rathbone's argument is persuasive because she bases it on the helplessness of the mother in existing conditions . . . the man is free to give her as little as he likes . . . and she has no redress.

But Ellen Wilkinson nevertheless opposed family allowances, concluding: 'Under capitalism the best way for the worker is to press through his trade unions for higher wages and shorter hours.' Ellen Wilkinson was in this article typical of the Labour Party in assuming that women's right to independence was secondary to 'working class issues' as the Labour Party defined them. The Labour Party opposed both birth control and cash payments to mothers throughout the 1920s and early 30s, in spite of the fact that in 1930 a special TUC and Labour Party Inquiry backed Family Allowances, believing they would be a point of power in wage bargaining by removing children 'from the firing line'.[203] (See p.93 below.)

Certainly there are dangers in any demand because the State always tries to recoup with one hand what it gives with the other. The wider availability of birth control does also mean that the State can use it to encourage forced or 'self-imposed' population control if women lack the circumstances to have the children they want. State payments to mothers can mean that the State will attempt more direct control over women. It may also try to use the payments to cut men's wages. Whether it will succeed depends on the strength and unity of the movement — as we have seen in the fight for unconditional Separation Allowances (pp.46-7 above).

There is no guarantee that the achievement of *any* demand will be an unambiguous victory. Even where it is a demand which speaks to the needs of those with least power, their organizing can be used to buy more powerful women off and so split the movement. This is what happened with the achievement of women's suffrage.

The vote and a measure of equal rights in law, great victories, did buy some women off. Eleanor Rathbone describes vividly who they were, not only in her speeches to NUSEC (see p.56 above) but in this book (see for example D.F. p.194). The involvement of women with independent means in the women's movement had been a vital factor in the flowering of a publicly feminist movement which was able to publicize the fights women were making and claim them for all women.

Their participation made possible the creation of women's newspapers and magazines, and women's organizations financed and controlled by women.[204] But by the 1920s, as Eleanor Rathbone points out (see p.56 above), 'Such women had mostly got all they wanted for themselves' as a result of their alliance with working class women, and they reneged on that alliance. Without their help, the struggles that working class women were making on their own behalf were no longer visible — hidden behind what the 'working class' (i.e. men) were doing. And the same power they had earlier brought to support working class women these middle class women now used against them, by claiming that their own priorities and demands were all there was to feminism.

The opposition of these middle class women limited the scope and influence of the New Feminists. In organizations as diverse as the Labour party and NUSEC, it acted as a brake on support for the New Feminists' specific demands, in particular State payments for mothers. And the possibilities for speaking openly about the need for the world to be completely transformed by women, according to all women's needs and experiences, were limited by this shrinking in what feminism was supposed to encompass into demands for 'equality' with men.[205]

Eleanor Rathbone's writing of the late 1920s and 30s reflects both the general working class defeats of the period and this narrowing of the women's movement. As we have seen, from the call for a State endowment of motherhood of the 1910s,[206] by 1924, in the midst of the severe economic depression (D.F. p.175), she is in this book more cautious about how she formulates the demand, leaving it to the reader to judge, for example, 'as to the relative merits of direct provision for families through occupational pools or State endowment' (D.F. p.376), and even backtracking, as I have already discussed, on whether the mother's and children's money should be paid as separate sums or merged into one sum. Despite the continuing currency of the idea of endowment of motherhood throughout the 1920s and 30s,[207] the narrow conception of feminism of many middle class women, especially many of the women in the political parties, meant that Eleanor Rathbone was thrown into greater dependence on men in those parties than had been the case in the 1910s. At the same time, the Labour Party and trade unions (with the notable exceptions of the Independent Labour Party [ILP] and the Miners' Union) dragged their feet on the question of cash for mothers throughout the 1920s and 30s.[208] The result, at a time when getting any money out of the State presented a major problem, was that Eleanor Rathbone was forced not only to press for 'family endowment' rather than the endowment of motherhood, but to fight for family allowances by any means possible, rather than calling unambiguously for the State to foot the bill.

Home Health

By the end of the 1930s, however, the general political climate was changing and the women's movement was once again coming together as a movement of all classes. Evidence of women's rising expectations hit the newspapers with headlines like 'Good-time girls won't have babies,' 'Selfish wives prefer cocktail bars to nurseries' and articles which joked about women who preferred Baby Austin cars to babies.[209] And demands for improved conditions of maternity, including State allowances for the cost of raising children and financial recognition for mothers, were once again a feature of large sections of the women's movement. Sylvia Pankhurst's book on maternity, *Save Our Mothers* was published in 1932; *Working Class Wives*, the Women's Health Enquiry Committee's report,[210] in 1939 — and it is interesting to see how much more wide-ranging are the demands of the later publication, despite Sylvia Pankhurst's undoubtedly more radical view of the world.

With a 50 per cent reduction in the infant mortality rate since the beginning of the century, the emphasis of campaigns around maternity and infant welfare was now clearly on the mother's health.[211] The experience of welfare and maternity clinics and the work of the Women's Health Enquiry Committee brought to light with some statistical clarity the experience that women knew only too well of continuous ill health and its relationship to poverty. Eleanor Rathbone had already recorded her impression of housewives' health in *The Disinherited Family* (see pp.184-5), but now there were surveys to back her up. And the fact that women in the home had no health insurance under the National Insurance Acts was increasingly recognized as a scandal, as the working conditions of housewives became a major political issue. Even those sections of the women's movement which had felt in 1919 that women's equality was now only a matter of achieving access to men's jobs, had by the late 1930s come to see that as long as millions of women were condemned to 'domestic slavery of mind and body',[212] the real choices open to all women were limited.

It was women who had 'made it' who constituted the Women's Health Enquiry Committee, set up in 1933 'to investigate the general conditions of health among women, especially among married working-women.'[213] They were JPs, an MBE, women with degrees and letters after their names, representing organizations as diverse as the Standing Joint Committee of Industrial Women's Organizations, the Women Public Health Officers Association, the Council of Scientific Management in the Home, the Midwives' Institute and others, as well as the ubiquitous Women's Co-operative Guild and the National Council of Equal Citizenship (as NUSEC was now called). Their attitude to the women whose lives they are describing is sometimes patronizing, for example: 'It is little comfort that these women have learnt to accept their lot with so little complaint . . .'[214] (which contrasts sharply with Eleanor Rathbone's assessment of women's aspirations [see D.F. pp. 191-5]). But nevertheless the variety and scope of their report and recommendations, the sympathy of their descriptions of the domestic slavery women faced, and the incidental information about the women's meetings attended by working class housewives, are all testimony to the fact that the women's movement was alive and well among those sections of society which were represented on the Women's Health Enquiry Committee, and among the 'working class wives' whose lives they are describing.

Their conclusions and recommendations clearly linked improvements in women's health to the provision of more money for 'the family' – in the form of both a cash Family Allowance to be paid to the mother and higher wages for men – and to improved social services to take some of the burden off women (including 'home helps' to relieve mothers not only in times of illness or crisis, but to enable mothers to take holidays away from home). They also recommended women's clinics, staffed by women doctors, to take care of all aspects of women's health; the extension of National Health Insurance to cover wives and children; and the establishment of women's clubs for 'recreation, holidays and leisure'.[215] They concluded that the fundamental cause of women's ill health is lack of money in women's hands and the domestic slavery that accompanies this poverty. And although they shied away from advocating money from the State for the mother in her own right, they came close, proposing that Family Allowances be paid direct to the mother on the grounds that:

In this way, not only would the anomalies as between employed and unemployed wage-earners vanish, but *the working mothers themselves would take their place in the economic system.* They control the family expenditure and perform the various tasks in connection with the care of the family. It is right, therefore, that they should be entitled, as they were under the system of separation allowances during the last war, to an income proportionate to the number of mouths they have to feed . . . The extension of the social services cannot go all the way . . . Power should be given to [the mother] to determine in some measure for herself, the needs of herself and her children, more than is possible if the help granted by the community is entirely in kind . . . For example . . . although there should be the provision of facilities for the performance of certain household tasks in a communal centre, the housewife should be free to choose whether to do these jobs herself, at home or at the centre, or to pay someone else to do them.[216]

They followed Eleanor Rathbone in clearly coming down on the side of cash payments to mothers,[217] as well as improved social services. (See D.F. p.366 ff.) In fact their recommendations are an index of the kind of respectability and wide-ranging support the demand for Family Allowances had achieved by 1939, which made legislation an imminent possibility.

CAMPAIGNING FOR FAMILY ALLOWANCES

This support for the demand for Family Allowances was the result not only of the demands and activities of women generally, but of steady campaigning by Eleanor Rathbone and the Family Endowment Society.

The first 'Family Endowment Committee', set up on Eleanor Rathbone's initiative in 1917 to spread the idea of endowment of motherhood, was made up of activists from the women's suffrage movement and the ILP and Labour Party.[218] It had in 1918 produced its conclusions, *Equal Pay and the Family: A Proposal for the National Endowment of Motherhood,* in the form of a 1/- pamphlet which called for 'a continuation and extension' of Separation Allowances and claimed that 'To-day . . . the endowment of motherhood [is] the most urgent question of the hour.'[219] Its work was sufficiently influential for Eleanor Rathbone to be invited in 1921 to address an all-party group of MPs in the House of Commons, and in 1924 a more permanent organization, the Family Endowment Society (FES), was set up. This new Family Endowment Society, however, was more heterogeneous, operating as a pressure group for the general principle of 'family endowment', rather than calling specifically for 'motherhood endowment by the State'.[220]

Eleanor Rathbone supervised the day-to-day running of the FES, and her gift for imaginative organizing was reflected in the wide range of activities which she saw as contributing to the campaign for Family Endowment. Operating as a campaigning pressure group, the Society kept the issue of Family Endowment alive by a stream of publications – from one-page leaflets, to pamphlets, to letters to the press; by providing evidence to numerous Royal Commissions and lobbying MPs; by a never-ending round of speaking engagements; and by constant pressure for immediate legislation.

Extra-Parliamentary Priorities

In keeping with Eleanor Rathbone's vision of organizing, the FES spent most of its financial resources on grassroots campaigning. Thus in 1925 (the year before the Miners' Lockout and the General Strike), the decision was taken to concentrate on the Mining Industry, and accordingly

19,000 copies of an FES publication entitled *Family Allowances in the Mining Industry* were circulated free of charge, in response to requests from branches of the Miners' Union, and another 11,000 free copies distributed at miners' meetings.[221] This publication dealt with the proposal, put forward to the Royal Commission on the Coal Industry by the FES, that employers in the industry should pay a family allowance to help families with children. Throughout 1925 and 1926, speakers were sent to speak to local miners' unions at all levels (in 1926 alone, Eleanor Rathbone spoke at Delegates' Meetings and individual Lodges in Lancashire, Cheshire, Durham, Northumberland, North Staffordshire and Cannock Chase, and to the Midlands and Northumberland Miners' Executives).[222] At the same time, research efforts were concentrated on finding out about Family Allowance systems in the mining industries of Europe. The efforts paid off. The Miners' Union accepted the principle of Family Allowances, and called for the State to pay them. They were thus the first union to support publicly a system of State Family Allowances, to be financed by the Exchequer and paid to the mother – a support which they maintained from 1926 onwards. (Helped no doubt by the fact that the needs of miners' wives and children have always been more than usually present in the men's demands, because the women have formed such an organized force in the closed community around the mines.) At the same time, in opposing the introduction of Family Allowances by *mine-owners*,[223] the Miners' Union strengthened Eleanor Rathbone's hand in pressing for State Family Allowances rather than the industry-wide payments which she saw as a compromise only, and much inferior to a State system (see D.F. pp.347-8 and 376-8).

It is worth noting, too, that Eleanor Rathbone, an upper class politician, and a woman, was not only invited to speak but well received at grassroots miners' meetings. It says much not only for her abilities as a speaker, but for her attitude to men, and working class men in particular. On the one hand, she refused to gloss over or romanticize the reality of hostility from working class men (like that of middle and upper class men) to women's independence; on the other, she recognized with great sympathy that working class men pay a great personal cost in order to support a wife and children financially,[224] and that wage-earners have much more of a right than employers to be cautious about any new proposals for changes in income distribution 'because they can least afford to take risks' (D.F. p.330). In general, for all her caution it is clear in this book that she hopes not only that State Family Allowances would benefit mothers and children, but that they would put the working class as a whole in a stronger position in relation to employers.[225] And her down-to-earth realism on the question of which class would ultimately pay for Family Allowances — that it would depend on the balance of power between classes at the moment of their introduction, and the skill with which each class 'uses its economic and political bargaining power to secure the equivalent of its contribution' (D.F. p.378) — would undoubtedly have appealed to working class people who know only too well that this is the reality of wage bargaining.

The impact of Eleanor Rathbone and the Family Endowment Society on the miners is also a clear indication of the effectiveness with which the FES organized, and of the grassroots working class interest in the principle of Family Allowances as a means of redistributing wealth to those whose need is greatest. With limited financial resources, the FES decided that the Head Office of the Society could manage with one full-time paid worker, and that priority should be given to paying organizers outside London, and to providing monthly 'speakers' notes' for all subscribers. From 1928 there were paid organizers in the North, the Midlands and Scotland, distributing FES literature, organizing conferences, addressing meetings, organizing articles and correspondence in the local press, and providing the campaigning groundwork that was so crucial in getting the idea of Family Allowances accepted as a practical proposal. The Society's Report for the year ending February 1930 gives some idea of their activities:

... in the Northern and Midland areas 64 towns have been visited and over 1,200 interviews effected with Trade Union officials, representatives of all the political parties, prominent individuals and others, while 105 meetings have been held.[226]

Between 1927 and 1930, because a Joint Committee of the Labour Party and the Trades Union Congress (TUC) was taking evidence on the subject of Family Allowances, the FES concentrated on trades councils and trade union and Labour Party branches, as well as relevant women's organizations — from Railwaywomen's Guilds, to Women's Co-operative Guilds, to Women's Sections of the Labour Party — and again the groundwork paid off. The Majority Report recommended that there should be an immediate State payment to mothers of 5/- for the first child and 3/- for subsequent children.[227] This Joint Committee, which had been appointed by the General Council of the TUC and the National Executive of the Labour Party, wrote in their report:

After a full Inquiry, the most exhaustive, we think, that has yet been made in this country on the question of Family Allowances, the signatories to this Report have arrived at the conclusion that the most valuable step that can now be taken to further the welfare of the nation's children is the institution of a scheme of Family Allowances to be paid in cash to the mothers ... in order to lighten the burden that now falls on the mothers who are trying to bring up a family on a hopelessly inadequate income . . . We are convinced that the money so disbursed would be spent both wisely and economically, since in our view the mothers themselves are best able, because of their own experience and training and their overwhelming personal interest, to apportion this expenditure in the way most calculated to secure the well-being of their children. No public authority can, in our view, make money go as far in the provision of food, clothing and healthy surroundings, as can the mothers who have learned economy in the hard school of experience . . . In our view the only satisfactory system is one financed and administered by the State, payments being made direct to the mother . . . through the Post Office. The allowances should be paid in respect of illegitimate children in precisely the same way as for legitimate children.[228]

They also pointed out that, since there was already an income tax rebate for children, middle class income tax payers were in effect receiving a Family Allowance from the State to the extent of the tax on £60 for the first child, and that it was only justice that this advantage should be extended to working class people whose wages were too low to bring them within the income tax bracket.

Eleanor Rathbone clearly believed that the success of Parliamentary lobbying and of maintaining the support of the intellectuals and Government advisers like Beveridge[229] was dependent on the pressure of public opinion outside Parliament and outside intellectual circles, and that this public opinion had to be mobilized by direct contact with as many organizations and groups of all kinds as possible. The reports of the FES give some indication of the range of organizations she and others addressed,[230] and of the growing demand for speakers and information which they had to meet.

Inside the Corridors of Power
From 1929, Eleanor Rathbone was also ideally placed to bring her extra-Parliamentary campaigning work to bear directly on Parliamentary debates and legislative planning. In that year, she was elected as an Independent MP, without ties to any of the political parties.[231] One of her first moves within the House of Commons was to organize an all-party Committee of MPs to press for Family Endowment — keeping herself firmly in the background since she was too identified as something of a fanatic on the subject usefully to take a public lead. She organized other people to put forward the case for Family Endowment to governments of the day, so that the proposal would be identified with as wide a range of support as possible. An obituary published in January 1946 records:

Her contribution to the legislative assembly was a distinctively feminine contribution. By this I do not mean only that she was at first mainly interested in the improvement of family conditions . . . I mean . . . the persistence and zeal with which she identified herself with her own causes . . . she would stalk through the lobby, one arm weighted with the heavy satchel which contained the papers on family allowances, another arm dragging an even heavier satchel . . . about refugees and displaced persons . . . Yet she was aware that her ardour was apt to create a mood of sales resistance. Again and again she would ask some other member to approach a given Minister on the ground that she herself had tried his patience too far . . .[232]

Her behind-the-scenes lobbying among MPs was highly successful. By June 1941, 152 MPs of all parties had signed the following Notice of Motion:

To move that this House would welcome the introduction of a national State-paid scheme of allowances for dependent children, payable to their mothers or acting guardians, . . . and urges His Majesty's Government to give immediate consideration to the formulation of such a scheme.[233]

This provided the climate which allowed and encouraged Beveridge to make State Family Allowances the cornerstone of his recommendations in the 1942 Beveridge Report.

Eleanor Rathbone was again behind the scenes in getting others to write letters to the press, and in orchestrating the wider Family Allowance campaign. Nevertheless she was widely known both inside and outside Parliament as the leading public advocate of Family Allowances and State payments to mothers. By 1945, when Family Allowance payments were introduced, she was a household name. Women who were adults in the 1940s remember her still, and there was widespread recognition that she had done more than any other individual to get this first universal payment to mothers on the statute book — recognition which was reflected in the press reports on the introduction of Family Allowances typified by the cartoon reproduced on p.120 below. And as the final stages of the Family Allowance Act were passed, the House of Commons paid tribute to Eleanor Rathbone for the years of work which had been vindicated.[234]

The Public Opinion Toll

By the early 1940s, there were few people that considered themselves 'progressive' who could argue against Family Allowances. Even those who had earlier argued that there should be an extension of social services *instead of* Family Allowances were being forced by the tide of public opinion to agree that mothers should get cash children's allowances[235] as well as access to free school meals for their children and other social services.

In 1938 Virginia Woolf, by now a famous writer, came out explicitly for a State wage for mothers. (See p.42 above.) That same year, the Married Women's Association was formed to press for the needs of wives, and the *Daily Herald* reported the event under a headline which read, 'Love, Honour & Obey — For a Weekly Wage', quoting the new Association as follows:

Men workers in trade unions would not allow their fellow members to work only for board and lodging, so why should they expect wives to work on these terms? . . . We are arranging a series of talks to women members of all political parties, Co-operative societies and other groups of women to put our case.[236]

The *News Chronicle* quoted their statement:

Millions of married women in this country make the home their trade or profession, and many of them give up good jobs for it. They have no wages, no National Health Insurance, no holiday with or without pay, and they go on working without any time limit.[237]

The Married Women's Association (MWA) fought to establish the principle that any family income left over after housekeeping expenses (a luxury unknown in most working class homes, but certainly available among skilled and professional workers), should legally be the joint property of wife and husband; that the matrimonial home should be the joint property of wife and husband; and that a wife should be entitled to keep any savings she was able to make out of the housekeeping money paid to her. On the whole, the focus of their demands was for a woman to be entitled by law to share in her husband's property and earnings; but while the MWA, representing primarily middle class women, at first emphasized a wife's right to her own money through a legal share in her husband's wage rather than a State payment,[238] any call for economic independence for housewives was bound to strengthen the Family Allowance campaign.[239] Press reports of their activities highlighted the poverty and financial dependence of housewives.

MP Wants Wages for Wives. Advocating wages for wives, Dr Edith Summerskill, MP, denounced at a London meeting of the Married Women's Association, 'the day-to-day humiliations' which wives experience in having to ask their husbands for money. 'The married woman, while she may have achieved political freedom, has a still harder task,' Dr Summerskill declared. 'She has yet to maintain her right to economic independence. While a woman is doled out certain moneys by favour of her husband, to which she knows she has no legal right, so long will her dependence be reflected in her acts and thoughts. Her whole manner of life will be dictated by her economic relationship to her husband. Her freedom of thought is shackled by the knowledge that her existence depends upon the pleasure of the one who controls the finances of her household. It is not cruelty, drunkenness, or even adultery which account for the greatest number of cases of domestic infelicity, but the resentment engendered in a wife by the knowledge of her complete dependence. Wages for wives, apart from its equity, would be the surest way of bringing happiness into the home . . .[240]

The MWA also made its own demands on the State. In March 1939 the *Daily Herald* reported a delegation they had sent to the Under Secretary at the Ministry of Health, to demand that wives and families of insured workers should be included in the National Health Insurance Scheme. He told them that:

... to bring in the wives and dependants would cost £10,000,000 a year, and the country could not afford it. To which Dr Summerskill retorted that over £8,000,000 was being spent on armaments.[241]

echoing Virginia Woolf's comments on the military budget (see p.42 above). *The Times* reported another deputation to the Ministry of Health in 1941 at which they pressed for direct State spending on mothers, this time 'to ask for allowances for foster mothers for the extra work involved by taking evacuated children'.[242]

The MWA was one of the first women's organizations to claim credit for the Beveridge Report's recommendations, seeing in them a response to their own campaigning:

The Beveridge Report is the first official document to treat husband and wife as a team, and the money coming into the house as a joint income, Dr Edith Summerskill, MP, told the Married Women's Association in London yesterday. That wives are recognised as partners and not dependants, she added, was a minor triumph for the Executives of the Association.[243]

They had undoubtedly contributed to that climate of opinion which is reflected both in the Beveridge Report (see p.85 ff. below) and in the speeches of women MPs of 1945 which seem so remarkable today (see p.89 ff. below) — as well as being themselves a sign of the times. And by 1946, with the Family Allowance Act already on the statute book and with a Labour Government in power, they were calling for 'a scheme for paying every housewife an allowance of from £1 to 25/- a week'.[244]

Two Jobs, Two Wages

In 1930, Women's Co-operative Guild members from twenty countries had debated at their International Conference 'whether the economic position of women should be best solved by State family allowances or factory work'.[245] The way in which this question was posed makes evident once again that the demand for State Family Allowances was seen as a demand for a State wage for mothers. It also reflected the split between mothers with a second job and mothers who were full-time at home.

Mothers working at home full-time wanted some money in their own right, and wanted the cash immediately. How they would use that money — to pay for help with the housework and have some 'free' time or get a second job; or to keep as income for themselves — was a question they would answer when they had the money.

On the other hand, mothers who had tasted the independence of a job outside the home wanted to be sure that a State wage would not be used to tie them down to housework and push them back into the home.[246]

From the way the question was posed at this Women's Co-op Guild Conference it is evident that some women assumed that only mothers working full-time at home would get the State family allowance/wage. Already in 1924, explicit in Eleanor Rathbone's work (see D.F. p.365) is the demand that a State endowment for mothers should be paid to women whether or not they were full-time at home; and that it was for women to use as they wanted. For example, it could be used to pay for childcare and help with housework by women who wanted to get out of the house, including women with a second job. But in general working class women were not demanding the right to motherhood *and* a job outside the home, as a possible option, because the burden of housework was so great that women did not readily contemplate a second job on top.

By the late 1930s, however, the dramatic fall in the birth rate made combining motherhood and a job outside the home a more positive proposition for working class as well as middle class women. This fall meant that the average number of children in working class marriages begun between 1925 and 1929 had fallen to between two and three.[247] Smaller families meant a new way of life for women, who only thirty years earlier could have expected ten pregnancies,[248] and by the end of the 1930s this new reality was increasingly expressed in women's demands. The recommendations of the Women's Health Enquiry Committee on Family Allowances (1939), already quoted, echoing Eleanor Rathbone, were quite explicit about the fact that Family Allowances might be used by women to relieve themselves of housework:

... the housewife should be free to choose whether to do these jobs herself ... or to pay someone else to do them.[249]

and when *Picture Post* magazine featured an article on 'Why Women Don't Have Babies', they recognized that women were demanding that the right to a life outside the home should not end with motherhood:

Women who want an all-round life can only find it outside the home. There ought to be more and more opportunities for women to combine a home and outside life.[250]

By 1942, a specific demand for State payments to mothers to be paid on top of wages from a job was being put forward by the London Women's Parliament (see pp.82-3 below). They campaigned for the

Government to increase the Separation Allowance paid to wives of servicemen during World War II to £2 a week, and for this allowance to be paid on top of any money a woman was able to earn outside the home.[251]

The importance of the fact that it was in this context that Family Allowances were being widely discussed and debated in the late 1930s and early 1940s cannot be overestimated. Family Allowances were introduced in 1945 as a universal payment, that is, for *every* mother who had two or more children, whether or not she also worked outside the home. With World War II, and the experience of women with young children massively going out to work, this dimension to the endowment of motherhood — two jobs, two wages — was unmistakable. At the same time, the level of power of women in the late 1930s and early 1940s, combined with the strength of the Unemployed Movement which by the late 1930s had the power to discredit the notorious means-testing of benefits, meant that there was no question of any test of eligibility for Family Allowances, either in the form of any 'inspection' of a mother's fitness to receive the payments, or in the form of conditions about whether or not she should be full-time at home.[252]

Yet paying Family Allowances to the mother whether or not she had a second, waged job made nonsense of the official rationale for payment, which was that on average a man's wage was enough to support a wife and one child only, so the State should help to support the second and subsequent children.[253] The Family Allowance payments as introduced in 1945 represented not simply a recognition that working class men's wages were in general insufficient to support a family, but a recognition — which the Government tried to avoid even at the final stages (see p.89 ff. below) — that the mother was entitled to some financial recognition from the State for her work in the home, whether or not she also worked outside. Although it is sometimes argued that Family Allowances were intended to buy women off and push them back into the home, the fact is that women won this money as an unconditional payment.

The principle that was won with the Family Allowance Act is so important that this point is worth reiterating. However much the State represented it as a simple welfare measure, conceded because most men's wages were too low to support more than one child, the fact remains that the Allowance was introduced as a payment to mothers regardless of family income *or any other test of eligibility*. It was to be paid to a mother whatever her husband's wage, and whether or not she also worked outside the home. Few women in Britain at that time, even among those who had opposed Family Allowances, would have doubted that Family Allowances represented a State endowment for motherhood — a fact which was reflected not in the amount paid, but in the principle behind the method of payment. And, however small, this payment to mothers had been won with 'no strings attached'. The Family Allowance could not be used to tie the mother to the home, as some women had feared, either by penalizing her if she took a job outside, or by subjecting her to any form of inspection for suitability.

In the 1980s, some politicians, faced again with the demand from women that a wage for housework should be paid whether or not they also have a job outside the home, are trying to suggest that these payments should be made only to full-time housewives, in other words they should be subject to a means and productivity test. In rediscovering the context in which Family Allowances were first introduced, their arguments can be seen to have no basis whatsoever in legislative precedent — in fact, just the reverse.

THE WAR EFFORT
Just how massive was the women's movement which produced a victory on this scale is still a well-kept secret, but women who remember World War II, or know of their mother's or grandmother's experience of the late 1930s and early 1940s, know that this was a time of an unprecedented level of women's power.

The Government's dependence on women was even more apparent in World War II than during World War I, not only as childbearers of future generations to replace those killed in the civilian as well as military slaughter, but as workers in industry and on the land, and as providers of social services in the home and in the community. During World War II, women's voluntary work provided on a massive scale the social services the Government had failed to provide — from food canteens to organizing the mass civilian evacuation. For example, in three days at the beginning of September 1939, one and a half million people were evacuated from the big cities, most of them unaccompanied schoolchildren with only luggage labels to identify them. This huge movement of people was organized and supervised by the Women's Voluntary Service (WVS), an organization of unpaid community workers formed in 1939, which by 1941 had over one million members.[254] It was they who dealt with the aftermath of mass bombing raids, feeding and comforting people, providing blankets and reassurance, preventing the breakdown of morale which would certainly have accompanied the bombing if they, and the hundreds of thousands of mothers who took charge of their families, had not kept the community together.

As in any wage bargaining, making the case that your work and your product are essential to the economy is especially easy to do — and carries added weight — when the product is in short supply or in particular demand, or both. Thus mothers, whose product is the workforce, have always chosen those moments in history when the State was most concerned about the supply of workers — 'citizens' and soldiers — to press their case. In the aftermath of the Boer War, the impact of a falling birth rate combined with a growing women's movement which articulated in specific demands what the birth strike had already demonstrated about mother's views and needs. The result was a flood of welfare legislation which provided the basis of the Welfare State in Britain. It was during World Wars I and II, when the Government was peculiarly dependent on women, and women were peculiarly organized and vocal, that women received what governments are always most reluctant to provide — not only social services in kind but cash payments. It should be clear that these social services and cash payments were a victory for women achieved by their own actions and demands, rather than the result of any sudden benevolence by the State.

During World War II the extensive Government propaganda to encourage women to work for the war effort — by 'cooking for victory' with limited ingredients, 'digging for victory' by planting their own vegetable gardens, and looking after children as 'its own form of National Service' — as well as the conscription of women into industry and agriculture to do 'men's jobs' — strengthened women's case. The propaganda undoubtedly persuaded women to do more work, but at the same time it recognized the importance of domestic work to the war effort and also created a climate in which it was not just acceptable but positively desirable for women to combine motherhood and homemaking with a job outside the home. Thus it inevitably had the effect of encouraging women to consider their skills and their rights in a new light. The accounts of women's activities and women's writings of the thirties make clear that these changes were already taking place before the war, but the six years of war highlighted and accelerated them at an unprecedented rate.

The number of married women with a job outside the home, for example, went up dramatically. By 1943 it was estimated that there were three million married women and widows in the waged labour force, more than double the pre-war figure, and that eight out of ten married women with children over fourteen had jobs outside the home.[255] At the same time most mothers of younger children were receiving Separation Allowances, since their husbands had been called up, and many were also being paid by the Government for billeting forces personnel or evacuee children.[256] This combination of payment to women full-time at home and access to jobs outside meant that for the first time most married women had access to some money of their own.

The tradition of Separation Allowances, begun in World War I, continued in World War II with payments reaching their maximum in May 1944. The allowance paid to the wife varied according to the rank of the husband, and compulsory deductions were made from his pay. But the allowance paid to the wife for each child, which reached 12/6 a week in 1944, was the same for all servicemen's families, and was financed entirely by the Government.[257]

The size of both the wives' and children's payments were a source of continuous campaigning by women. In September 1942, when the children's allowances stood at 8/6 a week each for the first two children and 5/- for each subsequent child, the London Women's Parliament was demanding an increase to 10/- a week for each child under fourteen and 16/- a week for older children still at school. At the same time, as we have seen, they were demanding £2 a week for wives and mothers of servicemen, to be paid whether or not they also had a job outside the house and to be financed entirely by the Government with no deductions from servicemen's pay.[258] These figures should be set against the average wage for women over eighteen working outside the home, which was estimated at £2. 4s. 4d. in July 1941, and would not have gone up substantially by 1942.[259]

Evacuation (which was often from the poorest slum areas surrounding docks and industrial centres — the priority bombing targets) provided overwhelming evidence for middle class people of the poverty and deprivation suffered by hundreds of thousands of children. Many of the children were obviously astonished at the regular appearance of meals, and put on weight at a rapid rate. The press was full of reports of the state of these children, but it was widely recognized that it was not 'maternal ignorance' or 'inadequacy' that was the problem but maternal poverty. Meanwhile, between 1939 and 1942, women and children were the highest number of war casualties — not until 1942 did military injuries and deaths begin to parallel those of the civilian population. The Government was therefore forced to assume financial responsibility for evacuees, as well as servicemen's wives and children, setting yet another new precedent in State payments.[260]

At the same time, precisely because this was a civilian as well as a military war, it was increasingly difficult for the Government to maintain a distinction between the benefits paid to the wives and children of servicemen and those paid to the wives and children of civilians:

> The distinctions and privileges, accorded to those in uniform in previous wars, were greatly diminished. Comprehensive systems of medical care and rehabilitation, for example, had to be organized by the State for those who were injured and disabled. They could not be exclusively reserved for soldiers and sailors, as in the past, but had to be extended to include civilians as well — to those injured in the factories as well as the victims of bombing . . . In this context, the Education Act of 1944 becomes intelligible; so does the Beveridge Report of 1942 and the National Insurance, Family Allowances and National Health Service Acts . . .[261]

Demands for equal treatment between members of the different war services, i.e. military and civilian, were paralleled by the demands made by women for equal treatment with men — from equal pay to equal compensation for injury, from health insurance to State payments to wives and mothers doing the war work of looking after children. The level of women's self-organization during the war was reflected not only in Social Service organizations like the WVS, which exploited the thousands of informal street networks women had created over the years, but also in the less orthodox organizations like the Women's Home Defence Unit, founded by Edith Summerskill and others in response to the Government's refusal to allow women to carry firearms in the Home Guard. (By 1942 the Women's Home Defence Unit had taught some thousands of women how to handle rifles and grenades to protect themselves and their families, as well as how to make Molotov cocktails!)[262] The scale of that self-organization is clear above all in the reports of the Women's Parliaments.

Women's Parliaments

In 1940 the first 'Women's Parliament' met in London, setting a pattern which was to be repeated in Lancashire and other parts of the country. Representatives from a wide range of organizations came together to work out detailed demands over a wide range of issues — nursery provisions, canteen facilities, food prices, overlong working hours, inadequate transport, equal pay with men and equal compensation for injury, the health service, maternity benefits, working conditions in local industries and services employing women, and working conditions in the home.

The Women's Parliaments represented a very high level of organization for women. They were a massive coming together of women working inside and outside the home, and of demands to meet the needs of women doing either or both of these jobs; the result of

the growing experience of a working day which spanned both the
domestic and the industrial workplace. The fact that so many women
worked both inside and outside the home was now bearing organi-
zational fruit, and it meant that the split between 'community'
demands and 'industrial' demands, which had always been a weakness
of both women's and men's organizing, was at last being confronted.[263]
Moreover, the combination of professional women and factory workers,
housewives and service workers, tackled the fragmentation of the
women's movement between women of different classes in a new way:

The London Women's Parliament, which represents nearly all women's organisations here, held a conference yesterday to discuss two bills on health and on
housing. The former dealt with industrial women, the hours worked, health committees and the extension of welfare and medical care. It was also concerned with
help for women at home, the provision of more home helps, of more midwives,
and maternity beds, with maternity benefit and improved local health services. It
demanded a national health service on the lines of the Beveridge Report . . . The
housing bill demanded, among other things the immediate control of all rents . . .
and was moved by an architect, Miss Elizabeth Denby, who said that bad housing
conditions caused hardship to women with young children . . .[264]

The meeting . . . was attended by nearly 1,000 London women representing groups
with half a million members . . . The delegates to the conference, speaking for
factory workers, business and professional women and housewives, also went on
record against juvenile court decisions to use the whip as punishment for
children, and against British laws that forbid housewives to keep for themselves
savings from household allowances . . . Under a large-lettered slogan, 'Women
of London – Fight for the London You Want Tomorrow,' aircraft workers in
their best slacks, nurses, town councillors, housewives and other working women
went onto the stage of the meeting hall and criticized conditions in their respective communities or described steps they had taken to improve them. The
housing programme that was adopted by the delegates included demands for
Government requisitioning of existing dwellings and the building of prefabricated
houses to relieve overcrowding in industrial areas, lower rents, more vigorous
measures in the repair of houses damaged in air raids, and a detailed plan for post-
war construction of roomy, modern homes. The health bill called for 'home-help'
agents, who would be paid partly by the local governments, to aid families where
the mother was ill . . . more accommodations for maternity cases . . . and more
sanitary factory conditions . . . This London Women's Parliament [November,
1943] . . . is the fourth since 1941 . . .[265]

The TUC characteristically called on trade unionists

. . . to have nothing to do with the so-called 'Women's Parliaments' . . . These
bodies, it is pointed out, are attempting to deal with many matters which are
the subject of trade union negotiations . . . they have circularised factory workers
and trade union supporters on wages questions. Bills have been produced on
wages, part-time working and training, and one dealt with wages and conditions
in the cotton industry.[266]

On the Dole

In organizing to press their own needs during the war, women were building on what had been won in the 1930s and before. For example, the mounting pressure for a universal State payment for children represented, as well as a demand for parity for the families of civilians with those of servicemen, a demand for an extension of the victories of the unemployed movement of the 1930s to the rest of the population.

Already in 1938, the 'Unemployment Insurance Statutory Committee', an official body supervising unemployment provisions,[267] had recommended in its Annual Report that dependants' allowances paid for the children of unemployed men should be extended to the families of the employed. This recommendation was to counter the new reality created by the women's movement and the unemployed movement. In securing Family Allowance payments as a component of unemployment pay in the wake of Separation Allowances, and in gradually pushing up the level of payments, the difference in income between families of men in work and those on the dole had been eroded. Government and employers were increasingly alarmed at this disincentive to work,[268] while the Unemployment Insurance Statutory Committee faced the awkward situation that if dependants' benefits were increased to meet the most recent estimates of the cost of maintaining a family in physical fitness, as the unemployed were demanding, unemployment payments would often exceed the wages of those in work.[269] Its report provided Family Allowance campaigners with a new round of ammunition.[270]

Beveridge and other social administrators have pointed to the approach of parity between wages and unemployment pay as being crucial to the reluctant support of the war-time Coalition Government for a State Family Allowance scheme. But they have obscured why the State was faced with this dilemma and who was behind the creation of this anomaly.[271] It was not a result of administrative failure or policy oversight, but an inevitable consequence of the strength of the unemployed movement in the thirties. That movement succeeded in putting a substantial part of the cost of an economic crisis on to the State by insisting on State compensation for the victims in the form of unemployment pay. This was in itself a major victory. The importance of the resulting near-parity between wages and unemployment pay to the introduction of universal Family Allowances in Britain cannot be over-estimated.[272]

With war-time demands for an end to social injustice as compensation for the war effort, and with the prospect of large-scale unemployment at the end of the war, it was clear that unemployment pay would have to approximate to subsistence costs for the whole family. It would then often be higher than wages unless State payments for dependants were extended to the employed.

At the same time, the Government was faced with women's evident reluctance to have children in poverty. Nobody could deny the importance of motherhood to the economy in replacing the popluation slaughtered in war. But women's action in reducing the birth rate had made evident that *without financial support from the Government* many women would refuse to perform this 'vital task' of making up for population losses.

The Housewives' Charter

In 1941 an 'Interdepartmental Committee on Social Insurance and Allied Services' was set up to make plans for post-war reconstruction, and in particular for a national insurance scheme. This was the Government's response to growing public pressure for a guarantee that there would never be a return to the poverty and inequalities of pre-war Britain:

> . . . in military terms, the war could not be won unless millions of ordinary people . . . were convinced that we had something better to offer than had our enemies – not only during but after the war . . . The effect on social policy of these ideas . . . was profound . . .[273]

At the end of November 1942 the Committee's findings were published as 'The Beveridge Report', with recommendations which went much further than the Government had intended. Beveridge dealt with the establishment of a social insurance scheme, but also made the case for Government responsibility for the maintenance of full employment, the establishment of a National Health Service to provide medical treatment for every citizen, and the immediate introduction of Children's Allowances to be financed directly by the Exchequer.[274]

The Government attempted to play down the importance of the Report and discourage publicity, but there was already considerable public interest in its rumoured recommendations and the Report became an overnight bestseller. Over half a million copies were sold to the public, and the newspapers and radio reported its contents in some detail.[275] One middle-aged housewife recorded her response to the BBC's coverage of the Report on Wednesday 2 December 1942 as follows:

> Never since I first listened to a speaker on the air have I felt as interested as I was tonight by Sir William Beveridge. I'll feel a bit more hopeful about the 'brave new world' now . . . His scheme will appeal more even to women than to men, for it is they who bear the real burden of unemployment, sickness, child-bearing and rearing – and the ones who, up to now, have come off worst. There *should* be some all-in scheme. As I listened, my mind went back to the days when the boys and their friends argued and set the world to rights . . . [They] thought I was a

visionary when I spoke of a scheme whereby women would perhaps get the consideration they deserved from the State . . .[276]

The Report was widely hailed as a 'Housewives' Charter' because one of its major premises was that women's work in the home was crucial to the economy and should be recognized. For example:

The census includes married women who do not work for money outside their homes among unoccupied persons. The unemployment insurance scheme recognises such women as adult dependants on their husbands . . . The health insurance scheme does not recognise such women at all, except at the moment of maternity. None of these attitudes is defensible. In any measure of social policy in which regard is had to facts, the great majority of married women must be regarded as occupied on work which is vital though unpaid, without which their husbands could not do their paid work and without which the nation could not continue.[277]

The popular tabloid, *Picture Post*, commented in a feature on the Beveridge Report:

The war has exploded the old idea that a married woman is a mere 'adult dependant'. Sir William Beveridge dismisses this idea as 'indefensible', says that most married women are occupied on work which is vital though unpaid . . . Hence, the Beveridge Report recognises the housewife . . . The recognition of the housewife, and the help for married women on marriage, in maternity, and at widowhood, are the proposals which particularly affect women . . . the Report . . . has become the Housewives' Charter.[278]

Beveridge recommended that housewives should be included in their own right in entitlement to social benefits, including a national health service, whether or not they also worked outside the home and paid National Insurance contributions. Whereas the social insurance principle when applied to men levied a compulsory tax to pay for insurance in sickness, unemployment and old age, for housewives the act of marriage (and the housework which was expected to accompany it) were assumed to be sufficient contribution to secure entitlement. The State in effect paid for housewives' insurance cover, since married men were not expected to pay extra for wives.[279]

But it was the most radical recommendation, for a 'Children's Allowance' to be paid directly by the State, which drew the most immediate support for Beveridge's Report.

Beveridge himself later commented on the major new principle it established:

In all the legislation of recent years in Britain the greatest break with old tradition under the influence of a new idea is represented by the Family Allowances Act of 1945 . . . The two National Insurance Acts of 1946 and even the National Health Service Act of the same year are no more than a completion of what was begun in Britain in 1911: the battle of Social Insurance for cash benefits and for medical treatment was fought and won in principle thirty-six years ago.
But family allowances in cash provided by use of the power of the State are a

new idea. They mean that part of the total national income . . . should by law be
directed down a new channel. . . . should be assigned to those individual citizens
who were undertaking the rearing of the citizens of the future . . .[280]

This was the only one of Beveridge's recommendations to bear fruit in
legislation under the wartime Coalition Government. Churchill bowed
to public pressure that this must be the first major move towards
'social reconstruction' and the Family Allowance Bill was introduced
to Parliament in February 1945. In addition, it is important to note
that Family Allowances paid directly by the State was the only measure
of the post-Beveridge Welfare State legislation to embody a wholesale
redistribution of income — because it was paid to women, the poorer
sex, and also because it was a redistribution of wealth to the working
class family, as a straight cash payment which did not depend on
insurance contributions, but came instead from the Exchequer.

Who Benefits?

Since the 1970s, the provisions made in the post-Beveridge Welfare State
legislation have been under attack by both Labour and Conservative
governments, with cuts in benefit levels, cuts in the National Health
Service and in other social services (for example, free school milk and
school meals), and threats to Family Allowances/Child Benefits. These
attacks have exposed in a dramatic way the degree to which the
Beveridge Report and the Welfare State legislation which followed it
were victories for women. In the face of cuts, even those who previously
saw the Welfare State only as a new level of State control,[281] and of no
real benefit to the working class, are forced to acknowledge that every
cut in social services or cash payments means more work, especially for
women. But if the cuts mean more work for women, then it is evident
that every extension in social services and cash payments took work off
women's shoulders, and represented an important gain.

It is certainly true that the State hoped to undermine the movement
of women which had achieved this victory through the *terms* of the
'Welfare State' legislation. In particular, as we shall see, the Government
was determined that all cash benefits paid in respect of women and
children, including Family Allowances (see p.89 below), should be
paid to men, as the 'heads' of the family, so keeping men over women
in the family and encouraging women to confront individual men for
money rather than the State. (Women defeated this plan.) And they
tried as far as possible to concentrate on the provision of benefits in
kind as an *alternative* to paying cash into women's hands, rather than as
a complement to it.[282]

But even with these (and many other) limitations, the post-Beveridge

'Welfare State' legislation provided for a new level of Government financial responsibility for housework — both through the provision of social services which took a huge burden of work off unpaid housewives, transforming it into paid work (for example as nursing in a hospital rather than caring for sick relatives at home); and in direct cash payments which the Government was forced to pay to mothers on an unprecedented scale.[283]

To say that women generally recognized the Beveridge Report as a major victory for themselves and welcomed it as a big step forward is not to glorify either its assumptions or its recommendations. For example, the recognition of housework embodied in the principle that women need not contribute in cash to the social insurance scheme applied only to women who were married; benefits paid during sickness and unemployment on behalf of a wife and children were to continue as payments to the man as 'head of the family'; married women with a job outside the home who opted to pay National Insurance contributions were to be entitled to reduced benefits only, on the grounds that their husbands provided financial support at least by paying the rent, i.e. the woman was dependent.[284] And while the Report's insistence on the importance of Children's Allowances provided an enormous boost to the pressure for immediate legislation, the suggested economies meant that many children and mothers were to be excluded. Beveridge recommended that Children's Allowances be paid for the second and subsequent children, but not for the first child (on the grounds of 'economy'); and that the 'universal' Children's Allowance payment should be deductable from other State benefits, and not paid on top of benefits as they were on top of wages.

This last proposal, which excluded the poorest families from the benefits of an additional payment, was widely attacked — for example, in floods of letters to the press (see plate 2 below). The Government backed it, however, holding firm to 'the principle, which was . . . accepted *by the leaders of all parties*, that there should be no duplication' with other State payments.[285] Aneurin Bevan, an ex-miner and the future Minister of Health, spoke up for his constituents in Parliament:

I would like to say a word about the excluded classes, and very important classes they are. It seems to me outrageous that the Government should have decided to exclude these classes . . . What justification is there for not supplementing unemployment benefit by these allowances . . . If the income going into a family as wages is so small that social insurance has to supplement it, the income is obviously smaller if the family is on unemployment benefit or workmen's compensation or is in receipt of one of the other forms of benefit . . . There is no reason why all the other allowances, pensions and rates of benefit should not have this allowance superimposed upon them.[286]

But the party leaders were adamant. Although in 1945 unemployment was negligible, they were determined not to set a precedent of paying Family Allowances on top of other benefits to either the unemployed or the growing number of single mothers claiming national assistance.

Governments were not challenged on these grounds again until 1973, when the Women's Family Allowance Campaign made one of its demands 'that Family Allowances be paid on top of social security', a demand added by single welfare ('unsupported') mothers active in that campaign, and pursued by the Wages for Housework Campaign in all its subsequent petitioning and lobbying on Family Allowances and Child Benefits.[287]

While the wartime Coalition Government was forced to respond with legislative proposals, at the same time it did everything possible to undermine the significance of Family Allowances. The rates of payment were to be 5/- per child after the first child, substantially less than the 8/- recommended by Beveridge, they would not be paid for the first child, and most important of all, they proposed in their Family Allowance Bill to pay the money to men. This was obviously intended to undermine the movement for economic independence for women which had been the driving force of the Family Allowance campaign.

Feminist Debates

Just how far they had miscalculated the strength of women's feelings on this issue, and the extent of public support for Family Allowances as the mother's due, was reflected in the Parliamentary debates.

On 8 March 1945 the House of Commons debated the Second Reading of the Government's Bill. Already a storm of protest had ensured that there was to be a free vote (i.e. no party line) on the question of which parent should receive the money. Eleanor Rathbone opened the debate by warning not only that *she would vote against the Bill if the money were not paid to women,* but that there would be a wave of women's anger and protest throughout the country on a scale which had not been seen since the days of the suffragette movement:

I think this is, in principle, indeed a very great Measure . . . For the first time it proposes that the State should make a money contribution, not merely to the bringing of children into the world and their education, but really for maintaining them. By doing so it remedies what I have always considered the fundamental injustice of excluding children from all share of their own in the national income, although children and their mothers together constitute between one-third and one-half of the entire population [sic]. It recognises that they have a claim to payment of money from the State. Yet this recognition comes in so strange a form that it seems actually to contradict rather than affirm that very principle. I shall concentrate my remarks very largely on the question of the recipient of the allowance. . . . because it is of immense importance. The proposal, in the way it is stated in the Bill, will not raise the status of motherhood but will actually lower it. It does so . . . because it treats the wife as a mere appendage . . . of her husband . . . Secondly, it is the one defect in the Bill which, if not changed now, will probably prove unchangeable later. . . . What does the wife do? . . . she spends her days and hours, as they say in my part of the world, 'All the hours God makes', in washing and cleaning for the children, clothing and feeding them – all the hours of the day and night. School holidays and the weekends bring her no remission, no time off; they actually increase the burden on the working class mother. All that is to go for nothing . . .

The Cabinet is composed of men, and they cannot be expected to realise how women think on this question. I want to warn them of the intensity of women's feeling about it . . . I took part in that long bitter struggle for the women's vote before the last war. We did not grudge all it cost us, because it was worth it . . . But I do not want to go through all that again. It was a very bitter struggle . . . Do not force us back into what we thought we had done with – an era of sex antagonism.

If the Bill goes through in its present form I cannot vote for the Third Reading, although I have worked for this thing for so many years. It would be one of the bitterest disappointments of my political life if the Bill did not go through. But I foresee too well the consequences if it goes through in a form which practically throws an insult into the faces of those to whom this country owes most, the actual or potential mothers . . . I beg members to think again, to beware of how they encourage sex antagonism . . . to become once more an issue in a General Election.[288]

Eleanor Rathbone was not the only one to take up this issue in strong terms. Mrs Adamson, Labour MP for Dartford, commented:

I speak as a practical housewife who has reared a family of four on a working man's wage . . . Some Members have ridiculed the point about the status of the mother. Of course we have had tributes paid, particularly during this war, to the women of this country and great tributes have been paid all down the ages to mothers. However the fact remains that the wife and mother has not the status to which she ought to be entitled. Her work is of the highest national importance, yet we have never valued her work, or given her that recognition which, in my judgement, was her due. We have always thought that her work was less important than that of her husband and less important than that of a woman in a factory or workshop . . . We shall have to give a greater recognition to the work of the mother in our legislation and in the community than has hitherto been done . . . and this new legislation provides an opportunity for recognition of that great status . . . I am glad the Government are to have a free vote of the House on this question . . . I shall not intimidate Hon. Members in this House by saying that on this issue the women of this country are waiting for them . . .[289]

Edith Summerskill, MP for Fulham West, also took the opportunity to put women's case in forceful terms:

I welcome the final acceptance of the principle of family allowances, but I must say that on a first reading of the Explanatory and Financial Memorandum, I thought, like others, that it was really a Bill which would in fact be an endowment of fatherhood. I am pleased to hear that the Minister has thought again and is to give the House a free vote. If he had not thought again and if he had foisted this Bill on the country in its present form, he would have become the most unpopular Minister in the country with women. I think he is very wise, and I feel that he will agree that the women Members are very generous in welcoming a free vote when it will mean that 601 men in the House will determine whether the mother should receive the allowance . . .[290]

As to the status of the mother. I was interested to learn from the Hon. and gallant member for Brighton that while he accepted the principle of paying 5s to the father, he had no time for women or individuals who talked about the status of women. It is very difficult for any man to understand that imponderable. One has to be a woman who is humiliated week by week when she has to ask her husband for necessities to understand it . . . He has never been put in this humiliating position. Therefore I say that a contribution of this kind, even of 5s a week, will enhance the status of the mother, who is, in my opinion, the most important person in the country, for she produces the potential workers. I would remind the House that the most important person in the country, producing the potential workers, is not legally entitled to one penny. This is the first opportunity that the House has had of recognising the services which the mother gives to the home and I ask the Minister to take full advantage of the opportunity.[291]

Beveridge himself, now MP for Berwick, felt it important to weigh in forcibly on women's side (although he had been carefully silent on this issue in his Report):

In coming to their regrettable decision to make payment to the father, I think the Government made a mistake in chronology. They did not realise that this was 1945; they thought we were back in the year 1879 — the year in which I was born — and in which, before the Married Women's Property Act, all money belonged to the husband.[292]

MPs were fortified in this debate by knowledge of the strength of the movement outside Parliament. Eleanor Rathbone, on behalf of the FES, had circularized women's organizations as early as July 1944 to warn them that the Government's White Paper would propose payment of Family Allowances to the father, and to urge them to put pressure on Ministers, MPs and the press.[293] That same month, she invited women's organizations to 'a lightning conference':[294]

. . . summoned to consider the point [of payment to the mother] at a few days' notice . . . it was attended, after one of the worst nights of fly-bombing, by representatives of nearly all the larger Women's Organizations, and passed a unanimous resolution.[295]

Plans were made to inform women all over the country of how their MP had voted on the issue of the mother's money, in preparation for an onslaught during the forthcoming General Election if the Government's Bill went through unchanged.[296] And there were also plans to lie down in the House of Commons, in good suffragette tradition, to get maximum publicity and so help to ensure that the press would report both the Government's plans to cheat women and the House of Commons' response.

Looking back at the tone of this debate in Parliament, what is striking is not that the Government should have tried to slip through payment of Family Allowances to men, but that the arguments put forward by women MPs should have been so explicitly feminist. In the 1970s and early 1980s the case for mothers has not been put forward in the House of Commons in this forceful way. In 1972, when the Government again tried to pay Family Allowances to the father and take money out of mothers' hands, MPs were astonished at the massive Family Allowance Campaign which sprang up overnight to defend mothers' money. MPs had to be educated in why it was that women felt so strongly on this issue. (See pp.94-5 below.) They found it hard to understand how such relatively small sums of money could mean so much to women,[297] and could be 'the only money I can call my own'.[298]

SHAPING SOCIAL POLICY: 1945 and 1973

A misunderstanding of the importance of Family Allowances to women, and consequently of the degree to which women might be mobilized to campaign for them, was evident not only amongst MPs of the 1970s, but in accounts of the history of Family Allowances written during that decade. So, for example, Hilary Land, who has written several articles dealing with the history of the Family Allowance Act, wrote in one of them:

On balance, therefore, the family allowances scheme introduced in 1945 only incidentally recognized the needs of mothers and children and then only to a limited extent. By excluding the first child and failing to make the value of the allowance equal to the subsistence cost of raising a child, the state was taking only a small share in the cost of maintaining its future citizens and workers.[299]

This belittling assessment of the significance of the legislation is at odds with that of women who remember vividly what the introduction of Family Allowances meant to them personally. Women alive today who were mothers in August 1946 can invariably still recount their memories of collecting the first payment from the Post Office, while many who were children at the time remember the excitement of going with their mothers on the first pay-day. Not only was 5/- per child a substantial sum in relation to average family income,[300] but this first payment from the State to all mothers was very clearly regarded by women as a major event in their lives and a major victory.

This failure to realize what relatively small sums of money might mean to women complements a frame of reference in which civil servants, MPs and Government advisers fill the screen:

. . . it would be a mistake to think that the introduction of family allowances in 1946 was *predominantly* a triumph for women's rights. On the contrary, only a minority supported family allowances as a means of recognizing and improving the status of mothers as a worthy end in itself.[301]

Of course the judgement of 'only a minority' comes from looking at Whitehall and the House of Commons and not the rest of the

population, where a majority, especially of women, clearly supported
Family Allowances as a means of 'recognizing and improving the status
of mothers'. In line with this same perspective the writer concludes:

The argument which finally convinced a government to consider a proposal for a
state family allowance scheme was that used by Keynes . . . that the introduction
of a universal scheme of family allowances, together with rationing and food
subsidies . . . would reduce the need and demand for overall wage increases.
Family Allowances, therefore, were taken seriously only when they were seen to
be relevant to the government's economic policy.[302]

Aside from the fact that this view of legislative history completely
leaves out the women's movement which put Family Allowances on the
Government's agenda, the implication here is that the introduction of
Family Allowances represented a defeat, since the only reason for their
introduction was an attempt to hold down wages. But the author cites
no evidence that Family Allowances had this — or any other — harmful
effect on women or men of the working class.

In fact the debate about whether Family Allowances would or
would not serve to hold down wages had been going on for over twenty
years. In 1930, the Majority Report of the Special Joint Committee set
up by the Labour Party and the TUC to consider Family Allowances
concluded:

We agree with those . . . Trade Union leaders who have told us that they are very
firm in their view that a system of [State] Family Allowances would not hamper
the Unions at all in their negotiations. Indeed, we believe that during industrial
conflicts the Unions will be very considerably helped by the existence of such a
scheme, since the workers' children will be removed from the 'firing line' and a
great factor of weakness will thus be removed.[303]

And by the early 1940s it was generally accepted in trade unions and
the Labour Party that the introduction of Family Allowances paid by
the State would not determine whether wages rose or fell, but that this
would be determined rather by the bargaining strength of the working
class, as Eleanor Rathbone had always argued. (See D.F. pp.329-31,
333-7 and 378.)

The assumption that it was the force of a particular argument,
rather than the weight of popular pressure, which finally 'convinced'
the Government is typical of most accounts of changes in social policy.
In this context, reportage of more recent Family Allowance history,
namely the battle over Family Allowance legislation in the 1970s in
which I was involved (along with thousands of others), is revealing.

In October 1972 the Government published a Green Paper, *Proposals
for a Tax Credit System*, which included the suggestion that universal
Family Allowances won in 1945 be abolished. As part of a system of
'tax credits', 'child tax credits' were to replace Family Allowances and

child tax allowances, but would be paid only to those families who came into the taxation system. In addition, the Green Paper suggested that to 'simplify' and 'economize' on administration, these child tax credits might be paid to the father.[304]

The response when women heard of these proposals was overwhelming anger at the proposed theft of Family Allowances from mothers. The Women's Family Allowance Campaign was launched to publicize the Government's plans and co-ordinate the protest activities of 'grassroots' women and organizations all over the country. It publicized not only the suggestion that the money be paid to men rather than women, but the impact the proposals would have on the 10 per cent of all families outside the tax system, including the families of strikers, students and Supplementary Benefit claimants who would not be entitled to child tax credits.[305] Petitions were circulated all over the country; there were numerous demonstrations of women and children at Post Offices, including a sit-in of some hundreds of mothers with children at the central Trafalgar Square Post Office in London; MPs and the Select Committee set up to examine the Green Paper were flooded with letters and deputations from a wide variety of organizations; and articles and letters appeared in the press.

Women who took part in that campaign were overwhelmed by the response from women in the street to the petitioning and leafleting, and tried to capture that response in the written and oral evidence presented by the Women's Family Allowance Campaign to the Select Committee,[306] as well as in lobbying, media coverage of the campaign, and other activities. And we saw the result of our campaign, and of women's activities and anger around the country,[307] in a gradual retreat from the Government's original proposals. By February 1973 the Government's Tax Credit Study Group saw fit to point out to the Select Committee that, on the grounds of 'social considerations', they felt that the payments should be made to the mother rather than the father, and that proposals to make payment of child tax credits dependent on full membership of the tax credit scheme in fact contradicted the principle of universal family allowances.[308] They summed up:

If the Committee conclude . . . that . . . credits should be paid to mothers they will wish to consider whether such payment should be made universally, regardless of whether the husband is entitled to be within the scheme.[309]

In other words, they proposed that the tax credit system as it applied to child tax credits should be abandoned in favour of universal payments, and that these should continue as payments to the mother.

As the pressure from women's organizations and individuals all over the country mounted, the Government discovered that they had unleashed not simply a defensive campaign, but widespread demands that the Family Allowance be extended to the first child, that it should be substantially increased and paid on top of other benefits, and also that women's work in the home should be recognized by a State payment independent of Family Allowances.[310] The immediate results were that the Select Committee Report of July 1973 recommended that child tax credits be dropped in favour of keeping a universal mother's benefit which would combine Family Allowances and tax allowances, and that payment should now also be made to the mother for the first child. (These recommendations were subsequently embodied in the Child Benefit Act of 1975.)

Yet only three years later, the impact of women's protest was being written out of accounts of these events, the campaign to keep the Family Allowance in mothers' hands passed over as 'much discussion', and the fact that the Government had originally proposed to pay child tax credits to the father completely lost. The result is that the changes in social policy achieved by women become invisible:

Proposals for a tax-credit scheme have been the subject of much discussion and quite properly much attention has been paid to provisions for children. As a result the 1970-74 Conservative Government had already promised that the child tax credit, which would replace family allowances, the family income supplement and the tax allowance for children, would be paid to the mother. Like family allowances they would be paid irrespective of the marital and employment status of the child's parents.[311]

To see the fight that women had made written out of history so quickly is a startling reminder both of how much remains to be uncovered of what actually happened in the past, and the importance of claiming the victories women have won, which are invariably hidden by the official accounts,[312] and which are rarely reported even by the contemporary press.[313]

The Mother's Share
Many things about the 1945 Family Allowances Act were a disappointment to Eleanor Rathbone. In particular, the amounts paid for children were much lower than she had hoped, there was no payment to the mother in her own right for her work in the home, and Family Allowances were to be deducted from other benefits. (She argued to the last that widows should be exempted from the 'No duplication' clause.[314]) During the final stages of the Family Allowance Bill, Eleanor Rathbone made clear, 'we are all making great sacrifices in accepting the compromise',[315] and in response to the tributes paid to her by other MPs summed up something of her attitude:

It is naturally a very great joy for me to see the end of the *first stage* in this fight, because I do want to make it clear, although it may seem rather ungracious when somebody is being congratulated upon her baby [I do want] to point out the defects in the baby . . . this baby is a very little one. We feel that it will have to be a good deal fattened and cossetted before it reaches its proper stature . . . the whole thing is on too small a scale.

There are many other respects in which we feel this Act . . . will have to be a bigger Act before it does its work. I would like to draw attention to one clause in it which was not amended . . . which lays down the extraordinary rule that no child is to have an allowance unless it is the child of someone born in Great Britain. This is going to have a bad effect on the reputation of this country . . .

But I would . . . say that this is to my mind a great day, because it lays down a great principle. In the early days I used to describe meetings of employers and employed, landowners and rentiers sitting round a table competing for a share in the national income with a woman coming from behind and holding out her hand, saying, 'I am the mother; the future citizens and workers depend on me; where is my share?' This Bill gives the mother through her children her share, although it is only a very little share so far.[316]

In trying to piece together something of the obstacles that Eleanor Rathbone faced and to understand her achievements, we must recall her starting point: mothers — unpaid, unrecognized, unrepresented, their work invisible. Against all the odds, against the lack of interest or hostility of those who have more power — from men of all classes to career women who often dissociate themselves — she pressed mothers' priorities to the centre of the political stage, establishing the 'great principle' of mothers' right to financial recognition for their work.

Something of the odds she overcame is suggested by what has happened since to the history of her achievements. Whatever the specific disagreements some historians may have had with Eleanor Rathbone and the endowment of motherhood, there is no doubt that the main reason that she has so often been undervalued is that she was a spokeswoman for mothers, who are assumed to have no history. For what is there that mothers could do or think or want that could count for much? That Eleanor Rathbone maintained her commitment and sensitivity to mothers, the poorest of the poor, through a lifetime of campaigning during which the public evidence of their power fluctuated, and during which she was often isolated even in the women's movement, speaks of an integrity, determination and political imagination which are the hallmarks of a great woman.

As mothers struggle once again to press their claim for economic independence, it is right that the women's movement today should recognize its debt to Eleanor Rathbone. For to go from nothing to 'a very little share', to go from having to beg for every penny to having by right some claim on the national income, was the first giant step on which everything that mothers now are demanding from the State is premised.

NOTES

1. She integrated the two issues by pointing out that at a time of fear of a declining population, financial help for mothers producing the next generation, and an open immigration policy whereby 'ready-made' citizens could enter the country, should complement each other. 'Though you can hurry up most things, you cannot hurry up the production of an adult citizen. But you can bring in ready-made citizens. That is largely . . . how Britain itself was built up. Many strains poured into our bloodstream and enriched it, adding enormously to our capacity to understand other races'. (Eleanor Rathbone, 'The Popular Peril', in *Local Government Service*, NALGO Official Journal, November 1943, reprinted by the Family Endowment Society.)

And she protested during the debate on the 1945 Family Allowances Bill at 'the extraordinary rule that no child is to have an allowance unless it is the child of someone born in Great Britain. This is going to have a bad effect on the reputation of this country.' (Hansard, vol. 411, 11 June 1945, col. 1419.) This is in striking contrast to the approach of some of the socialists to the same question. Beatrice Webb, for example, argued for family allowances on the grounds that 'if the nation wishes the population of Great Britain to be maintained *without recourse to alien immigration* on a large scale, it will be necessary for the State to provide, through the parents, for the maintenance of children during the period of their economic dependence;' my italics. (Quoted in *The Times*, 6 August 1946.)

2. Lord Beveridge's 'Epilogue' to Eleanor Rathbone, *Family Allowances: A new edition of The Disinherited Family*, Allen & Unwin, London, 1949, p.269.

3. ibid., p.277.

4. See, for example, Women in the Claimants Union, *Unsupported Mothers Handbook*, published by Highbury Claimants Union, London, 1972, and Milwaukee County Welfare Rights Organization, *Welfare Mothers Speak Out*, Norton, New York, 1972.

5. 'We invented the word "unwaged" to describe . . . housework. Although we got no wage for doing it, it wasn't entirely unpaid . . . Some of it is paid for in the form of food, clothing and shelter. But we get no money in our own right for expending *our* labour power in producing *other people's* labour power. We are deprived of . . . money in the form of wages which is . . . acknowledgement and reward for a social contribution.' (From Selma James, 'Marx and Feminism' in Kenneth Leech, After Marx – The Jubilee Lent Lectures for 1983, Jubilee Group, London 1984 p.54.) Selma James adds: 'We usually use the popular term, "unpaid work", which is increasingly used in Britain.'

6. *World Conference of the United Nations Decade for Women Programme of Action*, Copenhagen, July 1980, p.7. These figures, cited in passing, were published by the Wages for Housework delegation to the Conference, and have been widely quoted since.

7. House of Commons Debate of May 1975, quoted in the *Sunday Times*, 20 June 1976, p.17.

8. Reported in *The Guardian*, 27 September 1979.

9. *Agenda for the National Conference of Labour Women*, 12-14 June 1982, p.28. Norwich Constituency Labour Party had already in 1978 passed a resolution calling for a 'homemakers' allowance' for those with children under sixteen or adult dependants, to be paid whether the homemaker is full-time at home or not. 'This would give parents, especially women with children, the choice either to work at bringing up children themselves or to work at some other job' since the allowance could 'be used by the parents to secure the services of other persons during the periods when the parents were at work' if they chose to spend the money this way. The amount to be paid was 'to be determined by the average income level of the community' and to be paid on top of Child Benefits. This

resolution was circulated to other constituencies.

10.   *National Plan of Action* adopted at National Women's Conference, Houston, Texas, November 1977, p.28.

11.   *Displaced Homemakers Act*, HR 10270.

12.   *Equity in Social Security for Individuals and Families Act*, HR 3247. National Insurance 'credits' for women working full-time in the home were introduced in Britain in 1978.

13.   *The Bonnie Plan*, HR 7358.

14.   *Woman's Day* magazine, New York, 19 May 1978, p.24 ff.

15.   Cited in Norma Steele and Margaret Prescod-Roberts, *Black Women: Bringing It All Back Home*, Falling Wall Press, 1980, p.45.

16.   Monique Proulx, *Five Million Women: A Study of the Canadian Housewife*, Advisory Council on the Status of Women, Ottawa, 1978.

17.   *Programme of Action*, Copenhagen, July 1980, p.26, Paragraph 103. This became the major unifying issue of the 'Non-Governmental Organisations' Conference, organized by the UN to coincide with the gathering of official government delegations, and attended by 8,000 women. (See the Conference newspaper, *Forum 80*, Copenhagen, 21 July 1980.) A petition entitled 'Women Count – Count Women's Work' has now been launched (June 1984) by the International Wages for Housework Campaign and International Black Women for Wages for Housework, calling on all Governments to implement this Resolution.

18.   Krishna Ahooja-Patel (ed.), *Women at Work*, Bulletin of the International Labour Office, Geneva, July 1980, pp.v-vi.

19.   For discussion of the concept of 'family wage' and its limitations, see e.g. Doug Grieve, 'The Curse of Beveridge' in the *New Statesman*, 8 May 1981; Tess Gill, 'The Family Wage Debate' in *Link*, No. 35, 1982; Anna Coote, 'The AES: A New Starting Point' in *New Socialist*, December 1981. All of these articles tackle the question of dependent children without confronting the financial dependence of the adult who looks after them.

20.   The debate on housework in the women's movement, and in particular the stir caused by the publication of Selma James and Mariarosa Dalla Costa's *The Power of Women and the Subversion of the Community* in 1972 (Falling Wall Press, Bristol, 3rd edition 1975) launched an academic industry on housework. The bibliography in Rae André, *Homemakers: The Forgotten Workers*, University of Chicago Press, Chicago and London, 1981 provides a good guide to that industry. This book is unusual not only in breaking from the academic mould and stressing that 'without action, the theories are only so many words' (p.262), but because Rae André is scrupulous in acknowledging her debt to the women's movement, including the influence of the Wages for Housework Campaign and its publications.

21.   See e.g. the work of Hilary Land, discussed on pp.96-7.

22.   Mary Stocks, *Eleanor Rathbone*, Gollancz, London, 1949, pp.63-4.

23.   G.D.H. Cole and Raymond Postgate, *The Common People*, Methuen University Paperback, London, 1968, p.428.

24.   Margaret McMillan, writing of her sister's experiences in *The Life of Rachel McMillan*, London, 1927, p.137.

25.   Florence Nightingale, *Cassandra*, 1852, republished in Ray Strachey, *The Cause*, Bell & Sons, London, 1928, p.402.

26.   This financial independence was a key factor behind middle class women's organizing in the suffragette movement, where the kind of militancy for which the movement became famous was premised on not being totally dependent on fathers or husbands.

27.   A body of elected representatives which made policy for and administered the Poor Law in their locality.

28.   During the debate on New Feminism, Eleanor Rathbone commented bitterly on how many middle class suffragettes were ready to ignore the needs of working class women as soon as the vote was won. (See p.56.)
29.   i.e. those not covered by the 1911 National Insurance Act.
30.   Sheila Rowbotham, *Hidden from History*, Pluto, London, 1973, p.77.
31.   The same is true of the administration of Social Security/Welfare today. There are many districts in the UK where Social Security investigators either don't visit claimants to check up and 'snoop', or are very careful indeed about their behaviour for example, in many parts of Belfast, and in inner city areas like St. Pauls (Bristol), Brixton (London) and Liverpool 8, where single mothers and the families of the unemployed are concentrated in large numbers − and have the advantage of that concentration in confronting officials.
32.   Poplar in East London, the area which provided so much support for the suffragette campaign in East London led by Sylvia Pankhurst, was notorious for the degree to which working class Poor Law Guardians had been able to extend the payment of out relief to the 'able-bodied poor', such as widows, deserted wives and unemployed. (See Pat Thane, 'Women and the Poor Law', in *History Workshop Journal*, no. 6., Autumn 1978, p.41.)
33.   See pp.35-7 and 58 for more on the Women's Co-operative Guild.
34.   They stood as Labour Representation Committee candidates. The LRC, formed in 1900, was the precursor of the Labour Party.
35.   Quoted in Jill Liddington and Jill Norris, *One Hand Tied Behind Us*, Virago, London, 1978, p.139.
36.   Margaret Llewelyn Davies, *The Women's Co-operative Guild*, quoted in Liddington and Norris, *One Hand Tied Behind Us*, p.138.
37.   Sylvia Pankhurst, *The Suffragette Movement*, Longmans, London, 1931.
38.   Eleanor Rathbone, *Report on the Condition of Widows under the Poor Law in Liverpool*, published by the Liverpool Women's Industrial Council, Liverpool, 1913.
39.   Ibid., quoted in Stocks, *Eleanor Rathbone*, pp.62-3.
40.   See Selma James, 'Immigration and Population Control', in *Women and Capital* to be published in 1987 by Falling Wall Press. Major confrontations internationally are located on that battleground between what are the State's population needs and what are the needs of the parents who actually produce the children. The most obvious recent examples are the US government's concern to sterilize Third World women, and the success of the Indian people in forcing the fall of Indira Gandhi's government in the 1970s as a result of its attempt forcibly to sterilize millions of Indian women and men.
41.   The 1911 Census recorded industries and services in order of numerical importance. Domestic service topped the list, followed by agriculture, coal mining, building trades and cotton manufacture, in that order.
42.   See e.g. Steele and Prescod-Roberts, *Black Women: Bringing It All Back Home*.
43.   See e.g. Selma James, 'A Woman's Place', in James and Dalla Costa, *The Power of Women and the Subversion of the Community*. This essay records the experience of young women immigrants to Los Angeles, where the population rose by 29 per cent between 1940 and 1946 (p.20).
44.   James, 'A Woman's Place', p.69.
45.   Rathbone, *Report on the Condition of Widows in Liverpool*, p.10.
46.   In the Lancashire cotton mill districts, men's wages were lower than in many other parts of the country, so that women were usually forced to work in the mills after marriage as the man's wage was not enough to support a family.
47.   This duality is reflected in the divided attitude of Lancashire women to a State endowment for motherhood. (See p.51 and D.F. p.322.)
48.   Angus McLaren, 'Women's Work and the Regulation of Family Size: the

Question of Abortion in the Nineteenth Century', in *History Workshop Journal*, no.4, Autumn 1977, p.70. 'The number of children born to each hundred wives of textile families was until 1881-1886 in fact lower than the rate for every other class except that of the skilled professionals and businessmen, and was declining.'

49.　Quoted in G.A.N. Lowndes, *The Silent Social Revolution*, Oxford University Press, London, 1937, p.23.

50.　By 1913 some local authorities were paying maintenance grants to some secondary school children; the campaign continued to extend these payments and to win maintenance grants for all children. See Maud Pember Reeves, *Round About a Pound a Week*, London, 1913, republished by Virago, London, 1979, p.228.

51.　'We want 30s a week and less hours per day'; 'One hour schooling in the morning and one in the afternoon, and one shilling per week for attendance', as well as potato-lifting holidays; no home lessons; abolition of the strap; and free pencils and rubbers.' Quotations and demands from the *Weekly Express*, 15 September 1911, *Northern Daily Mail*, 15 September 1911 and the *Greenlock Telegraph*, 19 September 1911; quoted in Dave Marson, *Children's Strikes in 1911*, History Workshop pamphlet no. 9 Oxford, 1973.

52.　The statisticians didn't record the extent of this kind of work.

53.　Although most young girls would have handed over a portion of their earnings to their mothers, they would nevertheless have had more independence than at any other moment in their lives.

54.　'A single woman thinks twice about getting married and giving up the freedom that she has had before marriage. Before, she went out as she pleased and bought clothes as she needed them. She never had the freedom that men have but she was on her own. One young woman of twenty that I work with says she almost got married twice and she is certainly glad that she didn't. She told me . . . "I do what I want to do now." When she hears the married women talk, she says, "Hey, you're scaring me. You'll make me an old maid." ' (James, 'A Woman's Place' p.59.) This is Los Angeles in the 1950s, but that the same phenomenon was true of England at the end of the nineteenth century is amply reflected not only in the widespread (and horrified) reports on the independence of Lancashire mill girls who bought frills and ribbons and went out in gangs to the pub (see Margaret Hewitt, *Wives and Mothers in Victorian England*, Rockliff, London, 1958), but in the census statistics cited in the next note.

55.　Actual figures from the census: in 1871, 343 women in every thousand married by the ages 20-24; in 1911 the figure was 242 in every thousand. While statisticians have often attributed this change to the excess of women over men in the period, the proportion of women married by the 35-44 age group had hardly changed (1871, 762 per thousand; 1911, 753 per thousand).

56.　Patricia Knight, 'Women and Abortion in Victorian England', in *History Workshop Journal*, no. 4, p.59. The same point is also made by Angus McLaren in his 'Women's Work and the Regulation of Family Size': '. . . early birth control advocates . . . offered no new methods that were practical for the working class. The sheath was too expensive, the sponge unreliable, the douche required elaborate preparations and a water supply.' He concludes: 'Withdrawal and abortion were the only methods talked about by the birth controllers that basically concerned the workers.' (p.73.)

57.　See Marie Stopes, *Mother England*, 'A Contemporary History Self-Written by Those Who Have Had No Historian', London, 1929. Interestingly, surveys conducted in 'developed' countries as recently as 1966-72 showed that male withdrawal was the most common method of birth control in half the countries surveyed. See Charles F. Westoff, 'The Population of the Developed Countries', in *Scientific American*, September 1974, p.13.

58.   See e.g. McLaren, 'Women's Work and the Regulation of Family Size', pp.70-1: 'For the nineteenth-century working class the questions of fertility, infant and child mortality, and the economic utility of children would all bear on whether or not methods of control would be employed. The fact that working-class families remained larger than those of the middle classes did not mean that the worker was "ignorant" of means of family restriction. What it showed was that the two classes had different needs and aims. The usual high fertility of workers in general was "rational" given the particular conditions of high infant mortality and the fact that children raised frugally and put to work early could be valuable assets. Moreover, even in the large family birth control could have been used, not to restrict its total size, but to space births. When the working-class family declined in size it did so not simply because new means of control were available – withdrawal was their main form of contraception until well into the 20th century – but because new social and economic forces made a smaller family preferable.'

59.   Stopes, *Mother England,* pp.11, 83 and 114.

60.   See James and Dalla Costa, *The Power of Women,* for a devastating comment on the sexual repression at the centre of housework – in particular the section 'Dead Labour and the Agony of Sexuality' (pp.42-3).

61.   Stopes, *Mother England,* includes many letters from men concerned for their wives' health and well-being. Seeing the strain imposed upon them by frequent childbirth and the additional housework and poverty that resulted, they wanted to do something to help.

62.   See George Dangerfield, *The Strange Death of Liberal England,* London, 1935, republished by Paladin, London 1970, for an excellent account of the intertwining of male and female militancy in the years before World War I, and the Government's response.

63.   James and Dalla Costa, *The Power of Women,* p.45.

64.   Quoted in Rowbotham, *Hidden from History,* p.79.

65.   See e.g. 'Mr Barnet in Whitechapel . . . found that . . . the women . . . worked without adequate regard to their function as mothers' (1903), quoted in Anna Davin, 'Imperialism and Motherhood', in *History Workshop Journal,* no. 5, Spring 1978, p.16. For a detailed account of the Lancashire suffragette movement see Liddington and Norris, *One Hand Tied Behind Us,* and for the contribution made by the women of the East End of London see Pankhurst, *The Suffragette Movement.*

66.   Margaret Llewelyn Davies (ed.), *Maternity: Letters from Working Women,* London, 1915, republished by Virago, London, 1978.

67.   Ibid., p.14.

68.   'I read in *Vorwarts* that on that evening a mass meeting, under the auspices of the Social Democratic Party, would take place, at which the subject of the limitation of offspring would be discussed. This was to be the second meeting dealing with this subject. Another meeting had taken place the week before, August 22nd, at which several eminent Socialist women, among them Rosa Luxemburg and Clara Zetkin, spoke very strongly against the limitation of off-spring among the poor. In fact the title of the discussion was "Gegen der Gerburtstreik".' (Adelayne More, *Fecundity versus Civilisation,* London, 1920, p.40.) The Social Democratic Party was the German revolutionary socialist party.

69.   Eugenics is 'The science of race improvement' [sic]: *Chambers Twentieth Century Dictionary,* London, 1972.

70.   Sidney Webb, *The Declining Birthrate,* Fabian Tract 131, London, 1907, quoted in Davin, 'Imperialism and Motherhood', p.23.

71.   More, *Fecundity versus Civilisation,* p.40.

72.   Contemporary parallels are easy to find. For example the US Black Nationalists of the 1960s, while they opposed the US Government's sterilization

programme, countered the State's policy with one which urged Black women to have more children in order to swell the forces of the Black Liberation army. The Rastafarian pop group, Black Uhuru, is still singing this message today (1984) with their song *Abortion* which tells Black women not to use contraception or abortion.

73.   Llewelyn Davies (ed.), *Maternity*, p.46.
74.   Eleanor Rathbone, 'Family Endowment in its Bearing on the Question of Population', paper read before the Eugenics Society on 12 November 1924, p.4.
75.   Eleanor Rathbone, *The Ethics and Economics of Family Endowment*, Epworth Press, London, 1927, p.112 [my italics].
76.   She campaigned on behalf of Black women in India and Africa by pressing for more British government resources to go to women living under colonial rule (e.g. in the form of educational and training facilities); and for women's economic and civil rights (e.g. women's suffrage to be recognized in the Independence negotiations.)
77.   These were the instructions given to the four women health visitors appointed in Birmingham in 1899. See *Public Health*, August 1899, p.721, quoted in Davin, 'Imperialism and Motherhood', p.37.
78.   Recent legislation (the Children's Act of 1975) has increased these powers. For an example of how they are still penalizing women who are poor see Joan Leslie White, 'Nothing to Lose but my Children', speech given 4 July 1978 at a public meeting on 'Lesbian women, rape and custody'. Available from King's Cross Women's Centre, 71 Tonbridge St., London WC1. The speech describes Joan Leslie White's fight against Camden Council to retain custody of her children. See also Francie Wyland, *Motherhood, Lesbianism and Child Custody*, Falling Wall Press, Bristol, 1977.
79.   Thomas Gautrey, *Lux Mihi Laus*, London, 1937, p.91.
80.   Anna Davin, whose article on 'Imperialism and Motherhood' deals with this period, is much more ambivalent than Eleanor Rathbone on whether poverty or ignorance was the major cause: 'With hindsight, the conditions imposed by poverty *seem likely* to have been significant factors in infant mortality, to be ranked at least alongside "maternal ignorance" perhaps.' (Davin, 'Imperialism and Motherhood', p.36, my italics.)
81.   See the various descriptions of working class life of the period, especially Pember Reeves, *Round About a Pound a Week*; Llewelyn Davies, *Maternity;* Rathbone, *Report on the Condition of Widows under the Poor Law*.
82.   Women today make the same appeal, from Social Security/Welfare mothers saying, 'Our work as mothers raising the future generation is essential to the economy'; to mothers demanding more nursery provisions so that they can 'contribute to the economy' by going out to work, to teachers, nurses and other service workers doing socialized housework who argue their case for higher wages on the grounds that their work is essential to the economy. See e.g. Women in the Claimants Union, *Unsupported Mothers Handbook*, pp.14, 17 and 32; 'Women in labour keep capital in power . . . We're cooking, cleaning, looking after kids . . . All women, married or not, should claim unemployment benefit in their own right — it's a way of getting paid for the work we do at home . . . Right now we want . . . A wage to bring up kids — and we want bringing up kids to be everyone's job, not just women's.' And see the London Borough of Wandsworth Joint Shop Stewards' Committee, Public Bulletin, vol. 1, nos.1-4, 1977-8.
83.   See Stocks, *Eleanor Rathbone*.
84.   See e.g. Pankhurst, *The Suffragette Movement*, and Liddington and Norris, *One Hand Tied Behind Us*.
85.   See Margery Spring Rice, *Working Class Wives: Their Health and Conditions*, Pelican Books, London, 1939.
86.   Margaret Llewelyn Davies (ed.), *Life As We Have Known It*, by Cooperative

Working Women, London, 1931, republished by Virago, London, 1977, p.49.
87.   The high maternal mortality rate was the subject of campaigns in the 1920s, 30s and 40s. See p.68. As Eleanor Rathbone makes clear in this book, the *maternal* death-rate had been almost unaffected by these measures to help at the *end* of pregnancy and at childbirth because it was related to women's general poverty and ill health, which could not be sufficiently countered by short-term maternity benefits and medical attention. (See D.F. p.176.)
88.   It is interesting to note how the terminology has changed over the years to hide women's work in the home, so that 'working women' came to be applied only to women who worked outside the home for wages, and not those who worked at home unpaid. One of the first slogans of the Wages for Housework Campaign in the early 1970s, subsequently embodied in a badge, was 'Every Mother is a Working Mother'.
89.   Llewelyn Davies (ed.), *Maternity*, pp.153-4.
90.   See Gloden Dallas' Introduction to the 1978 edition of *Maternity*, pp.4-5.
91.   See *International Co-operative Women's Guild: Report of the Committee 1930-34*, p.22: 'The President acted as fraternal delegate of the Guild at the International Conference of Socialist Women at Vienna in 1931, where, on a motion for the formation of special Housewives' Committees to further the economic and public interests of the housewife, the Co-operative women present made a strong plea for the Co-operative Movement and its Women's Guilds to be recognised as the appropriate machinery . . . These developments showed the necessity for the Guild, which has always acted as the Housewives' International, to formulate and synthesise the needs, demands and objectives of the housewife in a comprehensive programme.'
92.   Though they did lend support at crucial moments. For example, during World War I the National Union of Women Workers called for an end to government supervision of women receiving Separation Allowances, and for the allowances to be called a wage. (See p.47.)
93.   Llewelyn Davies (ed.), *Life As We Have Known It*, pp.xxxvi-viii. The parallel between this description and the fact that Virginia Woolf recommended 'A Room of One's Own' (see the book of the same title, published in 1924) and £500 a year as a prerequisite for independent thought, is unmistakeable.
94.   See *Christian Commonwealth* newspaper, 28 October 1914.
95.   See the *Daily Herald*, 10 October 1914.
96.   'The Local Government Board offices were crowded with mothers and their babies, an unusual sight for Whitehall. They came to ask Herbert Samuel (Secretary of the Government's Local Authority Board) to recognise that, during the war, maternity was more important than ever.' (Llewelyn Davies [ed.], *Life As We Have Known It*, p.50.)
97.   A pound a week was defined as the poverty line by Charles Booth in his massive survey of *The Life and Labour of the People of London*, published in 1903. He estimated that one-third of the population lived at or below that line. In 1906, 48 per cent of adult men earned less than 25/- a week. See Pember Reeves, *Round About a Pound a Week*, p.212.
98.   *Ibid.*, p.xi.
99.   Mabel Atkinson, *The Economic Foundations of the Women's Movement*, Fabian Tract no. 175, London, 1914, p.18.
100.   *Ibid.*, p.15.
101.   *Ibid.*, p.22.
102.   See for example Mrs Wibaut, *Working Women and the Suffrage*, Independent Labour Party pamphlet of the 1890s, republished in Suzie Fleming (ed.), *Women in Rebellion*, Independent Labour Party, Leeds, 1973: 'One of the first reforms necessary for women to gain is Endowment of Motherhood . . . She whom

the State debars from earning in order that the welfare of its future citizens may be assured, should also be assured of a proper maintenance. The Socialist Party should demand a whole set of measures, which will include not only State Endowment of Motherhood, but . . . the procuring of pure milk by the community and an allowance for other necessities (clothing etc.); also the founding and arranging of good creches . . .' (1973 edn., p.7.)

103.   Llewelyn Davies (ed.), *Maternity*, pp.67-8.

104.   *Ibid.*, p.112.

105.   House of Commons, 6 March 1923. Speech by Mr Rhys Davies, MP. It is interesting to note that in proposing the mothers' pension be paid to mothers where the family breadwinner is incapacitated, these proposals went much further than today's provisions for unemployment and sickness where the money for the whole family is paid to the man.

106.   In expressing the demand for a State endowment of motherhood as modestly and defensively as possible, Eleanor Rathbone was reflecting a strategy which has always .characterized working class organizing, in which a subversive demand is presented as innocently as possible in order to attract maximum possible support and undercut the opposition. (A classic example is the demand for 'Peace, Bread and Land' which was the slogan of the Russian Revolution.) Right-wing opponents of motherhood endowment knew only too well what it would mean. (See p.44 above.)

107.   The experience of the 1970s, and since, has been that references like these to unpaid housework proliferate when women are also campaigning explicitly to get some financial recognition for the work.

108.   Llewelyn Davies, *Maternity*, p.6 and p.7.

109.   Margaret Llewelyn Davies, 'The Claims of Mothers and Children' in Marion Phillips (ed.), *Women and the Labour Party*, Headley Bros. London, 1918, p.32.

110.   Fabian Women's Group, *Statement of Aims*, London, 1913.

111.   See e.g. Mabel Atkinson: 'It is neither possible nor desirable that we should at this stage adopt a dogmatic attitude as to the length of time during which an expectant or nursing mother should be freed from ordinary industry and supported by a State grant. It will . . . vary from industry to industry . . . It would be easy under . . . Socialism to set aside excellently appropriate work for expectant mothers, and the State maintenance might then only need to cover a few weeks,' in *Economic Foundations of the Women's Movement*, pp.21-2.

112.   Victor Gollancz (ed.), *The Making of Women: Oxford Essays in Feminism*, Allen and Unwin, London, 1917. Contributors included Eleanor Rathbone, Maude Royden and Elinor Burns.

113.   Blanche Wiesen Cook (ed.), *Crystal Eastman on Women and Revolution*, Oxford University Press, New York, 1979.

114.   Virginia Woolf, *Three Guineas*, London, 1938, pp. 200-1. The argument in this book is that women's contribution to the anti-war movement lies in the achievement of financial independence for women, because women who are not dependent on men for money will be able to oppose men's pro-war stand.

115.   *Ibid.*, pp.202-3. For contemporary parallels see e.g. 'Pay Women Not the Military' in Wilmette Brown, *Black Women and the Peace Movement*, Falling Wall Press, Bristol, 1984.

116.   In her introduction to Llewelyn Davies (ed.), *Life As We Have Known It*, Virginia Woolf describes working class women's preoccupation with 'baths and money', with material necessities; and describes, too, the reluctance of middle class women, 'whose minds . . . fly free at the end of a short length of capital' (p.xxviii) to admit the degree to which their precarious freedom depended on that 'short length of capital'.

117.   See e.g. the continuity in the Women's Co-operative Guild (p.35 above).

118.   The editor's introduction to the 1979 edition of Crystal Eastman's essays

points out that what Crystal Eastman advocated would today be termed wages for housework: 'What is today referred to as "wages for housework" was featured in Crystal Eastman's feminist programme as a "Motherhood Endowment". In "Now We Can Begin", she wrote that the only way for women "at least in capitalist society" to achieve "real economic independence" was for the "political government to recognize and subsidize housework as skilled labour".' (Wiesen Cook [ed.], *Crystal Eastman*, pp.5-6.)

119. 5,754,044 women were 'occupied' and 13,132,246 'unoccupied' [sic]. (Cited in Gollancz (ed.), *The Making of Women*, p.202.)

120. Richard Titmuss, *Essays on the Welfare State*, Allen & Unwin University Books, 2nd ed., London, 1963, p.91.

121. William Beveridge, *Report on Social Insurance and Allied Services*, Emd 1604, HMSO, London 1942 p.49 and table XVI on p.123. Even allowing for the fact that the 'marriage bar' operating in the 1920s and 30s prevented many women from continuing or returning to jobs after marriage or motherhood; and the fact that the census figures took no account of paid work women did at home − either for small-scale manufacturers or by servicing other housewives − these figures are still quite startling.

122. Alexander Grey, *Family Endowment: A Critical Analysis*, Benn, London, 1927, p.34, quotes H.N. Brailsford, speaking at a conference on Family Endowment organized by the League of Nations Union in 1925: 'Frankly, I regard this proposal as a very heavy charge of social dynamite.'

123. Grey, *Family Endowment*, pp.33-4.

124. *Ibid.*, p.41. The quotation is from A.B. Piddington, *The Next Step*, London, 1921, p.29.

125. *Ibid.*, p.42. The quotation is from K.D. Courtney, and others, *Equal Pay and the Family*, Headley Bros., London, 1918, p.10.

126. Grey, *Family Endowment*, p.44. He is quoting *The Disinherited Family*, 1st edn., London, 1924, p.164, and H.N. Brailsford (see footnote 122 above).

127. Stocks, *Eleanor Rathbone*, pp.63 and 115, and D.F. p.257.

128. The principle of weekly payments in advance has only now been broken by the Thatcher Government, which in 1982 began to pay Family Allowances (Child Benefit) monthly, in arrears.

129. Government leaflet, *Separation Allowances for Wives and Children of Soldiers*, London, 1 March, 1915. The rates for officers' wives were higher, and so were their weekly deductions.

130. 'The extra 3/6 a week issuable to London Families in certain circumstances will continue as at present.' *Separation Allowances for Wives and Children of Soldiers*. There were twenty shillings to a pound, and so 3/6 − three and a half shillings − was about one-sixth of a pound.

131. See the book of the same name.

132. They should also be measured against the allowance of 5/- for the second child (none for the first) which was the rate at which the universal Family Allowance payment introduced in 1946 was paid.

133. The allowances were being paid for all children up to the age of sixteen, and for children over sixteen attending secondary schools, technical schools or universities.

134. *Co-operative News*, 26 December, 1914.

135. *Yorkshire Observer*, 26 November, 1914.

136. *The Nation*, 21 November, 1914.

137. *Daily News and Leader*, 19 November, 1914.

138. *Co-operative News*, 7 November, 1914.

139. *Yorkshire Observer*, 14 November, 1914. The importance of the Women's Co-operative Guild's work in securing these payments for unmarried mothers is described in Llewelyn Davies (ed.), *Life As We Have Known It*, pp.51-2. As the

voice of 'respectable married women', they persuaded the Government that married mothers felt that mothers who were not married should get the same treatment as themselves.

140. The non-contributory Old Age Pensions introduced before World War I were paid via the Post Office for the same reason.

141. *Northern Daily Telegraph*, December 1914 (no precise date on cutting) filed in the Gertrude Tuckwell Collection at the TUC Library.

142. *Daily News and Leader*, 19 November 1914, Parliamentary report: quoting Mr Barnes, MP.

143. It has sometimes been argued in the 1970s and 80s that a State wage for housework would mean more government control over housework and the women who do it. The experience of preventing government supervision of women receiving Separation Allowances was a major precedent, which must have had its own impact on the subsequent introduction of Family Allowances with 'no strings attached'. (See pp.46-7.)

144. See Dangerfield, *The Strange Death of Liberal England*, for a popular account of the militancy of the working class movement before World War I, written only twenty years later.

145. The suffragettes broke shop windows all over the country, including all the windows in Oxford Street in central London. The schoolchildren whose strikes have already been referred to (see p.25) also did their share of window breaking.

146. See Taylor Downing (ed.), *The Troubles*, Thames/Futura, London, 1980, p.77, for the way in which Irish hunger strikers capitalized on the political impact the suffragettes had with their use of hunger strikes as one of the tactics of their campaign.

147. Jessie Stephens, Glasgow domestic servant, Independent Labour Party member and suffragette organizer, was interviewed by Gloden Dallas and myself in 1974. She described how they prepared for a meeting in Glasgow at which Mrs Pankhurst, on the run from the police, was to speak. They placed barbed wire behind the flowerpots that lined the platform, which the police discovered only when they tore their hands and faces in trying to rush the platform to arrest Mrs Pankhurst. A part of this interview is reproduced in Marsha Rowe (ed.), *Spare Rib Reader*, Penguin, London, 1982, pp.553-61.

148. Emma Mahler, *The Social Effects of Separation Allowances: An Experiment in the Endowment of Motherhood*, Report of a Detailed Inquiry Organized by Liverpool Women's Industrial Council, Liverpool, 1916, p.8.

149. NUWSS understood that working class women could not afford to work full-time for the suffragette movement, however devoted they might be to the cause, unless they were paid. It therefore provided them both with a salary and, in Selina Cooper's case, a live-in housekeeper so that she could travel around even though she had a young child. (See Liddington and Norris, *One Hand Tied Behind Us*, pp.22 and 224.)

150. Pankhurst, *The Suffragette Movement*, pp.607-8.

151. In Gollancz (ed.), *The Making of Women*.

152. *Ibid*.

153. *Ibid.*, p.29.

154. Liddington and Norris, *One Hand Tied Behind Us*, p.260. The significance of Selina Cooper's speaking 'all for nothing' on behalf of the endowment of motherhood should not be missed. (See footnote 149 above.)

155. *Ibid.*, pp.259-60. The quotations are from *Common Cause*, 6 March 1914 and 27 February 1914.

156. Jane Lewis, *The Movement for Family Allowances*, 1917-45, typescript paper presented to the Memorial University of Newfoundland, 1974. This article has now been published in *Social History/L'Histoire Sociale* as 'The English Movement for Family Allowances, 1917-45'.

157. *Ibid.*, pp.3-4. The references cited are *Women's Leader* (newspaper of NUSEC), 17 July 1925, p.125; Mary Stocks, *The Case for Family Endowment*, London, 1927, p.37.

158. *Ibid.*, p.7. The reference cited is *Women's Leader* 11 February 1927, p.3.

159. NUSEC leaflet, circularized in 1927 and quoted in Jane Lewis, 'Eleanor Rathbone and the New Feminism During the 1920s', paper presented in September 1973 to the Memorial University of Newfoundland, and since published as 'Beyond Suffrage: English Feminism during the 1920s' in *Maryland Historian*, 1975.

160. Eleanor Rathbone in particular stressed repeatedly that equal pay for work outside the home would never be a reality as long as mothers working full-time at home and children were financially dependent on men. See *The Remuneration of Women's Services*, and D.F. pp.216-55. She also felt that communal facilities for childcare should be available – but that women should be in a position to decide for themselves whether or not to use them. (See D.F. pp.366-8 for Eleanor Rathbone's view of those who advocated communal services as an alternative to cash payments.)

161. Although in a recent article, 'The Mantle of Manhood', *New Statesman*, December 1981, Hilary Land comes close: 'Should the State provide more for children? Those who say yes must recognise the dangers of giving more power to the State to control the incomes and lives of families . . . more State provision could be used to the detriment of the rights and interests of working class women . . . Since [fifty years ago] State social services, in particular the social security system, have become far more centralised and bureaucratic. With this in mind, are cash benefits the best form of child support?'

162. There are those who have asserted that Family Allowances have nothing to do with a wage for motherhood or a wage for housework, without making any attempt to prove their case. Certainly that case cannot be made historically. It is impossible to account for the split in the women's movement over New Feminism without recognizing that Family Allowances, Family Endowment, Motherhood Endowment, as advocated by the New Feminists, was a demand for economic independence for mothers through the recognition of their work in the home, in the form of a payment for that work by the State.

163. There are many examples of the way in which the movement for money for mothers has been hidden. To cite just a few: Sheila Rowbotham's *Hidden from History* has two references to Eleanor Rathbone and 'her energetic' campaign, amounting to rather less than two paragraphs in over 100 pages dealing with women's history 1870s to 1930s. She mentions briefly the New Feminists' preoccupation with State payments for housework – and openly argues against them. Other writers are less straightforward. In her article on 'Imperialism and Motherhood', Anna Davin, in dealing with the demands being made by and for mothers at the beginning of the twentieth century, not only devotes less than a page to the question of cash payments through the endowment of motherhood, but dismisses Eleanor Rathbone as follows: 'Eleanor Rathbone was . . . its best known and longest-persevering proponent, using every possible argument, including that it would give the state the power to "manipulate the birth rate"'' (p.23). She gives no reference for this 'quotation', but it seems likely that she is misquoting the paper to the Eugenic Society referred to on p.31, where Rathbone, concludes, 'The manipulation of such a system would at least give to *the community* . . . an effective instrument for influencing the birth rate and guiding its flow, without violating the privacies or interfering with the liberties of individual citizens.' (p.6, my italics.) This six-page paper has taken on a disproportionate importance for historians critical of Eleanor Rathbone; it is cited without reference either to what her position on eugenics actually was or to any historical context for it – least of all the record of her socialist contemporaries which I have

touched on (see pp.21-2). At a Women's Research and Resource Centre meeting on the history of Family Allowances, a paper by Sylvia Mann began by characterizing Eleanor Rathbone as 'attempting to replicate the way Family Allowances had been used on the continent to regulate the birth rate'. She went on to claim that the starting-point for other supporters of Family Allowances in Britain 'was primarily their concern for child welfare'.

Eleanor Rathbone was herself aware that one of the most effective weapons of opposition is that of the 'oubliette' (D.F. p.343), whereby the movement and its ideas are never mentioned. One variation is to be highly selective, e.g. by citing Rathbone's advocacy of children's allowances but not her advocacy of a State endowment of motherhood. (See e.g. Beatrix Campbell, 'Women, Not What They Bargained For', in *Marxism Today*, March 1982.)

164.   Hilary Land, 'The Mantle of Manhood', *New Statesman* December 1981, pp.16-18.

165.   *Ibid.*, p.17.

166.   See Brown, *Black Women and the Peace Movement*, p.70, for more on this. And for an example of the white feminist population controllers she is referring to, see Maggie Jones interviewing Wangari Maathai of Kenya in Leonie Caldicott and Stephanie Leland (eds.), *Reclaim the Earth*, Women's Press, London, p.113. Maggie Jones ignores the reply, 'the greatest problem is poverty, not really the rate of population growth', and persists, 'what do you feel can be done to . . . reduce population growth?' This preoccupation with population control has been particularly evident in the ecology movement.

167.   See Lewis, *Eleanor Rathbone and the New Feminism*. She cites Mary Stocks' 1949 description of one particular meeting as evidence. (Stocks, *Eleanor Rathbone*, pp.117-18.) I think it likely that Mary Stocks, writing in the late 1940s, both imputed to Eleanor Rathbone her own motivations, and drew on what was in the 1940s the main plank of the Family Allowance campaigners – as advised by Eleanor Rathbone in *The Disinherited Family* – which was to appeal on children's behalf. In Mary Stocks' biography there is repeated evidence that feminism was the driving force in Eleanor Rathbone's life, and that the achievement of an endowment for mothers was her greatest and lifelong ambition. That she should have been concerned for the welfare of children as well as mothers is to my mind a mark in her favour; but she clearly believed that children's welfare was inseparable from mothers' independence, and was not amongst the army of 'do-gooders' who were (and are today) anxious to make a distinction between children's needs and mothers' needs in order to bypass mothers.

168.   This is matched today by those who object to any proposals for reform. 'We want "the revolution", "socialism", "the end of wages", "the end of house-work", "the end of the family"' have been arguments used not only against the campaign for financial independence for mothers, but against all kinds of demands which are of immediate use.

169.   Eleanor Rathbone, *The Harvest of the Women's Movement*, Fawcett Lecture given at Bedford College on 29 November 1935, quoted in Stocks, *Eleanor Rathbone*, p.113.

170.   1921 Presidential Address to the NUSEC, quoted in Stocks, *Eleanor Rathbone*, p.107.

171.   Rowbotham, *Hidden from History*, p.159.

172.   Both of these groups have in 1982 made front-page news, with the Occupation of the Church of the Holy Cross in King's Cross by the English Collective of Prostitutes, in protest against illegal and racist actions by the police against prostitute women working in the area (November 1982); and the 'Embrace the Base' demonstrations at Greenham Common, organized by the women of Greenham Common Peace Camp and attended by 30,000 women (December 1982). Interestingly, the two groups went out of their way to make contact with

each other. Women from the Peace Camp visited the Occupation in King's Cross to extend their support, and the English Collective of Prostitutes was among the many women's groups which came to surround the base.

173. Though it is interesting that, as I write, mass demonstrations of women are once more in the news, with the blockade of Greenham Common. (See above.)

174. To give just one example: the issue of rape has in January and February 1982 been treated with a seriousness by the media and Parliament which was inconceivable when in 1976 Women Against Rape led the first court invasions to protest at Judges' dismissal of rape as a serious crime, and organized a public trial of the judiciary and the Government for encouraging rape. (See Women Against Rape, *Women at W.A.R.*, Falling Wall Press, Bristol, 1978.) This is not to suggest that courts and governments no longer encourage rape (see Ruth Hall, Judit Kertész and Selma James, *The Rapist Who Pays the Rent*, Falling Wall Press, 1981, for an excellent analysis of this issue), but they cannot make light of the crime in the way they did in the mid-seventies.

175. See Vera Brittain, *Testament of Youth: An Autobiographical Study of the Years 1900 – 1925*, London, 1933, republished by Virago, London, 1978; and Dora Russell, *The Tamarisk Tree: My Quest for Liberty and Love*, Virago, London, 1975.

176. See Vera Brittain, writing of the 1920s in *Testament of Youth*, p.578: 'Where we had once spoken with polite evasion of "a certain condition", "a certain profession", we now unblushingly used the words "pregnancy" and "prostitution". Amongst our friends we discussed sodomy and lesbianism with as little hesitation as we compared the merits of different contraceptives, and were theoretically familiar with varieties of homosexuality and venereal disease of which the very existence was unknown to our grandparents.'

177. Dora Russell, *Hypatia, or Women and Knowledge*, Kegan Paul, London, 1925, pp.4-5.

178. *Women of the Rhondda*, film made in 1972 by Esther Ronay, Brigid Seagrave, Mary Capps, Mary Kelly, Mary Dickinson, Humphrey Trevelyan. The Rhondda Valley is in the heart of the South Wales coal mining area.

179. See Llewelyn Davies (ed.), *Life As We Have Known It*, pp.xxii and 136-40. One result was pit-head baths for the miners.

180. Almost four million houses were built in the years 1919-39. Local authorities rehoused over a million people in the slum clearance programmes of the 1930s. In York (the site of a series of social surveys by Seebohm Rowntree), for example, by 1939 almost every house had its own water supply and water closet, and one-third had baths. (See Charles Lock Mowat, *Britain Between the Wars 1918-1940*, Methuen University Paperback, London, 1968, pp.506-12.) Over the country as a whole, however, many of the poorest families were still living in overcrowded and slum conditions.

181. See e.g. Humphrey Spender's account of architectural students of the 1920s in *Worktown People: Photographs from Northern England*, Falling Wall Press, Bristol, 1982, p.12.

182. Letter from a Mansfield miner's wife in *The Woman Worker*, July 1926, no.4, p.4. The active participation of women from the mining community during miners' disputes is rarely reported in newspapers and therefore rarely appears as history – except where women write and produce their own reports. During the 1972 miners' strike in Britain a women's newsheet, *United Women* (produced in Betteshanger, Kent and London) was set up which recorded women's independent organizing, including their clashes with the union bureaucracy, resentful still of women's 'interference' in a dispute which in fact concerned not just the miner's livelihood, but the whole family's. In the current miners' dispute (1984) women's participation is so massive that the national media are forced to report it – including the numerous arrests of women, who this time are

also out on the picket lines.
183. Rowbotham, *Hidden from History*, p.135.
184. 'The original intention had been to confine this ["out of work donation"] to ex-servicemen, but . . . it was decided in 1918 to extend the "donation" to all workers covered by health insurance. Moreover, on the analogy of the Service allowances the donation was to include grants for dependants. *These were decisive developments.* The next step was obviously to broaden the scope of unemployment insurance and, the precedent having been established, to incorporate dependants' allowances in benefit. 1920 therefore saw the creation of a new unemployment insurance scheme, covering all workers except those on the land or in domestic service or the civil service. Dependants' allowances followed in 1921 . . .' (Maurice Bruce, *The Coming of the Welfare State*, Batsford, London, 1968, p.240, my italics).
185. Mowat, *Britain Between the Wars*, p.128. See D.F. pp.49-50 for the impact of these new methods of payment, in spite of the low level of the rates paid.
186. Mowat, *Britain Between the Wars*, p.484.
187. Mowat, *Britain Between the Wars*, pp.484-7. References cited are J.B. Priestley, *English Journey*, Heinemann and Gollancz, London, 1934, p.306; A.J. Lush, *Young Adult*, Cardiff, 1941, p.80; *Men without Work: A Report Made to the Pilgrim Trust*, Cambridge, 1938, pp.144 and 164-78.
188. The most famous action of the unemployed in Britain during the 1930s. The marchers walked from Jarrow, in the North of England, to London. Photographs of that march by Humphrey Spender have recently been on display in the travelling exhibition, 'The Thirties and After' organized by the Arnolfini Gallery, Bristol, 1981-84.
189. The urban riots of 1980 and 1981 in Britain have dramatically undermined any simple equation of unemployment with hopeless passivity.
190. See Jeremy Mulford's introduction to Spender, *Worktown People*, p.9, where he quotes for example a *Guardian* reviewer's impression of these photographs as depressing.
191. Alan Price, *Jarrow Song*, from the record *Between Today and Yesterday*, Warner Bros., London, 1974.
192. *The Guardian*, 1 May 1981.
193. Rowbotham, *Hidden from History*, p.136.
194. Quoted in Diane Gold, *Women in the Leeds Clothing Industry*, unpublished typescript, p.197. Gertie Roche became famous in 1970 as one of the leaders of the wildcat strike by women in the clothing industry, when 20,000 women came out on strike.
   Between 1931 and 1938, the numbers of women employed in the Leeds clothing industry went up from 24,000 to 37,000 (*ibid.*, p.21A).
195. *Ibid.*, p.25
196. *Ibid.*, p.77
197. *Ibid.*, p.81.
198. Quoted in Stocks, *Eleanor Rathbone*, p.243. Eleanor Rathbone was also active on various committees helping the Spanish refugees. As we have seen, during the 1930s and 40s she was to become famous for her work on behalf of refugees not only from Spain but from the territories occupied by Nazi troops in Europe. She was a vocal champion of the Jewish refugees interned in Britain, and led the campaign against the restrictive immigration laws whereby the British Government refused entry into Britain to hundreds of thousands of Jewish refugees.
199. Live births per thousand of population were 23.6 in the years 1911-15, and 15.1 in 1938. The all-time low was recorded in 1933 at 14.4. (Royal Commission on Population, *Report*, Cmd 7695, 1949, p.9.) One woman who

worked in a factory producing condoms in the 1930s recalled being ordered to allow a quota of faulty condoms through in order to up the birth rate. (Reported to me by her granddaughter, Lisa Longstaff.)

200.   The *Communist* newspaper, for example, debated the pros and cons of birth control in the 1920s. Some contributors argued that 'the capitalists had changed their attitude to contraception since the unemployed have apparently lost the habit of quietly starving.' (Rowbotham, *Hidden from History*, p.153.)

201.   See Stocks, *Eleanor Rathbone*, p.101.

202.   Ellen Wilkinson, 'Who Wants a Means Test on Wages', the *Tribune*, 8 July 1938.

203.   In 1924 the Labour Women's Conference passed a composite motion on motherhood calling for paid maternity leave for women with jobs, improved maternity care, some form of State payment to non-wage-earning mothers, and birth control information to be provided by local health authorities. But the Labour Party generally took longer to be persuaded on these issues. In 1925 the Labour Party Conference rejected a resolution from the Women's Conference calling for birth control advice for married people. In 1927 a Mrs Lawther appealed for support from the Labour Party Conference for birth control in return for women's solidarity with the miners during the lockout – but could not get it. In the same year the Independent Labour Party (ILP), already firmly behind cash family endowments, brought its own motion to the Labour Party Conference. The result was a Joint Committee of the Labour Party and the TUC to examine the question of State payments to mothers. Its Majority Report recommended in 1930 that cash allowances should be paid by the State to mothers for all children under school-leaving age (see pp.72-3) but in spite of this there was continued opposition in the Labour Party generally to the idea of cash payments to mothers, including from some Labour Party women.

204.   These women were able to publicly speak their minds about men, as Eleanor Rathbone does in *The Disinherited Family* (see for example, pp.196, 215 and 341-4), in a way that is impossible for women who are totally financially dependent. Eleanor Rathbone's outspoken criticism of men in general – her ability to say, for example, that all men resent women's independence, whatever their class or political colour – was a direct result of her own financial independence. She was dependent on neither a father nor a husband for either money or approval.

205.   Ray Strachey noted in 1936 that 'Modern young women know amazingly little of what life was like before the war, and show a strong hostility to the word "feminism" and all which they imagine it to connote'. (*Our Freedom and Its Results*, London, 1936.) Sheila Rowbotham comments, 'The feminists, like the Labour men and women, were let into Parliament and put on committees. Once inside the constitution they forgot that they had sought admission because they believed the world should be made anew . . . young women . . . inherited a feminism which had lost its glory, and forgotten its power, and thus saw little that could capture their feelings.' (*Hidden from History*, pp.162-3.)

206.   See Stocks, *Eleanor Rathbone*, pp.62-64; D.F., pp.257-8; Courtney and others, *Equal Pay and the Family* (1918); Rathbone, *The Remuneration of Women's Services* (1917).

207.   See pp.41-4, and the work of Dora Russell (e.g. *The Tamarisk Tree*, pp.175 and 177), Maude Royden's essays and pamphlets, ILP newspapers and pamphlets, the writing of Mary Stocks, Alice Heale, Margaret Llewelyn Davies and many others.

208.   Their record on other matters was similarly undistinguished. Trade Union membership fell by half a million in the years after the General Strike (see Cole and Postgate, *The Common People*, p.586) in disgust at the way trade union executives, and the TUC General Council in particular, had mishandled the Strike

and bowed to the Government. And most of the Labour Party leadership had by 1931 entered a 'National' coalition government and abandoned any pretence of socialist allegiance or commitment to a redistribution of wealth.

209.   Quoted in 'Why Women Don't Have Babies', an enquiry by Anne Scott-James, *Picture Post*, 13 November 1943.

210.   See Spring Rice, *Working Class Wives*. Margery Spring Rice wrote up the results of the Enquiry. The views expressed in her book were not necessarily those of the whole Committee, but the Committee approved the book as a summation of their work.

211.   Maternal mortality had even been rising in the 1930s.

212.   Spring Rice, *Working Class Wives*, p.14.

213.   *Ibid.*, p.21. The new awareness of the state of married working women's health which prompted this enquiry, and the agitation for health care for women full-time at home, were central to the creation of a National Health Service after World War II.

214.   *Ibid.*, p.95.

215.   *Ibid.*, p.207.

216.   *Ibid.*, pp.192-3 (my italics).

217.   Only one member of the Committee, trade unionist Gertrude Tuckwell, dissociated herself from the recommendation that there should be a 'system of Family Allowances paid [by the State] to the mother' on the grounds that 'I have never felt clear that family allowances would not adversely affect the raising of wages which is [also] advocated'. (*Ibid.*, p.207.)

218.   The original Committee of seven was made up of Kathleen Courtney, Maude Royden, Mary Stocks, H.N. Brailsford, Mr and Mrs Emile Burns and Eleanor Rathbone.

219.   Courtney and others, *Equal Pay and the Family*, p.11.

220.   Its membership was both more male and more respectable, though the permanent staff (the Secretary and the paid organizers) were all female. (See Reports of the Family Endowment Society, 1925-32.)

221.   Report of the Family Endowment Society for year ending 28 February 1927, p.2.

222.   Report of the Family Endowment Society for year ending 28 February 1926, p.2.

223.   Mine-owners in South Wales introduced Family Allowances at the height of the Depression as part of a package reducing wages. 'A meagre Family Allowance was embodied in the award of the South Wales Conciliation Board for the Coal Industry at the beginning of 1931. The award provided for a subsistence wage of 7/- a shift for a single man, 7/3 for a married man without children and 7/6 for a married man with children. It is unfortunate that practically the first industrial application of Family Allowances in this country should be associated with a wage reduction, should be so small in amount, and should be paid as an integral part of wages . . .' (Report of the Family Endowment Society for the year ending 29 March 1932, p.2.) This introduction of Family Allowances as part of a drop in wages was of course a measure of the defeat of the General Strike, and the Miners' Strike in particular. Like any other demand, at moments of defeat Family Allowances can be used against women and against men.

224.   See e.g. D.F. pp.163-4, where she refers to 'The exertions which are now wrung out of the married man by the fear of seeing his children suffer' and p.169, where she compares the magnitude of the price paid by middle class and working class men.

225.   For example because State Family Allowances would be paid during both unemployment and strikes. (D.F. pp.336-7.)

226.   Report of the Family Endowment Society for year ending 28 February 1930, p.2.

227. The Minority Report did not oppose the principle of State payment of Family Allowances to mothers, but recommended that the priority for State spending should be the provision of social services for the family rather than cash payments to mothers. See *Report on Family Allowances by a Special Joint Committee*, published by the TUC and Labour Party, London, 1930.
228. *Ibid.*, pp.1-2.
229. In his Epilogue to the 1949 edition (published under the title *Family Allowances*) he wrote: 'I read this book as soon as it appeared in 1924 – I was made to do so by being asked to review it – and I suffered instant and total conversion. Till that time . . . I had been apt to regard her [Eleanor Rathbone] and her Family Endowment Society as slightly tiresome . . . My own conversion was immediate and total . . . I became and remained one of Eleanor Rathbone's enthusiastic followers. It had become obvious to me that, whatever else was done or not done for social progress and the abolition of poverty, what Eleanor Rathbone wanted must be done.' (p.396.)
230. For example, the Report of the Family Endowment Society for the year ended February 1926 *includes*, under the heading meetings and conferences, etc. (and in addition to the various miners' organizations already listed on p.71 above), various universities and colleges, branches of NUSEC, Women's Citizens' Associations, Health Visitors and Sanitary Workers' Associations, the League of Nations, the Society of Friends, Adult Schools, the BBC – and a Conference on Family Endowment held at the House of Commons. The Report for the year ended February 1930 includes sections on the work of the Society in promoting Children's Rent Rebates (backing up Eleanor Rathbone's work in Parliament – see p.60), and School Maintenance Allowances (being proposed for children aged fourteen to fifteen as part of the Government's Education Bill for compulsory schooling up to the age of fifteen); as well as on the activities of that year in relation to the TUC and Labour Party's investigation into Family Allowances, and on general Family Allowances propaganda and organizing work.
231. She was elected as Independent MP for the Combined English Universities Liverpool, Manchester, Birmingham, Leeds, Sheffield, Durham, Bristol and Reading), and held her seat as a University MP from 1929 until her death in 1946. There is no doubt that as an Independent working without the backing of a party machine, it would have been very difficult for her to capture a constituency seat, even in Liverpool.
232. This same obituary continues: 'It was not only the feminine qualities of identification, of fanaticism and of persistence which rendered Eleanor Rathbone so formidable. Her position as an independent Member made her immune to the discipline and even to the conventions of party politics . . . And, finally, it was her immense, her insatiate industry which . . . gave such carrying power to her speeches and questions.' (Quoted in Stocks, *Eleanor Rathbone*, pp.143-4.) This indicates the advantageous position Eleanor Rathbone occupied as an Independent, free of party discipline. It also suggests why none of the parties courted her to join. Not only was she inconveniently 'fanatical', but the issues on which she was most fanatical – financial independence for women and an end to restrictions on immigration – were those that the political parties would have preferred not to have to discuss.
233. Quoted in *Family Allowances: the Case for a National Scheme*, published by the Family Endowment Society, London, July 1941.
234. Hansard vol. 411, 11 June 1945, col. 1415 ff.
235. Both the TUC and the Parliamentary Labour Party had given their support by 1942.
236. *Daily Herald*, 4 July 1938. I am indebted to Priscilla Allen for providing me with all the information that follows on the Married Women's Association, and for making available to me the numerous press cuttings from which I have quoted.

237. *News Chronicle*, 24 June 1938.
238. This was also the demand of middle class feminists in the early 1920s. See D.F. p.205.
239. They also supported the Family Allowance Campaign. Their aims were: 'To create a legal financial partnership in marriage. To help establish a comprehensive Medical Service for the whole family. To work for Family Allowance, social security, equal guardianship rights, equal pay. To awaken women to their political responsibilities as citizens' (quoted in *Wife and Citizen*, Journal of the Married Women's Association). And in 1942 Eleanor Rathbone was invited to address their National Conference (reported in *The Times*, 23 March 1942).
240. *News Chronicle*, 12 December 1938.
241. *Daily Herald*, 31 March 1939.
242. *The Times*, 9 October 1941.
243. *Daily Herald*, 17 December 1942.
244. *Manchester Guardian*, 20 April 1946.
245. *Life as We Have Known It*, p.xv (editor's introduction).
246. Eleanor Rathbone notes in *The Disinherited Family* (see p.322 footnote) that in the early 1920s women working in the Lancashire mills were opposed to campaigns for family endowment for this reason.
247. Titmuss, *Essays on the Welfare State*, p.89. During 1850-1900, 43 per cent of all couples, of all classes, had seven or more children. For marriages of 1925 or later the proportion of couples with seven or more children was 2 per cent.
248. '. . . the typical working-class mother of the 1890's, married in her teens or early twenties . . . and experiencing ten pregnancies, spent about fifteen years in a state of pregnancy and in nursing a child for the first year of its life. Today, [1952] for the typical mother, the time so spent would be about four years. A reduction of such magnitude in only two generations in the time devoted to childbearing represents nothing less than a revolutionary enlargement of freedom for women.' (*Ibid.*, p.91.)
249. Spring Rice, *Working Class Wives*, p.193.
250. *Picture Post*, 13 November 1943.
251. *Daily Herald*, 15 September 1942. They also campaigned for this money to be paid to mothers of servicemen and service women as well as wives
252. It is sometimes suggested that the only reason Family Allowances were introduced at the end of World War II was to lure women back into the home. I find it hard to reconcile this particular argument with the fact that the Government did not intend the money to go to women at all, and hoped that, having been forced to introduce Family Allowances, they could make the payments to men. (See p.89.) In any case, whatever the Government's intentions, they were unable to make Family Allowances conditional on women being at home full-time.
253. See e.g. Beveridge, *Social Insurance and Allied Services*, pp.155-6.
254. See R. Broad and S. Fleming (eds.), *Nella Last's War: A Mother's Diary 1939-45*, Falling Wall Press, Bristol, 1980, p.10.
255. R. Minns, *Bombers and Mash: The Domestic Front 1939-45*, Virago, London, 1981, p.15.
256. In 1939 women were being paid 21/- a week for billeting an adult and 10/6 a week for a child. These rates were considered very low and the Government was gradually forced to increase them, e.g. by adding a 3/6 laundry allowance to take account of the numbers of evacuee children who were wetting their beds in response to the shock of evacuation. (Minns, *Bombers and Mash*, pp.17-18.)
257. Information taken from H. Land, 'The Introduction of Family Allowances', in P. Hall, H. Land, R. Parker and A. Webb (eds.), *Change, Choice and Conflict in Social Policy*, Heinemann, London, 1975.

258. *Daily Herald*, 15 September 1942.

259. Broad and Fleming (eds.), *Nella Last's War*, p.317, citing Ministry of Labour Survey, July 1941. Another survey by the Ministry of Labour in July 1943 revealed that average wages for women over eighteen stood at £3 2s 4d, i.e. they had gone up less than £1 in the intervening two years.

260. At the beginning of the war, although the Government paid money to the women looking after evacuee children, parents were forced to contribute to this sum. This was a source of considerable bitterness and women all over the country protested. From May 1941 the Government took full financial responsibility. (Minns, *Bombers and Mash*, p.26.)

261. Titmuss, *Essays on the Welfare State*, pp.82-6, 'War and Social Policy'.

262. In February 1942 there were some fifty units, some of them with as many as 100 members, with an age range of eighteen to sixty. (Minns, *Bombers and Mash*, pp.54-6.)

263. See James and Dalla Costa, *The Power of Women*.

264. *Manchester Guardian*, 15 November 1943.

265. *New York Times*, 15 November 1943.

266. *Daily Herald*, 24 December 1942. The TUC's own record in relation to women working in industry during and immediately after the war was a source of great bitterness among women. They refused to defend women's interests (and men's) in pressing for equal pay, and colluded with Government and employers in using women as a temporary 'reserve' army of workers who would be laid off when men were available for jobs.

267. This Committee was set up by the Government to oversee the workings of the Unemployment Insurance provisions, and to make recommendations on rates, administration, etc.

268. The more so as more jobs became available with an expansion of the economy at the end of the 1930s.

269. A survey carried out in Bristol in 1937 had revealed that the families of the unemployed were better off than one third of the poorest families of men in work. (H. Trout *The Standard of Living in Bristol*, 1938.)

270. *Report of the Unemployment Statutory Committee*, February 1938. Beveridge was the Committee's chairman. The report quoted the memorandum submitted by the FES, which drew attention to the 'dilemma' of the overlap between unemployment pay and wages. (FES Report, 6 July 1938, p.1.)

271. See e.g. Hilary Land, 'The Introduction of Family Allowances', in Hall and others (eds.) *Change, Choice and Conflict in Social Policy*.

272. More recent victories in the campaign for higher Family Allowances/Child Benefits — including their introduction for the first child (see p.95) — were also due in some measure to the success of those drawing State benefits, particularly Supplementary Benefit, in forcing up their level relative to wages.

273. Titmuss, *Essays on the Welfare State*, p.82.

274. Beveridge, *Social Insurance and Allied Services*, pp.153-65.

275. See Broad and Fleming (eds.), *Nella Last's War*.

276. Broad and Fleming (eds.), *Nella Last's War*, pp.227-8. Nella Last was fifty years old when war broke out, a full-time housewife living in a rather drab provincial town, who had spent the last twenty-five years looking after her husband and two sons. Between 1939 and 1945, in response to an appeal from Mass-Observation, she kept a detailed daily record of her life which gives a unique and exciting picture of women's changing view of themselves during this period.

277. Beveridge, *Social Insurance and Allied Services*, p.49.

278. *Picture Post*, 6 March 1943.

279. In theory, wives' entitlement was based on their husbands' contributions. (See p.10 of the Report.) In practice, married men were not expected to contribute more than single men (para.23 p.14, and para.403 p.152), so that in

fact the married man was not being forced to pay for his wife.

A 'woman who lives as a wife' was in 1942 in a better position than a married woman in relation to the receipt of benefits, because since the 1931 'Anomalies Regulations' married women had not been entitled to draw any unemployment benefit in their own right, even if they had paid contributions. By 1942 Beveridge felt the need to propose a 'unified scheme [which] attaches advantages to the condition of marriage'. It included the abolition of the Anomalies Regulations (so that married women who had had a job and paid contributions would be able to claim unemployment and sickness benefits — albeit at only two-thirds the rate of men and unmarried women). (See para.115, p.52.)

At the same time, *all* women, married or not, were to be entitled to free medical treatment and to thirteen weeks' paid maternity leave from a job, to be paid at a rate of 50 per cent above unemployment pay (para.113 p.51, and para.115 p.52). These were major victories for women.

It is interesting that Beveridge's underlying assumption in dealing with married women was that most would make housework and motherhood their full-time occupations after the war as they had done before. (See e.g. para.108, p.49.) He was either behind the times, or attempting to justify plans for a post-war 'reconstruction' policy which would push women out of their war-time jobs. Yet, although he clearly felt that a woman should have a husband to support her, and that, once married, 'her attitude to gainful employment . . . should not be the same as a single women [sic],' nothing in his recommendation could be construed as a financial inducement to women to stay at home full-time. This is important because it is sometimes claimed that Beveridge favoured Family Allowance as a means of pushing women back into the home after World War II. I have already discussed the fact that the proposed Children's Allowances were not made conditional in any way on the mother being at home full-time. In addition, Beveridge remained studiously silent in this Report on the question of whether the mother or the father should get the Allowance.

280.   'Epilogue by Lord Beveridge' to *Family Allowances: A new edition of The Disinherited Family*, pp.269-70. See also the Government's *White Paper on Social Insurance*, Cmnd. 6550, HMSO, London, September 1944, Part I, p.6: 'The cost of these Family Allowances will be met wholly from the proceeds of [general] taxation; they are thus outside the bounds of the scheme of social insurance properly so called.'

281.   Elizabeth Wilson's *Women and the Welfare State*, Tavistock Publications, London, 1971, is a classic example of this analysis of the Welfare State. One result is that she presents the Beveridge Report ahistorically, e.g. quoting the passage reproduced on p.86 as an example of Beveridge's belittling of women in planning for the family as an economic unit (p.150), rather than the step forward and victory it was in its recognition of housewives' social and economic existence; and claiming that Beveridge's recommendation of Family Allowances was simply the result of his attitudes as 'a good Imperialist' (p.151). It is significant that her bibliography, listing over 250 titles, does not include *The Disinherited Family*. (See also footnote 283 below.)

282.   They argued that Children's Allowances need not cover even the full cost of subsistence because free school meals would be provided for all schoolchildren after the war. Eleanor Rathbone deals with the limitations of these provisions in kind in this book. (See D.F. p.366 ff.)

283.   To say this is not to harbour any illusions about the fact that the 'Welfare State' is still the State, and that welfare is first and foremost intended as the minimum necessary to keep the working population fit for work — so that it is no accident, for example, that hospital and social service provision for those too old to work does not match provision for those who have to be made fit for work again as soon as possible. The precise terms on which the welfare is to be provided

are a continuous battle ground. There is always a battle raging over whether cash payments can be used to discipline the working class, or whether the working class will use the money to further its own aims. A classic case in point is the way in which Supplementary Benefit and Child Benefit have been used by women to live independently of men as single mothers, and the Thatcher Government's response in proposing to cut Child Benefit for single mothers because it is 'subsidising immorality and illegitimacy'. (*The Guardian*, 9 May 1983.) The other classic case, much in the news (1983), is the battle over unemployment benefits. There is also a running battle about who the social services will serve. For example, women are demanding (in some cases successfully) that NHS facilities be provided to allow women to give birth in the circumstances that each individual woman deems best for her; while many doctors and NHS administrators are trying to insist that all babies should be born in hospital, and that doctors rather than mothers should decide about the nature of deliveries.

284.   It is important to recognize, however, that this was an improvement on the pre-Beveridge Report situation, when married women had no entitlement to benefits, even those they had paid for. (See note 279 above.) Interestingly, Beveridge notes that the reason for the introduction of the 'Anomalies Act' of 1931, barring married women from claiming benefits, was that there had been a widespread 'scandal in unemployment insurance: the drawing of unemployment benefit by women who were in no sense in search of employment. In districts and industries where married women were never accustomed to work and did not expect to find work, the Unemployment Fund . . . was tending to become a means of endowing young married life.' (*Social Insurance and Allied Services*, pp.52-3.) In other words, many married women had claimed a *de facto* State endowment by claiming unemployment benefit while working full-time at home.

285.   Hansard, vol.411, 11 June 1945. Debate on the Third Reading of the Family Allowances Bill, col.1401 (my italics).

286.   Hansard, vol.408, 8 March 1945, Debate on the Second Reading of the Family Allowances Bill, cols.2344-8. He was also vocal in his opposition to the exclusion of the first child from the payments.

287.   See Women's Family Allowance Campaign leaflets, 1972-3; Wages for Housework petition, *Increase Family Allowance Now!*, 1976; leaflets and statements of the Child Benefit for All Campaign, 1978, including resolutions passed at the meeting of the Child Benefit for All Campaign held in the House of Commons, 6 March 1978, organized by the Bangladesh Women's Association, the Union of Turkish Women and Black Women for Wages for Housework.

288.   Hansard, vol.408, 8 March 1945. Debate on the Second Reading of the Family Allowances Bill, cols.2275-82.

289.   *Ibid.*, cols.2294-7.

290.   *Ibid.*, col.2314.

291.   *Ibid.*, col.2319.

292.   *Ibid.*, col.2306.

293.   'A Call to Women's Societies. Children's Allowances. Payment to the Mother'. Letter from the Family Endowment Society dated 14 July 1944, signed by Eva Hubback and Eleanor Rathbone.

294.   Eva Hubback, in Rathbone, *Family Allowances* (1949 edn. of D.F.), p.285.

295.   Memorandum on Subjects for Discussion at the Deputation on Family Allowances to Sir William Jowitt (Minister without portfolio), Thursday 12 October 1944 (FES typescript). This description is a reminder that all this organizing was taking place in the context of the danger, and dislocation, of wartime Britain, in which women had to live with the ever-present horror of bombing.

296.   Hansard, vol.408, 8 March 1945, col.2282.

297.   In 1972 Family Allowances stood at 90p for the second child, £1 each for

the third and subsequent children. These rates were, relative to the cost of living, much lower than the 1945 rates, and were also subject to tax ('the clawback').

298.   At national meetings of the Women's Family Allowance Campaign, (see p.94) women from all over the country who were petitioning for Family Allowances to be kept, reported that word for word the same statement had been made repeatedly to them.

299.   H. Land, 'Women: Supporters of Supported?' in D.L. Barker and S. Allen (eds.), *Sexual Divisions and Society: Process and Change*, Tavistock Publications, London, 1976, p.115. In fact, of course, the major cost of maintaining 'future citizens and workers' excluded from Family Allowances was the cost of the mothers' time spent looking after them. Even today (1983), many of the organizations demanding an increase in Child Benefits, in response to the pressure from mothers for increased payment by the State, prefer to overlook the fact that even a Child Benefit which amounted to a full subsistence allowance would in no way cover the cost of raising a child, because the cost of the work of child-care is not included in any 'children's subsistence' calculations.

300.   In 1945, when the Family Allowances Bill was before Parliament, Unemployment Benefits were 24/- for a single man, 40/- for a married couple, 5/- each for the first and second child and 3/- each for other children – all paid to the father. According to the Ministry of Labour Gazette, *average* wages in January 1945 were 92s 9d a week, so there were many, especially women, who were earning much less. At a recent conference on 'Feminism, Economics and the State' in Bristol (March 1982), one woman recalled that in 1946 her mother was collecting 10/- a week in Family Allowances when her father, a Chief Inspector for an Insurance Company, was earning just over £4 a week before tax.

301.   Land, 'Women: Supporters of Supported?', p.112. Other historians of Family Allowances have followed Hilary Land in this view. Jane Lewis, in a recent article on Eleanor Rathbone ('Eleanor Rathbone and the Family', *New Society*, 27 January 1983) writes: 'When family allowances were granted in 1945, the legislation owed little to the arguments of Rathbone and the Family Endowment Society . . . both the FES and the Children's Minimum Council were primarily women's pressure groups. Government departments felt it safe to ignore them.' She cites as evidence the dismissive comments of one Government minister – but this is to judge women's impact on history through the eyes of those who would least admit that their minds, options and policies had in fact been changed by women's actions. She also follows Hilary Land in this article in the view that the reason 'the Government began to take family allowances seriously at the beginning of the war [was] as a means of holding down wages'.

302.   Land, 'Women: Supporters or Supported?', p.113. Keynes was not the only one to use this argument. Paul Douglas in the US based his case for the introduction of Family Allowances on the same kind of logic. (See Paul Douglas, *Wages and the Family*, Chicago, 1925.) Although Eleanor Rathbone at times uses arguments of 'economy' to make her case, the dividing line between Rathbone on the one hand and Keynes and Douglas on the other is wide and clear. For them, *the case* for Family Allowances is to save government and employers money. For Rathbone, *the case* for Family Allowances is women's right to financial independence and a share in the wealth they create, whatever ammunition she might use to get support.

The assumption that it is arguments rather than the force of popular pressure which change the course of history is common among policy-makers and academics.

303.   *Report on Family Allowances by a Special Joint Committee*, p.2. Family Allowances/Child Benefits have been crucial to the 1984 miners' strike.

304.   See, in particular, p.19 of *Proposals for a Tax Credit System*, Cmnd.5116, HMSO, London, 1972. 'The question of whether the child credits should be

paid to the father or the mother . . . is one of the more important issues raised by
the scheme . . . Although the Government regard the issue as entirely open . . .
*it has been assumed so far in this Green Paper . . . that the recipient of tax credits
would be the father* [my italics].

305.   See Suzie Fleming, *The Family Allowance under Attack*, Falling Wall Press,
1973, for an account of the Government's plans and the response of the Women's
Family Allowance Campaign; and London Family Allowance Campaign, *Implications for Women of the Government's Proposals for a Tax Credit System*,
London, 1972.

306.   See *Select Committee on Tax Credits, Minutes of Evidence*, 17 April 1973,
House of Commons Papers series 64, HMSO pp.373-83.

307.   Newspaper headlines reported 'Heath Loses the Women' (*Daily Express*
17 April 1973, quoted in Fleming, *The Family Allowance Under Attack*, p.7).

308.   *Select Committee on Tax Credits, Minutes of Evidence*, 15 February 1973,
House of Commons Papers, series 64 HMSO pp.70-95.

309.   *Ibid.*, p.72.

310.   See e.g. *Select Committee on Tax Credit, Minutes of Evidence*, 17 April
1973, pp.381-3; 'Pay Mothers to Stay at Home', *Sunday Observer* Editorial of
22 April 1973; 'Woman Power', article on the value of housework, in *New
Society*, 10 May 1973; and House of Commons debate of 30 April 1973, all of
which reflected the fact that a State payment to mothers for their work in the
home was once again firmly back on women's agenda. As we have seen (p.13),
in introducing the Second Reading of the 1975 Child Benefit Bill, Barbara
Castle, Social Services Secretary, also talked explicitly about a wage for mothers.

311.   Land, 'Women: Supporters or Supported?', p.127. Elsewhere in the same
article (p.112) she refers to the fact that 'family allowances were threatened with
abolition in the tax credit proposals', and to the evidence of the Women's Family
Allowance Campaign that 'Family Allowance is the only form of income all
women with two or more children are entitled to: however inadequate it may be,
it is for many mothers the only source of money of their own. It is also the only
recognition they get for the work they do in looking after children'. It is in
answer to this evidence that she continues, 'This is true, but it would be a mistake
to think that the introduction of family allowances in 1946 was *predominantly* a
triumph for women's rights.' This suggests that her account of the introduction
of Family Allowances is intended to make a political as well as historical point,
namely that women who see Family Allowances as a financial recognition by the
State of their work in the home should not think that it was a campaign based
on these assumptions which was responsible for the introduction of Family
Allowances in 1945 — lest this lend encouragement to today's campaigning for
State payments for housework, which she has actively opposed.

312.   Characteristically, the Select Committee Report of July 1973 gave no
indication that there had been a major change in the proposals since the original
Green Paper. Governments and their officials are always anxious to gloss over
U-turns in 'thinking' which are the result of political pressure.

313.   The press coverage of the first pay-day under the Family Allowances Act
(6 August 1946) paid tribute to Eleanor Rathbone but hid the movement behind
her. *The Times*, in particular, suggested that although feminism had been the
starting point for the Family Allowance campaign, the achievement of Family
Allowances had nothing to do with either feminism or the women's movement.
This article by a 'special correspondent' (*The Times*, 6 August 1946, p.5) set the
tone for future misrepresentations of the history of Family Allowances, already
cited. At the same time, at the very moment of first recognition by the State of
women's work in the home, *The Times* leader that day suggested that this work
should be seen as a joint responsibility for both parents, and implied that Family
Allowances should be seen as the parents' money rather than the mother's:

'. . . the community . . . is attempting to collaborate with both parents and not exclusively the mother.' This is the view of many of those in the Establishment, including the Feminist Establishment, today. They would rather put the money in men's hands than allow each woman the economic freedom to decide for herself whether or not she wants to share that money from the State with a man. It is the opposite view to that of Eleanor Rathbone, who fought for Family Allowances as a *foot in the door* of State payments to mothers for their work in the home, and economic independence for housewives.

314. Hansard, vol.411, 11 June 1945, cols.1406-7.
315. *Ibid.*, col.1406.
316. *Ibid.*, cols.1418-20 [my italics].

ACKNOWLEDGEMENTS

I am grateful to Housewives in Dialogue for the support which enabled me to write up what I had researched; the women on the rota of the King's Cross Women's Centre in London, especially Solveig Francis and Gigi Turner, for invaluable help with gathering information; Jack Rathbone for his continuing patience and support; the late Brian Jackson for his creative encouragement; Molly Ladd-Taylor for her productive questioning; Denise Green for deciphering and typing succeeding drafts; Petra Schaefer for her caring for Rachel and Joe; Caroline Barker, Pauline Battson, Sue Hill and Lisa Longstaff for help with proof-reading; Mary Fuller, Judith Matthew, Anne Neale for their reading and comments.

Above all, I want to thank Selma James whose work on this introduction has been invaluable, and whose organizing, speaking and writing has provided more of the ideas than I could ever hope to footnote; and the women who have made International Black Women for Wages for Housework and the International Wages for Housework Campaign. It is the day-to-day practice, experience and achievements of that Campaign since 1972 which have shaped my view of history, and caused me to re-evaluate whatever I had learned from books and papers.

For an account of the perspective and organizing of the Wages for Housework Campaign, the reader will have to look elsewhere, since there is no attempt to describe either in this introduction.

Suzie Fleming

ELEANOR RATHBONE
1872 – 1946

RATHBONE'S DAY

FIRST pay-day under the Family Allowances Act took place yesterday. For more than 30 years Eleanor Rathbone advocated financial aid for parenthood. Before she died last January, aged 73, she saw her major proposals accepted and about to become law.

But if she were alive today it is likely that her voice would be heard in protest against one aspect of the new Act. That is the decision to reduce relief payments for tuberculosis and public assistance from families receiving family allowances. A selection of letters below shows what readers think of this new Means Test.

Cartoon by Vicky from the *News Chronicle*, 7 August 1946.

THE
DISINHERITED
FAMILY

INTRODUCTION

I doubt whether there is any subject in the world of equal importance that has received so little serious and articulate consideration as the economic status of the family—of its members in relation to each other and of the whole unit in relation to the other units of which the community is made up. I say "articulate consideration" because what appears haphazard in our present arrangements for the family is probably the result of more deliberate purposing and choosing than appears on the surface, but it has been a sub-conscious and therefore inarticulate purpose and choice. The reasons for this we shall come to later on. For the present we are only concerned with the fact itself. If the reader doubts it, let him consider any of the other units or classifications that have to be taken into account in framing the economic structure of society, that is, in providing material means for its maintenance—capital and labour; rent, profits and wages; production and distribution; collective and private enterprise, and so forth. Not one of them but has been the subject, in general and in detail, of a never-ending stream of writing among economists, industrial experts, politicians and pressmen. The family too has, of course, been written about—as a problem of population by Imperialists; of breeding by eugenists; in relation to endless problems of health, housing and child welfare. But of the family as an economic unit— something which has its own claim, based on its own value to the nation, to its own share in the nation's wealth—there has been next to no consideration at all. The claim has been not so much disparaged or negatived as ignored. In saying this I do not forget the work, to which this book itself owes much, of Mr. Seebohm Rowntree and of the sociologists and labour leaders who have followed him in pleading for the claim of the wage-earner to "a living wage" based on the needs of a family. But unfortunately their plea assumes acceptance of a supposition which it is one of the main objects of this book to refute—that all men are heads of families and that all families are of the same size, or rather can justifiably be assumed to be so for the purpose of regulating wages. As I shall try to shew, this fiction bears so little relation to the real facts that the attempt to base a wage system upon it inevitably breaks down. Or rather it does worse than break down. It exerts just enough pull on the industrial machine to drag it off the high road of a remorseless but efficient commercialism into a morass of confused thinking and frustrated, because impracticable, humanitarian purpose.

Further, those who have put forward this theory of the "living wage" regard the family not as it really is—an aggregate of individual human beings, each with an actual or potential value to the community—but as "the dependants" of the wage-earner. The very word suggests something parasitic, accessory, non-essential. A wife and children, and the wherewithal to keep them, are conceded to the wage-earner as though they were part of the "comforts and decencies promotive of better habits" for which he may reasonably ask as necessary to his development as a full human being. But if he prefers to use the margin thus allowed him for breeding pigeons or racing dogs or for some other form of personal gratification, instead of for keeping a family, that is assumed to be his affair, not the State's or his employer's. His wages are his remuneration, earned by the sweat of his brow or the travail of his brain, and how he spends them is no one's business but his own.

Yet when we are considering society from any other point of view than the economic, we can all see well enough that, of all its institutions, the family is after all the institution that matters most. It is at once indispensable as a means to all the rest and, in a sense, an end in itself. Pluck from under the family all the props which religion and morality have given it, strip it of the glamour, true or false, cast round it by romance, it will still remain a prosaic, indisputable fact, that the whole business of begetting, bearing and rearing children, is the most essential of all the nation's businesses. If it were not done at all, the world would become a desert in less than a century. To the extent that it is done badly, a nation finds itself confronted, in wartime, with the problem of making an A.1 army out of a C.3 population; in peacetime with the competition of rivals that manage better.

To do it superlatively well, so that the rank and file of citizens should be well born and well bred, would go further than anything else to ensure national greatness, intellectual prestige, material prosperity, efficiency, productivity—everything that appeals most to the mind of the plain business man. It is another indisputable fact—bordering on a platitude—that the strongest emotions, the most enduring motives, the most universally accessible sources of happiness, are concerned with this business of the family; perhaps (though here we are straying from platitude into conjecture) because it is in self-reproduction that the average man finds the surest satisfaction for the instinct of immortality, for the desire to be quite certain that death will not end everything for him.

It being so generally recognized that the well-being of the family concerns the community as a whole, there seems something strange in the assumption so commonly made, that the question of the maintenance of families concerns only individual parents and can be safely left to them; or that, at most, society need only take cognizance of the matter by, as it were, mixing a little philanthropy with its business and influencing employers to pay wages which will enable their male employees to indulge in the praiseworthy leisure-time occupation of keeping families. The mere magnitude of the economic problem involved might have preserved it from so haphazard a treatment. When we remember that wives and dependent children constitute nearly half of the entire population, surely it is worth considering whether the problem of rationing this vast National Reserve cannot be solved in a more economic and efficient fashion than through the above-mentioned conception of " a living wage", based on the needs of a family, and ladled out indiscriminately to all male wage-earners of average capacity and industry.

One object of this book is, as it were, to put the present method of providing for families on the dissecting table and subject it to a thorough examination. I have set myself to trace its history; to examine its implications in theory and its consequences in practice; to discuss its effect on the distribution of wealth; on the character of national expenditure; on the efficiency of the workers; on the well-being of their homes, their wives and their children; on the quantity and quality of the birth-rate; on the status of women as mothers and as wage-earners.

The second object of this book is to discuss alternative methods of providing for the family; to describe the experiments, projected or actually in being, which other nations are making in the endowment of families; to consider how far these experiments are applicable to the conditions of this country, and how the difficulties and objections which impede them can best be met.

But behind these two definite objects lies an even larger, if vaguer, aim. This book will have failed if it does not convince the reader that Family Endowment involves something much greater than a scheme of child welfare, or a device of wage distribution—that it offers a hope, not dependent for achievement on a revolution or a scientific miracle but realizable here and now, of making attainable by every family, even the lowest on the industrial ladder, the material means for healthy living, and of placing the service of motherhood in the position of security and honour which it merits but can never reach under the present system.

In attempting such a task, I am conscious of the risks I run. Without any pretensions to be a trained economist or statistician, I have ventured to criticize economists on their own ground, and to put forward and support by a large use of figures proposals for a re-distribution of a portion of national resources. I have tried to escape the possible consequences of my rashness, by making an extensive use of others better equipped than myself. Wherever possible, I have used facts and figures drawn from writers of established authority, but the considerable number of supplementary calculations required have been nearly all worked out for me by Miss M. E. Bulkley, formerly of the London School of Economics, who has also collected many of my social data. A few facts were supplied by Miss E. M. Scott, of the Women's Information Bureau, Effingham House, Arundel Street. The material relating to continental experiments was collected principally by Miss Olga Vlasto, Hon. Secretary of the Family Endowment Council, who has received much help from the British Consuls and from numerous foreign correspondents in the countries concerned. Their help has been acknowledged in the appropriate places, but I should like specially to mention M. Bonvoisin, of the *Comité d'Études des Allocations Familiales* in Paris, who has been unweariedly kind in answering enquiries on special points. Three friends, Mrs. Eva M. Hubback, Mrs.

J. L. Stocks and Miss E. Macadam, have read nearly the whole script and helped me with many criticisms and suggestions. As the two former have the economic training I lack, I hope they have saved me from falling into any palpable blunders, though I must not saddle them with responsibility for my deliberate heresies.

For the benefit of those who are anxious to gain a working knowledge of the subject of Family Endowment, but have not time to wade through the whole of this book, I may suggest that the table of contents will indicate the portions of it likely to interest them. All who read any of it, however, should read the second chapter, which contains the kernel of the case against the present system.

NOTE TO THIRD EDITION

I have added a supplementary chapter, tracing the developments in the Family Allowance movement at home and abroad during the three years which have elapsed since this book was first published, in March 1924.

E. F. R.

PART I

THE PRESENT ECONOMIC STATUS
OF THE FAMILY

CHAPTER I

THE GROWTH OF THE DEPENDENT FAMILY

Most people are accustomed to think of the arrangement by which wives, and children up to the period of adolescence, are normally dependent on the earnings of the male head of the family as though it were one of immemorial antiquity, almost inseparable from the existence of the family as a social unit.

Yet in fact, at least in its present extent and as concerning the manual workers, it is a quite modern arrangement, less than a century old in this country, newer than that in most civilized countries and not yet existent in countries which are still in a primitive stage of civilization. Until public opinion steps in to prevent it by laws and customs, the struggle for existence usually forces the wives of the manual workers and their children at a very early age to labour either for wages or at the production of food and necessaries for home consumption. Many writers have described the use and abuse of child labour in the factory system of the early nineteenth century and the long struggle which led to the gradual emancipation of the children. But the labour of children and their mothers did not begin with the industrial revolution. Miss Dunlop in her history of child labour and the apprenticeship system shews that " in mediæval England, children were employed as freely and at as early an age as ever they have been under the factory system,"[1] though probably under more natural and humane conditions. The records of many trades in the Middle Ages shew that children were indentured

[1] *English Apprenticeship and Child Labour*, by O. J. Dunlop (T. Fisher Unwin, 1912), p. 15.

as apprentices under ten years old, though the best trades did not take them till twelve or fourteen. Agriculture, which then absorbed the great majority of the population, provided many tasks at which children of a much tenderer age could be employed, such as tending animals, picking stones, weeding, scaring birds. Indeed the temptation to use children in these ways is so great when poverty presses hard, that I have heard it said of children in the Black Forest today that they have no childhood, every moment spent out of school being occupied. As shewing the value set on their labour in early times, there is an English statute of 1389, designed for the protection of agriculture, which lays it down that no child who has " used husbandry " till twelve years old may leave it for any industrial occupation.

As for the children's mothers, the evidence, though more scanty, indicates that they also habitually did hard work in the fields and, like every one else " meet to labour," could be compelled to work there at harvest time under penalty of two days in the stocks. But their duties in their own homes cannot have left them a great deal of time for anything else, since in addition to the work of the modern housewife, they were responsible for most of the spinning and weaving of clothes, baking and brewing, making of preserves and medicines and ointments for the use of their households. In the days when the diet and clothing of the labourer consisted almost entirely of a few simple articles, mostly home-made, and when a large part of the production of the country was production for direct use and not for exchange, the question of the " dependency " of wives can scarcely have arisen. They must have produced fully the value of their keep and this was probably true of the wives (though not of the children) of the greater part of the middle classes also.

In the working class the family was regarded as the unit of labour and the share of each member was hardly distinguishable, although doubtless the father's was normally the largest and was probably the main source of support for the infant children.

Adam Smith, discussing the basis of wages for manual labourers, quotes opinions from three earlier writers which illustrate this point.

" Lord Chief Justice Hales, who wrote in the time of Charles II, computes the necessary expenses of a labourer's family, consisting of six persons, the father and mother, two children able to do something and two not able, at ten shillings a week, or twenty-six pounds a year. If they cannot earn this by their labour, they must make it up, he supposes, either by begging or by stealing. He appears to have enquired very carefully into this subject. In 1688, Mr. Gregory King . . . computed the ordinary income of labourers and out-servants to be fifteen pounds a year to a family, which he supposed to consist, one with another, of three and a half persons." [1]

In another passage he quotes Cantillon, a French writer of the early eighteenth century, said by Jevons to be the founder of modern political economy.

" A man must always live by his work, and his wages must at least be sufficient to maintain him. They must even upon most occasions be somewhat more; otherwise it would be impossible for him to bring up a family, and the race of such workmen could not last beyond the first generation. Mr. Cantillon seems, upon this account, to suppose that the lowest species of common labourers must everywhere earn at least double their own maintenance, in order that one with another they may be enabled to bring up two children ; the labour of the wife, on account of her necessary attendance on the children, being supposed no more than sufficient to provide for herself. But one-half the children born, it is computed, die before the age of manhood. The poorest labourers, therefore, according to this account, must one with another, attempt to rear at least four children, in order that two may have an equal chance of living to that age. But the necessary maintenance of four children, it is supposed, may be nearly equal to that of one man. The labour of an able-bodied slave, the same author adds, is computed to be worth double his maintenance; and that of the meanest labourer, he thinks, cannot be worth less than that of an able-bodied slave. Thus far at least seems certain, that, in order to bring up a family, the labour of the husband and wife together must, even in the lowest species of common labour, be able to earn something more than what is precisely necessary for their own maintenance; but in what proportion, whether in that above mentioned, or in any other, I shall not take upon me to determine." [2]

All this suggests that the burden of the family's dependency was, when compared with that of the present day, a relatively trifling addition to the man's needs and that the wife rather shared in than increased it.

To the great industrial developments of the eighteenth and nineteenth centuries, the labour of women and children contributed to the top of their strength. Defoe, writing in 1724, describes the home workshop of the Yorkshire cloth-makers, and it must be remembered that their industry and that of the later cotton textiles, though chiefly centred from the first in Yorkshire and Lancashire, was much less localized then than now, the manufacturers distributing their bundles of yarn through middlemen all over the country. The combination he describes of agricultural with industrial work was also general, in varying proportions, agriculture being merely supplementary to industry in the northern counties and vice versa in the southern.

[1] *Wealth of Nations*, Book I, Chap. VIII (1920 edition, Vol. I, p. 79).
[2] *Ibid.*, pp. 69-70.

" We saw the homes full of lusty fellows, some at the dye vat, some at the looms, others dressing the cloths ; the women and children carding or spinning, all employed from the youngest to the oldest; *scarcely anything above four years old, but its hands were sufficient for its own support.* Outside as every clothier must necessarily keep one horse, at least, to fetch his work and his provisions from the market, to carry his yarn to the spinners, his manufactures to the fulling mill, and when finished to the market to be sold and the like ; so everyone generally keeps a cow or two for his family. By this means the small pieces of enclosed land about each house are occupied ; and by being thus fed, are still further improved from the dung of the cattle."

Another writer, describing a " tour through the manufacturing districts," suggests a darker side to these " hives of human industry " when he says, " the creatures were set to work as soon as they could crawl and their parents were the hardest of taskmasters".[1]

When the work was taken into the factories the children and many of their mothers followed it there. The story of the long struggle for the emancipation of the children and protection of the women has been told so often that I have no need to repeat it. I will only remind the reader of the extreme youth of some of the children who even in the nineteenth century were thought " sufficient for their own support " in and out of the factories.

Thus the number of children between nine and thirteen who were employed in textile factories in 1835 amounted to 47,000, this being 13 per cent. of the total number of employees.[2] The children under nine had by then been excluded from these factories by the Act of 1819, after a fierce opposition from the employers which shewed the value they set on their labour.

In the mines, until the Act of 1842 which excluded children below ten years old, " the employment of children of seven was common, in many pits children were employed at six, in some at five . . . Even babies were sometimes taken down into the pits to keep the rats from their fathers' food."[3]

The Commission on Employment of Children appointed in 1862 found that the employment of children at four, five and six, was still common in many industries such as pottery, glass, metal ware, pillow-lace and hosiery.[4] Thus in the Birmingham hardware manufactory, about 2,000 children

---

[1] *Notes of a Tour in the Manufacturing Districts of Lancashire*, by W. Cooke Taylor, 1842; quoted in *A History of Factory Legislation*, by B. L. Hutchins and A. Harrison (2nd edition, 1907, p. 5).
[2] Hutchins and Harrison, *History of Factory Legislation*, pp. 304-7.
[3] *Lord Shaftesbury*, by J. L. and B. Hammond (Constable & Co., 1923), p. 70.
[4] Hutchins and Harrison, *op. cit.*, Chap. VIII.

were employed, a fourth of them being probably under eight. In hosiery, children of three to five were kept at work till 11 or 12 at night, being pinned to their mothers' knees, " so that they cannot fall when they are slapped or fall asleep".[1] In the cottage workshops, miscalled " schools," straw plaiting and bobbin lace-making were found specially suited to the nimble fingers of tiny children from two or three upwards.[2] We even find Lord Shaftesbury moving an amendment to the Education Bill of 1870 to lower the age of leaving school from thirteen to ten and urging that " the extent to which persons in London depended on the labour of their children their Lordships would scarcely be aware of, and it was impossible that a man could maintain wife and family on 9s. a week, unless he was assisted by such labour ".[3]

The money value of all this child labour cannot be estimated, but that it was considerable is shewn by the tenacity and ingenuity with which every successive restriction was resisted, not only by interested parents but by important employers and even by economists such as Edward Baines and Nassau Senior. One of the earliest writers on the subject, Sir William Petty, says it was estimated that " the children of Norwich, between six and sixteen years old, do earn £12,000 per annum more than they spend "—no inconsiderable sum in the seventeenth century; he suggests seven as the age below which children, generally speaking, might be expected to be maintained by their parents.[4]

In any case, it is plain that the labours of the children and their mothers, both in production for use and production for exchange, must have reduced the financial burden of fatherhood to a modest level, at least for all who were sufficiently near subsistence level to be tempted to use this resource. When it was gradually withdrawn from them, partly by protective legislation and partly by the changes in processes and the growth of towns which diminished the opportunities of production for direct use, the responsibility for the support of the family was thrown on the men. Those who resented this were blamed for their short-sighted selfish-

[1] *Ibid.*, p. 158.
[2] *Ibid.*, p. 155. I have myself seen such a lace-making " school " in Italy, where none of the workers looked over seven. When told to rise to greet the visitors, they did so without stopping their work and barely raised their eyes to glance at us.
[3] Hammond's *Lord Shaftesbury*, pp. 257-8.
[4] Hutchins and Harrison, *op. cit.*, p. 4.

ness. The reformers, influenced by the *laissez-faire* economics of their day, although they had been fighting one of its applications, seem to have taken it for granted that the wages of the men would adjust themselves to their new responsibilities. It is generally assumed that this in fact happened, as real wages were rising throughout the period of the struggle. They would probably have risen in any case, as the period was one of great wealth and increasing assertiveness on the part of the wage-earners. Whether the amount of the rise balanced, or more or less than balanced, the value of the work of the women and children who had been displaced I have never seen discussed. When the rise in wages is mentioned, the counteracting loss is almost always forgotten.

One thing however is certain, that whereas the labour of wives and children, whatever its evils, did at least help to proportion the income of the family to its numbers and needs, the rise in wages was spread out thin over the general body of men wage-earners, without regard to family responsibilities. This involved a consequence which—obvious as it is— seems to have passed unnoticed or at least undiscussed (so far as I have been able to discover) both at the time and since. By prolonging the period of care-free, unproductive youth and encouraging mothers to give themselves up wholly to the care of their homes, yet making no provision for this vast army of non-producers except through wages, the new system postulated an immense increase in national productivity, if the welfare of the children and the community of which they are the future producers was to be really safeguarded. It required not merely that fathers should earn as much as the whole labouring unit of the family had earned before, but that men without wives or without dependent children should earn enough for the needs of an imaginary family, since it was not possible (or so it was universally assumed) to discriminate between the wages of married and unmarried men.

Does not such a commitment involve problems worthy of the consideration of economists, employers and politicians? Might one not expect to find in their works and recorded speeches many discussions as to whether the product of industry was adequate to meet the strain, and, if so, at what minimum standard of living, and for what size of family? And if the discussion shewed that the national income, so considered, was likely to be an uncomfortably tight fit, might one not look for some controversy as to whether a more economical method of providing for families could not be found than one which assumed some millions more than actually existed ?

But in fact one finds nothing of the sort, except in two or three very recent works of which I have made much use in the next chapter. The question of the maintenance of the family in relation to wages, to national resources and to problems of population, occupies a diminishing instead of an increasing place in the economics of the later nineteenth and early twentieth centuries. One cannot say that the early classical economists neglected the subject altogether. In a sense, the needs of the family were the basis of the structure they raised. They believed (though they did not use the terms) in a " living wage," a " basic minimum," established not by statute but by Nature in ordaining that a man could not live unless he ate and that the share of the labourer in the product of industry could not be less than would enable him to maintain himself and " keep up the population." But, as we have seen from the extract already quoted from Adam Smith, the amount of financial responsibility which this involved, over and above the man's own maintenance, was vaguely conceived by him and evidently not expected to be very heavy. Nevertheless it was an important factor, from its supposed influence on the growth of population and through that on wages. He contended that in countries where wealth was stationary, wages could not rise much above subsistence level, as the demand for labour in such countries will also be stationary and if higher wages tempt the labourer to produce more children than are necessary to maintain their number, the competition for employment will drive wages down again. On the other hand, if wages fall much below this level, more children will die of want and more labourers be deterred from marriage and propagation, until scarcity of labour and competition for it drive wages up again. But he recognized that this stratification of wages at the level of subsistence did not necessarily hold good oi countries in which wealth was increasing and instanced the Great Britain of his own day as a country where wages were in fact on the whole above that level.

In Malthus and Ricardo the subsistence rate was represented as the normal level to which wages were always tending to fall. Malthus in his famous *Essay on the Principle of Population* in 1798 laid down that " population, when unchecked, increases in a geometrical ratio ; subsistence increases only in an arithmetical ratio".[1]   Hence population was always pressing upon subsistence and was " kept down " by the positive checks of starvation, war and pestilence. One of the objects of his book was to urge that these positive checks should be made unnecessary by the preventive check of late marriages and continence in marriage.

Ricardo took broadly speaking the same view.   In expounding his " iron law of wages " he says that the " natural price " of labour is that which will enable labourers " to subsist and to perpetuate their race without either increase or diminution".[2]   But he evidently did not consider that these needs which were to determine wages were a fixed quantity, for he urged that a taste for " comforts and enjoyments " should be stimulated in the workers as one of the best securities against a superabundant population.[3]

The elastic character of the standard of living and the importance of it in determining wages is much more elaborated and insisted on by J. S. Mill.[4]   But like his predecessors, he held that the lowest level of wages was in the long run determined by the subsistence needs of a family large enough " to keep up the population " and like them he was obsessed by the fear of over-population and of any measures he thought likely to stimulate it.   He admits that " since no one is responsible for being born",[5] it would be right to tax the rich in order adequately to support all existing children, if it could be done without encouraging people to bring as many others as they thought fit into existence and so suspending one of the ordinary checks to population; but this he assumes to be impossible.

All these writers are as vague as Adam Smith as to the extent of the responsibilities which a man must be able to meet out of his wages if " the population is to be kept up " and take no account of the variations that must occur in different countries, different parts of the country and different generations according to the use made of women's and

---

[1] *Essay on the Principle of Population*, 1798, p. 14.
[2] *Principles of Political Economy and Taxation*, Chap. V (3rd ed., 1821, p. 50).
[3] *Ibid.*, p. 54.
[4] *Principles of Political Economy*, 1848, Book II, Chap. XI.
[5] *Ibid.*, p. 427.

children's labour. Nor do they explain by what force labourers of one generation are impelled to ask, and employers to concede, the rate of wages needed by the small minority of labourers who are at any one time responsible for the size of family needed to keep up the population of the next generation.

Professor Marshall throws no further light on this subject. Reviewing the Physiocrats' theory of wages he says:—

" On these suppositions the normal wage in any trade is that which is sufficient to enable a labourer who has normal regularity of employment, to support himself and a family of normal size according to the standard of comfort that is normal in the grade to which his trade belongs ; it is not dependent on demand except to this extent, that if there were no demand for the labour of the trade at that wage the trade would not exist." [1]

But what is " a family of normal size " ? Elsewhere Marshall defines " normal " as " in general accordance with the 'normal', the type or standard or general rule of the people whom we are at the time considering." [2] But there is no general rule as to the size of dependent families. The number of dependants on a labourer's wages varies from zero to ten or eleven. Even if it were possible to fix on a family of a particular size as necessary to keep up the population to an actual or desired figure and to treat that as the normal for which wages do or should provide, families would still pass through various stages of dependancy in arriving at the normal and receding from it as the children grow up.

In another passage Marshall says, " with £150 the family has, with £30 it has not, the materials of a complete life".[3] Is this statement then equally true whether the family consists of two or ten persons ? Probably Professor Marshall was again thinking of his " normal family." As I shall shew in the next chapter, it has become customary in sociological writings to treat as the " normal " or standard the five-member family, consisting of husband, wife and three dependent children, which happens in fact to be one of the smallest groupings.[4] Nowhere in these classic authorities do I find any recognition of the waste of resources at the one end and the human suffering at the other involved in a system which stretches families of all sizes and stages of development to fit the Procrustean bed of a uniform wage.

No doubt the minds of economists during the later nineteenth century were influenced against a recognition of the

[1] *Principles of Economics*, 1890, Vol. I, p. 556.
[2] *Ibid.*, p. 87.   [3]*Ibid.*, p. 2.   [4] *See* below, pp. 16-17.

disadvantages of the present system by the evil repute of the only alternatives to it which had hitherto been experienced or proposed. There were the communistic schemes of Godwin and his followers, associated in men's minds with revolution and the levelling of classes. There was the disastrous experiment in subsidizing wages known as the Speenhamland system, which made up the income of the labourer's family to the sum judged necessary for its support. Modern critics of this system are apt to forget that the new and demoralizing feature about it was not that it proportioned income to family needs— for that was normally done by the labour of wives and children —but that it put the idle or inefficient family on the same level with the industrious.[1] Recollection of these things combined with the high birthrate of the nineteenth century and fear of over-population to create a strong tradition of distrust of any proposal for providing for families otherwise than through wages.

In the work of still more recent economists, the family sank out of sight altogether. The subsistence theory of wages was superseded by theories in which wives and children appear only occasionally, together with butchers' meat and alcohol and tobacco, as part of the " comforts and decencies " which make up the British workman's standard of life and enable him to stand out against the lowering of his wage. I do not think it would be an exaggeration to say that, if the population of Great Britain consisted entirely of adult self-propagating bachelors and spinsters, nearly the whole output of writers on economic theory during the past fifty years might remain as it was written, except for a paragraph or phrase here and there, and those unessential to the main argument.

The family reappears in the writings of the group of sociologists, headed by Charles Booth, who by laborious investigations have laid bare the concrete conditions of life in the wage-earning classes and revealed how great a proportion of them were living in poverty of graded degrees of blackness. It appears again in a shadowy form in recent wage-negotiations as reinforcing the demand of the workers for " a living wage " adequate to the needs of " our wives and families". This shadowy conception I will now proceed to grasp and examine.

[1] Mr. and Mrs. Hammond shew that " the abolition of the Speenhamland system and the introduction of the new Poor Law had been followed by a slight rise in wages, but the most important consequence had been a great extension of the labour of women and children " (*Lord Shaftesbury*, p. 90).

CHAPTER II

THE DOCTRINE OF A UNIFORM " LIVING WAGE "

During the last quarter of a century an uneasy conscience, quickened by the revelations of sociologists as to the conditions under which the poor live and by a growing fear of the working-class vote, has compelled employers to allow the question of the human needs of workers and their families to intrude itself into discussions on wages. The doctrine of the living wage has thus found its way into popular acceptance, though in a vague and rough and ready form. It has gradually come to be assumed almost without discussion that a trade in a healthy condition should, under normal circumstances, yield to full-time men workers of average efficiency not only enough for their own maintenance, but for that of their wives and children.

Even in times of depressed trade and falling wages it would probably be difficult to find an employer who would openly maintain that, except as a temporary and deplorable necessity, the rate of wages could legitimately be fixed at a level which made this impossible. But as a rule both employers and employed have been content with these vague statements of the principle. There have been few attempts to define either the size of the family for which a " living wage " should provide or the standard of living at which it should be maintained. When circumstances have obliged the disputants to face up to these questions, they have generally fallen back on the hasty assumption that by " a family " was meant what they describe as a normal, or typical, or average, or standard family of husband, wife and three children, and the awkward question of why this particular size of family should be so described has not been so much as asked. For example, it is stated in the report of the Court of Enquiry into the Wages and Conditions of Employment of Dock Labour (1920)[1] that this assumption as to the necessity for paying a living wage and basing it on this size of family was assumed practically

[1] 1920, H. C., No. 55

without question by all participants—employers, port authorities and workmen. The discussions of the Court, which were long and heated, turned on the question of what rate of wages would be necessary to satisfy such a standard at the current cost of living.

I propose in this chapter to examine this conception of a living wage and ask certain questions about it. First: how far does it correspond to the facts as to the actual size of workmen's families? What proportion of workers would, under such a standard, have their living needs exactly met and what proportion would enjoy a surplus or suffer from a deficiency? Secondly: to what extent has the proposed standard been actually achieved in this country in the past or at present? Thirdly: if not so far fully achieved, could it conceivably be achieved out of the present product of industry and if so by what readjustments of distribution? Incidentally in this and more systematically in later chapters I shall discuss the effect of trying to apply this conception of a living wage, its defects, and the possible alternatives to it.

(a) Does it Fit the Facts?

First, then, how far does the conception fit the facts? The reply is that a family consisting of husband, wife and three dependent children is in fact one of the smallest groupings. This may be seen from the following table, which is based on the materials compiled by Dr. Bowley for use in his book *Livelihood and Poverty*,[1] being the result of a scrutiny of roughly one-twentieth of the working-class households in Reading (1912), Northampton, Warrington and Stanley (1913); supplemented by a scrutiny of one-tenth of the working-class households in Bolton (1914) and one-fifteenth of the Census sheets (1911) for Bethnal Green, Shoreditch, Stepney, Bristol, Leeds, Bradford, Newcastle-on-Tyne. The number of working-class men earners about whom particulars were obtained was 13,475, representing by sample a total number of 448,000. It will probably be agreed that such a sample is sufficiently large in quantity and representative in quality to be taken

[1] *Livelihood and Poverty*, by A. L. Bowley and A. R. Burnett-Hurst (G. Bell & Sons, 1915). Further information based on all the investigations mentioned above is given by Dr. Bowley in "Earners and Dependants in English Towns in 1911," in *Economica*, May 1921. For the Table given in the text I am indebted to the London School of Economics, which however has no responsibility for the use I have made of the figures.

as indicative of the whole. Assuming this to be so it shews that, of men workers over twenty in England, roughly speaking,

27 per cent. are bachelors or widowers without dependent children.

24.7 per cent. are married couples without children or with no dependent child below fourteen.

16.6 per cent. have one dependent child.

13 per cent. have two dependent children.

8.8 per cent. have three dependent children.

9.9 per cent. have more than three dependent children (i.e. 5.5 per cent. have four children; 2.8 have five; 1.1 have six; .4 have seven; and .1 eight or nine).

These figures include the households where there is more than one wage-earner, e.g., a wife or child over fourteen working. If the households be taken which consist solely of husband, non-earning wife and three dependent children, the proportion is still smaller. Dr. Bowley found that " a household so constituted only occurs in 56 households per thousand in the skilled group, in 52 per thousand in the un-skilled."[1] So much for the claim of this type of household to be described as normal, standard, average or typical!

Ignoring the possibility of a second wage-earner, it follows from the above table that " a living wage " based on the needs of the five-member household might be expected to be just adequate in about one household in eleven; it would be less than adequate in one household in ten; it would leave a margin in about four households out of five. These figures may seem at the first glance " not so bad " to those who think it highly desirable that the great majority of workers' families should have a margin above what is necessary for bare existence. But their contentment will vanish on a closer inspection. Although only 9·9 per cent. of the families were found to have more than three dependent children at the time of inspection, these being the larger families include a large proportion of the children; in fact the proportion is about 40 per cent.[2] Further it must be remembered that a considerably higher percentage of families must have passed through the stage previously, before some of the children became wage-earners, or would pass through it in the future, when more children were

---

[1] *Economica*, May 1921, p. 107.

[2] *See* the figures given for seven boroughs by Dr. Bowley in *Economica*, May 1921, p. 110 (Table VII).

born. In Rowntree's *Human Needs of Labour*[1] (Chap. I) he illustrates this point elaborately from his investigations in York, which indicated that 33 per cent. of working men have more than three children simultaneously dependent on them during part of their married life and that if only three children were allowed for in fixing minimum wages, 62 per cent. of the children of men in receipt of such wages would be in a condition of privation for varying periods and 54 per cent. would remain in such condition for five years or more.

It is true that Mr. Rowntree defends the five-member family basis for wages on the ground that, as shewn by his figures, about 50 per cent. of the families include three or more dependent children for some period. But he proposes to provide for the needs of the children in excess of three by an allowance paid by the State to the mother for each such child. The surplus in excess of minimum needs which the five-member basis would allow to the smaller households, he defends on the ground that it should be of value to the young man in preparing for his future family and to the elderly couple in saving for their old age. This does not sound very convincing; nor somehow, as one reads Mr. Rowntree's argument, does one feel that he is quite convinced of it himself. It is clearly unsatisfactory, assuming that minimum wages are to be based on the needs of the worker, that the basis chosen should be the needs of five persons, merely because half the families concerned will consist of this number at some stage or other. The " human needs " of a family are its present needs, not its past nor its future needs, and as we have already seen, the five-member basis fits the present needs of about one family in eleven, not one in two.

As for the claims of the young bachelor and the elderly couple, it seems unnecessarily artificial to budget for one purpose in order to meet another. Does experience lead one to suppose that the surplus enjoyed by the bachelor is in fact generally spent on saving for the equipment of a future home or on immediate football or cigarettes ? And why suppose that the amount allowed for three fictitious children will be just right to provide for the old age of their parents ? The reader will be in a better position to consider these points and also the proposed subsidy to families over three children, when

[1] *The Human Needs of Labour* (Chap. I), by B. Seebohm Rowntree (Thos. Nelson & Sons, 1918).

we have estimated the limitations of the national income and are considering the social effects of the uniform wage and the proposed alternatives to it. It is I think quite clear that when Mr. Rowntree put forward his proposal, these alternatives had not occurred to him, for as the rest of this chapter will shew, there is no one whose works afford richer material for demonstrating the failure of the theory of a uniform family wage to fit the facts.

Perhaps the simplest and most graphic illustration of that failure can be found in the following calculations:

Assuming that the number of adult male wage-earners in the United Kingdom was about 8 million[1] in 1911 and that they have since increased in proportion to the increase of population,[2] the number may now be taken as approximately 8,360,000. According to the 1911 Census there were roughly 10¼ million men over twenty and 6½ million wives in the total population. If we assume that the proportion of married couples is approximately the same among the working classes, the number of wage-earners' wives would in 1921 be about 5,300,000. The number of children is about 9½ or 10 million according to the figure taken as to the average number of children per man.[3] To pay every man on the basis of the five-member family wage would mean providing for a population of 8,360,000 men, 8,360,000 wives, and 25,080,000 children. Under such an arrangement provision would be made for 3 million phantom wives, and for over 16 million phantom children in the families containing less than three children,[4] while on the other hand, in families containing more than three children, those in excess of that number, over 1¼ million in all, would still remain unprovided for.

The provision for phantom wives may I think be defended on the ground that a man who has not a wife to keep has

[1] This is the estimate of the number of " men in situations " given by Mr. Sidney Webb (*New Statesman*, May 10, 1913, *see* below, p. 25). The total number of wage-earning men and boys he estimates at 10,600,000. This corresponds fairly closely with Dr. Bowley's estimate of 11,000,000 wage-earning men and boys in 1911 (*The Division of the Product of Industry*, 1919, pp. 7, 11).

[2] The population of the United Kingdom was 45¼ million in 1911. No figures are available for the population of Ireland in 1921, but assuming that it had increased slightly (as in Great Britain) the population of the United Kingdom in 1921 was about 47¼ million.

[3] The number of children per 100 wage-earning men over 20 years of age will be found from the figures given by Dr. Bowley in " Earners and Dependants in English Towns" (*Economica*, May 1921, pp. 109, 110) to be 119. In the table given above (p. 16) the proportion works out as about 115 per 100 men. The former figure is probably the more accurate, being based on more numerous data.

[4] *See* the figures given above, p. 16.

to pay someone to do his cooking, washing and housekeeping for him, whether it be a landlady, a mother or some other woman relative. But considering the provision for children, we arrive at the surely amazing result that if the efforts of Trade Unionism were successful in securing—as they have certainly not secured at present—the payment of " a living wage " based on the needs of a five-member family as a minimum to every male worker of twenty years and over, and if no one received more than the minimum, we should in fact be providing in the nation's wage-bill full rations for over 16 million phantom children while we provided inadequate rations for 1¼ million of the real children. Further, out of the total 9½ or 10 million children, over 5 million (54 per cent.) would be insufficiently fed and clothed for five or more years sometime in the period between birth and leaving school.[1]

It should be noted that these figures do not furnish any argument against the doctrine of a living wage, but only against a living wage based on the needs of a uniform family. Any system of wages, whether consciously influenced by family needs or not, must inevitably be either wasteful or socially disastrous so long as it is the only means of providing for families, yet does not adjust itself to their varying sizes. This would only cease to be true in a community so wealthy that it could afford to provide for everyone on the scale adequate to the needs of the largest size of family. Later on we shall try to measure the extent to which this country fails to be such a community. Meantime it is notorious that it does fail, and the general acquiescence in so monstrous a misfit as the present plan of providing for families can only be explained by the infinite power of custom to blind men's eyes to even the most obvious facts. During the Great War, the problem of the moment was to make not the money income of the nation but its food supply go round. Suppose that the Food Controller had dealt with this problem by assuming that every man over twenty was the head of a family of five and that every woman had only herself to keep and had issued his food cards accordingly ? What would have been thought of the economy and equity of such an arrangement and how long would the Ministers responsible for it have remained in office ?

[1] *See* above, p.18.

(b) Has it been Achieved ?

The second question we have to ask is whether the five-member family subsistence standard of wages has in fact been achieved in industry as a working minimum. The answer is emphatically that it has not, and this holds good whichever we accept of several widely varying estimates of the subsistence cost of such a family. For example there are Mr. Rowntree's two estimates; the one contained in his *Poverty*[1] and adopted with slight modifications and in terms of current prices by Dr. Bowley in his *Livelihood and Poverty* (1914); and the later and rather more generous estimate of the *Human Needs of Labour* (1918). Higher standards than either of these have been put forward by Sir Leo Chiozza Money,[2] and by the exponents of the Labour point of view who gave evidence before the Court of Enquiry into Dock Labour.[3] I have taken Mr. Rowntree's two estimates as the basis of discussion, because they are probably the best known and the most scientifically worked out, and as they are also the lowest, everything that is said of our failure to achieve them in practice applies in even greater measure to higher estimates.

In *Poverty* the primary cost of maintaining a family of husband, wife and three children is assessed at 21s. 8d.[4] The standard assumed is a very meagre one, allowing only for the minimum of food, clothing and fuel necessary to the maintenance of physical health, with the addition of 4s. for rent, this being the lowest current rent for necessary accommodation for such a family in York. The dietary suggested is based on various scientific estimates of food values and is less generous than that allowed for paupers in workhouses. It is assumed that every penny is spent to the best advantage and nothing wasted. Nothing is allowed for expenditure on butcher's meat, alcohol, tobacco, insurances, fares, postage or recreation. The mode of life which this would entail is thus described by Mr. Rowntree:—

" A family living upon the scale allowed for in this estimate must never spend a penny on railway fare or omnibus. They must never go into the country unless they walk. They must never purchase a halfpenny newspaper or spend a penny to buy a ticket for a popular concert. They must write no letters to absent children, for they cannot afford to pay the postage. They must never contribute anything to their church or chapel, or give any help to a neighbour which costs them

[1] *Poverty : A Study of Town Life*, 1901.
[2] Quoted in *Wages, Profits and Prices* (published by the Labour Research Department, 1922), p. 26.
[3] H. C., No. 55 of 1920.   [4] *Poverty*, Chap. IV.

money. They cannot save, nor can they join sick club or Trade Union, because they cannot pay the necessary subscriptions. The children must have no pocket-money for dolls, marbles, or sweets. The father must smoke no tobacco, and must drink no beer. The mother must never buy any pretty clothes for herself or her children, the character of the family wardrobe as for the family diet being governed by the regulation, ' Nothing must be bought but that which is absolutely necessary for the maintenance of physical health, and what is bought must be of the plainest and most economical description.' Should a child fall ill, it must be attended by the parish doctor ; should it die, it must be buried by the parish. Finally, the wage-earner must never be absent from his work for one day." [1]

Of course, this is not how families with incomes " round about a pound a week " actually live. The fascinating studies of such families collected by Mrs. Pember Reeves shew that even when the husband is nearly as self-denying as Mr. Rowntree's model man and the wife as good a manager as her overtaxed strength and inadequate household equipment make possible, the income is very differently spent. Burial clubs always, and pocket money for the man's fares, tobacco, etc., nearly always, figure in the budgets at the expense of the food bill. This will be seen from the following Table :

	Mr. Rowntree's Model Budget for family of 5.	Actual Budgets :				
		Family of 5 with income of 21s.	Family of 8 with income of 20s. to 26s.	Family of 6 with income of 22s.	Family of 8 with income of 25s.	Family of 4 with income of 14s. (evening work).
	s. d.	s. d.	s. d.	s. d.	s. d.	s. d.
Food	12 9	8 1 (less than	7 0½	9 9½	10 6½	4 11½
	(say 11½d. per head per day.)	3d. per head per day.)	(1½d. per head per day.)	(2¾d. per head per day.)	(2¼d. per head per day.)	(1½d. per head per day.)
Rent	4 0	7 0	8 0	6 0	7 3	6 0
Clothing . . .	2 3	1 2	1 0	Nil	0 6	Nil
Fuel	1 10	1 10	1 3	1 5	1 8	0 11½
Household sundries, gas, cleaning materials, etc. .	0 10	1 5	1 0½	1 7½	1 2	0 6
Insurance . .	Nil	1 6	1 8	1 2	1 10½	0 7
Retained by husband . .	Nil	Nil	Nil to 6 0	2 0	2 0	1 0
	21 8	21 0	20s. to 26s.	22 0	25 0	14 0

The above particulars are taken from some of Mrs. Pember Reeves' budgets.[2] The families were all those of South Londoners, men of good character in regular work.

[1] *Ibid.*, pp. 133-4.
[2] *Round About a Pound a Week*, pp. 133-5, 201-2 (G. Bell & Sons, 1913).

Such records however must not be taken as discrediting Mr. Rowntree's calculation of minimum food needs, since the facts given as to the health of these London families shew how severely they suffered from the privations of their lives. If we accept his figures and add to them, say 2s. 4d. to cover all the items he omits, that gives a pre-war subsistence wage of 24s.

But public opinion as to the needs and rights of the worker has moved on a long way since 1900, even in the well-to-do classes, and although at the present time of depression many amongst the latter are trying to force the wage-earners back to or below pre-war standards, there is no sign that the wage-earners themselves will abandon their claim to a share of the comforts and decencies of life as well as its necessaries. Mr. Rowntree in his later book, *The Human Needs of Labour*, published in 1918 but based on pre-war figures, abandons his poverty basis and substitutes an estimate which, though still assuming the strictest economy, allows for a modest expenditure on meat, insurance and personal and household sundries. The sum he arrives at for the family of five is 35s. 3d.

How do these two estimates, 24s. and 35s. 3d., compare with actual pre-war wage level ? Public opinion was shocked at the revelation that in York 10 per cent. of adult men received less than 20s. for a full week's work; 16 per cent. between 20s. and 22s.; and 10 per cent. between 22s. and 24s., i.e., 36 per cent. below subsistence level. The proportion below the " human needs " level is 91 per cent. But the most complete figures published are those given by Mr. Sidney Webb in the *New Statesman* of May 10, 1913. They are admittedly only approximate. Mr. Webb's estimate however of the total wage bill, £740 million, corresponds fairly closely with Dr. Bowley's estimate of £782[1] million in 1911, while his

[1] *Distribution of the Product of Industry*, p. 30. Dr. Bowley quotes other estimates ranging from £730 to £881 million. Mr. Webb's estimate of £740 million is made up as follows :—

		Million £
8,000,000 men in situations	. . . . .	564
700,000 casuals	. . . . . .	18.5
1,900,000 boys	. . . . . .	44
All males	. . . . . .	626.5
3,000,000 women	. . . . . .	85
500,000 casuals	. . . . . .	.5
1,500,000 girls	. . . . . .	28
All females	. . . . . .	113.5

estimate of the number of men in situations (8 million) is the approximate figure quoted to me by Dr. Bowley as the number of adult male wage-earners in the same year. The figures may therefore be regarded as not very wide of the mark. The wages of men in situations are as follows:

ESTIMATED EARNINGS OF EMPLOYED MANUAL WORKING WAGE-EARNERS IN THE UNITED KINGDOM IN THE YEAR 1912.

Class.	Numbers.	Average Rate of Earnings in a Full Week, including all Emoluments.		Average Wages Bill for a Full Week.	Yearly Wages Bill (allowing 5 weeks for Short Time, Sickness, Involuntary Holidays and Unemployment).
		s.	*d.*	Million £	Million £
Men in Situations:					
Below 15s.	320,000 = 4%	(abt.) 13	0	0.21	10
15s. to 20s.	640,000 = 8%	(abt.) 18	0	0.58	27
20s. to 25s.	1,600,000 = 20%	22	6	1.80	85
25s. to 30s.	1,680,000 = 21%	27	6	2.31	109
30s. to 35s.	1,680,000 = 21%	32	6	2.73	128
35s. to 40s.	1,040,000 = 13%	37	6	1.95	92
40s. to 45s.	560,000 = 7%	42	6	1.20	56½
Over 45s.	480,000 = 6%	50	0	1.20	56½
Total	8,000,000 = 100%	30	0	12.0	564

This shews that 32 per cent. earned less than 25s. when in full work and 74 per cent. less than 35s.; with a proportionately lower average income when a normal amount of time off work is allowed for.

To so great an extent did pre-war wages fail to realize the ideal of a minimum wage for men sufficient for the support of a standard family.

Of greater practical interest however is the question how far these wages satisfied the needs of really existent families. The question can be answered by referring once more to the researches of those invaluable sociologists, Mr. Rowntree and Dr. Bowley. It is worth noting that although both of these accept the prevailing assumption that " a living wage " ought to conform to the five-member family basis,[1] yet when it comes to measuring the actual extent of poverty they both tacitly abandon this artificial basis and count as

[1] *See* above, p. 18, for Mr. Rowntree's defence of this standard.

living in " primary poverty " every working man or woman
whose income from all sources is insufficient to provide
subsistence, according to the exiguous standard of physical
needs already described, for himself and his actual dependants.   So estimated, the number of families found to be
living in primary poverty in York amounted to 15.46 per
cent. of the wage-earning class and to 9·91 per cent. of the
whole population of the city.[1]   In Northampton, Warrington, Stanley and Reading (Dr. Bowley's four sample towns)
the proportions varied considerably, but regarding the four
as one city, 13½ per cent. of the working-class households,
containing 16 per cent. of the working-class population
and 27 per cent. of the workers' children, were reckoned
to be living in primary poverty.[2]   If the more generous
" human needs" standard had been taken, the proportion
falling below it would of course have been very much
larger.

It will be noticed that these proportions, though shocking
enough to those who realize the amount of suffering and
wastage they denote, are less than half what would have
to be taken if we were to reckon as " poor " everyone whose
wages fell below the fictitious uniform standard of needs
that is implied in the conception of a uniform living wage.
Probably it is owing to the confusion that exists in the public
mind between the two standards, that although Mr. Rowntree's and Dr. Bowley's figures attracted considerable attention when published, no one (so far as I know) drew the
conclusion that leaps to the eye, that by far the greatest
cause of primary poverty is the failure of the wage system
to adapt itself to the needs of the variously sized households
actually dependent on the wage-earner.   Even these two
able writers, while in the act of giving the facts and figures
which prove this, help, I venture to think, to obscure the
truth by continuing to talk of " low wages " and " large
families " as the cause of poverty as though there were some
absolute standard of lowness and largeness.   This will be seen
from the following table, which is based on their figures.[3]
It shews the immediate cause of poverty in the households
found by Mr. Rowntree in York (1899) and by Dr. Bowley
in Northampton, Warrington, Stanley and Reading (1912-13)

[1] *Poverty*, p. 111.
[2] *Livelihood and Poverty*, pp. 46-7.
[3] See *Poverty*, Chap. V; *Livelihood and Poverty*, pp. 47 and 173.

Immediate Cause of Poverty.	Percentage of households affected	
	In Dr. Bowley's 4 towns together.	In York.
Chief wage-earner out of work	2	3
Chief wage-earner in irregular work	2	3
Chief wage-earner ill or old .	11	10
Chief wage-earner dead .	14	27
Chief wage-earner in regular work but at wages insufficient to support his actual family of dependent children . .	71 (i.e. 3 children or less, 26%; 4 children or more, 45%)	57 (4 children or less, 44% ; 5 children or more, 13%)

to be living in " primary poverty," i.e., on incomes insufficient to maintain even the low standard laid down in Rowntree's *Poverty* (see above, p. 17).

Considering that these two sets of figures were collected at an interval of about fifteen years, by investigators using different methods, the coincidence of their results is remarkable. The one important difference—the much larger proportion of poverty in York caused by widowhood—is probably due either (or both) to a difference in the amount of wage-earning occupations available for widows in the respective towns or (and) to a difference in the policy of their Boards of Guardians in regard to the extent and scale of out-relief granted to those who are willing to apply for it. Both investigations were carried on during years of fairly prosperous trade and this no doubt accounts for the very small extent of unemployment and irregular employment recorded. Under the conditions of exceptional trade depression which have prevailed during the last two years, these two causes would no doubt bulk very much more largely in any analysis of the conditions of poverty-stricken households. The point which matters is that, during the years of ordinary good trade in the decade before the war and at the standard of real wages then prevailing, roughly about 15 per cent. of working-class households were found to be living on incomes insufficient for their bare physical needs however exiguously estimated, and by far the largest cause of their poverty—a cause outweighing all the others put together—was the inadequacy of the wage to meet the needs of the household actually dependent on it. Yet it may safely be said that if one were to put off-hand to an audience of middle-class men, including employers, social workers and economists, the question: "What, excluding personal misconduct, are the chief immediate causes of privation in working-class families ? " nine out of ten of them would enumerate:—unemployment or irregular employment, sickness, old age, widowhood. The tenth man (and a much larger proportion if one's audience were itself of the working class) would add " low wages "; or the failure of employers to pay a living wage. But even these would assuredly think of the living wage (if they thought of it precisely at all) in terms of some uniform standard fixed by trade unionism or some other negotiating or legislating body with a vague reference to the needs of an imaginary uniform family.

(a) Is it Achievable out of the Present National Income ?

There remains the third question which I set myself to answer at the beginning of this chapter:—How far is the conception of a minimum wage for men workers based on the needs of a five-member family realizable out of the resources of the nation? Granted that it has not yet been achieved, could it be achieved in the future through a redistribution of the product of industry between the wage-earning and other classes; or through any probable increase in the amount of that product ? A great mass of public opinion, including apparently the whole of that of the organized Labour movement in this country, holds that it could be so achieved. While rejecting impatiently as inadequate the estimates of minimum needs put forward by " middle-class " sociologists such as Mr. Rowntree and Dr. Bowley, this opinion relies for the enforcement of the much higher standard it desires on the double device of redistribution and an increasing productivity, both contingent on some form of workers' control of industry. It is not my purpose here to discuss the ground of this faith, so far as it relates to the effect on production of as yet untested changes in the economic structure of society. These effects are obviously a matter for prophecy rather than for dogmatic assertion and every one will prophesy differently, in accordance with the bias given him by his economic position and political prejudices.

But the question of how the present sum of the nation's wealth could conceivably be redistributed so as to give the largest possible share to the wage-earners and with what results, is one of fact which has been quite recently explored by the writers who are perhaps our greatest authorities on the statistics of national wealth and wages—Dr. Bowley and Sir Josiah Stamp. Although best known as a statistician, Dr. Bowley by his investigations into the actual conditions of working-class homes, in the book *Livelihood and Poverty* from which I have quoted so often, has done as much as any man to expose the extent, incidence and evils of poverty due to low wages, so that he cannot be suspected of any bias against efforts to raise the standard. Sir Josiah Stamp is a statistician whose former position at the Inland Revenue Board gave him special facilities for estimating national resources, and he was referred to by the then Chancellor of the Exchequer (Mr. Chamberlain) as the " highest authority we have on such questions at the present time."

Both these authors have within the last few years published books [1] in which they analyse the amount and distribution of the national income, defined by Sir Josiah Stamp as " the aggregate money expression of those goods produced and services performed by the inhabitants of the country in a year which are, in fact, generally exchanged for money." [2] They also make an arithmetical estimate of a possible redistribution between the wage-earning and other classes of this income, or rather of that portion of it which is available for the current expenditure of individuals, national and communal charges and reserves of saving remaining as before. Those who wish to know the bases of the calculations should read both books for themselves; or at least the chapter on " Distribution " in Sir Josiah Stamp's book in which he summarizes Dr. Bowley's conclusions and gives his own. Put as shortly as possible, their conclusions are as follows:—

Dr. Bowley estimates that in 1911 there were in the United Kingdom approximately 11 million wage-earning men and boys, with an aggregate wage-bill of £631 million and an average wage for a week's earnings in ordinary industry of £1 9s. 2d. for men over twenty, 10s. 7d. for lads and boys, and £1 6s. 3d. for all males. There were also 4,650,000 wage-earning women and girls, with an aggregate wage-bill of £151 million and an average wage for a week's industry of

[1] Bowley, *The Division of the Product of Industry* (Clarendon Press, 1919, 2s. 6d.); Stamp, *Wealth and Taxable Capacity* (P. S. King, 1922, 10s. 6d.)
[2] *Wealth and Taxable Capacity*, p. 40.

13s. 6d. for women over eighteen, 7s. 3d. for girls, and 11s. 10d. for all females.[1]

He further estimates [2] that in the same year (1911) the aggregate income of the residents in the United Kingdom, derived from home sources, was £1,900 millions or less, and of this nearly 60 per cent. (£1,158 millions) was in the hands of persons whose annual income was below £160; 42 per cent. being received as wages, 13 per cent. as small salaries (this included earnings of independent workers and small employers) and 5 per cent. as old age pensions or receipts from property in the hands of very small people.   Of the remaining 40 per cent. (£742 millions) " £145 millions certainly was earned as salaries or by farmers, and £190 millions certainly was ' unearned ' (in the sense in which the word is currently used), and obtained from the ownership of real property or securities.   The remaining £407 millions is the total of all profits of trade and professions (excluding those which go to persons whose incomes are under £160), and a considerable part (whose amount cannot be ascertained) goes to shareholders and others who take no active part in the business."   Dr. Bowley goes on to suppose that all earned incomes above £160, including those of active employers, were reduced to that figure and concludes:—

" When we have subtracted the incomes so reduced, farmers' incomes and the incomes of endowed charities, from the £742 millions of tax-paying income, we are left with about £550 millions. This may be taken as a maximum estimate of surplus and unearned income that could be regarded as transferable to national purposes. Actually the cutting down of earned incomes would in fact seriously diminish the power as well as the will to work, and a good deal of income would disappear in the process of transfer.   £550 millions is then an outside estimate of the part of home-produced income that is the target of attack by extreme socialists.

" Out of this sum, however, the great part of national saving is made and a large part of national expenses is met; when these are subtracted only £200 to £250 millions remain, which on the extremest reckoning can have been spent out of home-produced income by the rich or moderately well-off on anything of the nature of luxury. This sum would have little more than sufficed to bring the wages of adult men and women up to the minimum of 35s. 3d. weekly for a man and 20s. for a woman which Mr. Rowntree, in *The Human Needs of Labour*, estimates as reasonable." [3]

---

[1] *The Division of the Product of Industry*, Chap. III. Dr. Bowley makes it clear that this estimate of wages is based on figures that are not entirely complete, and that there is therefore a margin of error, but a small one.

[2] *Ibid.*, Chap. V.

[3] *Ibid.*, pp. 48-9. The cost of bringing adult *men* up to the minimum is calculated by Dr. Bowley as £130 million (*ibid.*, p. 20). He does not specify the exact sum required for the women, but from Mr. Webb's estimate of three million women earning £85 million per annum (*see* above, p. 25 n.), we may calculate that to bring all women wage-earners up to Mr. Rowntree's standard of 20s. would cost £56 million per annum.

It should be noted that this hypothesis of Dr. Bowley's involves not only the cutting down of all the higher earned incomes to £160, but the confiscation of all unearned incomes not belonging to people already below the £160 limit, including those derived from the savings of retired people. But as neither Dr. Bowley nor anyone else who has seriously considered the matter believes such a drastic measure of expropriation to be either practicable or desirable, this is equivalent to saying that the establishment of a legal minimum wage, based for men on Mr. Rowntree's later estimate of the needs of a five-member family and for women on the needs of an individual, would be—given our pre-war National Income, or an income equivalent to it in purchasing power— a practical impossibility.

These calculations are of course concerned with the national income as it actually was. Dr. Bowley explicitly excludes consideration of changes in the amount of the product of industry that might take place subsequent to the redistribution and as a consequence of it—such as changes due to the increased efficiency of those whose wages had been raised; the slackening of effort and enterprise on the part of those whose salaries and profits were cut down; the enlistment in industry of previously idle people; the disappearance of apparent income when the effort was made to transfer it; the adoption of better or worse methods of production and distribution; the elimination of waste due to competition, etc. He also excludes consideration of the changes due to the redistribution of spending power.

From these abstract calculations of the possible results of a social upheaval, Dr. Bowley passes on to consider how far it would have been practicable, under the existing economic system, to increase the pre-war rate of wages. He concludes:—

" In fact, while in some industries a considerable advance may have been practicable, in the majority no such increase as would make possible the standards of living now urgently desired, and promised in the election addresses of all the political parties, could have been obtained without wrecking the industry, whether by stopping the source of further investment or closing down firms whose profits were low. This statement in its general terms cannot, it is thought, be reasonably denied by anyone who has studied the facts."[1]

He next points out that if all this was true before the war, there is no reason to suppose that the situation has altered for the better since. While in some directions there is

[1] *Ibid.*, p. 53.

improved efficiency due to the elimination of waste and the skill acquired by women and other workers previously kept to unskilled processes, this has been more than balanced by the loss and deterioration of man-power and of material.

"At the best it can only be hoped that the loss in productive power is not very serious nor permanent. . . . The wealth of the country, however divided, was insufficient before the war for a general high standard; there is nothing as yet to show that it will be greater in the future." [1]

Sir Josiah Stamp examines and endorses Dr. Bowley's conclusions and in the course of his analysis of national resources gives the following calculation of his own:—

He estimates that in 1919-20 the national income lay between £3,700 millions and £4,100 millions, and was probably about £3,900 millions.[2] He considers what would be the effect of pooling and dividing equally the excess of all income over £250, after first deducting the taxation now borne by this section and assuming the same relative proportion of national income to be set aside for capital extensions, increased production, etc., as before the war. He estimates that the amount available for division "would not exceed £150 millions, which would not give each family more than £14 a year rise, or say 5s. a week," in the first year of distribution. In following years he suggests—though he admits it to be guess-work—that owing to the effect of the distribution on effort and on values, the amount of increment per family would shrink to £5 a year or a little less.[3]

He further gives some interesting calculations (too complicated to summarize here) of which the purport is to shew that, while the nominal and real value of the national income and the share of every class in it have increased greatly since 1800—the bulk of the increase in real values having been secured during the first part of the nineteenth century—yet the "slope" of distribution, i.e., the relation between the share of one class and another, has hardly altered, the increase having surged up evenly through all classes of the population. It is implied that this holds good of all civilized countries for which figures are available, and that the scheme of distribution of wealth between classes apparently follows fairly closely a mathematical rule or formula

[1] *Ibid.,* pp. 54, 58.   [2] *Wealth and Taxable Capacity,* p. 75.
[3] *Ibid.,* pp. 95-8.

known after the name of its discoverer as " the Pareto line "; so that a statistician knowing the total amount available for distribution and the number of incomes in certain groups would be able to predict the distribution of the remaining income holders over the intermediate figures.[1]

To the plain observer of social phenomena, this statement must seem at first sight not only curious but astounding and confounding. When we remember the great shifting in the balance of power and influence between the classes since 1800, it seems almost incredible that it should have effected no change in the relative proportions of wealth secured by the employing and wage-earning classes respectively. On reflection, however, perhaps the statement is less startling than it sounds. It does not of course necessarily mean that all the effort that has been expended on trying to improve the lot of the manual workers has had no effect on their wages, since we have no evidence that they would even have kept their place in the " slope of distribution " without these efforts. It may be contended that it has only been through the improved bargaining power due to their political, economic and educational enfranchisement that the wage-earners during the past century have succeeded in securing that increases in wages have been roughly proportionate to the increase in national wealth. Further, Professor Pareto himself points out that no general law applicable to all circumstances can be deduced from his formula and that we cannot assume " that the form of the curve would not change if the social constitution were to change radically."[2]

The figures I have quoted from Dr. Bowley and Sir Josiah Stamp further prove that even if the redistribution could be brought about, its effect on the rate of wages would be totally inadequate to produce a standard of comfort which the workers themselves would accept as satisfactory, at least so long as we proceed on the assumption that no advantage can be given to the family of three, six or eight persons that

---

[1] *Ibid.*, pp. 78 *seq.* Sir Josiah Stamp illustrates this by telling how when he was in the Inland Revenue Department and super-tax statistics were first published in 1913, he found that the number of income tax payers in a certain group was not quite what it should have been according to the Pareto rule. He therefore told his colleagues that they had missed over a thousand payers in the class £5,000 to £10,000. They were annoyed, but they promptly set about looking for the missing thousand and found them.

[2] *Manuale di Economia Politica*, quoted by Pigou in *Economics of Welfare*, p. 697.

is not equally extended to the single man and even (if " equal pay for equal work " be conceded) to the single woman.[1]

There remains the hope that as a result of workers' control, or the progress of discovery or both, the product of industry may itself be increased—some day, somehow—so greatly as to allow of the payment to every one of a wage at least sufficient to provide everything that a reasonably large family can reasonably want even at the period of greatest dependancy. If this hope be some day realized, no one probably would grudge to the bachelor or spinster the luxuries that they would be able to purchase out of the surplus allowed them for imaginary children.

But meantime, what of the real children—the millions of them who here and now " in Rome or London, not Fool's Paradise " are struggling up to maturity with bodies stunted and faculties atrophied by privation ? What of their over-worked mothers and harassed fathers ? Have we nothing to offer them but the hope, spun out of " ifs " and " ands," that they or their descendants may some day dwell in an economic castle in the air ? Very bitter things have been said in the past by leaders of working men about those leaders of religious thought—more influential a generation ago than now—who sought to distract the poor from troubling about their present remediable wrongs by encouraging them to set all their hopes on a Better Land to be reached after death. It was pointed out that that kind of teaching served very well the ends of the privileged classes who wanted to keep their privileges. I suggest that the leaders of working men are themselves subconsciously biassed by prejudice of sex as well as of class, when they cling persistently to the ideal of a uniform adequate family wage, even when acknowledging that its attainment belongs to a distant and speculative future. Are they not influenced by a secret reluctance to see their wives and children recognized as separate personalities, " each to count for one and none for more than one " in the economic structure of society, instead of being fused in the multiple personality of the family with its male head ? There can be

---

[1] It does not of course follow that a measure of redistribution is not a thing desirable in itself and well worth working for; not only as a means of mitigating hardship, but for the sake of its moral results in getting rid of the profound sense of injustice roused by the spectacle of the excessive inequalities of wealth and the contrasts of privation and luxury. I do not see how anyone can doubt that this dissatisfaction is responsible for much industrial inefficiency.

no doubt, I think, that this complex does exist. But I have satisfied myself by experiment that when it is no longer repressed but by an exposure of the real facts and figures is dragged to the surface, a large proportion of men recognize it for the base thing it is and are as willing as any woman can be to examine fairly the case for a system of providing for the family more in accordance with its needs and the resources of the nation.

In Part II it will be shewn that such a system exists, not merely on paper, but already realized in several countries—in a rudimentary and imperfect form it is true, but still in a form which has shewn vigorous life and rapid growth and has involved a minimum of disturbance of the existing economic structure. Another more complete and, as I believe, in the long run a better system of provision on national lines will be discussed and it will be suggested that this too could be realized out of existing resources, on a modest scale, but in a form which might reasonably be expected to promote that increase in productivity which alone will make really adequate provision possible.

But first let us complete our examination of the existing system and its results.

CHAPTER III

THE SOCIAL EFFECTS OF THE PRESENT SYSTEM

We have hitherto been considering the uniform family wage and the possible alternatives to it almost entirely as a problem of distribution, as a question of how best to ensure that a sufficient portion of the wealth produced by the community will be applied to the maintenance of those of its members—the mothers and children—who are not engaged in the immediate production of wealth but are essential not only to its future production, but to the continued existence of the community itself. From this point of view I do not think that it can be denied that the case against the uniform family wage is irrefutable and overwhelming. Regarded as a device of distribution, what can anyone find to say in favour of a device which never yet has been anything like completely achieved; which could not be so achieved except on the assumption that the product of industry is, by some unknown or at least untested means, doubled or trebled; but which if and so far as achieved out of the present product would mean that provision cannot be made for the needs of $9\frac{1}{2}$ or 10 million real children without budgeting for over 16 million imaginary children, and even then leaving half the real children insufficiently rationed for over a third of their childhood? Does not the whole thing suggest some lunatic's plan of irrigating his plot of seedlings by arranging for an unguarded flow of water over several barren fields in such a manner that the stream is nearly exhausted by the time his plot is reached?

During two years I have repeatedly brought this aspect of the question before the public in articles, letters to the press and speeches. No one has attempted to refute or belittle the facts and figures, but every unfavourable commentator has simply walked straight past them to criticize the alternative proposals, arguing that these are open to certain risks and difficulties—that their adoption would be opposed by bachelors and elderly men, or would weaken the motive to industry in fathers, or loosen the bonds of the family, or unduly increase the population. These objections raise social and moral issues quite different from those we have been discussing, although they (or at least the two latter of them) have their bearing on the problem of production and consequently of distribution. Before they can properly be answered, it is necessary to consider how the present wage system works out from a social and moral point of view; in its bearing on the capacity and the will to produce; on the harmony of the family and the welfare of its individual members; on the problem of population. We shall then be in a position to discuss the relative merits of the two systems.

It is obvious that a wage system which, whether based or not on the needs of a family, is all that is available in the great majority of cases to cover the maintenance of families, involves a sort of cycle of prosperity for the average working man and his household. Professor Marshall [1] calculated that in unskilled or casual labour a man usually attains nearly his full wage-earning capacity at eighteen; in skilled occupations at twenty-one. Whether these figures are accepted or not, it may be assumed that a man over twenty if fully employed is normally earning the standard rate recognized for adults in the occupation and grade in which he is working. He may or may not pass in subsequent years into a higher grade, by being put to work involving greater skill or supervision of others. But in a large proportion of cases he will remain one of the rank and file of his occupation all his life, and it is with regard to the rank and file that minimum scales are normally fixed. While single he lives with his parents or in lodgings. In the former case he may or may not, according to his mother's circumstances or disposition, be expected to contribute as much as, or more than the actual cost of his maintenance to the household expenses. In the latter, his landlady will certainly expect some profit for her trouble in " doing for " him. But his wage, even if small, probably leaves him a more or less comfortable margin for his personal pleasures. When he marries, unless his wife is also a wage-earner, he incurs the whole expense of the joint household. This may leave him rather less pocket-money to spend, but he obtains instead greater comfort and more attention to his personal tastes. The young couple take a

[1] *Principles of Economics*, 1890, Book IV, Chap. IV, p. 230.

pride in their home and hope to embellish it by degrees, obtaining one piece of furniture or household gear after another on the hire-purchase system. When the first baby comes, the strain on the husband's purse and on his forbearance in other respects begins to be felt; but it is still bearable and the satisfaction of fatherhood more than makes up for it. As the family increases the pressure tightens. Every new arrival means pinching a bit either off the husband's pocket-money or off the comforts and necessaries available for the rest of the household or both. As the figures relative to actual earnings shew,[1] this means in a very large proportion of families that even when the husband is self-sacrificing and the wife a good manager, the food and clothing and fuel will be less than is necessary for bare physical health. The period of greatest privation will be reached during the years of greatest dependency; and it is in these years that it will be least possible for the wife to eke out her husband's wages by her own exertions, by going out to work or taking in a lodger. As child after child reaches the age of fourteen and passes into the labour market, the pressure lightens, and the circumstances of the family may again become comparatively easy, until old age and failing capacity bring another period of straitness. This indeed may be averted if some of the grown-up sons or daughters remain at home, or contribute substantially to the support of their parents. Or again it may be accelerated by the premature breakdown in health of the wage-earner or any other member of the household. Such a breakdown may of course occur at any period during the cycle, and very often it can be traced to the privations that have been endured just at the time when such privations are most injurious—while the children are young and tender, the wife bearing the double strain of child-bearing and looking after a young family, and the husband stimulated to exert himself even beyond his strength by the needs of his household.

Such is the normal economic cycle through which the normal rank and file workman's family passes. Most of those who have themselves passed through it take it as a matter of course, as do we who look on. Habit has inured and to a great extent blinded us to the anomalies it involves, the hardships it produces, and the demoralizing tendencies

[1] *See* Chap. II.

it fosters, while we are still open-eyed to the possible corresponding disadvantages of any disturbance of it.   Let us
therefore go back to the beginning of the cycle and examine
it in greater detail, considering how its various stages react
upon the different members of the family and upon their
contributions to the general well-being.

(a) The Effect on the Wage Earner, and on Production

It may be assumed that in the majority of cases the young
wage-earner has sprung from approximately the same industrial and social grade which he joins.   If his father has
been an artisan, he will have endeavoured to put his son to
a trade; if an unskilled labourer, the son is likely to become
the same.   There are many exceptions but this is the general
rule.[1]   His childhood therefore will probably have been
passed in a home maintained on a sum no larger, very likely
smaller, than that which he earns when first he receives an
adult's wage.   In such a home there will not probably have
been much room for quiet or privacy or much encouragement to studious habits.   His mother, whatever his natural
inclinations, will not have had time or means to foster such
tastes in herself or her children.   If he is an ordinary youth
with nothing exceptional about him, who takes colour from
his surroundings, he is not likely to have acquired during
these most impressionable years the wide mental outlook, or
fastidious personal habits, that will make him ambitious about
his future.   He will have been accustomed to escape from
the overcrowded little home to the streets, and his idea of
happiness will be to have plenty of money for the pleasures
they offer—for cigarettes and beer, football and betting,
picture-shows and dancing, possibly if some social or religious
organization has got hold of him, for cycling and camping out.
On such things he will have become accustomed to
spend a good deal of money—more or less according to his
wages and the amount of his contribution to home expenses.
If he is regularly employed, and especially in times of prosperous trade, when wages are rising and overtime plentiful,
he can often make enough to satisfy his wants without working a full week.   Naturally he does not see why his convenience
should give way to his employer's, if extra leisure seems

[1] See *The Nature and Purpose of the Measurement of Social Phenomena,* by A. L. Bowley
(P. S. King & Son, 1915), pp. 88-9.

more attractive to him than extra pay. But in most occupations, the various forms of labour are interdependent and the absence of a considerable proportion of the young, strong men from a shift may make it impossible for the work to be carried on. Hence the older married men, who ask nothing better than to work full time and overtime too in order to meet the needs of their households, are obliged to stand by with the rest and to share the blame so freely meted out to the British working-man for his supposed failure to allow British trade to rise to the level of its opportunities.

During the coal strike of 1920 the miners' case for increased wages rested mainly upon the inadequacy of existing rates to maintain their families at a satisfactory standard. The owners replied that the effect of previous increases had been a lessened production owing to slackened effort and short time. Both arguments were probably true. The miners guilty of short time were not, it may be safely surmised, the men with families to support, but the young unmarried men and the elderly men with several sons contributing to the upkeep of the household. This has indeed been admitted to me by several mine-owners, and by two of the best known of the miners' representatives.[1] The latter, in discussing the possible introduction of family allowances into their industry, remarked incidentally that in fact there was more grading of incomes in proportion to family needs than appeared on the surface owing to the larger proportion of time put in by the men with families. The influence of the same factor has been frequently admitted and never denied by employers and Trade Unionists in other industries.[2] Several employers have explicitly attributed to the slackness of the younger men the failure of their industries to take full advantage of the opportunities for securing foreign trade offered by periods of exceptional demand, and have alleged this as a reason for refusing an increase or pressing for a reduction of wages, while owning that the existing rates pressed very hardly on the men with families.

It may be argued that in their relation to the proposal for family allowances these facts cut both ways. If it is

[1] It is also borne out by the table of miners' wages, quoted in *The Times*, March 2, 1923, which shewed that absenteeism was greatest among the men paid at the lowest rates, i.e., presumably the youths.

[2] The same fact is alleged of the German workman (*see* below, p. 223).

by the needs of their wives and children that the married men are stimulated to greater exertions, why deprive them of this motive power by putting them on the same level as the childless men with regard to satisfaction of need?

The answer is twofold:—First, it does not follow that the adoption of a system of family allowances, whether paid by the State or by the industry, would allow the family man to enjoy the same surplus for his individual pleasures as the childless man had previously enjoyed. Whether it did so or not would depend on whether the allowances were given as an addition to the existing wage-bill or as part of a redistribution of it, and this in turn would depend on two factors—the product of industry and the power of the worker to secure a greater or less share of it. In the latter case—i.e., if the allowance were the result of a redistribution of an existing wage-bill—the bachelor's surplus would be cut down for the benefit of his comrade's family; but the amount received by the latter would not be likely to allow him much margin for joy-riding on workdays, after paying the family's boot and milk bills.

But even if the allowances were given under such circumstances and in such a way that they came as a pure gain to the workers—a net addition to previous wage rates—so that the married man would be able, if he so desired, to choose between more pocket-money or more leisure as the bachelor did before, does it follow that the latter's easy-going ways and somewhat unprofitable methods of spending his surplus, which the employer deplores and the fair-minded worker to some extent admits, would simply be extended to all workers? I suggest that it does not follow, and that human nature being what it is, it is not even probable. The demoralizing feature about the present system is not that it gives young men a considerable surplus above the minimum necessary for the satisfaction of primary physical needs, but that they come into the enjoyment of that surplus at a time when their habits and standards have already been formed, amid the wrong environment and at a low level. Born of an underfed, over-worked mother, bred in an over-crowded home, with a constitution enfeebled by early privation, with an appetite vitiated by ill-chosen and ill-cooked food and accustomed to respond only to the stimulus of strong coarse flavours, with mental faculties atrophied by neglect and æsthetic perceptions blunted by constant contact with ugly, depressing, sordid surroundings, what chance has the average young worker to realize the potentialities of living and its concomitant spending? Naturally he is unambitious, content to stick to a routine job and to do only sufficient of that to secure him his bed and board and enough pocket-money to spend his leisure pleasantly according to his lights. Most members of the middle-classes, including nearly all brain-workers, even the worse paid, earn when employed a larger surplus over minimum physical needs than the average manual worker. But so far from admitting that this acts as a damper on their productive energy and ambition, very many of them would claim quite truly that the surplus is insufficient to enable them to make the best of themselves as efficient workers; that they need more margin for physical comfort and mental culture and seeing something of the world if their powers are to reach full development.

In every age and class of life a sudden burst of prosperity is demoralizing, at least when the life-habits have been formed at a lower level. The vulgar extravagance of the war profiteers, the munition girls' fur coats and expensive chocolates, the char-a-bancing on workdays and the duck and green peas of the young miners, which have been the theme of so many not wholly undeserved gibes—all are quite natural manifestations of the same characteristic of human nature; that it takes time for it to adjust itself satisfactorily to new conditions, and that a deluge of wealth is more likely to run off the surface after drowning the crops than to swell the seed and fill the springs of well-being.

It may further be pointed out that it is not only the rising generation which would gain if by making special provision for families, the position of married men and bachelors was equalized. The exertions which are now wrung out of the married man by the fear of seeing his children suffer, may find favour with his employer when contrasted with the slackness of the care-free young men, and on the principle that "human nature is as lazy as it dares to be", it is no doubt good for all of us to have a strong motive for exerting ourselves. Nevertheless, it has not been found that the best work is done under the overseer's lash, and it may be doubted whether the whip of starvation is the most lasting and wholesomely effective kind of incentive either. Apart from the considerations of human happiness involved, and regarding men for the moment simply as beasts of burden, would any team owner or farmer approve a system which required the heaviest loads to be drawn by animals which were just beginning to be past their prime, and simultaneously reduced the quantity and quality of the feeds given these animals? The experience of the war, I believe, shewed that men of from thirty-five upwards were distinctly less able to endure very prolonged spells of exposure and hardship than men in their twenties. Dr. Bowley's figures regarding the conditions in working-class homes [1] prove that married men between thirty-five and forty have the largest number of dependants, and these ages are consequently the height of the privation period in their families. There can be no doubt that a good many cases of premature breakdown or death are caused by the fevered anxiety of affectionate husbands and fathers to add to the family income. This leads them to seize every opportunity of overtime, walk to their work to save fares, and neglect slight illnesses and symptoms of impending trouble.

To sum up: I conclude that it would be entirely to the benefit of industrial efficiency if the workers were all to secure a substantial surplus over subsistence needs, provided that the surplus was normally constant throughout the working life, so that the rising generation should benefit by and be trained to its use. But under the present system, the surplus enjoyed by the average young unmarried workman rather injures than improves his productivity and that of the industry to which he belongs.

This is not the only respect in which the present method of providing for families injuriously affects production—in quantity, in quality and in distribution. In a future chapter I shall discuss the position of the woman wage-earner and shew how her productive capacity is thwarted and curtailed by the jealousy of the male worker—a jealousy due partly to his well-grounded fear that her lesser family responsibilities will enable her to undersell him. But the lower rate of pay of the woman worker has another side to it which may be mentioned here. As the vast majority of wives and children are dependent on men wage-earners, it follows that the cost

---

[1] " Earners and Dependants in English Towns," in *Economica*, May 1921 pp. 109-10.

of rearing the future generations from which *all* industries draw their recruits is thrown mainly upon those industries which employ chiefly adult males.   It happens that these industries include most of those essential to future production— mining, the iron and steel trades, shipbuilding, all the building and transport trades.   On the other hand, the trades which employ a high proportion of female and juvenile labour (labour which is cheap partly because it has, broadly speaking, only itself to keep) are mainly those which provide for immediate consumption—the clothing trades, tobacco, confectionery, the retail distributive trades, hotels and restaurants.   By escaping their share of a charge which is essential to their future existence, these trades are in effect drawing a subsidy from the male trades.   This is a consequence of the present system which has been generally ignored.[1]

(b) The Effect on the Wage-Earner as Husband and Father

What is the effect of the bachelor's surplus on his character as a prospective husband and father?   Again I must repeat that the case we are considering is that of the average youth, destined to remain all his life a member of the rank and file, rather than of the brilliant exception.   Mr. Rowntree suggests that the surplus will be useful to provide the equipment of the future home.   But he answers this argument very effectively himself when he says:—

" I know too much about human beings to assume that we can count upon the voluntary savings of young married people to any appreciable extent.   It is easy for the armchair moralist to charge the working man with being thriftless; but after all, it is harder for a young man to save than for one who is older.   He is at an age when the demand for full life runs high.   His physical vigour is at its maximum; his instincts are generous rather than prudent; and he relies upon himself to cope with fresh demands as they arise by getting more remunerative work, or perhaps by working harder.   He may not wilfully mortgage the future, but he refuses to mortgage the present.   As for children, they may not come, or they may not live; why sacrifice tangible satisfactions day by day to a mere contingency?   Why, again, the finer type of worker may say, refuse help to a comrade who is in actual need, for the sake of preparing to meet a need that is problematical ? "[2]

Everything that is said here of young married men may be said still more truly of young men before marriage.   Indeed it is doubtful whether the youthful bachelor workman usually saves anything at all towards his future home, until the time comes when " that not impossible She, who shall possess my

[1] In their section on Parasitic Trades, *Industrial Democracy*, Part III, Chap. III (d), Mr. and Mrs. Sidney Webb come very near it, but they speak only of trades which pay their workers insufficient for their own healthy maintenance.
[2] *The Human Needs of Labour*, pp. 45-6.

heart and me," has materialized into an individual Gladys Brown or Joyce Robinson. Even then, he probably finds that courtship is an expensive affair, involving presents and outings and—since even the dingy human male must have some mating plumage—visits to outfitters and haberdashers. Unfortunately, perhaps, the extravagant but convenient hire-purchase system has made it possible to set up housekeeping, without even saving up towards the necessary minimum of furniture and household gear.

All this sounds very human and harmless and pleasant, and thrift is by common consent a plain-headed virtue. But in fact it means, that under present conditions a young man usually forms habits of personal expenditure which he finds it impossible to keep up after marriage and when the children begin to come, except at the expense of his family's welfare. And a habit formed at seventeen or eighteen and sustained till twenty-five or thirty is not an easy thing to break.

The influence which this unpretentious-looking little fact has had upon the direction of national expenditure and production would be an interesting and, so far as I know, an entirely novel subject for speculation. Those people of the prosperous classes whose consciences have been made uncomfortable by the revelations of sociological investigators as to the proportion of working-class families who live in poverty, have been wont to reassure themselves by quoting the enormous sums that are spent in public-houses and on the cheaper sorts of tobacco; the takings at football matches and cinema theatres and music halls; the betting that goes on, not only in the parts of race-courses frequented by the plebs, but in every workshop and dockside.

They remind us, for example, that in 1921, a year of depressed trade, the National Drink Bill was £402,726,000, representing an expenditure per head of not less than £8 10s., and per adult of twenty-one years and upwards (including abstainers) £14 4s.;[1] the national expenditure on tobacco was well over £70 million[2] and the expenditure on enter-

[1] " The National Drink Bill for 1921 ", by G. B. Wilson, in *Alliance Year Book* for 1922, p. 89. The taxation on intoxicating liquors was £190,700,000, and the net Drink Bill, therefore, £212,026,000.

[2] The estimated value of tobacco imports retained for home consumption in 1921 was £13.9 million, and the duty paid £56.8 million (*Annual Statement of Trade* for 1921, Vol. II, pp. 455-6); i.e. the value at the port of entry plus duty amounted to over £70 million. The price of the tobacco when it reaches the consumer's hands, and consequently the national expenditure on tobacco, is, of course, considerably greater.

tainments some £50 to £70 million.[1] This, to be sure, is the expenditure of the total population, but they hasten to point out that a very large proportion comes from the pockets of the working classes; that, for instance, out of the total Drink Bill, £263¾ million represents the expenditure on beer —the working-man's drink.

If the working-classes can afford to spend these colossal sums on this sort of thing, they cannot (these critics think) be so very badly off. In any case, why raise wages, if it only means setting more money free to be spent in ways which help to unfit the workers for their work? But have these complacent people ever asked themselves, how much of the luxury expenditure of the working classes is incurred by the bachelors and the childless couples out of the wages which their Trade Union has secured them on the plea of "our wives and families", and how much by the real fathers of real children, who having been wont in their gay young days to spend 50 to 75 per cent. of their earnings on their *menus plaisirs*, fail to see why they should deprive themselves when, after all, "a man's money is his own" and "other fellows' wives have to manage on less."

The question of how much of their wages husbands give their wives is a delicate one, into which no systematic investigation into social conditions has, so far as I know, attempted to probe. A vast amount of evidence on the point, drawn from every section of the wage-earning classes, lies buried in the case-papers of Soldiers' and Sailors' Families Associations and War Pensions Committees all over the country; for it was the duty of these bodies, in assessing the claims of wives to supplementary separation allowances during the war, to ascertain from the wife how much "husband gave" and then to check this, by obtaining from the employer the amount of wages paid. But even this evidence is not entirely reliable, owing to the tendency of claimants to let their replies be coloured by the judgment they had formed as to whether they would secure most from the Government by making out their pre-enlistment condition to have been one of prosperity or poverty.[2] Broadly speaking, the evidence

[1] The receipts from the entertainments duty amounted to £10,313,600 in 1921-2 (*Report of the Commissioners of Excise and Customs*, 1921-2, p. 44). The rate of tax varies according to the price of the tickets (e.g. 3d. on tickets costing from 7d. to 1s., 4d. on tickets from 1s. to 2s., 6d. on those from 2s. to 3s., and so on).
[2] Compare as illustrating the same tendency in another class the difference in the valuation of household effects for probate and insurance.

shewed that the ways of husbands and wives vary like the circumstances of their households, almost infinitely. At one end of the scale comes the type of husband usually described by the humble sort of matrons in my own part of the world as "a proper good husband, Miss; one of the best", who empties into his wife's lap every payday the whole of his earnings and receives back from her, meekly and with gratitude, as much as she thinks proper to allow him. At the other end are husbands whose estimates of family needs resemble those of one individual known to me, earning according to his employer seventy shillings a week besides overtime, whose wife exclaimed ecstatically on first receiving her separation allowance, "Twenty-three shillings a week and only myself and the three children to keep! Why, it will be like sailing on the edge of a cloud". Between these extreme types are vast numbers of men who treat marriage as a real partnership, who regard "my wages" as "our wages" and who plan out the expenditure of the joint income with their wives, so as to ensure that the very smallest amount possible of the suffering that comes during periods of economic stress shall be borne by the children. But there are also large numbers who have another method of smoothing out for their families the ups and downs of their own industrial prosperity, by keeping their wives in a convenient ignorance of the amount of their earnings and habitually handing over to them the minimum sum on which experience has shewn that they can contrive to manage. And these two groups shade off into each other by infinite gradations. I forbear from any attempt to suggest what proportion the selfish bear to the unselfish husbands. Everyone will estimate it differently according to the amount and kind of his experience—and customs vary in different districts and occupations.

Probably those whose experience has been derived from any kind of "social work" will tend to take too pessimistic a view, because such workers are apt to come into intimate contact chiefly with those in whose lives there has been some kind of breakdown. On the other hand class loyalty, and the fact that they themselves associate chiefly with the intellectual aristocracy of the workers, often lead those who profess to speak from "the labour point of view" to minimize the evil of the selfish and self-indulgent husband, as though he were a rare exception in a community of paragons. Neither the facts of individual experience nor the figures of luxury expenditure make such a view tenable.

A drink bill of £402 million is not really explainable in a community where, as shewn in Chapter II,[1] a large proportion of the wage-earners are living below the " poverty line " and a still larger proportion below the level of reasonable " human needs," except by admitting that in a very substantial proportion of households the expenditure is incurred at the cost of going without many things which are necessary to the well-being of the home and children. Nor surely need any working-man feel that in making this admission he is reflecting on the habits of his class in comparison with that of other classes, for in no other does parental affection demand quite the same quantity and quality of self-sacrifice. Middle-class parents whose incomes are low in proportion to the standard of their class have to forgo many pleasures which their fellows enjoy—foreign travel, entertaining, theatre-going, motoring. But they have seldom to choose, even in exceptional circumstances of unemployment or sickness, between going short themselves of nourishing food and warm clothing or seeing their children go short; nor need they feel that even a modest expenditure on the machinery or the ordinary comforts of a full life in a civilized community—on tram fares and postages, tobacco, beer and holidays—must be at the expense of a really adequate food and milk bill. If this were their normal experience in normal times, a subconscious instinct of self-preservation would probably lead them to cultivate a certain insensitiveness to the hardships of their dependants and to acquiesce in a very low estimate of their needs. In claiming a higher standard for himself, the man is supported by the valid plea that the wage-earner's strength must be kept up, as well as by the traditional sanctions of male predominance. Many collectors of working housewives' budgets have noticed how general is the recognition of this by the housewives. Thus Mr. Rowntree says:

" Extraordinary expenditure, such as the purchase of a piece of furniture, is met by reducing the sum spent on food. As a rule, in such cases, it is the wife and sometimes the children who have to forgo a portion of their food—the importance of maintaining the strength of the wage-earner is recognized, and he obtains his ordinary share." [2]

Miss Anna Martin, whose standpoint is that not of an investigator but of one who has lived for many years in close and affectionate familiarity with the married women of a district in South-East London largely inhabited by dock and warehouse labourers, writes:—

" Any increase in the family expenses only touches the father after every other member of the family has been stinted. As the income of the family depends entirely on his health and strength, this is not unreasonable. Nor can he be expected to relinquish his few small luxuries. The members of the Lodge reported considerable dissatisfaction among their husbands over the increased tax on tobacco under the Budget of 1909. When asked what other impost would have been preferred, the women replied : ' The men would rather have had it on the tea or on the sugar; *we* should have had to pay that ; the halfpenny on the ounce of tobacco comes out of their bit ' " [1]

Mrs. Pember Reeves, analysing the expenditure of families living "round about a pound a week", calculates the cost of the man's food alone at 4*s*. 6*d*. to 5*s*. a week, the food for wife and children working out at less than 3*d*. a head per day.[2] Mr. Rowntree estimates the physiological food needs of a woman as ·8 those of a man[3]—a much larger proportion than she actually gets according to the above reckoning.

While not denying the supreme importance of keeping the wage-earners in good health, it may be suggested that a wife who during a large part of the period of maximum dependency is either pregnant or nursing a child has also her " special need " of nourishment. The right of a man to a higher standard of living being however so generally acknowledged, the transition from that into excessive expenditure is only a matter of degree, and he may easily be led into keeping for himself an unfair share of the family income. Everyone knows from personal experience how easy it is to persuade oneself that little self-indulgent habits formed during a period of holiday or ill-health have become necessary to one's health and efficiency. The uniform wage system encourages the formation of such habits, not only by the amount of pocket-money which it gives to young unmarried men, but by the mental confusion it engenders. This enables them at one moment to fight the battle of higher wages from behind the petticoats of their hypothetical wives and children and the next to claim the wages thus won as their exclusive property, earned by the sweat of their brows, which they are free to spend at will on keeping a wife or backing a winner.

[1] ";The Married Working Woman," by Anna Martin, in *Nineteenth Century*, January 1911, pp. 113-14.

[2] *Round About a Pound a Week*, pp. 140, 142-3.

[3] *The Human Needs of Labour*, p. 87.

(c) **The Effect on the Children**

Although the foregoing reflections have been necessary to a complete treatment of my subject, it would be a mistake to attach too much importance to them, or to suppose that the case against the uniform wage-system rests to any considerable extent on the imperfections of husbands—those very human and sometimes apparently even endearing imperfections. Suppose that every husband and father belonged to the type assumed in Mr. Rowntree's earlier model budget—that he " turned up " every penny of his wages to his wife for housekeeping purposes and neither drank nor smoked. Suppose that every such husband was mated to a wife of corresponding perfections as a housekeeper, who in the intervals of doing all the work of her household found time to study scientific food values, to buy everything in the cheapest market and to use it to the best advantage. Even such a model couple as that is not a match for the laws of arithmetic. Not having the secret of the widow's cruse or the table spread in the wilderness, they cannot make an income of 30s. or 50s. or 70s. yield as satisfactory results when spread over the needs of seven persons as over the needs of two or three. Working-class mothers, I grant, come nearer to performing miracles than most people, but they are miracles of appearance rather than of reality. Margarine can be made to look like butter and flannelette like flannel, but it is not so easy to give the same nourishing and warming qualities. The more ordinary type of housewife does not even succeed in cheating appearances. Most experienced observers at a mothers' meeting could pick out first and possibly second babies by their frilled and spotless get-up. Later comers in the family have to put up with the limp and faded cast-offs of their predecessors. And as it is with their outward raiment, so with all the other circumstances of their lives. Everything that the third, fourth, fifth child consumes—its food, its clothing, its share of bedding, soap, and mother's care—is filched from a supply which seemed only just to go round before it came. Everyone acquainted with well-to-do nurseries knows that the attitude of the ex-baby to the baby is not always impeccable, but that is due to an unworthy jealousy. The grievances of the ex-baby in a poor home are all too real, though having learnt from the first to expect little of life it makes less fuss about them.

Mrs. Pember Reeves, discussing the children of her low-paid workers' families living on about a pound a week, says:—

"The ex-baby, where such a person existed, was nearly always undersized, delicate and peevish. Apart from such causes as insufficient and improper food, crowded sleeping quarters and wretched clothing, this member of the family specially suffered from want of fresh air. Too young to go out alone, with no one to carry it now the baby had come, it lived in the kitchen, dragging at its mother's skirts, much on its legs but never in the open air. One of the conveniences most needed by poor mothers is a perambulator which will hold, if possible, her two youngest children. With such a vehicle, there would be some sort of chance of open air and change of scene so desperately necessary for the three house-bound members of the family. As it is, the ex-baby is often imprisoned in a high chair, where it cannot fall into the fire, or pull over the water-can, or shut its finger in the crack of the door, or get at the food. But here it is deprived of exercise and freedom of limb, and develops a fretful, thwarted character, which renders it even more open to disease than the rest of the family, though they share with it all the other bad conditions.

"There is no doubt that the healthy infant at birth is less healthy at three months, less healthy still at a year, and often by the time it is old enough to go to school it has developed rickets or lung trouble through entirely preventable causes." [1]

Of the other children covered in her enquiry Mrs. Pember Reeves says

"The outstanding fact" about them "was not their stupidity nor their lack of beauty—they were neither stupid nor ugly—it was their puny size and damaged health . . . The 42 families investigated . . . have had altogether 201 children, but 18 of these were either born dead or died within a few hours. Of the remaining 183 children of all ages, ranging from a week up to sixteen or seventeen years, 39 have died, or over one-fifth. Out of 144 survivors 5 were actually deficient, while many were slow in intellect or unduly excitable." [2]

The ex-baby, in common with its brothers and sisters, had a much better chance in war-time, at least if its father was serving. Then the arrival of a new-comer in the family meant that a few weeks later the mother would draw on her ring-paper the first instalment with arrears of the little weekly income of 5s. or 3s. 6d. or 2s.[3] assigned for its special use by a grateful nation which had become conscious of the father's actual and its own potential value as a defender. Often one of the earliest uses made of the timely increment was to negotiate the hire-purchase of that perambulator which, as Mrs. Pember Reeves observes, is so badly needed if the young members of a family housed in cramped and sunless quarters are to enjoy that air and sunshine necessary to all young growing things. More often still, the extra money meant simply that the household expenditure on the neces-saries of life expanded with its increased numbers, instead of, as in pre-war days, remaining always the same quotient with a different divisor and a shrinking dividend.

[1] *Round About a Pound a Week*, p.179.
[2] *Ibid.*, pp. 193-4.
[3] The amounts for first, second and subsequent children were different and the scale was increased several times during the war.

The good effects of separation allowances on child welfare have been generally recognized, but the magnitude of their influence has been to some extent obscured by the number of other conditions peculiar to war-time which pulled in the opposite direction. These conditions were familiar at the time to everyone who was in touch with the lives of working-class families, but the impressions of the war period seem to be fading so fast that it is well to remind ourselves of some of them. For example, in war-time scavenging was at its worst owing to the scarcity of labour. Streets were left unswept and the ashbins left unemptied so long that their contents overflowed into the yards and back streets. Refuse was blown by the wind through the windows and down the throats of the passers-by, especially the children whose heads are so near the ground. Housing conditions, always atrocious among the lower-paid workers, grew steadily worse throughout the war. House building entirely stopped and four years' growth of population spread itself into every crevice of an already insufficient house supply. The landlords, feeling themselves hardly used by the Rent Restriction Act, and urged on all sides to avoid employing labour, usually refused to execute even the most necessary repairs. Cleaning materials and all other articles of a housewife's equipment became scarce and dear. Visitors entrusted with the payment of allowances to soldiers' wives came back with scandalized accounts of the conditions of overcrowding, dilapidation and vermin amid which they found respectable women were struggling to keep their families healthy and clean.

As to food, the restricted supply of meat and fresh milk were comparatively unimportant to the poorer class of women and children, who usually consume little of either. But the coarseness of war bread and the dearness and scarcity of fats and sugar made a great difference in the daily diet, while the food-card system and the demand of the well-to-do for " offal " and other odds and ends of food usually left for the poor, severely limited the housewife's opportunities for picking up savoury morsels, which in normal times do so much to make coarse and monotonous fare masticable by overtired women and delicate children.

Besides all these material discomforts there was the mental strain, reacting on the nerves and temper of the whole family, of continual anxiety for husbands and sons at the Front and (in some parts of the country) of fear of air-raids. There was also the physical strain on the large numbers of married women who undertook industrial employment of an unaccustomed and often very strenuous kind.

Bearing all these facts in mind, the following statements, picked out from a mass of similar evidence, surely speak volumes for the steadying effect of economic security and especially, as regards the large section dependent on separation allowances, of incomes proportionate to family needs:—

From the reports of the Chief Medical Officer of the Board of Education :—
" With few exceptions there is a clear statement on the part of School Medical Officers that war conditions resulted in substantial improvement in the physique of the children," e.g. in London, Birmingham, Bradford, Sheffield, Swansea, Newcastle-on-Tyne, Cornwall.[1]
The report for 1916 notes that children, generally speaking, were better clothed than at any time since medical inspection was introduced.[2]
The report for 1918 notes that the number of children receiving school meals was the lowest on record.[3]
From the report of the Medical Officer of the London County Council :
" The story is . . . one of continuous amelioration throughout the whole period of the war. Whether judged from the state of the children's clothing, from their health as expressed by their nutritional well-being or from the conditions found as regards cleanliness, the result is the same, practically steady improvement in each particular . . . In both sexes and at all ages there was a continuous decline in the percentage of children returned as poorly nourished and in each section the number of such children was in 1918 less than half the number found in 1913."[4]
From the reports of the Registrar-General for England and Wales :—
The Report for 1916 says: "The very considerable mortality of the first year of life has declined in a most interesting manner since the outbreak of war . . . The conditions under which confinements take place, may, for instance, have been improved by separation allowances." [5]
The report for 1917 says: "The war employment of women in industry has thus been accompanied by an actual fall in infantile mortality from premature births", in spite of the increased employment of married women. " The fall may conceivably be explained as the consequence of improvement in other circumstances under war conditions neutralizing the harmful effects of increased industrial employment." [6]
The figures for the pre-war and war years shew that the number of deaths of women from alcoholism and of infants from overlying decreased steadily and rapidly throughout the war.[7]

During 1919, the army was rapidly demobilizing. There was considerable prosperity; yet the report of the Chief Medical Officer of the Board of Education notes that

"there are not lacking some signs of slight deterioration at all ages during 1919 and 1920, particularly among infants entering school life and in London also amongst boys of eight . . . and girls of 12 " [8]

and there is a similar note of uneasiness in the report of the Medical Officer of the London County Council.[9] Before 1920

[1] Report for 1922, p. 120.   [2] Cd. 8746, p. 142.   [3] Cmd. 420, p. 174.
[4] Report of Medical Officer of Health of L.C.C. for 1918, pp. 25-6.
[5] Cd. 8869, p. xxxiv.   [6] Cmd. 40, p. xxxviii.
[7] See especially the discussions in the Reports of the Registrar-General for 1916 and subsequent years. I have not forgotten that there were other causes contributing to these results. The reader will form his own opinion of their relative importance.   [8] Cmd. 1522, p. 146.   [9] Reports for 1919 and 1920.

was over a period of unemployment had begun and through the relief measures taken to cope with it the country entered on the second great experiment in incomes proportionate to family needs. The significance of the facts in relation to our subject has I think been generally overlooked.

As everyone knows, the depression has been the severest experienced in living memory. At its height over $1\frac{3}{4}$ million persons were unemployed, and including the under-employment of those on short time it is reckoned that a fifth of the labour power of the country had been running to waste. Yet after the strain had continued for three years, the testimony of experts was unanimous that on the whole the physical condition of the children was well maintained. For example:—

" The broad conclusion at which School Medical Officers arrive is that the general health and physique of school children is at least as good now as it was before the war." [1]

Abundant and detailed testimony to the same effect is contained in a report recently issued by a number of well-known sociologists, after an enquiry in a number of typical towns and country districts. They agree that

" The widespread physical distress, which was the normal accompaniment of unemployment in previous depressions, has been prevented . . . In the past two winters, with unemployment far more extensive and severe than in any other pre-war depression, this physical distress is not noticeable." [2]

A good deal of the evidence quoted goes further than this and compares present conditions in some respects favourably not only with previous periods of depression but with times of normal employment, and with regard to the health of the children this view is practically unanimous. The reports from the various districts are also unanimous in attributing the saving of the situation in this respect to insurance allowances, Poor Law Relief and school feeding, helped out by savings from the period of separation allowances and high wages. Further they make it clear that the class which has suffered most, not merely in relation to their previous position but absolutely, is that of the upper grade workers—artizans, clerks, etc.—whose savings were largest but who were prevented by pride from accepting Poor Law relief or school meals for their children unless they were absolutely forced to do it.

But only in a single passage, and without apparently

[1] Report of the Chief Medical Officer of the Board of Education for 1922, p. 121.

[2] *The Third Winter of Unemployment:* Report by J. J. Astor, A. L. Bowley, Henry Clay, Robert Grant, W. T. Layton, P. J. Pybus, B. Seebohm Rowntree, George Schuster and F. D. Stuart (P. S. King, 1923), p. 69.

appreciating its supreme importance, do they allude to the feature common to all three forms of public assistance which has made them jointly so surprisingly effective in proportion to their money cost, that they are all adjusted to some extent, though in the case of unemployment benefit only to the meagre extent of 5s. for the wife and 1s. for each child, to the real needs of real human beings instead of being, like wages, based on a fiction.

"The reason everywhere given is the same. Health is better than in pre-war depressions, because the pre-war starvation is prevented. The unemployment insurance benefit, *especially since it was proportioned to need by the allowances for dependants*, has relieved many who would have endured months of privation before resort to the Poor Law ; while the greater resort to the Poor Law, and the more generous scale of relief awarded, have ensured a regular supply of good food in many homes that were not too well fed when trade was good . . . . It is even possible that in some cases, those in the lowest ranks of self-supporting workers, the real position of the family has been improved ; *relief allowances are usually proportioned to size of family, which wages are not*, and Poor Law authorities usually see that their relief takes the form in large part of wholesome food." [1]

From all this emerges the remarkable conclusion, that an army of about 1½ million wage-earners, with over 2½ million dependants, have been tided over three years' unemployment without apparent injury to the children and with relatively little deterioration in their social condition. This has been achieved by the help of an expenditure of money which could not conceivably have yielded the same result if distributed in wages in the ordinary way. The following figures will roughly illustrate this.

The Report shews the amount spent on Unemployment relief during the year ending March 31st, 1922, to have been as follows:—[2]

Unemployment Insurance Fund .. £67½ million.
Poor Law Relief .. .. .. £7½ to £8 million.
Relief works .. .. £6 million.
Miscellaneous (school meals, etc.) .. £1½ to £1¾ million.

making a total of £82½ to £83¼ million.

The average number of unemployed of both sexes and all ages during the same period is estimated to have been 1½ millions, with 2,580,000 dependants. Of the unemployed, 1,130,000 were adult males. As the report points out, to have maintained these men at the minimum used in *Livelihood and Poverty* (a standard very near Mr. Rowntree's " poverty

[1] *Ibid.*, p. 70. The italics are mine. [2] *Ibid.*, p. 62.

line "[1]) would have cost, at current prices, £160 million.[2] By common consent, the good value obtained for the sum expended is due largely to the fact that the grant made was to some extent proportioned to the size of families and safeguarded for the provision of necessaries.[3]

(d) The Effect on the Wife

It is customary among the well-to-do classes to attribute the high rate of mortality and the low standard of health among the children of the poor to the ignorance and carelessness of their mothers and every improvement in their condition to the efforts made in recent years to instruct and train them. The days are passed when it was assumed that mothers could attain perfection in their art aided only by the light of nature and by the traditions handed down by old wives to young wives. We have now an elaborate machinery of pre-natal and post-natal clinics, health visitors, and domestic science teachers, designed to supplement the meagre and half-forgotten information given to little girls at school. The development of this kind of organization reached its high water mark during the war, when the public conscience became seriously alarmed about the dangers of a C 3 population. It is to this period we owe the institution of Baby Week—that annual festival at which all manner of societies and individuals engaged in teaching the working-class mother draw together for mutual encouragement and for a collective effort to glorify the functions of motherhood and impress on those who discharge it the truth that theirs is indeed " work of national importance". At the present time, it is the general public and the politicians who seem to stand most in need of the reminder; the sense of the importance of the child population having been almost obliterated by the overwhelming desire for economy. But even when the propaganda was most fashionable, its value was to some extent spoiled by the tendency of the propagandists to overestimate the educational aspects of the problem and to

---

[1] Not the more generous estimate of *The Human Needs of Labour*, but the one based on the barest physical necessities (*see* above, pp. 21-22).

[2] *The Third Winter of Unemployment*, pp. 65-6.

[3] In saying this I have not, of course, forgotten that the army of the unemployed is not a standing army, but is constantly being recruited from, and itself recruiting, the army of employed. Nor have the unemployed been living only on relief, but also on savings, help of relatives, etc. But this is also true to some extent of wage-earners in normal times.

underestimate its economic side. It may be questioned whether it has ever occurred to any but a negligible fraction of Medical Officers of Health, inspectors, councillors, committee men and subscribers, concerned in child-welfare schemes, that if motherhood is a craft (as doubtless in a sense it is), it differs from every other craft known to man in that there is no money remuneration for the mother's task, no guarantee of her maintenance while she performs it and (most important yet most ignored of all) no consequential relationship recognized by society between the quantity and quality of her product and the quantity and quality of the tools and materials which she has at her disposal. Children are the mother's product, food, clothing, and other necessaries her materials and tools; but a plumber's wife with one puling infant has power to purchase more of these necessaries than the plumber's labourer's wife, though she be the efficient mother of a hungry family of six. Her command of materials depends in fact not on her own skill or productivity, but on a circumstance entirely irrelevant to her personality, on her husband's occupational value to the community and his power of extracting that value from his employer.

We are all so familiar with this arrangement that scarcely anyone, except a few feminists and recently a few of the working mothers themselves, sees anything anomalous about it. The husband, if a trade unionist, is insistent on his claim for a " living wage " sufficient for the needs of a family, but he thinks of the family as part of his own multiple personality. It is *his* family that has to be kept out of the fruits of *his* toil, the remuneration of *his* value to the community. The sentimentalist, who has taken motherhood under his special protection, is shocked at the bare suggestion that anything so sordid as remuneration, anything so prosaic as the adjustment of means to ends, should be introduced into the sacred institution of the family and applied to the profession of motherhood. Yet is it not much as though there were some kind of unwritten tradition, handed down from antiquity, which compelled the members of one guild of craftsmen, let us say hatters, to carry on the business of their craft only by entering into individual partnership with the members of some other craft; the hatter asking no price for his hats, but being maintained and supplied with materials by the partner of his choice according to the latter's ability and goodwill? One can imagine that if such an arrangement had lasted for several generations, it would acquire a sort of religious sanctity in the eyes of the majority of mankind, to whom custom is as a religion. Members of other crafts would uphold it, because it ministered to their sense of dignity and importance and because it enabled them to claim remuneration enough for the support of two crafts, while remaining free to maintain only one if they chose. Hatters would be induced to acquiesce by representations that just because it was their function to clothe the noblest part of the human frame, the seat of the brain, it would be an insult to offer them remuneration like ordinary trades-people. Occasionally someone of independent mind would point out that the arrangement was not calculated to encourage efficiency among hatters nor to secure a satisfactory supply of hats, but the protest would carry little weight with a community which in addition to being prejudiced by tradition, had never been accustomed to pay directly for its hats and so did not realize that it was paying for them indirectly and in the most wasteful possible way. Objectors would be invited to notice that the craftsmen who actually supported hatters and enabled them to exercise their craft, in fact worked harder than those who merely drew the money and used it for other purposes, and the ridiculous arrangement would be praised for the industry of the former section instead of being blamed for the idleness of the latter.

To make this parallel complete, it would be necessary to add certain flourishes to which it is difficult to give verisimilitude, as, for example, that the contract between the hatter and the other craftsman was usually entered into in youth, when both parties were in a state of intoxication induced by a certain strong sweet wine; that it was a lifelong contract which could not be broken without incurring severe social penalties; that the clauses in it ensuring the hatter's right to maintenance were extremely vague and nearly impossible to enforce, but that among the higher grades of craftsmen it was customary to supplement these by a voluntary settlement arranged by the parents of the parties; and finally, that society, or at least all its more conservative sections, frowned severely on any attempt by the hatter to limit his production of hats to the number he could achieve satisfactorily out of the material allowed him by his partner and encouraged him to spin it out into as many head-coverings as possible, while never ceasing to scold him for the progressive deterioration in their quality.

I think it must be admitted that this is not a travesty but a fair representation of the economic conditions under which the delicate operation of bearing children and the highly-skilled work of rearing them through infancy to maturity is carried on.

The position of the wife and mother in this and most other western countries according to theory and sentiment, according to law, and according to prevalent practice is a curious example of human inconsistency. Popular sentiment places her a little lower, than the angels; the law a little higher than a serf. In life as it is lived in four households out of five or nine out of ten, her position is neither that of angel nor serf, but of an extremely hard worked but quite adequately valued member of the family; her husband's partner with functions different from his but recognized as equally or nearly equally important; the administrator of the bulk of the family income; with a hold on the affections of her children usually stronger than his and on their obedience (so far as that virtue is practised at all by the modern child) only a little less strong. In the fifth or tenth household— the proportion is important but as it is unprovable I will not discuss it except to say that I incline myself slightly to the more pessimistic view—the husband uses his power to make her position nearly or quite as bad as, or worse than, the law permits.

The case against the present economic system as it affects wives and mothers is seen in its ugliest aspect in the latter group of households, but it does not depend for its existence upon them. It is concerned mainly with those anomalies in the married woman's lot which depend neither on the law nor on husbands, but upon the failure of the machinery of distribution to adapt itself to the conditions brought about partly by the industrial revolution and partly by our modern conception of what is due to a child—conditions which have changed her and her children from producers into dependants without making any provision for their maintenance except through the imperfectly realized theory of the family living wage.

I will deal first with these anomalies as they affect the

normal household, and afterwards with the position of the unhappily married wife.

(i) *The Wife in the Normal Home*

The physical effects of the present system on the mother have already been touched on in a previous section.[1] We saw that when the food money is insufficient to provide enough for everyone (and as our comparison between estimates of needs and actual wage-rates shewed, this is the normal state of things in a very large proportion of families during the years of greatest dependency) the mother's way of making it go round is first of all to stint herself. This does not necessarily imply extraordinary unselfishness on her part. It is the natural expedient to which probably any normally conscientious person would resort, who had the responsibility of buying, cooking and serving the food of a hungry family. But of course working-class mothers are unselfish to a fault, where the needs of their offspring are concerned. Also (though that is much less generally recognized) necessity has made many of them very resourceful. The children in many homes are so much accustomed to see their mother produce a dinner out of the most inadequate resources that they no more expect her to fail, than well-to-do children expect a conjurer to fail in producing the usual rabbit out of an empty hat.

Popular sentiment from the Old Testament downwards has never failed to pay its tribute to the devotion of mothers, but only a few women observers, so far as I know, have called attention to the steadily increasing strain on their resources and endurance caused by the rising standard of educational and social requirements. Compulsory education, prohibition of wage-earning by school-children, abolition of half-time, restriction on home work which tends to drive it into the factory, have reduced the wife's chance of supplementing what her husband " turns up " by her own or the children's earnings. Through medical inspection at school, the visits of a health visitor when a baby is born, her own attendance at a child-welfare centre, her attention is continually being called to some fresh requirement said, perhaps with truth, to be essential to a healthy home, but involving on her part more labour in cooking, washing, scrubbing, sewing and

[1] *See* above, p. 43.

contriving and demanding better utensils and materials than she has money to buy. Miss Anna Martin records the contrast between old standards and new drawn by one of her Rotherhithe mothers:—

" When I was ten years old I was helping my parents by gathering stones for the farmers; now, I send four girls to school every day with starched pinafores and blackened boots. Except on Sundays, my father never had anything but bread and cold bacon, or cheese, for his dinner ; now I have to cook a hot dinner every day for the children and a hot supper every evening for my man".[1]

How often it happens that there is in a family a small child who has to be carried once or twice a week to an outpatient department (each attendance involving several hours' waiting), a baby requiring to be nursed, and several children to be got off to school punctually. If the mother neglects to take the child to hospital, or leaves the baby alone in the house, or keeps an older child at home to attend to it, she is liable to be prosecuted and fined. Even if she escapes that, she is almost certain to be scolded by the aggrieved official responsible for the particular department of child welfare she has flouted.

Mrs. Pember Reeves and Miss Anna Martin have both collected time-tables from some of their friends among working housewives, shewing how their days are usually spent. Each time-table varies in detail, but the collective result is so much the same that a single specimen may suffice. It is the day of one of the South London wives who kept house on about a pound a week. She had four children, the eldest eight and the youngest a few months old; but as she lived in buildings, with her room and water supply on the same floor, and had an old mother who came in to help daily, it is one of the easiest time-tables of those recorded. This was her day:—[2]

4.30.—Wake husband, who has to be at work about 5 o'clock. He is a carman for an L.C.C. contractor. Get him off if possible without waking the four children. He has a cup of tea before going but breakfasts away from home. If baby wakes, nurse him.

7.15.—Get up and light fire, wake children, wash two eldest ones. Get breakfast for self and children.

8.0.—Breakfast.

8.30.—Tidy two children for school and start them off at 8.45.

9.0.—Clear away and wash up; wash and dress boy of three ; bathe and dress baby.

10.0.—Nurse baby and put him to bed.

10.30.—Turn down beds, clean grate, scrub floor.

11.30.—Make beds.

12.0.—Mother, who has done the marketing, brings in the food ; begin to cook dinner.

[1] "The Married Working-Woman," *Nineteenth Century*, Dec. 1910, pp. 1105-6.
[2] *Round About a Pound a Week*, pp. 164-6.

12.15.—Children all in, lay dinner, and with mother's help tidy children for it.
1.0.—Dinner, which mother serves while Mrs. G. nurses baby who wakes about then.
1.30.—Tidy children for school again.
1.45.—Start them off and sit down with mother to their own dinner ; wash up ; tidy room ; clean themselves.
3.0.—Go out, if it is not washing-day or day for doing the stairs, with baby and boy of three.
3.45.—Come in and get tea for children. Put boy of three to sleep, nurse baby.
4.15.—Children come in.
4.30.—Give children tea.
5.0.—Wash up and tidy room. Tidy children and self.
6.0.—Go out for a " blow in the street " with all four children.
7.0.—Come in and put children to bed. Nurse baby.
7.30.—Husband returns ; get his supper.
8.0.—Sit down and have supper with him.
8.30.—Clear away and wash up. . . . Get everything ready for the morning. Mend husband's clothes as soon as he gets them off.
10.0—Nurse baby and go to bed.

After reading these time records one sympathizes with one of the mothers—one with eight children—who, when asked what she had most enjoyed during a fortnight's convalescence at the seaside, replied after some reflection, " I on'y 'ad two babies along of me, an' w'en I come in me dinner was cooked for me".[1]

Public opinion—wiser than the statisticians who classify these women as " unoccupied " and " non-producers "—recognizes that " a woman's work is never done." Nevertheless it may be compatible with happiness and health; but not when complicated by all the discomforts and restrictions of extreme poverty; when her workshop is a dark and insanitary little house in a court or back street; when every penny spent on soap and cleaning materials, on the most necessary utensils of her craft, on repairs, clothing and recreation, is taken off the food money; when the routine of incessant drudgery goes on from year to year without break or change except those brought about by the recurrent episodes of birth, sickness and death.

It is much easier for obvious reasons to measure by statistics the health of husbands and children than of wives and mothers. As they are not entitled (unless wage-earners themselves) to compensation for accidents, or insurance during sickness or invalidity, no public record is kept of their lapses from health. They are not subject to medical inspection like the children, and suffer less from infectious diseases requiring notification. For similar reasons, their illnesses and ailments far seldomer come under medical treatment. The man, if unfit to work,

[1] *Ibid.*, pp. 168-9.

must consult his doctor and make some show of following his advice, or lose his sick-pay, and he gets his treatment free. The child, whether sick or merely suffering from a " defect", must be put under the doctor, because the law and public opinion and parental affection combine to require it. The mother of a young family with small means seldom calls in the doctor unless absolutely compelled. She cannot afford the fees of a private doctor or the time wasted in attending a dispensary. When actually ill, the man knows that he serves his family best by allowing himself to be taken to hospital and allocating his sick pay to his dependants. The wife in like case calls in the nearest cheap doctor and continues to direct the household from her sick-bed.

For these reasons no doubt it is in vain that the records most likely to contain evidence as to the health of working-class mothers have been searched, without furnishing any evidence worth speaking of, except the grim fact that the deaths of mothers in child-birth have decreased not at all during the last twenty-five years,[1] and a few remarks testifying that mothers, unlike children, have not escaped unscathed from the physical effects of recent years of unemployment.[2]

In default of official evidence therefore I will venture to give my own impression [3] of the health of married working-women. It is that among those of the poorer sections, from early middle age onwards, the standard of health is deplorably low and that, if any method existed of testing their condition comparable to that of the medical examination of school-children or recruits for enlistment, the proportion of those found suffering from some definite defect or chronic ailment would startle everyone. The physical appearance of many of them, the lines round their mouth and eyes, their complexion and the texture of their skins, dry and brittle or moist and flaccid, the prematurely thinned or whitened

---

[1] Annual Report of the Chief Medical Officer of the Ministry of Health, 1922.

[2] E.g. in *The Third Winter of Unemployment* (see above, p. 49 n.) it is reported that in Glasgow, " the midwives say they have to get more medical assistance now because the women are not as strong as they used to be. Our opinion is that this is due to under-nourishment. The mothers always are the first to suffer " (p. 202). In Stoke-on-Trent " the increasing evidence of malnutrition of mothers is unmistakable " (p. 297).

[3] I.e. an impression based on about thirty years' intermittent experience as a social worker, investigator of industrial conditions, and (during the war) organizer of assistance to soldiers' and sailors' wives in Liverpool. In these various capacities I must have interviewed several thousand married working-women of various grades and had more or less prolonged dealings with several hundreds of them.

hair, the stooping shoulders and dragging gait all seem to testify to an endurance of physical discomfort and weariness so habitual and so habitually repressed that it has become subconscious. They are like the outward and visible embodiment of all the circumstances of their own hard and sunless lives.

It is often necessary for sensitive people, when imagining conditions which they have not personally experienced, to remind themselves of Pascal's saying: "Il ne faut pas attribuer a l'état où nous ne sommes pas, les passions de l'état où nous sommes". But many well-to-do people carry the spirit of the saying a great deal too far. Conditions which would seem to well-to-do women an intolerable injustice and cruelty if they themselves, or those they care for, had to live under them for a week, do not move them to the least pang of pity when they see them endured by people of another class or race or sex. Those of their friends who worry about the conditions of the slums, or starving children in Russia, or over-worked women at home, seem to them as unreasonable as children who pity the poor fishes for living in the cold sea. They have a set of comfortable maxims to preach down all such scruples. "These people are used to it." "They have no nerves and do not suffer like educated people." "Working-women enjoy poor health." "They like being never alone." "If you gave them baths they would use them to keep coal or ducks." "See how they waste their money in drink." And every bit of evidence that human nature adjusts itself to bad conditions and is not always utterly miserable under them, or again that it has succumbed and been deteriorated by them, is stored up and triumphantly quoted to prove that there is no need or that it is of no use to change them. Those who have been in real touch with the lives of the poor—at least of those of them who have not been hopelessly degraded to the level of their environment—know how fundamentally untrue beneath their superficial truth are the consolations offered by these easy optimists. Suffering cannot be measured by its outward expression or even by the extent to which it is expressed in the conscious mind of the sufferer. To express a feeling even to oneself usually implies some hope of relief and is itself a form of relief. It may be questioned whether almost the worst sort of suffering is not subconscious, instinctive, unlocalized, like the "feeling ill all over" of which people dying of some incurable chronic complaint often complain, when roused out of their torpor by questionings about their symptoms. The facial expression of many middle-aged mothers in their normal health, with its look of repressed endurance, is often curiously like that of these chronic invalids, and when they do fumblingly express themselves, it becomes clear that they too are feeling ill all over, mentally and morally if not physically.

As regards mental suffering, it seems probable that educated women of another class, if driven by misfortune to live under the same physical conditions as the poor, would suffer quite differently, but I doubt whether they would suffer more, unless their misfortunes were their own fault and so intensified by the worst pain of regret. They would probably become bitter and angry, or despairing and distraught, as the working woman seldom does. But they would have consolations not so open to her; the hope of climbing out of their conditions, or of helping to change them for others through some political or social movement; or at least the power of detaching themselves occasionally from their surroundings and calling up before their minds the beautiful things in literature and nature with which they are stored. Most educated people, I think, hardly realize how much of their daily satisfactions they owe to this power, exercised semi-consciously at all the duller moments of life, in the wakeful hours of night, in trains and trams, when the babel of surrounding voices merges itself into the babble of streams over stones and the roar of passing traffic into the surge of the sea and the wind in the trees. But the possession of this sort of private listening-in apparatus implies not only a store of the right kind of experiences to draw on, but the power of reconstructing them which belong, I fancy, chiefly to the cultivated mind. Here again it is dangerous to generalize, but so far as one can tell, the mind of the ordinary working-woman is occupied with what is immediately present to her in place and time. While it is not tormented, as the mind of "her betters" would be in similar circumstances, by the sense of injustice or by anxiety about the future, neither is it lit up by the rays of imagination or of hope.

So far we have been considering the present system chiefly as it affects the physical well-being of the women, especially in the poorer households. But it would be a mistake to suppose that its effects are only physical, or that they are limited to cases of poverty. The tacit refusal of Society to recognize that the services of the wife and mother have any value to the community which entitles her to a share in the national dividend has also indirect consequences, which affect in varying degrees all ranks of married women.

One of these indirect consequences is connected very closely with the questions of health and well-being which we have just been discussing. The system leads to an immense amount of wasted and misapplied domestic labour and consequently to a far lower standard of comfort than would be attainable, if the same resources were better applied. This is true in a slight degree even of servant-keeping homes, but it applies chiefly to all ranks below the servant-keeping class. Many writers on wages, such as Professor Pigou, Mr. J. J. Mallon, Mrs. Sidney Webb and Mr. R. H. Tawney, have pointed out that one of the effects of an abundant supply of cheap, unorganized labour is to encourage slovenly and antiquated methods of production and that when employers have been compelled by Trade Boards, or war-time scarcity, to raise wages, one result has been seen in better organization and improved machinery. Similarly, the dearness and scarcity of domestic service in the United States compared to this country has led to a much more extended use of labour-saving contrivances. But if cheap labour leads to waste, how much more true is that of labour which is altogether unpaid? It may be said that this should not apply to the unpaid labour of the housewife; since she is in effect her own employer. Few husbands actually exercise their legal right absolutely to control " the management of the house, the allotment of the rooms for various purposes, the arrangement of the furniture, the style of the decorations, the hours of meals",[1] etc., of the households they pay for. But the laws and customs which not only set no price on the labour of a wife, but give her no claim to any return for it except to be protected, as a dog or a cat is, from starvation or cruelty, naturally have affected the wife's sense of the value of her own time and strength. In a community where nearly all other services are measured in money, not much account is taken, at least by uneducated people, of unpaid

[1] *Husband and Wife in the Law*, by E. Jenks, p. 48.

services. It is not only of the labour of wives that this is true. Everyone who has had much to do with philanthropic committees knows how recklessly they often waste the services of voluntary workers, sending a visitor several miles to visit a single case in a street which will be visited by another visitor an hour later, doing every letter by hand to save buying a typewriter and so on.

In a hundred ways our social customs, our domestic architecture, our ideas of decoration and dress, shew signs of the undervaluation of domestic work, especially that of housewives of the present and the servants of the past. A clever little pamphlet on *The Uses of Costing*, issued as one of a series by the Ministry of Reconstruction during the war, began by demonstrating the waste of labour caused by a badly planned house. It compared, with illustrative charts, the real labour cost as measured by the number of feet walked by a housewife in preparing afternoon tea for five people, in a badly equipped, old-fashioned kitchen (340 ft.) and in a compact well-equipped one (34 ft.), and suggested that an average of an hour per day for every British housewife is a modest estimate of the waste of human brain and energy caused by ill-planned homes, lacking in even the cheaper and more obvious kind of labour-saving devices. No one acquainted with the usual types of working-class and middle-class houses will think this estimate too high. Assuming there to be roughly about eight million separate dwellings in the United Kingdom [1] this implies a waste of fifty-six million hours per week, which if the modest value of sixpence an hour were put on the housewife's services would be equivalent to a loss of £73 million per annum. It may be said that this is unsound, because a housewife's wasted odds and ends of time have no value in the labour market. If saved to her, they could not be used anywhere else. Not for wages, though even that is not strictly true in neighbourhoods where skilled domestic help is in great demand. But they could be used in her own home in rendering services—now undone or done badly—of very great value, economic as well as moral.

There is, I suppose, no occupation in the world which has an influence on the efficiency and happiness of the members of nearly all other occupations so continuous and so per-

[1] The Census of 1911 gave 7,142,000 inhabited houses.

meating as that of the working housewife and mother. On nearly every day of his life, from cradle to grave, the future or present wage-earner is affected in his health, his spirits, his temper, his ambitions, his outlook on Society and judgment of its arrangements, by the conditions of his home and the personality of the woman who runs it. Potentially, the work of that woman is as highly skilled as that of half a dozen ordinary craftsmen. If the minds of Soyer and Eustace Miles, Paquin and Liberty, Froebel and Mme. Montessori, Dr. Coué, Mrs. Carlyle and Mrs. J. S. Mill were rolled into one and embodied in one working housewife, they would find scope in her job for their united abilities. Actually, that work is performed in most households by the feminine equivalent of an industrious but untrained workman, who has picked up his trade by rule of thumb and is equipped with an insufficient number of atrociously bad tools.

The most vivid and suggestive account known to me of these households is contained in Mrs Eyles' book *The Woman in the Little House*. The book is not free from crudities. It has a tendency to dwell on the depressing side of the life it describes and to ignore its happy moments and the many evidences it affords of the irrepressible power of human nature to rise above environment. But like the collection of working-women's letters in *Maternity*,[1] it has the unmistakable savour of personal experience, which is wanting from the more ordered records of scientific sociologists like Booth, Rowntree and Bowley. It describes the routine of life as Mrs. Eyles saw it lived by her neighbours in a little street of Peckham inhabited by respectable working-class people.

We are shewn the type of houses in the street:—jerry-built; with walls so thin that every sound could be heard not only all over the house, but by censorious neighbours on either side; with ill-fitting doors and windows; no place for bicycle or pram except in the parlour or kitchen; no cool and well-aired cupboard for perishable food; inadequate storage for coal, and chimneys that smoked; no hot water supply except that boiled in the kettle or the copper; a copper, pipes and taps all too small and generally leaking; an iron stove of an old-fashioned pattern needing constant blackleading, and so forth. One sees the unlikelihood that

[1] *Maternity: Letters from Working-Women collected by the Women's Co-operative Guild* (G. Bell & Sons, 1915).

a woman who has to be cook, housemaid, laundress, seam-stress, nurse and nursery governess in such a home and who spends about every second twelve months in expecting and recovering from a confinement, will have the leisure of mind and body for the study of hygiene and food values, the care-ful and discriminating shopping and the skilful cooking, using and costing, that would enable her to make the best of her small income. The diet is described: made out of meat that has been exposed outside a shop where street-dust and flies can cover it and passers-by paw it, of stale vegetables and fruit similarly exposed, of cheap qualities of groceries and tinned fruits and condensed milk and margarine —prepared and served by an overtired mother in the intervals of half a dozen other occupations, with the help of two or three pots and pans and an inadequate stove.

It is not only the wife's inadequate housewifery that reacts on her husband and children. It is also the monotony and confinement of her life, resulting from narrow means and lack of domestic help. Mrs. Eyles dwells much on this:—

" The cloistered state of the married woman is a very perilous thing for her and for the community. We hear much about the damnable effects of prison life on the individual. But the married woman's life, in her little home, is worse than a convict's because, while the convict is always thinking of the times when he will get out, she does not think it likely she will ever see anything different. She has nothing, literally nothing, on which to feed spiritually. The country woman has the green trees, the flowers, the song of birds and the wind on the heath. The town woman has nothing. She is too exhausted to dress and go out into the park with a crowd of children. Usually she is so much conscious of shabbiness that the bright days of spring and summer, that call her to the green places, drive her the closer indoors ; for her there are no " fires of spring " into which she can fling her winter garment. Imagine oneself shorn of all poetry, literature, history, science and even the memory of travels one has made, pictures, plays, beauties one has seen. Imagine oneself stripped bare by pessimism of religion—as the working-class woman is—and not yet wise enough to make a philosophy or religion of one's own. . . . She has nothing at all in the way of spiritual resources, and her brain, quite a fine machine really, is unused and untrained".[1]

Naturally these physical and mental conditions result frequently in hysteria and loss of mental balance. This leads to further domestic discomfort which drives the children into the streets and the man to the public-house, or to the political club or trade union meeting, in a frame of mind which is graphically described by Mrs. Eyles:—

" Here perhaps half-a-dozen men are discussing politics calmly and with clarity of judgment that would astonish many upper class people to-day. Smith comes in from a badly cooked and served meal in a hopelessly disordered house, suffering from chronic dyspepsia and from a severe raking-up because his wife was cross. He bursts in on the cool political discussion with a thoroughly black, hopeless

[1] *The Woman in the Little House*, by M. L. Eyles (Grant Richards, 1922), pp.16-17.

" grouse " and the coolness gives place to heat ; revolution takes the place of evolution. *I believe that the political revolutions that end in bombs and massacres begin with the tired, neurotic women* in the Little Houses ; they so rake up the men folk, who have not the comprehension to see that they are grievously overburdened and ill, that red murder enters the men's hearts. But the primitive instinct, that usually makes a man protect his own, forbids him, in most cases, from murdering the poor woman ; he goes about with murder in his heart against society ". [1]

Mr. H. G. Wells has observed much the same thing though, manlike, it is only to the ill-cooked dinner that he ascribes the mischief.

" Mr. Polly sat on the stile, and looked with eyes that seemed blurred with impalpable flaws at a world in which even the spring buds were wilted, the sunlight metallic, and the shadows mixed with blue-black ink. . . . Drink, indeed, our teachers will criticize nowadays both as regards quantity and quality, but neither church nor state nor school will raise a warning finger between a man and his hunger and his wife's catering. So on nearly every day in his life Mr. Polly fell into a violent rage and hatred against the outer world in the afternoon, and never suspected that it was this inner world to which I am with such masterly delicacy alluding, that was thus reflecting its sinister disorder upon things without. It is a pity that some human beings are not more transparent. If Mr. Polly, for example, had been transparent, or even passably translucent, then perhaps he might have realized, from the Laocoon struggle he would have glimpsed, that indeed he was not so much a human being as a civil war.

" Wonderful things must have been going on inside Mr. Polly. Oh ! wonderful things. It must have been like a badly managed industrial city during a period of depression ; agitators, acts of violence, strikes, the forces of law and order doing their best, rushings to and fro, upheavals, the Marseillaise, tumbrils, the rumble and the thunder of tumbrils ". [2]

But the married woman's effect on her husband is not her only contribution to the growing forces of social discontent. She herself has her discontents, less articulate than his but quite as deep-rooted. No one who has been closely connected with married working-women during the last ten years can doubt that a large proportion of them are profoundly dissatisfied with their lot. Their resentment fastens itself first of all on the conditions of their maternity; secondly on their economic conditions generally; lastly on the subtler question of their status. Of course I do not suggest that all or any of these discontents are universal among them. In a group numbering several millions there are infinite varieties of circumstances, characters and opinions. There are many women still who, being happily married and comfortably placed, are quite satisfied with their lot. There are others who, whether happy or not, are instinctive Conservatives, who feel that established customs must be right and that the existing economic order, including the subordination of women, is divinely ordained. Others grumble at the economic order, but not at women's place in it; for they

[1] *Ibid.*, pp. 15-16.   [2] *Mr. Polly*, pp. 10-12.

never think of themselves as subordinate, having achieved either equal partnership or the upper hand over their own husbands. Others do not generalize at all, but are as instinctive as animals, though animals whose instincts have been confused by an unnatural environment and have lost their rhythm.

But there are also a very large and growing number—probably no one is qualified to say what proportion of the whole they represent—who are either consciously or subconsciously in revolt. These find their most articulate expression through the membership of such bodies as the Women's Co-operative Guild, the Women Citizens' Associations, the Women's Institutes and Village Councils and similar purely local organizations. But their numbers far transcend such membership; for the habit of joining societies and attending meetings is comparatively new among women and is limited by the circumstances of their lives. Those who are most encumbered by children and household cares have not the time for it, and those who are poorest or unhappiest have not the clothes or the spirits for it. Hence most of those who do attend are the older women whose children are at school or at work. But what the younger women are thinking can be gauged by one significant fact, the decline of the birth rate. The question of maternity is very naturally the one that lies uppermost in their minds. Those who are accustomed to speak to meetings of these women's organizations must have noticed its tendency to crop up on all occasions, irrespective of what the subject immediately on hand may be. I noticed this first in meetings connected with the Suffragist agitation before the war. A speech dealing chiefly with the political or industrial aspects of the question would be followed, after the usual pause, by woman after woman rising to her feet and asking apparently irrelevant questions which began with, " Will Mrs. So-and-so tell us what is the use of a woman bringing children into the world when," etc. The grievances which followed ranged over all the hardships and uncertainties of the wage-earners' lot, as it affects themselves or still oftener their children. If asked to name their remedy, they would do so in terms that implied their own dependency, for it is only beginning to dawn on the more advanced of them that there is any alternative to it. They would suggest higher wages, or (if unhappily married) that a man should be compelled to keep his wife, or State maintenance of the unemployed, or the overthrow of the capitalist system. Their economic theories, so far as they have any, are still derived chiefly from their husbands or from the books they bring into the house. But even in the less advanced and articulate among them, there is often a very unmistakable sense of sex-grievance as well as class-grievance; a feeling that women are having unfairly the worst of it, and an uneasy desire for more control over their own destinies. From asking why their husbands are not better able to keep them, they are passing to the stage of asking whether it is just that they and their children should be so completely dependent on his power and will to do so. Their experience of separation allowances during the war and all that was said then of the importance of healthy children to the community, followed by their political en-franchisement and the many efforts it has brought with it to instruct and appeal to them, have all helped to quicken in the working-woman a dim sense that she is " an end in herself and not merely a means to an end". She feels that society is not treating her as though it recognized this when it reckons all its other services in terms of economic values, but simply takes no account at all of her except as a " dependant", or synonymously an appendage or hanger-on of someone else, when it pays tribute in plenty of sugary phrases to the value of her services, but pays for them in nothing else, and parcels out all its wealth among those who provide it with land, or capital, or services of brain and hand other than hers.

The development of this sense of sex grievance into a sense of sex solidarity and an articulate demand for the economic independence of women is I believe only a question of time. It is slow because it is hindered by the competition of other loyalties; family loyalty and class loyalty. The women who have sufficient leisure of circumstances and ease of mind to become leaders among their fellows are usually, though not always, either unmarried or those who have been fortunate in their own marriage. Often it is their husbands who have fostered their public spirit and encouraged them to use it in organizing others. Naturally such women have no sense of sex antagonism themselves. It is difficult for them to separate in their minds the personal issue from the impersonal and to see that their own security, far from imposing a taboo, entails an obligation towards those who are not secure. Biassed by their own experience, the vertical cleavage of class seems to them much more important than the horizontal cleavage of sex. In the organization of class activities which are common to men and women, the more ambitious women find a larger and more conspicuous field for their abilities than in organizing women for their own ends. Very often such women, especially when they have themselves had difficulties to overcome, have a contempt for women who have failed where they have succeeded and find much more congenial fellow workers among men. In the same way, clever and ambitious men often prefer to climb into the ranks above them than become leaders of their own class, and this was still commoner in the days when the labour movement had few well-salaried or conspicuous positions to offer. But the parvenu of sex, as of class, is not an attractive person; being usually too nervously anxious to commend herself to her new associates by shewing indifference to the special interests of women and belittling their capacities. Now however that women have become a political force, the special mission of this type of woman in the eyes of the men of her political party and consequently of her own, is to marshal the women voters behind the party banner and to prevent their energies being " dissipated " or their minds " confused " by mingling with women of other parties than their own and so discovering the bond between them. This tendency is especially strong in the extreme right and extreme left wings of opinion; those whose propaganda is most concerned with defending or attacking the privileges of wealth and class. Incidentally the anxiety of these political parties to keep women from " fraternizing with the enemy " and to prove to them that " Codlin is their friend, not Short " helps to secure for them some occasional crumbs of reform. But so far as their policy is successful it hinders the development of the demand for economic independence, which offends a prejudice common to men of all classes.

The married working-woman however is apt to have a shrewd if a narrow mind. Her success in her particular job depends largely on humouring her household, especially its male members, and getting her own way while seeming to give them theirs. Hence it is much harder for those not in personal contact with them to judge their real opinions, especially about matters affecting themselves, than those of men. New ideas are passed from one woman to another in confidential talk instead of being at once rushed into print and on to the platform and the movement of opinion is consequently slow.

A striking instance of this is seen in the history of birth-control. Most observers agree that the coincidence between the propaganda of Mr. Bradlaugh and Mrs. Besant and the beginning of the decline in the birth-rate was not accidental. But after the great burst of publicity occasioned by their prose-cution in 1877, the subject sank almost completely below the surface of public expression. The women like Brer Rabbit " kep' on sayin' nuffin " about it in public. But the hint that had been dropped in their midst was passed from one to another, with the result of an almost perfectly unbroken decline for forty-four years. Can anyone doubt that if the question had affected men to anything like the same extent in their work, health and almost every detail of their lives, there would have been a flood of talk about it—canvassing of pros and cons and hows—which not all the Judges and the Mrs. Grundys in the land could have quelled. The result would probably have been the same; but accomplished much more quickly and without some of the evils due to imperfect knowledge.

The movement for economic independence is still subter-ranean. The desire is there, repressed partly by masculine taboos but still more by lack of knowledge of the means. When this is supplied, nothing I believe can stop its progress, which will probably be much more rapid than that of birth-control. There are not the same reasons for reticence and their newly gained citizenship is slowly making women bolder and more articulate.

(ii) *The Wife of the Bad Husband*

If the present system tells hardly on the wives and children of the wage-earner even when the latter is ordinarily indus-trious and affectionate, how do they fare when he is a shirker or a bully ? Few people who have not been in contact with the facts realize how completely such a man has his family at his mercy, and how little the law does to protect them against anything but his worst excesses. The impressions of the lives of the poor given by the reports of the well-known investigators from whom I have quoted so often are sometimes thought by those who do not know to be too pessimistic, but in fact they tend to be too favourable, because they describe almost exclusively the well-ordered homes. The broken-spirited wives of brutal or drunken husbands and those who themselves drink or are hopeless muddlers or slatterns cannot be got to keep accounts or time-tables. " Why not, since there is nothing to be ashamed of " is the reflection by which the timid housewife encourages herself to let strangers into the secrets of her domestic economy, and those who have not this consoling consciousness can seldom be persuaded to make the attempt, or be relied on if they do make it. Light is only let in on their households when some evil occurs which compels an appeal to the relief society or police court, and then the facts seldom find their way into print in any detail, unless some unusual incident catches the attention of the press or makes a moving paragraph in an annual report. Usually they are too commonplace to be sensational and too sordid to be picturesque. But to anyone with knowledge and imagination it must seem that hardly any form of suffering can be worse than that which goes on day by day in a working-class home, where either husband or wife is really bad. The bad wife is worse for the children; the husband can escape from her all day and most of his evenings. But take the much commoner case where the husband drinks, gives his wife as little as possible of his earnings, and ill-treats her. Scarcely any ingredient of human suffering is wanting from such a home—hunger and cold, dirt and ugliness, fatigue and pain, fear and shame. Imagine what the life of the woman must be like—shut up all day in two or three tiny, airless, sunless rooms; with children always with her and always more to do for them than she can possibly manage; seeing them hungry and cold and ailing with no money to buy for them what they need; trying to keep clean without soap or cleaning materials; liable to be inspected at any time by school visitors, health visitors and district visitors, who blame her for her failure to make bricks without straw; never certain whether the little money her husband has given her this week may not be less or nothing next week; generally expecting her next confinement or re-covering from the last one; always overtired; always suffering from an ailment in some part of the body, rheumatism, dragging pains, nausea, swollen feet, aching back, bad teeth, bad eyes; dreading her husband's return from work at night, his blows and curses. Then the nights! Mrs Eyles in her book on *The Woman in the Little House*[1] gives a very plain-spoken account gathered from the talks in confidential moments of her married women neighbours in Peckham, of the suffering caused by cramped sleeping quarters and by the primitive ideas of marital rights which still prevail among the worst sort of husbands. The same sort of facts, expressed with more reticence and dignity, peep out from some of the letters published in *Maternity*.[2]   It is clear that what J. S. Mill described as " the lowest degradation of a human being, that of being made the instrument of an animal function contrary to her inclinations",[3] is still enforced by a good many men on their wives as part of the price they are expected to pay for being kept by them.

It may be said that all this, whether true or not, is irrelevant to the subject of this book. The unhappiness of homes where there is a bad husband is due to his character, not to his wife's dependency. Partly of course this is true, but character is influenced by circumstances and nothing so fosters a disposition to tyranny and self-indulgence as the power of exercising it unchecked over the members of a man's own family, those who cannot break away from him so long as he keeps his behaviour within very elastic limits. As J. S. Mill long ago pointed out:—

" The almost unlimited power which present social institutions give to the man over at least one human being—the one with whom he resides, and whom he has always present—this power seeks out and evokes the latent germs of selfishness in the remotest corners of his nature—fans its faintest sparks and smouldering embers— offers to him a licence for the indulgence of those points of his original character which in all other relations he would have found it necessary to repress and conceal, and the repression of which would in time have become a second nature".[4]

Most people accustomed only to the conditions of life among the middle and upper classes think that this has ceased since Mill's day to be a true description of the power of a husband over his wife. They know that a series of Acts have been passed designed, some of them to give a married woman complete control over her own personal property and earnings, others to provide her and her children with several means of escape from a cruel or neglectful husband.   It

[1] *The Woman in the Little House,* by M. L. Eyles (1922), Chap. VII.
[2] *See* above, p. 63 n.
[3] *The Subjection of Women,* 1869, p. 57.   [4] *Ibid,* p. 67.

is quite common to hear the married woman's position described as though she were the spoilt darling of the law, especially by lawyers who have a thorough knowledge of its provisions but very little experience of their working out as they affect the poorer classes. Thus Professor Jenks in his *Husband and Wife in the Law* after enumerating a number of " privileges " enjoyed by the wife, remarks that it is difficult to speak of her " disabilities " except in the terms of the famous chapter on snakes in Ireland.[1] In actual fact, several of these so-called " privileges " are so only to dishonest and unscrupulous women, whom they enable to escape paying the debts they have run up. Their only effect on other married women is to make it harder for them to obtain credit, if they need it for some legitimate purpose such as starting a business.

The position of the married woman in some respects is indeed considerably better than it was before these various Acts were passed. Their effect in raising the standard of public opinion and so preventing the commission of wrongs has probably been even greater than in providing a remedy. But it is untrue that she now suffers from no serious disabilities imposed by the law, and preposterously untrue that it gives her all the protection she needs against a tyrannical husband. It is surely, except possibly in a purely technical sense understood by lawyers, a great positive disability that a wife, so long as she nominally lives with her husband, has no legal right to any say or part whatsoever in the management of their children, or any remedy (so far as those over five are concerned) against being totally separated from them ! In the words of Mr. Jenks, none of the recent changes in the law " affect the primary right of a father, who is not guilty of any misconduct, to the sole control, during his life-time, of the custody, maintenance, education and religious upbringing of his infant unmarried children—at least till the age of sixteen".[2] These exclusive rights of the father are in fact not interfered with by his misconduct, unless its character and the wife's circumstances make it possible for her to obtain a legal separation from him. Nor are they, so far as the law can prevent it, dissolved by death, since even when he leaves his children entirely unprovided for, he has the power of directing by will

---

[1] *Husband and Wife in the Law*, by Edward Jenks (J. M. Dent & Co., 1909), p. 71.

[2] *Ibid.*, p. 41.

the religion and manner in which they are to be brought up and of appointing a guardian who, acting jointly with the wife, must see to it that so far as possible the father's wishes are carried out.

This disability is not directly connected with the question of economic status, for legally it continues even when the family is entirely maintained out of the wife's income or earnings. But it is easy to see that in practice the parent who holds the purse strings will inevitably have a great power of control over the arrangements for the children's upbringing. If those who built up the fabric of British law had been guided less by sex bias and more by considerations of natural equity, they might have been expected to use the law to redress the unfair balance of advantage which the economic arrangements of society give to the father who supports his children by his remunerated labours outside the home, over the mother who supports it by her unremunerated labours inside. Instead, they acted on the principle " to him that hath shall be given " and rested the whole weight of the law on the side of the father. If comparatively few husbands abuse their power in this respect, it is because the sense of justice of the ordinary man refuses to let him take seriously the monstrous legal fiction that a man has " a primary right to the sole control " of the children whom a woman has borne with great suffering and at the risk of her life and to whose care Nature and custom require her to devote herself as the chief work of the best years of her life.

It would be outside the scope of this book to discuss in full detail the proposals that have been made for remedying this injustice by giving the husband and wife equal rights of custody and guardianship. No one probably will seriously argue that a change is unnecessary because the vast majority of wives do not suffer under the law. When a law affects millions of people, a tiny percentage of sufferers may mean absolutely a very large number. Further, there is no means of telling what this number really is, since very few women care to speak of domestic grievances for which they know that there is no redress. But even if it could be proved very small, that is no reason why these women should continue to suffer, since to reform the law would cost next to nothing and would merely bring it into line with the almost universal sense of what is right and fair.

By far the most serious failure of the marriage laws, however, in point of the number of families practically affected, is their treatment of the questions of maintenance during the lifetime of the husband and after his death. With regard to the latter, the rights of wives and children may indeed be described in the terms of the chapter on snakes in Ireland. They have no rights, except in the case of the husband's intestacy. He may if he chooses marry a wife in her youth, promising (if they are married by the rites of the established church) to love and cherish her and endow her with all his worldly goods, give her children and then—perhaps when the children are still totally dependent, perhaps when the wife has long passed the age when she could earn her living—leave them and her entirely unprovided for and without assigning a reason will everything he possesses to his mistress. During the husband's lifetime, his wife and young children are legally entitled to be supplied by him with food, necessary clothing and lodging, provided of course he has the wherewithal to do it. But the law is very vague and unsatisfactory in defining the extent of the obligation and utterly ineffective in the machinery it provides to enforce it. In fact, so long as the family continues to form one household, no practical means of enforcement exists. There are in theory two indirect and partial means. First, the wife may, if she can, obtain necessaries from the tradespeople on credit or borrow money from a friend to purchase them. The burden will then rest on the tradesmen or lender of proving both that the articles purchased were in fact necessaries and that the husband had left his family unprovided with them. Some confusion in the public mind arises from the fact that in cases where a tradesmen sues a husband for his wife's debts, the articles that have been supplied are often not necessaries in any reasonable sense of the word, and thus the impression has arisen that the law is even too lenient to extravagant wives. The explanation is partly that the tradesman's case sometimes rests not on the doctrine of necessities but on the plea, intended for his protection, that he had reason to believe that the wife was acting as her husband's agent. If, for example a husband has habitually paid his wife's dressmaker and has given no notice of his intention to cease doing so, the plea might be admitted. But in considering what he is likely to have sanctioned the Court usually takes into consideration the means and position of the husband. Hence this method of providing for the household may sometimes prove fairly effective in the

case of a wife who is both able and willing to involve un-
suspecting tradespeople in debts which she knows they may
be unable to recover. A scrupulous or proud woman will not
be thus willing, and a working-man's wife, even if willing,
will almost certainly not be able.

Her other resource (in theory) is to appeal to the Guardians,
who have power to give relief and recover the cost from the
husband. This is occasionally done when the husband is
absent from home, e.g., if he is a seaman or working at a
distance. If he is at home the Guardians will only relieve,
if at all, by taking the wife and children into the workhouse
and proceeding against the husband. But this is very rarely
done and then only as a preliminary to applying for a separation order. A more usual plan in extreme cases of neglect
is to remove the children and prosecute the man for causing
them unnecessary suffering. He may then be sentenced to
a short term of imprisonment and on release called on to pay
something—usually a very small weekly sum—for their maintenance in an industrial school or other institution. This,
besides depriving the mother of their care, leaves her to get
on as best she can.

The only effective remedy for a working-class wife tied to
a cruel or neglectful husband is for her first to leave him and
then apply to a Court of Summary Jurisdiction for a separation
order with maintenance and custody of the children. The
fear that she will do this is indeed in many cases some check
on a man's disposition to tyranny or to self-indulgence, and
this is the one respect in which the much vaunted improvements
in the marriage law since Mill first drew attention to its
harshness have substantially benefited working-class women.
But the conditions under which such orders are granted are
in many respects very gravely unsatisfactory. Space will not
allow of a full discussion of the defects in the system, but the
following summary will give an idea of some of the chief of
them.

The grounds on which a woman may obtain a separation
order with maintenance are that her husband has failed to
maintain her and her children, or has treated her with
persistent cruelty, or has committed an aggravated assault on
her, or has deserted her, or is an habitual drunkard. Orders
given on the first two grounds are subject to the proviso that
the wife must shew that the neglect or cruelty complained of

has caused her already to leave her husband and live apart from him. This frequently debars the worst sufferers from seeking redress. The wife has no legal right to take her children with her and even if she could do it by stealth often knows no one whom she could ask to take in the whole family without payment. The worse the husband, the less likely that she will be willing to leave the children alone with him. A still more serious bar to applications is the inadequacy of the amounts obtainable and worse, the uncertainty whether they will ever be paid. The maximum that can be granted is 40s. weekly for the wife and 10s. for each dependent child. In deciding what to grant, the magistrates should be guided by the man's earnings, but usually they have no evidence as to this but his own statement and he naturally makes himself out as poor as possible. The wife does not know the amount, and even if aware that she had the power to subpœna the employer, would be afraid to do so, lest his annoyance should lead to his sacking the man. A written statement of the employer cannot legally be accepted, as it ought to be, as prima facie evidence of earnings. Some Benches rarely give the maximum, on the ground that if the burden on the man is made too heavy he will evade payment. If he is sufficiently determined, he can almost always do this. His wife knows, and he knows that she knows, that if she proceeds against him for non-payment he may be sent to prison. But as this wipes out the arrears already due, besides causing him to lose his employment during his imprisonment and probably after it, she will be no better off. Therefore she is more likely to hang on indefinitely in hopes of persuading him to pay. For the same reason, the magistrates will probably give him several chances before proceeding to extremities. When he sees that the patience of both is on the point of wearing out, he can finally elude them by going abroad, whence he cannot be extradited, or almost as finally by moving to another town, or even by merely changing his address and place of employment.

Another obstacle which deters many wives is the difficulty —often since the war amounting to sheer impossibility—of finding lodgings that will take children, or furnishing them with the necessary bedding and equipment when found. The household plenishings that mean so much to a working housewife have usually been bought in the early days of marriage out of the housekeeping money which she considers hers, though legally it is not so, or scraped together out of her earnings or separation allowance, though she seldom has any proof of this. Justice would seem to demand that when the joint household is broken up, it should be the guilty partner and not the innocent who should be driven out of it, and it has been proposed by Mr. Lieck, Clerk to the Thames Police Court, that the Bench in granting a separation order should have the power to arrange for the transfer of tenancy to the wife and for an equitable division of the household goods.

All this seems to assume that it is always the husband who is in fault. In fact, the only ground on which the husband can obtain a separation order against a bad wife is, under the Licensing Act of 1902, that she is an habitual drunkard. Even then he is usually ordered to pay maintenance to her. This is a hardship and it seems also unfair that in cases where a wife, though not a drunkard, has made her home miserable by the gross neglect of her duties or ill-treatment of the children, her husband should have no legal means of getting rid of her. It is probable that in this matter legislation has been inspired less by tenderness for the wife than by the reflection that a drunken or worthless woman is likely to become chargeable to the ratepayers.

The machinery of separation orders might easily be improved on the lines that have been indicated and proposals for doing so have been for some time receiving the intermittent attention of Parliament.[1] But even if brought into full operation they would only go a short way towards solving the problem of the neglectful husband. What seems needed is legislation that will ensure the maintenance of the wife and children without resorting to separation except in extreme cases. A separation, at least in working-class marriages, is always a desperate expedient, for there it involves, not only the break-up of the home and the severance of the children from one parent or the other, but the splitting up into two of an income which is usually barely sufficient for the upkeep of one household. This often leads to the forming of an illicit connexion by the man who has lost his housekeeper or by the woman who has lost her home.

Why should not the magistrates, if the wife can satisfy

[1] A Bill drafted by the National Union for Equal Citizenship has been before Parliament since 1921.

them that her husband has persistently failed to maintain her, be permitted to give her a maintenance order without separation, and if the husband obdurately refused to obey the orders, why should they not be able to take the further step of ordering the employer to pay a portion of his wages direct to the wife? There seems no difference in principle between forcing the husband's hand in this way and forcing it by allowing the wife to pledge her husband's credit for necessaries, except that the former provision would benefit the working housewife without risk to tradesmen and the latter is of use only to less scrupulous types of well-to-do women.

The objection is sometimes raised that if a maintenance order were given to a wife while still living with her husband, he would so resent it that he would make her life intolerable. But the wife surely is the best judge of that. She knows her husband's disposition as no stranger can know it and if satisfied that separation was the only possible remedy, it would still be open for her to apply for it. Those who are best acquainted with the type of man who is the subject of police-court proceedings know that he is often unexpectedly amenable to the pressure of public opinion as exercised through the law. It might be expected, on the analogy of the above objection, that a father or mother who has been punished for cruelty to a child will come out of prison bursting to be avenged on the child by any means short of risking another punishment. But the experience of the N.S.P.C.C. seldom bears this out. Frequently the shock of seeing his conduct through other people's eyes, or more probably his dumb sense that society and the opinion of his fellows is against him and that it will be easier for him to swim with the tide, seems to pull the offender up. He may relapse again, but he seldom seems to shew a special grudge against the child or even against the Society which has been the instrument of his punishment.

But the value of such a provision would lie less in cure than in prevention. As everyone knows who has had experience of local administration, the efficiency of most of our social legislation concerning health, child welfare, conditions of employment, etc., depends very little on resort to penalties, and very much on its influence on the standard of behaviour of ordinary citizens. To take a single example, in 1921 there were in Liverpool 94,451 nuisances reported to the Medical Officer of Health, each of them representing an offence punishable by fine against the local bye-laws. The total number of prosecutions for the offences in that year was 218 and the number of fines inflicted was 44. One may take it that a substantial proportion of the remainder of the nuisances were remedied when the attention of the offenders had been sufficiently often called to them. For one person who is obstinately anti-social in his conduct, there are a dozen who are merely careless, rather selfish, very unimaginative about the feelings of others, but susceptible to the pressure of public opinion, especially the opinion of their neighbours and fellow-workers.

There is perhaps no relation in life as it is lived in a modern industrialized community where the temptations to selfishness are greater and the checks on it fewer than the relation between a wage-earning husband and a wholly dependent wife. The man's money is so small, his control of it so absolute, the enticements to spend on himself so many, the hold they have got on him during his care-free bachelor years so strong. What has his wife to set against these things that will appeal to a man who happens to be naturally self-indulgent or cross-grained, when once her physical attraction has prematurely faded under the strain of incessant childbearing and overwork? She has her tongue; but the more she uses it the more she will drive him out of the home into money-spending places. She has nothing else but the chance of a separation order, and he knows that he can carry his neglect to almost all lengths before she can or will resort to this. If it were open to her to apply for maintenance without separation, and the order could be enforced if need be, by attachment of wages, five neglected wives out of six would never have to make the attempt. Shame and the fear of their fellow-workmen's ridicule would induce the husbands to supply at least enough for bare necessaries.

Another method for securing provision for wives which would apply to all types and classes, not merely to the victim of the bad husband, would be to give the wife a legal right to a definite share of her husband's income. This is the plan usually advocated by English feminists. So far as I know it is only in use in Sweden, where by the Marriage Law of 1920, the estates of husband and wife at marriage are combined into one collective estate, of which each owns one-half, but administers only the portion which he or she has brought into the marriage. This separate administration however is subject to conditions giving the other party a certain amount of control. Thus they are conjointly responsible for household debts; neither may sell or mortgage any part of his share which has to do with the household or working conditions without the consent of the other. For example, if the husband is a carpenter and the wife a dressmaker, he may not sell his planing machine nor she her sewing machine without the written and attested consent of the other. If a dissolution of the marriage is brought about by divorce, each takes half the joint estate, irrespective of whether the portions administered by each have increased or diminished. At death, the survivor takes one-half, or the whole if there are neither children nor living parents of the deceased. This is the legal system; but by agreement or trust, husband and wife may obtain absolute rights over their own property.[1]

The working of this remarkable law will be watched with close interest by the women of other countries. Some such arrangement as it embodies seems to be the logical outcome of the theory of marriage embodied in the law and the marriage services of all religious denominations in this country. A contract which is binding for life and supported by every kind of religious and social sanction, which theoretically ties together the parties to it in the closest possible union, physical, moral and economic, ought surely to involve some real sharing of economic prosperity or poverty—not merely an obligation on each not to let the other starve. The fact (where it is so) that the wife has not contributed any part of the money income ought not to deter her from sharing, since the functions implicitly assigned to her in the contract, as in the social customs and traditions it embodies, are such as to impede her from contributing. This moral right to share is of course recognized in the practice of all successful marriages. What is lacking is the means of legally enforcing this moral obligation on the husband who refuses to recognize it. To represent such enforcements as an insult to husbands in general and an " interference " in private life is absurd. Parents in general do not feel insulted because they know that there are laws which make the ill-treatment of children punishable. Such laws simply do not affect them at all, because they have never felt any desire to ill-treat their children. But in practice

[1] These facts are taken from a pamphlet by Fru Elizabeth Nilsson ; published by the International Woman Suffrage Alliance.

the fixing of a definite arithmetical proportion does present difficulties. Whatever proportion was fixed would probably lead to individual cases of hardship. If fixed at too low a figure, it would often be unjust to the wife. If absolute equality were insisted on, there would be situations such as that described in H. G. Wells' novel *Marriage*, where a brilliant young man of science who acts on the theory of equal partnership, finds that the hard-earned money designed for his researches is squandered by his wife on fashionable extravagances. It is difficult to maintain that a wife has a moral right to an equal share of earnings which are the result of exceptional ability and above those on which she could have reasonably counted when entering into the contract of marriage.

Probably a law which, without defining an exact proportion, gave the wife an enforceable right to be maintained in reasonable accordance with the means and social position of the husband would meet most of the hard cases and result in a rough measure of justice. Here as before, the test of the law's success would not be the number of cases brought into Court, but the number of those in which the fear of possible publicity obliged an ill-conditioned husband to behave as his fellows do without compulsion.

The whole problem would be immensely simplified by a system of direct provision for families. This might or might not include an allowance for the mother as well as for the children. Whether it should do so will be discussed in the last chapter. But even if it did not, the securing of provision for the children would take the worst of the sting out of the sufferings of an ill-treated wife. It is their helplessness and the knowledge of her inability to support them that so often obliges her to endure in silence. Their future secured, she would gladly dare all for herself. But the cases where she would be driven to extremities would be fewer. The brutal or insatiable husband is largely the result of a system which encourages a man to believe that his wife and children are his appendages, kept as he might keep animals, out of the wages of his labours and protected only as animals are, from the worst extremities of cruelty or neglect.

(e) The Effect on the Widow and Orphan

Of all the many forms of injustice into which the nation has been unwittingly led by the refusal of the leaders to think out the question of family maintenance, the most cruel and indefensible has been its treatment of widows and fatherless children. The contrast between this treatment as it is in fact and as it ought to be, in accordance with the principles in which we believe ourselves to believe, because we have been brought up in them, is a most striking instance of discrepancy between theory and practice. For centuries before the foundation of Christianity, the widow and the fatherless served as the very symbol and embodiment of all that should stir the bowels of compassion. It was said to be an attribute of the Deity Himself that " He is the Father of the fatherless and defendeth the cause of the widow".[1] " To visit the widow and fatherless in their affliction "[2] was to be part of the definition of true religion. One might expect to find in a nation bred on this kind of teaching that widows and orphans were a first charge on the good services of the community; that they were comforted, protected, cared for. One finds in fact that of all the innocent victims of our clumsy, blundering social system, they are the most undeservedly humiliated and unnecessarily distressed. Those who think this statement an exaggeration are invited to study the following facts:

Under social conditions as they are and have been for several generations, the sole resource of a widow with young children, other than her earnings or the charity of relatives and neighbours, is to apply to the Board of Guardians for relief under the Poor Law. No other form of State assistance is provided for her. In order to realize the implications of this it is necessary to remember the theory on which the Poor Law of 1834 was based—a theory which has never been repudiated or abandoned, although in some respects the practices based on it have been modified to suit changing circumstances of time and locality and changing phases of public opinion. This theory is that the State recognizes its obligation for the livelihood of the individual citizen to the extent of ensuring that no one shall be condemned by poverty to death by starvation. Those reduced, whether by their own fault or otherwise, to the extreme of destitution are granted the right of free maintenance by the State. In this way the instinct of pity is satisfied and the citizen released from the necessity of indiscriminate almsgiving. But for fear lest the provision of State aid should weaken the motives towards exertion and self-reliance and lead to certain sections

[1] Psalm lxviii.   [2] St. James' Epistle.

of the people becoming willing parasites upon the community, it is provided that the conditions under which the aid of the State is given shall be " deterrent " and that the situation of those in receipt of it shall be distinctly less eligible than that of even the poorest self-supporting citizens. In other words it is intended that the position of the pauper shall be humiliating and disagreeable, in order that no one shall be tempted to remain a pauper a moment longer than he can help.

This general principle is in its working out made subject to qualifications and modifications; the conditions under which relief is given being made more or less "deterrent" according to the classification to which the applicant belongs as well as according to the temper of the individual Board of Guardians.

Since the publication of the report of the Poor Law Commission of 1909 and its revelations as to the conditions of widows and orphans, their treatment by most Boards of Guardians has tended to become humaner and less niggardly, and this tendency has been accelerated during the past four years by the agitation for widows' pensions. But the older and harsher tradition has never been wholly lost sight of by the administrators of the Poor Law; still less has it lost its hold on the minds of the working classes themselves. It has made " the stigma of pauperism " a very real thing; so real that many widows, the best of their kind, those in whom the tradition of self-help is strongest and who are most sensitive to slights, are indeed " deterred " from seeking the help so grudgingly offered and prefer to drag along somehow, allowing their own and their children's health to be undermined by insufficiency of food, clothing and house room.

This abhorrence of the Poor Law on the part of the respectable poor is so well recognized that gradually Parliament has been forced by public opinion to provide a machinery of public assistance, independent of the Guardians, for sufferers from all the other chief causes of undeserved distress, except widowhood. For the old, there are old-age pensions; for the sick, health insurance; for the unemployed, unemployment insurance. The reluctance to force the unemployed on to the Poor Law is shewn by the adoption of the clumsy and confusing device of " uncovenanted benefits " for those who have exhausted the insurance to which they are entitled. Only the family man—always the hardest hit under the present system— has been forced in many cases to apply for the hated out-relief to supplement the inadequate allowance made him, of five shillings for the wife and one shilling for each child. But for the widow who devotes herself to the care of her fatherless children, not even that scanty provision is made. For her alone, the Poor Law is still thought good enough.

Yet it surely is incontestable that of the four classes her claim to be emancipated from the Poor Law is the strongest, and that which could be granted with least risk of undermining the self-reliance and energy of any part of the community. With regard to the other three it is at least possible to argue with some plausibility that if the State had left them alone, only offering the aid of a deterrent Poor Law as a last resort, their need—at least in times of normal employment—could conceivably have been met by the exercise of co-operative thrift and that, indeed, in thousands of cases it was being so met—for the unemployed through trade unions, for the sick through friendly societies, and for the aged through savings and insurance and the help of grown-up children.

But the widowed mother of young children! Did anyone ever hear of a practicable scheme for enabling a thrifty young workman to provide, not only for unemployment, sickness and old age, but also for the contingency of his own premature death, by leaving such a sum as would keep his widow and children until they have all reached wage-earning age? Would not such a scheme without State aid be a sheer actuarial impossibility? If it were possible, would not some of the great Friendly Societies, including as they do the most thrifty and far-sighted of the working-classes, have before this provided this sort of benefit? Surely if anyone's poverty and need is " the Act of God", it is the poverty and need of a widow with young children, and to make the grant of public assistance to such a one " deterrent " and surround it with humiliating conditions, is as irrational as it is cruel, as contrary to public policy as it is unjust.

Those who wish to study the actual conditions of these widowed mothers who have accepted poor-relief will find plenty of material to their hand. The Poor Law Commission of 1909, besides devoting considerable attention to the subject in their general survey, appointed special women investigators whose reports were published in two appendix volumes.[1]

---

[1] Reports on the Condition of the Children in Receipt of Poor Law Relief, Cd. 5037 (London and the Provinces), and Cd. 5075 (Scotland),

Their general verdict is summed up in the following paragraph from the main Report:

" Some Boards endeavour to act upon the principle of sufficient enquiry and adequate relief ; but the large majority still give wholly inadequate allowances, and rely upon the insufficiency of their enquiries for ' unrevealed resources'. If these resources happen to exist all is well ; if they do not then the recipients inevitably suffer. Committees of our number have been present at many Relief Committees where hardly any enquiry had been made as to the means of the applicants, and where the Guardians habitually relied upon ' unrevealed resources' in fixing the amount of relief."[1]

The condemnation expressed in the Minority report was even more sweeping. The detailed facts and the figures revealed an amount of suffering and of mental and moral deterioration among the widowed mothers and their children which make these blue books most painful and depressing reading. " Nothing," comments the Minority report, " can add to the force of these terrible figures".

Up till that time, the policy encouraged by the Local Government Board and pursued by " strict " Boards was that of taking into the workhouse schools those children whose mothers were unable to support them by their own exertions. The growing sense of the cruelty and unnecessary costliness of this policy led to the issue by the Local Government Board of several circulars, in which Guardians were incited to use full discretion and not to deprive mothers of the care of their children without due cause. Various suggestions were made to ensure better administration, especially the appointment of special committees and women visitors to deal with this class of case. In 1919 a further detailed investigation was set on foot by the Ministry of Health. Their report, as might be expected from an official document, is cautiously worded and takes the most optimistic view possible of the facts cited. But it shews that the Board's recommendations as to women visitors, etc., had been ignored by most Unions,[2] and while finding " a growing endeavour to see that the family income is sufficient to meet all reasonable needs " admits that " there are still too many places where the sums granted are sufficient only on the unverified assumption that they are supplemented from undisclosed resources".[3] This is certainly borne out by the reports from the county districts, which reveal the most

[1] Majority Report, p. 148.
[2] The report on one group of counties says: "Guardians think that they have always given adequate relief, and they have no wish to employ women officers ; and in some cases are even very much averse to having women members on the boards " (Survey of Relief to Widows and Children (1919), Cmd. 744).
[3] *Ibid.*, p. 4.

startling variations in the standards adopted in different parts of the country. Perhaps the most extreme types are represented by a Union in the industrial north which allowed 23s. for a widow with one child, 63s. for one with six; and a Union in the midlands whose scale for a widow with seven children was 10s. Samples of other figures given are—for Cornwall, Devon and Somerset, an average of 2s. 10d. per head per week; for Oxfordshire and six other counties, from over 4s. to 1s. 8d.; for Gloucestershire and six other counties, an average of 6s. per head; for Lancashire, Cumberland and Westmorland, an average of 4s. 5½d. per head. These general averages conceal much greater discrepancies between the standards of different Unions in the same district, and it is noticeable that the highest figures are often found in districts where the opportunities for supplementary earnings seem likely to be greatest.

While the detailed reports shew abundant evidence of a fairly generous spirit in some Unions—sometimes accompanied by care and discrimination, sometimes by reckless and slovenly methods of administration—they also abound with instances of excessive penuriousness and its inevitable results in underfeeding, bad clothing, overcrowding, ill-health and moral deterioration—all the evils in short of which the Poor Law Commission of just ten years previously had complained so bitterly. Yet the report was produced at a time when the country was in the height of its short period of post-war prosperity and enthusiasm for reconstruction, when wages were at their summit and before the cry of " anti-waste " had produced its crop of short-sighted economies at the expense of all forms of social administration. It seems probable therefore that the lot of widows and orphans has grown harder rather than happier during the ensuing four years.

It is impossible however to judge of the effects of the present system merely by studying the case of those who receive poor-relief. The success of the Poor Law in being " deterrent " in respect to widows may be judged from the fact that, of the total number of civilian widows with dependent children in Great Britain, which may be estimated as 244,700,[1] only about 61,500 or 25 per cent. receive poor-

[1] According to figures supplied by the Census Office there were in 1921 306,000 widows with dependent children, the latter numbering 606,500. The number in Scotland may be taken as approximately 41,500 widows and 75,200 children. If we deduct the service widows with dependent children (103,000 widows, with 217,800 children) we have a total of 244,700 widows, with 463,900 dependent children.

relief.[1]   The rest have " managed somehow," some of them
no doubt fairly well, with the help of parents, wage-earning
children, charing, letting lodgings, etc., but others at what cost
to themselves and the future labour power of the nation only
those can guess who have been in close touch with the striving
poor.   One of my earliest experiences as a social worker
was as chairman of a committee started to prevent boys
and girls drifting into blind alley occupations by guiding
them into skilled employments.   When an unusually diminu-
tive and peaky-faced aspirant after a high-class occupation
presented him or herself, it became common form for some
member of the committee to say " Widow's child, as usual "
and, in spite of all our efforts, either personal disabilities or
the imperative need to earn something at once resulted in
most of such applicants slipping into the army of unskilled
casual workers.

To provide each of the 244,700 widows and their 463,900
children with pensions, calculated on Mr. Rowntree's " human
needs " standard of 12s. a week for a widow and 3s. 6d. for
a child,[2] or at the present cost of living (November 1923)
21s. and 6s. 1½d. respectively, would cost the nation £13¼
million per annum for the widows and £7¼ million for the
children—a total of £20½ million, or £17½ million more than
the amount now spent out of the poor rates on the relief of
widows and their children.[3]   But it would be possible—
whether desirable or otherwise—to devise a considerably
cheaper scheme.   For example, the pensions might be skilfully
graded on the assumption that a widow with—say—only
one or two children of school age was capable of doing something towards her own support.   Or a slightly lower general
scale might be adopted.   But most people with practical
experience will agree on two principles; first, that a woman

[1] The number of widows receiving poor-relief (institutional and domiciliary)
on January 1, 1923, in England and Wales was 54,794, with 123,406 children
(H.C. 121 of 1923, p. 27); I have added an estimated number for Scotland.

[2] In calculating 35s. 3d. as the minimum for a five-member family, Mr.
Rowntree allows 3s. 6d. for the woman's food and 1s. for her clothing.   If we
allow 4s. for rent and 2s. for fuel, and 1s. 6d. as her share of household and personal
sundries, we have a minimum of 12s.   For the figure of 3s. 6d. per child, see below,
p. 246.

[3] In addition, to make provision for total orphans, who have been estimated by
the Government Actuary as numbering about 50,000, at say, 12s. a week, would
cost roughly another £1½ million.   In all the above calculations the age limit
for the children has been taken at 16.   If a limit of 14 be taken, the cost would
be a little over ¾ of the above.   Any rates embodied in legislation would probably
be made subject to a cost-of-living sliding scale.

with even one young infant to look after in addition to all her house-work should not be forced into the labour market, and that day nurseries are from the financial and every point of view a doubtful economy; secondly, that the troublesome, unjust and demoralizing device of the income limit should not be introduced into the system of widows' pensions.

Opinions may differ as to methods and scales, but there seems no room for differences as to the need for some provision more honourable and adequate than that of the Poor Law. The impediment has hitherto lain not in any reasoned or organized opposition, but in the same failure and reluctance, on the part of those in authority, to think the matter out, that has been noted with regard to the general question of the economic status of the family. Now that the influence of the woman's vote has forced the question to the front, a solution cannot be much longer delayed.[1]

The attitude of the male electors to the question offers a curious problem to the psychologist. On the face of it, it would seem that provision for widows and orphans concerned men nearly as closely as women. To an affectionate husband and father, what should be more intolerable than the thought that, if an accident or illness should cut him off prematurely, those he left behind would be plunged into penury, tempered only by the humiliation of poor-relief or the scanty earnings possible to a woman who has to play the part of both parents. Yet one is faced with the stubborn fact that the enfranchisement of working men preceded that of women by over half a century and that during that period many social reforms, including old-age pensions and accident insurance, were passed into law and many others made the subject of active agitation, but the subject of widows' pensions was (so far as I can trace) never once debated in Parliament or pressed on the hustings.[2]

Probably the explanation of this apparent apathy lies

[1] At the General Election of 1923, pensions for widows with dependent children were included explicitly in the programme of the Labour Party and implicitly in that of the Liberal Party. The Unionists, at the famous Plymouth Conference, passed a resolution in the same sense, but their leaders merely promised " further consideration".

[2] Since 1918 it has been twice debated on resolutions introduced by the Labour Party. In 1919 the principle was accepted by the House without a division. In March 1923 it was opposed by Mr. Baldwin's Government on grounds of economy and rejected. Before 1918, resolutions in favour of widows' pensions were carried at several of the Annual Conferences of the Labour Party, the earliest occasion being in 1908.

partly in the instinct which makes all men turn away from the thought of death and its consequences as long as possible. Their respect for property has forced the well-to-do classes to overcome this distaste and has created the custom of making wills. The wage-earner has not been so constrained. But in addition one cannot but remember that, as the homely phrase goes, " human nature is the same all the world over " —in the West as in the East. The Indian custom of suttee, or failing that the lifelong servitude of the widow to her husband's parents, probably has its roots in an instinct which in the more sophisticated West yields a milder flavoured fruit. Perhaps Western men, who have been accustomed to hear the relationship between husband and wife compared to that between Christ and His Church, find nothing strange in the thought that when the giver of all good gifts is withdrawn, the dependants on his bounty should shiver and go hungry. Perhaps this thought, which brings pain to what is best in them, yet ministers to a sense of self-importance which lies very deep down. Perhaps some men are even conscious that they have not given their wives much other reason to regret their loss, and would rather be mourned for such a reason than none at all.

CHAPTER IV

THE WOMAN WAGE-EARNER

In previous chapters the doctrine of " a living wage " has been discussed mainly as though it concerned men wage-earners and their " dependent " wives and children. Women wage-earners have been almost ignored. It is necessary now to ask how they stand towards a wage-system which attempts to serve the double purpose of remunerating the services of producers and of providing for the rearing of future generations. Obviously the two great groups of women producers —those who perform remunerated services of hand and brain in the labour market and those who perform unremunerated services in the home—stand in a very close relationship, since about five out of six of the former group pass after a few years into the latter.[1]

Yet by a curious irony of fate, our present wage-system makes these two groups, economically speaking, rivals and enemies of each other, destined without desiring it and without knowing it, to balk, frustrate and injure each other at every turn. This unnatural and involuntary warfare has had, I believe, baleful effects upon society which have to a great extent been unrecognized even by feminists. Its immediate effects on the immediate material prosperity of the two groups are only part of the evil. It has hindered the full development of the productive capacities of the nation to an extent which cannot be measured, but of which the experience of the war, when an unconscious truce took place between the unconscious combatants, enables one to form some notion, and it has given a wrong twist to the outlook and ambitions of women, especially the abler and more ambitious among them, which cannot fail to have a harmful influence on the eugenic prospects of the race. I will try to justify these assertions, which I know will seem to most readers at first sight not very intelligible or convincing.

[1] *Educated Working Women,* by Clara E. Collet (P. S. King, 1902), p. 34.

216

(a) The Double Standard

Everyone knows that, broadly speaking, there is a double standard of pay for the two sexes. With the exception of a few occupations, of which the medical profession and the textile industry are the most conspicuous, women receive a lower rate of pay than men, even when they are engaged in the same occupation and do work which is equal in quantity and quality. Every one knows too that there is among men workers a strong dislike and fear of the competition of women in nearly every calling where such competition is an actual or possibly impending danger. This dislike has no doubt been greatly intensified in the past, and is to some extent intensified still, by sheer sex prejudice—by a feeling among the members of the dominant sex that it is belittling their own strength and skill to admit that any woman can attain to the like. Partly also, no doubt, it is dislike of any fresh addition to the number of competitors, without reference to the question of whether the competition is fair or unfair. But there can, I think, be no doubt that the most formidable and permanent part of the opposition—that which encourages the less worthy part by giving it a cloak of reason and equity in which to disguise itself—is the feeling among men workers that, as things are, the competition of women is not fair competition.

This feeling is made up, I think, of two elements. Partly it is the direct and inevitable result of the double standard of pay. Women are regarded as a dangerous class of blacklegs, who because they can afford to take and do take lower pay are a standing menace to the men's standard of life. Partly it is the belief that men have a better right to employment, because they represent not only themselves but their wives and children and the fact that some women have and many men have not dependants[1] is ignored or disposed of by saying that " normally " men are heads of families, while with women such a condition is exceptional or " abnormal". The married women naturally tend to share this view, though when they have themselves been wage-earners it is tempered by loyalty to their fellow workers and knowledge of their difficulties. It is even shared to some extent by the women wage-earners themselves, especially the young ones who expect soon to be married and look on their present occupation

[1] *See* the figures on p. 13.

as merely a way of keeping going until the right young man comes along. So long as the women remain in the few trades—mainly the needle trades and domestic service—which are traditionally and nearly exclusively their own, they are accepted as a matter of course, but whenever women are engaged in occupations where there is actual or potential masculine competition, they are conscious of being looked at askance, not only by those actually in rivalry with them, but by the whole body of organized male workers, and to a certain extent by general public opinion as expressed in the press and in social intercourse.

This is obviously not a comfortable nor an economically wholesome state of things. It is unpleasant for the women workers, who find themselves treated in the world of employment as alien interlopers or a kind of army of occupation. It cannot be good for " productivity " that any great section of workers should be barred out from certain callings and forced into others by considerations which have nothing to do with their productive efficiency. All the usual arguments in favour of free trade as against protection apply here. Just as, in the long run, it is best for the prosperity of the world as a whole, and of the individual nations composing it, that the channels in which a country's trade flows should be determined by its natural aptitudes and not by political considerations; so the prosperity of the community will be best served if the productive capacities of its citizens are allowed to find their natural level, uninfluenced by the question of sex.

Nevertheless, it is plain that, as things now are, those who are hostile to the competition of women workers with men have a case. Their hostility cannot be brushed aside as though it were wholly due to old-fashioned sex prejudice or selfishness. *As things now are*, it is true that the presence of women in the same occupations with men is a menace to the wage standards of the men. *As things now are*, it is true that, on the whole, unemployment or low wages among men brings greater suffering and more social damage than unemployment and low wages among women; because although not all men have dependent wives and children, yet the vast majority of wives and children are dependent on men.

The whole subject of the competition between men and women workers has been damaged by the prejudice and exaggeration shewn on both sides—by the opponents of the women and by their defenders—and the arguments used by both have tended to obscure the real extent of the injury caused by the introduction of sex considerations into the question of production. The women have either ignored the question of undercutting, or have sought to dispose of it by the airy suggestion of "equal pay", without I think sufficiently appreciating the practical difficulties of carrying this into effect, and the inequitable distribution of resources which, *as things now are*, it would intensify. The men have oscillated between a policy of denying the capacity of woman for serious competition, and of protecting themselves against her competition by every device known to the strategics of trade unionism. Or perhaps it would be truer to say that they have pursued both policies simultaneously, the former ostensibly and the latter subterraneously. Neither side has faced the problem fairly and squarely, as a real difficulty, arising out of the present wage system, and bound to go on causing damage to both sides and to the common weal, unless some means can be found of finally solving it. I suggest that the only possible solution is through a system of direct provision or family allowances that will, once for all, cut away the question of the maintenance of children and the reproduction of the race from the question of wages and allow wages to be determined by the value of the worker's contribution to production, without reference to his family responsibilities.

But to make this clear it is necessary to consider first the alternative solutions that are usually put forward and to see whether the difficulty can be got rid of, either—as most Trade Unionists desire—by limiting the industrial employment of women as much as possible and segregating them in occupations that are definitely given up to them, or—as most feminists are agreed in demanding—by allowing them to compete freely in all occupations, but on the condition that the competition is fair, i.e. that there is no undercutting but "equal pay for equal work".

Those who advocate the plan of segregation or delimitation of occupations usually represent it as merely the codification of a process which Nature and economic forces have themselves set up. For example, when, twenty-six years ago, Mr. and Mrs. Sidney Webb wrote their *Industrial Democracy*, they belittled the difficulties arising out of the competition of the sexes, by pointing out that there were in fact very few instances of trades where men and women were employed on identical processes. They admitted that the Unions were strongly hostile to the admission of women and would have instantly gone on strike rather than permit it. But they suggested that the policy of exclusion was unnecessary and futile—unnecessary, because over by far the greater part of the field of industry, men and women workers were separated by the force of a kind of natural fitness; futile, because " wherever any considerable number of employers have resolutely sought to bring women into any trade within their capacity, the Trade Unions have utterly failed to prevent them".[1]

The experience of the war has shewn the fallacy of this presentment, which has always seemed to me rather like arguing, that, because all the besiegers are outside the city wall and all the besieged inside, no hostilities can be going on. The success or failure of the policy of exclusion cannot be gauged by the few cases where " a considerable number " of employers have " resolutely sought " to bring women inside their trades. Such an attempt is not likely to be made unless the proposed substitution of women for men is on a large scale, and the advantages to be obtained are clearly established. Employers in the past have usually known that any introduction of women to a process hitherto reserved for men would be resolutely opposed, openly and covertly. A strike is by no means the only resource. It must be remembered that the more skilled a process is, the more teaching it requires. As a rule, a boy picks up his trade by watching, helping and receiving more or less definite instructions from the ordinary journeyman. Only a very small employer teaches his apprentice himself. Obviously an employer would find it very difficult to compel his men to impart their skill to girls. Any workman who did so would be severely penalized by his Trade Union and scowled on by his fellows. At the best, unwilling instructors are found to make very inefficient instructors. As for technical classes supported out of public funds, the Unions have in most places taken very good care that they shall not be used, by women or other· unprivileged persons, as a back door into the trades. An

[1] *Industrial Democracy* (1902 edition), pp. 498-9.

employer therefore who contemplates breaking new ground by the substitution of female for male labour in a skilled process knows that even if ultimately successful he will have to face a period of friction, dislocation or even suspension of his business, lasting until he has either brought the men to their knees or has somehow or other had enough women taught to be able to run his business with them and with non-unionists. There is also the possibility—one which no employer of the dominant sex is likely to under-estimate—that after all his trouble the women will prove incompetent. Clearly he is not likely to make the experiment, unless the saving he expects to make by it is very great, or unless—and this is perhaps the commoner case—demands and exactions which he considers unreasonable have provoked him to " show the men that he can do without them " by securing a more docile as well as a cheaper set of employees. But for one trade where there can be any question of such wholesale substitution, there are probably a hundred trades and thousands of employers who would like well to introduce women in small groups, to work either at the same processes with men or exclusively at subsidiary processes for which their qualities are likely to give them special aptitude, but who do not think that even the saving of from 40 to 60 per cent. on the wages of a few workers, much less the mere advantage to be obtained from a wider choice of workers, is worth the friction and unpleasantness with their men which would certainly ensue, even if they did not venture on an open fight.

(b) War-time Experience

That this is so was evident even before the war to those who were closely on the look-out for women's industrial opportunities. But the overwhelming proof of the extent to which their opportunities have been limited by masculine opposition is afforded by war-time experience. Then, under the pressure of national necessity, the barriers of sex prejudice and of Trade Union exclusiveness gave way—by no means so universally and completely as the outside public believed at the time, but still to a very considerable extent. The Government, as the need for more men at the front became urgent, did their utmost to encourage the substitution of women for men at home. The Trade Unions, naturally anxious to safeguard the interests of their members, obtained guarantees; first, that women engaged on men's jobs should be paid at men's rates; secondly, that Trade Union rules and practices, including of course those which excluded women, should be restored by force of law at the end of the war—a promise subsequently carried out by the Pre-war Practices Act of 1919. Under cover of these guarantees, women were admitted into a large number of occupations and sections of occupations, previously reserved for men. By July 1918, the total number of occupied women had increased by $22\frac{1}{2}$ per cent., or from just under 6 million to nearly $7\frac{1}{2}$ million,[1] the great majority of the additional women workers directly replacing men.[2] A brochure issued by the War Office in 1916 [3] for the purpose of encouraging women to offer themselves and employers to accept them, enumerated over 1,600 trades or processes in which women had been successfully employed, including such heavy occupations as sawmilling, heavy work in shipyards, loading props into trucks, loading and weighing coal, stoking, butchering, driving steam rollers, and such fine work as piano tuning and finishing, finishing motor cycles, acetylene welding, moulding artificial teeth, delicate electric drilling. Cabinet Ministers and others vied with one another in gorgeous tributes to the value of the work accomplished [4] and the country grew weary of hearing that "the women are splendid".

More balanced and elaborate estimates of the success achieved by women in these new openings, and surveys of the whole question of the relation of their work and pay to that of men, are contained in the reports of two Committees set up by Government—the Women's Employment Committee of the Ministry of Reconstruction, appointed in August 1916,

[1] Report of the War Cabinet Committee on Women in Industry, Cmd. 135, p. 80.

[2] Report of Board of Trade on Increased Employment of Women during the War . . . up to April 1918, Cd. 9164, p. 4.

[3] Women's Work in Maintaining the Industries and Export Trade of the United Kingdom, 1916.

[4] E.g., Mr. Lloyd George, December 25th, 1915: " I have seen women performing tasks hitherto allotted to skilled engineers—performing them successfully, swiftly—and yet it had only taken them, some two days, some a week and some a fortnight to learn how to do that work " ; the Earl of Derby, July 13th, 1916: " Women are now part and parcel of our great army: without them it would be impossible for progress to be made, but with them I believe that victory can be assured " ; the Earl of Selborne, July 5th, 1916: " If it were not for the women agriculture would be absolutely at a standstill on many farms in England and Wales." One expert on shipbuilding, whose name I forget, made a much-quoted assertion that if the war had gone on a little longer he could have undertaken to build a Dreadnought entirely by the work of women.

and the War Cabinet Committee on Women in Industry, appointed in September 1918. Both reports [1] were published in 1919, before the generous glow which seemed for a time to dissolve both sex and class prejudice had faded away, and I think it would be admitted by the keenest feminists that the tone of the Reports shews no signs of prejudice against women on the part of the members of the Committees, although in both cases the large majority of them were men. At the same time it must not be forgotten that by far the greater part of the evidence they examined was supplied by witnesses who represented either Associations of Employers or Trade Unions, and both of these classes had a distinct motive for laying stress on the defects of women workers which could scarcely fail, even though unconsciously, to colour their evidence. The employers were concerned to use women's work, but to get it cheap; the trade unions were concerned to prove that women's work was only fit to be used as a war-time makeshift. It would not serve the purpose of either to admit (even supposing it were true) that in any given case women workers were of equal or greater value than men. In saying this I am not impugning the honesty or patriotism of the witnesses. Everyone who has tried to collect evidence on a disputed question must know how extraordinarily rare it is to find an interested witness who is capable of keeping a perfectly even keel. The ultra-conscientious witness in his desire to be impartial heels over to the other side. The rest are ingenuously and unsuspectingly biassed in favour of the views that best serve their own prestige and pockets.

Another point which must be remembered in studying these war-time experiences is that the women workers who were brought into comparison with men were selected and trained under very abnormal conditions. At the beginning especially many employers, supposing apparently that all women were " much of a muchness", selected their female workers by methods similar to those of one head of a Government department who, having been often vainly urged by the wife of his chief in the Cabinet to introduce women clerks, at length reported that he had done so with very disappointing results. The women, it seemed, were frivolous and spoilt

---

[1] Cd. 9239 and Cmd. 135. *See* also the pamphlet issued by the Home Office on *Substitution of Women in Non-munition Factories During the War* and the detailed reports of Factory Inspectors on which the pamphlet is based (both published by H.M. Stationery Office, 1919).

the discipline of the office. When asked how they had been recruited he replied ingenuously, " We just asked our young men if they knew of any young ladies who would be suitable". Another head of a famous war-time organization, selecting women candidates for responsible and difficult work abroad, rejected the testimonials offered by the heads of their schools and colleges and the women chiefs under whom they had directly worked, saying " we prefer testimonials from men", and accepted instead references from clergymen and bankers with whom they, or sometimes only their parents, had had occasional professional dealing. Only gradually did the general run of employers learn the necessity of entrusting the selection and supervision of women to those who had experience in such work.

Undoubtedly also many women were held back, especially from the more highly skilled processes which required the most instruction, by the jealousy of men workers who could not bring themselves to impart to females skill which had a high monopoly value.[1]

To those who read the evidence with these facts in mind, it must I think be evident that—after making every allowance for the exuberance of war-time tributes—the success achieved by women in occupations previously thought only suitable to men was at least sufficient to shew that a vast amount of productive capacity must in pre-war days have been running, and is now again running, to waste, as a result of the policy of exclusion. The clearest and most unanimous testimony refers to occupations where manual dexterity and delicacy of manipulation are called into play. For example, Mr. Greenhalgh, Staff Officer of the Ministry of Labour and former secretary of the Rishton Weavers' Association, told the War Cabinet Committee:—

[1] For instance, in the pamphlet on Substitution issued by the Home Office, it is pointed out that " where the women—as most frequently happened—were entirely dependent on the skilled men for instruction, and these men were opposed to their introduction into the process, substitution was effected with difficulty, if at all. Even the existence of an agreement with the men's organization did not always solve the difficulty, since it was open to the individual male worker to put up a passive resistance to the instructions of his own leaders. Such passive resistance played some part in preventing effective substitution in the Nottingham lace trade; and in the Electro-plating Trade as long as that trade continued busy with the manufacture of its own products. The open opposition of the Glasscutters' Union for a time held up the substitution of women in the lighter decorative processes—perfectly suitable for them—of the flint glass industry, but in the end the matter was finally and amicably settled by agreement" (*Substitution of Women in Non-munition Factories During the War*, H.M. Stationery Office, 1919, p. 12).

" Take women altogether as compared with men, I venture to say that women upon weaving take home more money than the men. That is because of the nature of the work. The more adept you are in the use of your hands, the smaller your hands, the better you can handle twist and weft, and the better you can draw in ends that are broken, so that a man who has big hands is hampered in comparison with his daughter and the daughter takes home more money at the week-end than he does". [1]

Mr. John Taylor speaking of the same trade said:—

" I think the employers would be inclined, if there was sufficient female labour, to give females the preference, although it is a system which has gone on for such a large number of years that the employers have no feeling in the matter at all". [2]

This of course refers to one of the few trades where women had a really equal chance with men even before the war. But the same qualities are shewn in many trades where women's employment only began with the war.

" ' Women for ammunition work,' states the Manager of a Metal Works and National Filling Factory, ' are much more suitable than men . . . . They have more delicacy of touch and their fingers are more supple. Discipline and scrupulous cleanliness are difficult to obtain in either sex, but once a woman has acquired these habits she can be relied upon to maintain them. I think that ought to be qualified—with supervision—but they are much more cleanly. Shops where women work are really quite models compared to those where men work. They are very adaptable and train more quickly than men '." [3]

A Committee of the British Association reported in 1919 that

" There are few processes in industry on which women have not been employed, and few in which some women have not proved successful". [4]

The Report of Miss Anderson, H.M. Principal Lady Inspector of Factories, for 1915 says:—

" While comment is made on the unequal progress comparing factory with factory in one and the same industry and varying degrees of success in some industries are mentioned, the Inspectors are unanimous in speaking of the admirable spirit and natural skill shewn by the women . . . . In wire-drawing and engineering industries it is remarkable, considering the half-heartedness of the initial experiment, how general is the satisfaction over its success. It is an everyday occurrence to be told frankly by foremen that the women are doing ' very well indeed, much better than I ever thought they could '. . . . To myself, a managing foreman in a great shell factory said with emphasis, ' There is more in this than people think, *women have been too much kept back* '." [5]

The Home Office pamphlet on the substitution of women, in summing up the position, declares:—

" The Inspectors' reports show . . . that in a great preponderance of cases substitution has proved satisfactory. It is clear that in certain trades already largely employing women, such as the clothing and boot and shoe industries, women have shown capacity to take up and carry out completely and satisfactorily many of the more skilled processes hitherto reserved for men and have acquired mastery of the whole range of operations in other trades, like light leather tanning, which they had barely touched before the war". [6]

[1] Report of War Cabinet Committee on Women in Industry (Cmd. 135), pp. 88-9.   [2] *Ibid.*, p. 89.   [3] *Ibid.*, p. 281.
[4] *Industry and Finance* (Supplementary Volume), issued by the British Association, 1920, p. 10.
[5] Cd. 8276, pp. 14-15.
[6] *Substitution of Women in Non-munition Factories During the War*, 1919, p. 15.

The Report of the Women's Employment Committee says of the lighter operations in process work, such as " light engineering and wood-work in munitions, boots and shoes, clothing and light leather tanning in non-munitions trades", that " the women's success has been so complete and so notorious that little need be said " of their operations.[1]

Next to the occupations where manual dexterity and nimbleness, cleanliness and neatness were of advantage, the commercial openings appear to have been those where the success of women was most complete. There women before the war had found some footing, but chiefly as stenographers or telephonists. The typewriter and the telephone having been invented at a time when the employment of women was recognized as a possibility, they obtained a vantage ground from the first in this kind of work. As Professor Cannan pointed out:—

" If such things had been invented long ago, and owing to the conditions of that ime, the occupations connected with them had been made men's employments, women would probably have still been shut out from them". [2]

They still were shut out till the war from nearly all the more skilled and from some of the less skilled forms of commercial work. Their war-time success in banks was specially marked. Mr. Ingram of the L.C.C. Education Offices reported that, of 1,200 women placed through him in banks and in offices, only two complaints had been received. A London bank manager, writing in 1917, declared that the question as to the success of woman labour in banks

" is, I think, largely answered by the fact that a complete and efficient banking service has been maintained during two and a half years of war, when banking conditions have been abnormal and full of difficulties and complications entirely without precedent. . . .During this period, especially during the last twelve months, a large proportion of the total clerical work of the whole of the banks in the United Kingdom has been done by women clerks. . . . The net result is overwhelming evidence that, where women clerks have been carefully trained in their new duties, the results have been highly satisfactory". [3]

(c) Post-war Period

All this evidence indicates that there must have been much potential capacity for productive services among women that was never called into play before the war. What has become of it now ? To what extent have the new forms of service through which it found expression become a permanent

[1] Cd. 9239, p. 11.
[2] Committee on Women in Industry, Summaries of Evidence, Cmd. 167, p. 175.
[3] " Women in Banks," by Thomas C. Newman, in *Englishwoman*, April 1917, pp. 42-3.

addition to the labour power of the nation, and to what extent has the stream of women employed shrunk back again within the old channels ? It is impossible to answer these questions fully at present. The statistical material is not available, although when the occupation volumes of the 1921 Census are published, they will supply it in a very rough form. Further, the circumstances of the last four years have been so abnormal, that in any case it would be a mistake to assume that the present attitude towards the woman worker will be permanent. When a period of prosperity comes again, if the present generation of employers are alive to see it, they may remember their war-time experience of women's work and take courage from it. But for the time there is no doubt that they have capitulated practically without resistance to the forces which regard women very much as a fleet of merchant-men might be expected to regard a pirate ship, whose aid they have been obliged to accept to pilot them through strange waters during a storm.

Where women were actually replacing men at the Front it was of course part of the bargain that they should give up their places on the men's return. So far as I can ascertain there have been very few complaints of failure on the part of the employers to keep the bargain, or of women to acquiesce loyally in it. But in a great many cases the men did not return, and during the war and the brief prosperity which followed it many new branches of business were opened and new processes discovered. A great many of the unallocated posts then created were filled by women, and scattered through the professions and the trades there are still a sprinkling of women who have held their ground. It is difficult to gauge how many, because the employers who have kept women often behave as if they were ashamed of it and anxious to say as little as possible about it. But unquestionably the number retained are a handful compared to the great numbers who have been driven out; some to be replaced by youths with much less claim than themselves to war service. Thus in engineering—the field where the most conspicuous success of women was achieved—there appears to have been almost a clean sweep. There are instances of individual women who have held their own and who are working for firms who have insisted on retaining them; some of these being firms run by or specially for women. But these are only specks on the surface of the vast engineering industry. The munition works where the greatest number of women were employed have of course for the most part gone out of existence. But there are other kinds of engineering work where the special aptitude of women for delicate manipulative processes, to which such high testimony was borne during the war, would surely find vent, if there were no explicit or implicit taboo on their employment. An equally clean sweep—again with a few individual exceptions—has been made of the women employed in various capacities on railways, tramways, buses and motors.

In banks and commercial houses, the exclusion seems to have been rather less complete, probably because the opposing forces are less thoroughly organized. Some large banking firms and commercial houses have retained a portion of their women staff in departments reserved for men before the war, but only to a small extent and mainly on the more routine jobs. The women who did responsible and highly-skilled work, apparently to the complete and even enthusiastic satisfaction of their employers, have been mostly discharged. So far as those I have consulted can tell, most of those retained in responsible positions are in private firms which are comparatively independent of trade union pressure and able to use their own judgment. The same holds good of accountancy, where women found an opening for the first time during the war and have been retained to a very limited extent. In all these occupations the exceptionally fortunate women who have kept their footing have often been those who had either family influence or some capital at their back. In agriculture, where a small amount of capital can be made to go further than in most industrial and commercial undertakings, a sprinkling of women have been able to establish themselves as dairy or poultry farmers or market gardeners; and in catering (restaurants and tea-shops) there are many small ventures run successfully by women.[1]

The small amount of achievement in these and other forms of individual enterprise is no doubt partly due to the fact that the women who have any large amount of capital have so far usually preferred and been encouraged by social opinion to live on their dividends, and either occupy themselves with various forms of strenuous idleness or with unpaid philan-

[1] For most of the above details of the post-war position, I am indebted to the London Society for Women's Service.

thropic or public work. The girl of the wealthy middle class very rarely indeed enters the family firm, even in cases where the lack of sons, or the perversity of sons in preferring other occupations than business, is a family grievance. Here partly tradition and partly natural laziness are to blame, but partly also a reasonable sense of the risk involved in taking up a whole-time occupation which may be interrupted by marriage. Similarly in professional circles where the money available for expensive forms of training or for business investment is limited, parents not unnaturally feel that if a choice has to be made, the money is better spent on sons who will certainly wish to remain in their profession all their lives than on daughters who may only possibly do so. The same consideration undoubtedly has some deterrent influence on employers, who fear to place too much dependence on a class of workers whose tenure of office is so uncertain.

But making allowances for all these influences, it is true of even the upper grade of occupations and much more generally and emphatically true of the middle and lower grades, that the narrow channels within which the employment of women was confined before the war, is now again confined and is likely to remain confined if nothing helps it to break through, are due much less than is generally supposed to the free play of economic forces, which select from the available supply of labour the more efficient sex for the more skilled job and the less efficient for the less skilled, and much more to the steady pressure of men's hostility to women's competition.

(d) Sex Antagonism in Industry. Is "Equal Pay" the Cure?

What are the underlying causes of this attitude of the man worker towards the woman worker? I repeat that it cannot be explained solely by the age-long tradition of masculine domination, nor solely by the inevitable resentment felt by vested interests at a new class of competition, though both play their part. It is also due partly to the conviction that men have a right to all the best paid jobs, because they have to support wives and children out of their pay; partly to the fear that women, because they have no wives and children to support, can afford to take less, will be forced to take less, and so will undercut men.

Of these four motives, the first two are unreasonable, selfish, anti-social. To give them free play would be unjust not only to women but to the community, because they tend to check the full development of its productive resources. The last two are not unreasonable and to a considerable extent are justified by facts. If women are to fight the two former motives, they must find some way of getting rid of the two latter.

Curiously enough, both the women who lead the professional and trade organizations of women and most of those who speak for the political side of the women's movement have perceived clearly the danger of undercutting and propose to meet it by insisting on equal pay; but have ignored or belittled the other difficulty which equal pay would actually intensify. Apparently they have done this because they believe that to acknowledge the extra family responsibilities of men as a factor influencing wages would weaken their claim for equal pay. Yet most of them, even those who lead organizations of industrial women, belong themselves by origin to the middle classes, and might have perceived that in the professions the "families to keep" motive is very much stronger than the fear of undercutting. In the medical profession there has in fact been no undercutting, the women doctors having from the first insisted successfully on receiving the same rate as men. But masculine jealousy, though doubtless mitigated by this circumstance, has not been averted, as the determined movement to exclude women students from some of the largest hospitals has quite recently reminded us. In the teaching profession, the claim for equal pay is being energetically pushed by a section of the women; but the men, so far from regarding this as an evidence of loyalty and a method of safeguarding their own standard of life, are passionately resenting the claim and clamouring for greater differentiation between men's and women's salaries than already exists, on the plea of their family responsibilities. In the Civil Service, where the battle for equal opportunity has been waged with great ability and pertinacity on both sides,[1] the whole pressure of the astute officials who have wanted to keep women out of the higher sections of the service has been exerted to secure that they shall be separately graded and differently recruited and paid from men.

On the other hand, in the industrial occupations, the leaders of the men's Unions, though avowedly they would prefer that women should be kept altogether out of the factories or confined

[1] *See* the reports of the London Society for Women's Service for 1919-22.

to separate jobs, [1] have begun in some cases to feel that this is impracticable or at least that it is incompatible with democratic principles.[2]   They have frequently signified that their objection to open competition between men and women would be mitigated if not removed, if there were no sex differentiation at all in pay; that is if women, whenever they worked in the same occupation and same grade of occupation as men, received the same rates, whether the work was paid for by time or by piece.   " Equal pay " in this sense was urged by some of the representatives of skilled Unions before the Fair Wages Committee of 1908 [3] and again before the War Cabinet Committee on Women in Industry in 1919.[4]   It was also pressed on the latter Committee by a number of Women's Unions and Societies connected with Labour and by some of the feminist societies.   There is no doubt that it represents the most generally though not unanimously accepted view of the Trade Union world of women as well as of men. The question of the effect which the adoption of " equal pay " according to this definition would have on the prospects of women in industry is very fully and very ably discussed in the sixth chapter of the Majority Report of the War Cabinet Committee.   They state that the evidence placed before them had shewn that in occupations involving heavy or fatiguing manual work or technical skill, the average output of women is as a rule less than that of men and that where time rates were paid, the enforcement of the principle " the rate for the job " would in effect involve paying women the same rate as men for work of less value.

" Of the results of the universal adoption of this policy of equal time rates we were left in no doubt. There was complete unanimity on the part of the employers in every department of industry proper that it would drive women out, and the opinion of the general Unions was that it would have this effect on trades unsuited to women. The skilled men's Unions were now, as, according to the evidence before the Fair Wages Committee, they had been in 1908, of opinion that the policy would involve exclusion and it was frankly admitted by some of them that this was what was desired. The Management Committee of the General Federation of Trade Unions, however, appear from the evidence of the Federation's representative to have seen the hardship of this on the women displaced and the difficulty of the situation involved by paying equal time rates to the woman merely because

[1] Mr. Hutchinson, representing the A.S.E. before the War Cabinet Committee on Women in Industry, said that personally he did not " wish to see women in factories at all " (Summaries of Evidence, Cmd. 167, p. 59).

[2] In 1919 the Labour Party introduced a Women's Emancipation Bill (afterwards torpedoed by the Government Sex Disabilities Removals Act), of which the first clause ran:—" A woman shall not be disqualified by sex or marriage from holding any civil or judicial office or place of profit or trust."

[3] Cd. 4422.   [4] Cmd. 135.

she worked equal time. The women's Unions most connected with industry took the view that the principle of the ' rate for the job ' meant the exclusion of women from certain trades, but laid stress on this exclusion being either the result of insufficient training, which was remediable, or of the work being specially laborious and therefore only suitable for exceptional women. They thought that under any other system the entry of women into new occupations would be looked upon with suspicion and resisted. . . . Outside industry proper, where physical strength and technical training told less, e.g., in clerical duties, the evidence was less in support of the view that women would be driven out of occupation by the same rates being paid to both sexes. In the teaching profession, it appeared that the same rates paid to men and women would have the result of attracting women with a higher standard of qualification, and so of either driving out men or forcing a new differentiation of salary if men of equal qualification were required". [1]

The evidence thus summarized bears out my view that women are cherishing a vain hope if they think that merely by enforcing the principle of " equal pay " in the sense of " the rate for the job " they can buy off men's hostility to their competition. It is only in trades where this would mean in effect " equal pay for work of inferior value " and would consequently bar women out, that men have shewn any enthusiasm for the principle. It is sometimes argued that if a woman is not capable of the average output of a man, this very fact shews that the occupation is not suited to her, but the Committee point out very truly that this is fallacious. Who will contend that tennis and golf are unsuitable for women because their play is in general inferior to that of men ? A woman may be able to produce four-fifths of a man's output with ease, but if required to produce five-fifths as a condition of remaining in the trade she is likely to be tempted to overstrain herself. From the point of view of the interests of the industry, it is equally untrue to assume that the employment of women is economically unsound merely because their output is less, provided that they are allowed to be paid in proportion. This becomes obvious if we consider the case of the one great industry— the Lancashire cotton weaving—where men and women are and have been for several generations paid equal rates for the job, without causing the exclusion of either sex. This has been possible, first, because the industry was originally carried on in the home, the whole family taking part in it, and when it went into the factory women as well as men followed it there; secondly, because piece-rates prevail and women, where their output is less or they work fewer or lighter looms, earn less though getting exactly the same rates. But supposing that time-work rates had been the custom of

[1] Cmd. 135, p. 186.

the trade as it is in engineering, would women, if paid at the same rates, have retained the opportunities they enjoy at present and would the trade have profited as it has done by being able to utilize to the full the productive capacities of both sexes, without either sex being exploited or undercut by the other ? It was the Amalgamated Society of Engineers who most insistently pressed on the War Cabinet Committee the principle of the occupational rate,[1] but it was this Society which, after the war was over, refused the application for admission to the Society of women acetylene welders, although these had not only stood staunchly and loyally for the principle of the occupational rate,[2] but had proved their exceptional fitness to compete on the men's own terms.

The majority of the War Cabinet Committee were convinced by the evidence before them that the adoption of the principle of " the rate for the job," where this signified equal time rates, would bring " doubtful advantages to men " and would be fraught with " serious injury to women".   It would also be to the disadvantage of the nation, since it would tend to keep women out of employment, even in times of expanding trade when their work was required " to make the productiveness of the country more equal to the requirements of an increased consumption".   They therefore rejected the formula of " the rate for the job " in favour of " equal pay for equal work " in the strict sense of " equal pay in proportion to efficient output". [3]   They accepted the principle of equal piece rates and proposed that lower time rates should only be allowed when the employer can produce evidence to the satisfaction of the workpeople or the Industrial Council or Arbitration Court that the output is definitely lower.[4]

This they considered to be the utmost that was necessary to safeguard the men against undercutting, and the only doubt was whether the effect might not be to weigh the scales a little against the women.

When these discussions took place the memory of women's war-time achievements was still fresh in men's minds. So were the lavish promises of social reconstruction and a higher

[1] Cmd. 167, pp. 58-9.

[2] Miss Tynan told the War Cabinet Committee that " if it should prove that at equal rates employers preferred men, the Society's view was that they would rather fight for the equal rate than undercut their men colleagues by accepting a lower rate " (*Ibid., p.* 60).

[3] Cmd. 135, pp. 187-8.   [4] *Ibid.,* p. 190.

standard of life for all workers. Employers—disquieted by the lassitude and disaffection shewn by the returning soldiers —were sparing no effort to impress on the public that increased comfort would only be possible if there were increased production, and the same warning, over the names of some of the most respected Trade Union leaders, was blazoned on every hoarding.   Since then, four years of depressed trade and unprecedented unemployment have made the question of the exact terms on which women should take their proper place in industry seem nearly as unreal as arrangements for the coronation of a prince who has become a hunted fugitive. The women who are lurking in the corners of the disputed industries are, with a few exceptions, not anxious to call attention to themselves by demands for equal pay, and the men workers—except when they are also politicians—no longer feel it necessary to disguise the formula of exclusion under a euphemism.

When a period of expanding trade comes again the question may revive with it.   If at that time the Labour Party are in power or at least powerful enough to exercise a dominating influence in questions of industrial legislation, it is quite possible that equal pay in the extremest form of the occupational rate may be given legal sanction, either as a general principle governing all occupations, or in those occupations where rates of pay are already regulated by statutory bodies, or only for the employees of the Government and local authorities.

I suggest that, except under such compulsion, there is very little chance that equal pay, either in that form or according to the other interpretation, will make much headway, so long as the forces which have led in the past to unequal pay remain unchanged.   I suggest further that if compulsion were introduced as things now are, the effect would be to perpetuate and intensify the existing tendency of the two sexes to become segregated in different occupations and to give women even less equality of opportunity than they have at present.   Those who claim to speak for women usually couple together equal pay and equal opportunity, as though they were as inseparable as concave and convex.   But as a matter of hard fact, most of the small measure of equal opportunity which the woman-worker has hitherto enjoyed has been secured by accepting unequal pay.   Her cheapness has been the one effective weapon she has possessed when matched against the traditional domination, the vested interests, the trade organization, the political influence, and the physical superiority of the male. At the same time, it has been a two-edged weapon with which she has frequently cut herself and a poisoned weapon with which she has injured her potential future self and mate and children. How can such an unnatural conflict be prevented, and what are the forces which make competition between men and women, which shall be at once free and fair, so difficult to secure?

In order to give the answer it is necessary to revert to the theory—discussed at considerable length in Chapter II—of the " living wage " and to ask what effect this theory itself, and the facts with regard to family responsibilities which lie behind it, have had on wage rates. We saw then that it has become established as a kind of recognized truism—passionately believed in by the workers, unhesitatingly though somewhat unthinkingly endorsed by the general run of public opinion, and tacitly though sometimes grudgingly admitted by most employers—that an industry in a healthy condition and under normal circumstances " ought " to pay a " living wage " to its workers, and that where men workers are concerned this is interpreted as meaning a wage that will enable a man of average industry and capacity to support " a family " —that actually elastic entity being standardized, when further definition is pressed for, as though it consisted invariably of five persons. We saw further what a sloppy and ill-thought out theory this is; how badly it fits the facts, how imperfectly it has been and is being achieved in industry and how impossible it would be to achieve it adequately out of the existing national income. Nevertheless the theory exists, and clumsy, mis-shapen, shambling, stuttering thing that it is, it is the only living offspring to which the thought of economists, industrialists and moralists has given birth, which expresses the fact that society has to provide somehow for its own reproduction, and that as long as there is no way of doing this except through the wages of men, those wages must bear some relation to the needs of families.

But how far does this theory, or the facts which it attempts to express, actually influence wages? As we saw in Chapter I, the earlier economists assumed that the subsistence cost of a family was the main factor in determining wages. If the labourers did not earn sufficient to maintain themselves and enough children to " keep up the population", their numbers would be thinned by starvation; or, as Mill put it, by the refusal of the labourers to marry and have children; and the competition of employers for labour would raise its price. If, on the other hand, labourers earned more than the necessary amount, they would have larger families, and the over-supply of labour would lead to a fall in its price. This theory may have been approximately true to facts a hundred years ago, but if so it is true no longer. None of the suggested checks now work as the economists anticipated. Falling wages are not checked by the starvation of children, for humanitarian sentiment steps in to keep them alive. Labourers are not induced by low wages to refrain from marriage and procreation, nor tempted by high wages to produce large families. Thanks to some (at least to economists) unaccountable perversity in human nature, the actual tendency is apparently just the reverse. The families at the bottom of the social scale have the largest number of children and the number diminishes steadily right upwards to the top.[1] But this does not necessarily mean that the needs of the workers have no influence on their wages. Most modern economists agree in laying stress on the standard of life of the workers as a factor in determining wages, though they differ considerably in describing its operation. By " standard of life " they mean, not the minimum of physical necessaries on which the worker can sustain existence, but the total of the needs, including physical necessaries, which they expect to be able to satisfy out of their wages and without which they either will not consent to work at all or will work grudgingly and inefficiently. This " standard of life " may be merely tacit and informal, determined by the customs and habits that have somehow or other established themselves among the workers in a particular occupation and district at a particular time, or it may have been made explicit and crystallized by being embodied through Trade Union action into a set of standard rates and conditions of employment. But the point for us to notice is that the power of the Trade Union to enforce the standard rate will depend largely on the firmness with which the standard of life which it embodies has established itself, the tenacity with which the workers cling to it and the amount of suffering which they will be prepared to endure

[1] See pp. 188 et seq.

rather than accept anything else. That of course is not the only
factor, for no amount of tenacity or organization will enable a
Trade Union permanently to sustain a rate of wages which is
permanently and genuinely beyond the capacity of the industry
to bear, because of the strength of foreign competition or
because the demand is one that will wither away if prices rise
beyond a certain level. But granted that it is possible for an
industry to meet a certain wage-bill, the chance that the
employees will be able to extract the full amount will largely
depend on the staying power of their standard of life.

What bearing has this on the power of women to enforce
their claim to equal pay and equal opportunities ? When a
movement first began to train educated, middle-class women
as gardeners, it was obvious that whatever the ordinary
working-class male gardener might think of the experiment,
it contained no menace to his standard of life. The wages
on which he had been satisfied to rear a family seemed to the
ex-high school girl all too small to satisfy her individual
customary needs. I know of one garden where the war-time
introduction of two women to work alongside two elderly
men was the means of securing for the men higher wages,
shorter hours and a summer holiday. Contact with the
higher standards of the women infected the men. But in
the ordinary case the women who find their way into a trade
previously male belong to the same class as the men. They
have probably been reared in homes where the whole family
income has been no more than that which " equal pay "
would secure to them for their individual use. If later on
one of them married a fellow worker or a worker in a trade of
equivalent standard, she would have to revert again to her
earlier scale of living and to keep her whole household on
what her husband chose to give her out of a wage no larger
than that which she earned before marriage. That wage in
fact would not have been based on needs and customs that were
indigenous to her. It would have been based on a dogma.
What chance have women workers of enforcing such a demand
on employers who are indifferent to dogma and bent on getting
their labour cheap ? It may be done in times of exceptional
expansion of trade or shortage of labour, such as occurred
during the war. Or it may be done under normal conditions
by a few exceptional women of tenacious purpose. But what
employer,   contemplating   the   employment   of   women

in large numbers on a process hitherto monopolized by men, would forgo the temptation of beating them down to a level of wages corresponding with what he knows, and they know, and all the world knows, to be their real standard of life? I may be reminded that, as I made plain in previous chapters, the young bachelor workman and the elderly workman with wage-earning children enjoy a standard of comfort which is just as artificially inflated as that of the woman worker would be under a régime of "equal pay". But in the first place, these workmen obviously occupy a vantage ground for bargaining which is not open to the women. Even if they have no dependent wives and children themselves, they are indistinguishably lumped together with those who have and they can fight the battle of high wages from behind the petticoats of their comrades' wives and children. In that fact, indeed, lies the chief strength of the opposition to family allowances. But secondly, it is not true that the artificial prosperity of the childless workman has been enjoyed without injury to his comrade's family. Far from it! In the words of Mr. Commissioner Piddington, Chairman of the Australian Minimum Wage Enquiry, "from the produced wealth of the country, its children have less than enough, in order that the unmarried childless may have more than enough." [1] The resources out of which wages are paid are not a shoreless and bottomless sea. We have seen that even if capitalists' profits were eliminated altogether, and equalization of earnings carried out to an extent which even the extremer Socialists do not think possible or desirable, the whole wealth of the nation is at present barely enough to raise the worse paid workers to the by no means extravagant level of comfort suggested as desirable in Rowntree's *Human Needs of Labour*—so long, that is (never let us forget this qualification) as we proceed on the present assumption that no concession can be made to the parents of a family of three, five or seven young children unless the same advantage is simultaneously extended to the irresponsible youth of twenty. Handicapped by that supposed necessity, not all the forces of Trade Union organization, backed by humanitarian sentiment in favour of "a living wage", has sufficed or will suffice to secure an adequate standard of life for families. But what is impossible already would become

[1] Report of the Royal Commission on the Basic Wage (Australia), 1920, p. 90.

still further removed from possibility if the unmarried woman worker made good her claim to equal pay.[1]

(e) **The Test-case of " Equal Pay "—the Teaching Profession**

To illustrate this, let us suppose that the contingency already foreshadowed has arrived and that, by the joint pressure of trade unionist and feminist opinion, equal pay has been established by law; without any accompanying provision for wives and children. What would be the effects on social welfare and on the employment of women ? Clearly they would vary in different occupations according to their conditions. Let us consider first the occupation which more than any other seems to offer a favourable field for the experiment—teaching in public elementary and secondary schools. This has characteristics which at once get rid of some of the usual difficulties in the way of equal pay. In the first place, both sexes have always been employed in it in large numbers, the women (at least in the elementary schools)[2] being at present about three times as numerous as the men, so that there is no question of a prejudice against their employment. Secondly, the work they do is generally admitted to be equal in quantity and quality and identical in kind, except that the women teach chiefly the older girls and the juniors of both sexes and the men chiefly the older boys.[3] Thirdly, the danger of either sex totally or to any large extent displacing the other as a result of the adoption of equal pay, though not negligible, is probably less than in any other profession, because of the special fitness of men for the teaching of big boys and of women for the teaching of big girls and infants. Fourthly, the women in the profession are as strongly organized as the men and mainly in the same organization—the National Union of Teachers. They are educated, trained to express themselves and have leaders and spokeswomen well able to hold their own in the struggle for improved status. Lastly, the employing bodies—the local authorities and the State—are

[1] For the arithmetical proof of this, *see* below, p. 247 n.
[2] According to the Report of the Board of Education for 1921-22, about 78 per cent. of the teachers in elementary schools are women. The proportion in secondary schools is more difficult to ascertain, but would be somewhat less.
[3] Thus the report on Teachers in Elementary Schools says:—" Men and women often work side by side in the same schools; even if they are relatively seldom in competition for the same posts their duties are similar if not identical; and we are satisfied that the work of women, taking the schools as a whole, is as arduous as that of men and is not less zealously and efficiently done " (Report of Departmental Committee on Scales of Salary for Teachers in Elementary Schools, Cd. 8939, p. 9).

much more susceptible to political pressure than any body of private employers and are unable to use either the argument of foreign competition or the argument that "the industry cannot bear it", which are found so effective in profit-making enterprises. Bearing these points in mind, I think it may be said that the teaching profession is the test case for equal pay and that if it would not work well there unless accompanied by family allowances, it would be most unlikely to succeed in any other occupation, except those where the numbers affected are so small that economic considerations are outweighed by personal ones. It seems worth while then to examine the situation with regard to teachers in some detail.[1]

As before stated, about three-fourths of the profession are women. I do not know the proportion of the men teachers who are married with dependent children. But as, on the one hand, their children probably remain dependent to a later age than those of wage-earners, while on the other hand, they have a decidedly lower birth rate, it seems probable that the proportion does not greatly exceed the 48·3 per cent. estimated for the wage-earning population.[2]   The scale of pay now in use is (with slight modifications) that fixed by the Burnham Committee and it accords to women salaries amounting to four-fifths of those given to men doing the same grade of work in the same district. Although drawn up by a Committee on which the National Union of Teachers was largely represented, and agreed to by that body, the scale has given rise to bitter dissatisfaction among the men teachers, many of whom have left the N.U.T. and formed a separate Association of School Masters. They allege that the rates given place them in a position of inferiority compared with men belonging to professions of equivalent standing and are inadequate for the support of their families at the standard of comfort they may reasonably expect. On the other hand a considerable number of the women have seceded from the Union and formed a separate organization for the purpose of demanding equal pay.

On our hypothesis that they succeed in securing this, it is obvious that either the women's rates will have to be raised to at least the present level of the men's, or the men's depressed to the level of the women's. In view of the men's discontent with their present rates and their powerful organization, the

[1] See below, p. 190.   [2] See the figures given on p. 13.

latter alternative is extremely unlikely to be adopted, but if it were there can be no doubt that it would inflict considerable hardship on men with families and would probably tend to deter able young men from joining the profession. If on the other hand the women were raised to the men's level it would impose a heavy additional burden on the rates and taxes. It would mean in effect that the scale of pay for the whole profession was being adjusted to the standard of life of less than one-eighth of its members; for roughly speaking three-fourths are women, about one-eighth are men without dependent children and about one-eighth are men with such children. Other inevitable consequences are easy to foresee. The increased cost of staffing would be a serious impediment in the way of needed improvements in education—smaller classes, more scholarships, a raising of the school age, the coming into effect of the Fisher Act, etc. The tendency to reserve all the plums of the profession for men candidates, even when women were theoretically eligible, would become even more marked than at present. Most members of education committees are male and many of them are fathers of families. The feeling that is so strong among them that a salary of £500 or £700 is " too much for a woman " is not entirely due to sex prejudice. Behind it lies the conviction that the £500 or £700 will be expended to better advantage on the needs of a family than on those of an individual. An instance of the operation of this motive in educational appointments was given me many years ago by one of the pioneers of Welsh secondary education. He was chairman of the committee of management of a newly established school. The school was to be co-educational. The Committee by a unanimous vote decided that the post of Principal was to be open to men and women. It happened that outstandingly the best candidate—in academic qualifications, in previous experience and in force of personality—was a woman. This was generally admitted, but first one committeeman murmured that £500 was a large salary for a lady; then another remarked reflectively that Mr. A (the second best candidate) had a wife and five children. The Chairman reminded the Committee of their previous decision and of the importance of securing a Principal of first-rate qualifications. They shook their heads sadly and without further argument proceeded by a large majority to appoint Mr. A.

In face of these tendencies it appears to me that it is neither justifiable nor politic for women teachers to press for " equal pay" without making it clear that it must be accompanied by some system of family allowances. It may be said that this would not of itself dispel the desire of men to keep the plums for themselves, nor obviate the methods, avowed and unavowed, by which they seek to achieve this. No; but it would remove everything which at present gives justification to that desire both in the minds of those who feel it and of the general public. On the other hand it would be peculiarly unfortunate if any group of women, especially one whose profession is concerned with the welfare of children, should seem indifferent to the welfare of their own colleagues' families, or should range themselves with the hard-faced school of thought which would like to see all considerations of " living needs " eliminated from the question of wages. It is not in fact logically possible for the advocates of " equal pay " to join this school, for it has for its central dogma the very principle of " laissez-faire " which has brought the difference between men's and women's wages into existence. Women cannot " have it both ways". Either wages should be regulated entirely by the " blind economic forces " of supply and demand, or those forces must be bridled and guided by ethical considerations. If society is to lend its ear to the plea that justice demands that those who do work of equal value shall receive equal pay, it must also listen to the plea that the service of parenthood has likewise its value. There is, I suggest, only one possible way of satisfying both claims and of reconciling them with the interests of the ratepayers and the efficiency of the educational service, and that is by coupling with the concession of equal pay a system of direct provision. Such a system could be adapted to the special needs of the teaching profession. The scale of allowances and the age of dependency recognized might be such as would be suitable to a profession whose members naturally expect to give their children an education which will fit them for a status at least as good as their own. To avert any possible fear that an economy-loving education committee would be led to discriminate against teachers with dependants, it might be arranged that the payment of family allowances be defrayed by the Treasury and not by the ratepayers.

Such a settlement would make it possible to apply strictly

to the teaching profession the principle of equal pay, without injustice to the married man and without imposing an undue burden on the ratepayer or hampering the efficiency of the schools. The latter indeed would gain in efficiency, because it would become for the first time possible to fill every appointment with a teacher of the personal qualifications and of the sex best suited to it, without being biassed either by considerations of sentiment or of economy.

It is difficult to believe that in the long run this would not be an advantage to the men as well as to the women; and not only to the married men, but to the prospects of men generally in the teaching profession. But at present the men do not see this and the extremist section among them as among women is affording to the world a melancholy demonstration of the fact that a high level of education is not necessarily incompatible with a narrow and short-sighted form of professional selfishness. Unlike nearly every other profession or industry, this group of men teachers have apparently made up their minds that they have more to gain than to lose by " unequal pay". To justify it, they make great play with the argument of " our wives and families " and argue quite truly that the service of the mother in the home is as valuable as that of the teacher in the school, but turn a deaf ear when it is pointed out that this is not adequately recognized by a system which gives to an unmarried or childless schoolmaster the same salary as that received by a father of four and a higher salary than a schoolmistress with orphaned brothers and sisters dependent on her. From the point of view even of their own interests, it is difficult to believe that the teaching profession is exempt from the general rule which makes the presence in an occupation of a double standard of pay a menace to those receiving the higher standard. Education Committees may have a bias in favour of male candidates, but they are also influenced by considerations of economy which are likely to become more potent as the ratepayers become better organized; and so long as there is a difference and the greater the extent of the difference between the pay of men and women, the greater the likelihood that the relative proportion of the two sexes in staffing arrangements will be determined for reasons other than their special suitability. Though there are some positions in schools for which men or women respectively are clearly preferable, there are a good many others which could be filled almost equally well by either sex, and in these the question of economy is likely to be the determining factor, rather than, as it should be, the merits of a candidate selected from a wide field open to both sexes.

I conclude therefore that equal pay, though needed in the interests of everyone concerned in the teaching profession, would not work equitably or satisfactorily even in this especially favourable field, without provision for family maintenance.

(f) "Equal Pay" in Industry

How would " equal pay " work in the industries, where at least it is nominally desired by men as well as women? Would it lead to the withdrawal of men's opposition to the entry of women to their trades and would it secure to them equality of opportunity?

It is true that one of the two chief grounds of men's dislike of women in their trade—the fear of undercutting—would be to some extent allayed and this might lead in some occupations to the removal of the Trade Union interdict. But is anyone sanguine enough to hope that the opposition to women, which can make itself effective in other ways besides formal interdict, would vanish altogether? In the first place the men would still be apprehensive, and with some reason, of the influence of women on their rate of pay. In the long run, the presence in an occupation of a large number of workers who could afford to take less than the rest would exercise a downward pull on rates by weakening the power of the men to press for a rise or resist a fall. There might even be the possibility that if the employers were pressed too far they might eliminate men entirely from the grade in question and so escape the rule. Secondly, the other ground of men's hostility, the belief that because of their family responsibilities they have a right to the cream of the work, would be strengthened and not weakened by equal pay. As we have already seen, it is only in the trades where it is expected to act as a barrier to women's employment that the demand has been put forward. When, as in the case of the teachers, men have not this hope, it is not likely that the sight of a woman " taking the bread out of a man's mouth " by competing for his job will be sweetened to him merely by the knowledge that the loaf which she earns is as large as that he had hoped to share with his family. Illogical creature that he is, he would have scolded her if she had taken less, but he will not love her any better because she has got as much.

To turn to the other side of the question, what would be the effect of equal pay on the employer? Clearly, in those occupations where he has not been induced to employ women even by the certainty that he could get them for two-thirds or a half of the men's rates, he is not likely to begin when he has to pay them equally. There might be exceptions in a few highly skilled occupations, where the employers find it difficult to get a sufficient number of really competent workers and where the offer of a man's pay might tempt into the occupation women of better quality and education than the average of men available. In this way the change might result in opening to women some careers which are now closed. On the other hand in some occupations where both men and women are now employed, the men at the higher and the women at lower rates, it would probably suit the employer best, if he had to pay them equally, to eliminate either the one sex or the other. Judging by past experience this would tend to the lower paid and less skilled occupations becoming, even more than they are at present, reserved exclusively for women and the better paid and more skilled for men. Women often shrink from admitting this, as though it implied an admission of natural inferiority, and there can be no doubt that men very generally draw this conclusion. But surely this is to overlook the very heavy handicap on the industrial efficiency of women which results from their " marriage mortality". The fact that five women out of six[1] and, if we take the working class only, a considerably higher proportion, get married sooner or later—the majority of them in the early twenties—is an insuperable obstacle to their capturing the whole of any highly skilled occupation, except those few for which they are very unmistakably marked out by nature. On the other hand in low skilled occupations, or those where the only form of skill required is the nimble-fingered dexterity in which young girls excel, it is often a positive advantage to the employer that his workers discharge themselves after a few years' service.

It would conduce to much clearer thinking and would save a good deal of recrimination, if those who discuss the

[1] *See* above, p. 90.

relations of the sexes, in industry and every other department of life, would pay more attention to obvious differences of sex circumstance and would not hastily jump to the conclusion that every instance of inferiority on the part of women was due to some innate difference of sex character. Let those who are disposed to think disparagingly of the capacities of working women, because so few of them rise to high places, or because so many of them are unambitious and disinclined for responsibility, or because Trade Unionism among them has made such slow progress, reflect how men would be likely to show up in any of these respects, if all of them knew, from the time they first entered their occupation, that the chances were at least five to one against their remaining in it for more than a few years, after which they would pass on to a quite different calling which would be the main work of their lives; if, moreover, the whole weight of tradition and public opinion was against their promotion in the first occupation and in favour of their taking only the second seriously; if lastly, this public opinion had taken shape in a whole host of palpable impediments and impalpable influences, all tending to hinder them in their first occupation and push them into the second. It is difficult to form a vivid conception of men in such a situation because nothing analogous to it actually exists among them. But anyone whose imagination is equal to the task will be, perhaps for the first time, in a position really to appreciate the blighting influence which the prospect of marriage and motherhood has on the industrial careers of women. Perception of this even by women is I think hindered by the fact that in the class which does most of the thinking, or at least most of the writing and talking of the world—the educated middle and upper class—the proportion of permanent spinsters is very much larger than in the wage-earning class. The girl who looks forward as a matter of course to a University education followed by a professional career knows as a rule that it is more likely than not [1] that she will remain unmarried and have to depend on her profession not only for her livelihood but for the main occupation of her life. Her career means at least as much to her as her brother's means to him, and she often throws herself into it, and into the friendships and the intellectual

---

[1] *See* the figures given by Mr. and Mrs. Whetham in *The Family and the Nation* (p. 143), regarding the proportion of University women who marry.

interests which it brings her, with a whole-heartedness which makes the possibility of its interruption by marriage scarcely more worth taking into account, than the chances of inheriting a fortune or being killed in a collision. With the working-class girl it seems probable that this is very rarely true. In any case it is undeniable that the proportion of such women who remain unmarried is so small that an employer who contemplated staffing the higher positions in his works from among them would have a very restricted field to choose from. He could indeed enlarge it by bringing in married women, but that again entails disadvantages, real or imaginary, actual or potential which tend to discourage him.

Returning to our imaginary régime of equal pay, I conclude therefore, that if, in order to escape from the necessity of paying his women workers equally with men and so forgoing what has hitherto been a powerful inducement to employ them, employers desire to eliminate the one sex or the other, it will tend to be the men who disappear in the unskilled and the women in the skilled occupations.

Whether women, in any given occupation, would retain the foothold they had already won or even extend it would depend on the following considerations:—first, whether there was a scarcity in the trade of skilled male workers; secondly, whether the women's work was really equal, or better still had sex advantages (e.g. greater dexterity or docility) which more than compensated its sex disadvantages (e.g. marriage mortality, legal restrictions, etc.); thirdly, whether the weakening of the employers' motives to employ women when they were no longer cheap were counterbalanced by the weakening of the men's hostility to their employment. It is impossible to predict with certainty what results would be produced by the interplay of these various forces. Even the opinion of the experts in each occupation cannot be taken as final because it is almost invariably biassed by prejudice and self-interest. What can however be said with certainty is that a state of perfect competition between men and women workers (i.e., competition that is both perfectly free and perfectly fair and therefore calculated to produce the best productive results without inequity) could only be reached if, first, equal pay could be achieved in the sense of equal pay for work of really equal value, and secondly, if there could be eliminated from the

minds of everyone concerned—employers as well as workers—
the "men have families to keep" complex which at present
operates so strongly against women.

It may be said that this is an unattainable counsel of
perfection. The first condition could never be completely
achieved because it would involve a separate bargaining in
each individual case. True; but we could get a very long way
towards it—as near indeed as need be for practical purposes,
if it were recognized that where, in a given occupation or
grade of occupation, the work of women was on the average
and in the long run demonstrably inferior (or superior) in its
net productiveness to the work of men, they should be allowed
to receive rates of pay lower (or higher) than the men's rates
to an extent which reasonably represented the extent of the
difference. To carry out the feats of mensuration which such
a principle implies does not seem likely to present more difficulty to a Trade Board, or a Joint Industrial Council, or a
Trade Union negotiating with an Employers' Federation, than
many feats which are actually accomplished by these various
types of negotiating bodies, when they draw up their very
complicated piece-work lists. Professor Edgeworth, quoting
from the First Report on Wages and Hours of Labour (1894,
C. 7567) explains that:—

"The wage-rate proper to each kind of work is obtained by numerous extras
and deductions corresponding to variations from a standard article or process with
specified price—a standard which is itself far from simple. Here, for instance, is, or
was, the definition of the standard woman's boot: 'Button or Balmoral, $1\frac{1}{2}$ in.
military heel, puff toe; 7 in. at back seam of leg machine-sewn, channels down or
brass rivets, pumps or welts, finished round strip or black waste.' The extras (and
likewise the deductions) may be presumably calculated on the principle described
by Mr. and Mrs. Webb as 'specific additions for extra exertion or inconvenience'
so as to obtain 'identical payment for identical efforts' ".[1]

When Trade Boards were first under discussion, Mr. and
Mrs. Ramsay MacDonald, who were then opposed to them,
made great play with instances similar to this description
of a standard boot as illustrating the impossibility of fixing
and enforcing rates nicely adjusted to the innumerable
variations of process in a complicated trade, through the
machinery of Trade Boards. Yet the thing has been done,
and the party Mr. Ramsay MacDonald leads passionately
opposed the curtailment of the functions of Trade Boards
by the Government of 1923. When one considers what are
the actual drawbacks to women's labour put forward by

[1] "Equal Pay to Men and Women for Equal Work," by Prof. Edgeworth in
Economic Journal, December 1922, p. 441.

employers—smaller output, irregular timekeeping, legal restrictions on overtime, higher overhead charges due to the
above three causes, inability to perform some minor detail
of the work—it is difficult to believe that the task of verifying
and working out the costing of these deficiencies presents
any very serious difficulty in a trade sufficiently organized
and under control to be susceptible of wage-regulations at
all. Even the disadvantages attendant on "marriage
mortality", as tested by the proportion of women workers
who leave for marriage soon after attaining proficiency, and
the importance in the industry in question of retaining a high
proportion of experienced workers, must surely be roughly
estimable by the experienced officials representing employers
and Trade Unions who are accustomed to negotiate wage
questions. It would doubtless be difficult to set a price on the
discomfort which the employer feels in dealing with a class of
employees whom he cannot swear at comfortably, but that
may perhaps be written off against the satisfaction it must give
him to know that they are much less likely than their male
colleagues to go on strike or spend Monday in recovering from
a week-end spree. Does not the real difficulty in working out
rates which would represent equitably the comparative value
of men and women's labour arise from the fact that none of the
parties concerned have hitherto wanted to do it ? The employers have seen their profit in exaggerating the women's
deficiencies; the men if they cannot exclude the women *de jure*
hope to do it *de facto*, by insisting on their claiming more than
they are worth; and inexperience, vanity and above all desire
to placate the men have led women to acquiesce in the claim.

Then, again, it may be said that the second condition
essential to perfect competition—elimination of the "families
to keep" reason or excuse for preferring men—would never
be perfectly achieved, even by the adoption of family allowances, because in spite of the allowances, it would still be felt
that an individual who is a parent as well as a worker is
(if equal in other respects) of more importance than an
individual who is only a worker, and that his unemployment
or underpayment is more socially injurious. True again;
but family allowances would carry us a great part of the way,
especially if the system adopted were such that the allowances
were adequate in amount and graded to meet the needs of
workers in occupations of varying status, and provision

was made for their continuance during periods of at least involuntary unemployment. Society would then know for the first time just where it stood with regard to family maintenance. It would no longer feel that money was being filched out of its pocket in the shape of higher wages or increased cost of living on the plea of " wives and families " which was really spent on football matches or silk stockings. At the same time it would be much harder for it to ignore the needs of the real children, when it saw them numbered and budgeted for individually, instead of as a blurred and shifting background behind every man's head. Employers would have lost their one valid excuse for paying women less than men, when their work was really equal. This would not by itself secure equal pay or equal opportunity for women, but it would make it possible to achieve both by resolute organization, helped possibly by legislation. This done, employers would gain by being able to concentrate on efficiency. They would no longer be tempted to economize by substituting inefficient female for efficient male labour, nor find themselves compelled to restrict their field of choice to one sex or the other by Trade Union opposition. A kind-hearted employer when considering questions of promotion or of dismissal in slack times, would not feel constrained to give preference to an inferior workman with a family over a superior one without dependants.

Before leaving the subject of equal pay and its bearing on family maintenance, there is one neglected and one disputed point which call for discussion.

(g) "Equal Pay" for Equivalent Work

I have hitherto tacitly assumed, as others writing on the subject have done, that the claim for equal pay concerns only those occupations in which both sexes are employed. But in fact the claim, if conceded at all, must as a matter of justice be extended to occupations where the work of women is different from that of men but equivalent; by which I mean that it calls for about the same or similar qualities of body, mind or character and imposes about the same strain on those qualities. For example, one might say that the work of a tailor or tailoress and a dressmaker, or of a trained elementary school teacher of either sex and a trained sick nurse, are about equivalent. The workers in these two pairs of occupations belong as a rule to about the same social status as the other member of the pair; go through about the same number of years' training before they arrive at proficiency; require in the case of the first pair, about the same amount of manual dexterity and taste, of the second, about the same high qualities of character and brain. There are of course differences in the kind of aptitude required. The tailor requires more accuracy and neatness and the dressmaker more delicacy and taste; the nurse's work is more arduous, dangerous and responsible; the teacher's makes a greater demand on purely intellectual qualities. But roughly probably no one would deny that there is an equivalence. And probably there is not one of the whole range of occupations now monopolized by women which has not, if we searched them out, several equivalents among occupations now shared between the sexes or monopolized by men. If then, the claim for " equal pay " is founded on " justice ", on the principle that those who are contributing a service of equal difficulty should receive an equal reward, surely it ought to be extended to all women's occupations which are equivalent to any man's occupation. Why, merely because there are men as well as women in the tailoring trade and the teaching profession, pay the tailoress more than the dressmaker, the schoolmistress more than the nurse ? Why should the scavenger who cleans our streets get more than the charwoman who cleans our houses? Again from the point of view of preventing undercutting and securing really free and fair competition, it is evidently not enough to demand equal pay for workers in identical occupations. There should be equal pay in equivalent occupations; otherwise there can be no certainty that the women may not be keeping the men out by means of their cheapness, or the men keeping the women out for fear of their cheapness. It is not safe to assume, as Mr. and Mrs. Webb do in *Industrial Democracy*, that when the besieging sex is outside the walls and the besieged sex inside, the sexes cannot be at war. About twenty years ago when investigating the conditions of the cigar-making trade in Liverpool, I found in progress a nearly complete capture of the trade by women. The handful of men still left spoke bitterly of the women as blacklegs. I do not know what has happened since but if, as seems likely, those few men have long since passed out, the woman cigar-maker is probably no longer regarded as a blackleg. Yet potentially she is just as much (or as little) " taking bread out of the men's mouths " as though she had just clambered into some citadel of masculine exclusiveness.

There is another disadvantage arising incidentally from the assumption that it is only when a woman does precisely the same work as a man that she is entitled to the higher scale of pay customary among men. It leads unobservant people to form a quite wrong estimate of the relative difficulty and importance of " men's jobs " and " women's jobs". When women took up men's work during the war, it was amusing, but it was exasperating too, to hear the naive astonishment expressed by men when they found that women could actually perform delicate manipulative processes in engineering; or that they had physical endurance and good humour enough to do the work of a tramway conductor for nine hours a day; or that they were clever at handling live stock on a farm. Yet all their lives men have been accustomed to see the wonders of delicate manipulation wrought by women's fingers in dressmaking, millinery, lace making, embroidery, cookery. Every day working men see their wives and mothers toiling for twelve to sixteen hours at scrubbing, sweeping, cooking, sewing, tending young live things. Their attitude is but a fresh illustration of the truth that a people accustomed to measure values in terms of money will persist, even against the evidence of their own eyes, in thinking meanly of any kind of service on which a low price is set and still more meanly of the kind of service which is given for nothing.

For all these reasons it is clear that a true equilibrium between men and women workers could not be achieved merely by vindicating the claim of women who are doing the same work as men to be paid at rates equal to those of men but higher than those paid to women rendering equally valuable services which only women can render. It could only be reached by getting rid altogether of the double standard of pay for the two sexes.

When however we pass from what is desirable to what is practicable, what hope is there of attaining this end, so long as the causes which have brought about the double standard remain untouched? It may be possible, though as I have tried to show, it would work out badly all round, for the women working in the same occupations as the men to hitch their trailer on to the men's car and so get themselves dragged up to a level of pay in excess of their real standard of life. Trade Unionism and legislation might together accomplish this. But what motive power can the women in the equivalent occupations command which will bring them up to the same level? We may know that a charwoman's work is as skilled as a scavenger's, but who is going to force the householder to pay the same? Who is going to trace out for each of the many ill-paid women's trades the parallel grade in men's occupations? Again, even if the machinery existed, we are up against the old difficulty that the wealth of the country is insufficient to pay really adequate family wages even to all men workers and that the childless male workers who are now enjoying an approximation to a family wage are doing it at the expense of their comrades' children. It will not mend matters to admit the women to a share of their undeserved gains. Nothing can really redress the balance except to remove the weight that is pulling it down against the women. This does not of course mean that the men would be dragged down to the women's level, nor necessarily that the women would be pulled up to the level of the men. It might conceivably be that the relation of the total of women workers' incomes to the total of men workers' incomes would remain much as at present, though both totals would probably rise as a result of the greater efficiency and productivity that would result from giving every child a fair chance. But we should know what part of each income was wages and what part society's method of providing for its own reproduction—and the latter portion would be paid to the wives and mothers on whose shoulders rests the real burden of that special task.

(h) **The Responsibility of Women Workers for Dependants**

Those who are concerned in defending the claim of women to equal pay have laid much stress on the fact that women are often responsible for dependants. The extent to which this is the case has been so much investigated and discussed lately, that I need not deal with it at any length. I will merely refer my reader to the previous investigations;[1] and will say, that of the three estimates worked out, which differed in a somewhat startling fashion, I think myself that that arrived at by

---

[1] *Wage-earning Women and their Dependants*, by Ellen Smith (The Fabian Society, 1915). "Dependants on Women Wage-earners," by M. H. Hogg, in *Economica*, January 1921. *The Responsibility of Women Workers for Dependants*, by B. Seebohm Rowntree and Frank D. Stuart (Clarendon Press, 1921).

Miss Hogg, of the London School of Economics, is probably the most reliable.   The estimate of the Fabian Women's Group, who concluded that 51·13 per cent. of working women where wholly or partly responsible for dependants, has been widely quoted.   But the methods used in the enquiry, which made its object known to the women wage-earners from whom information was sought, would inevitably lead to a biassed result, as the women who replied would be mainly those who desired to substantiate their claim to equality of treatment with men.   On the other hand, Mr. Rowntree reached the conclusion that only 12·06 per cent. of women workers were wholly or partially supporting others.   But his enquiries, as his Report shows, were made chiefly from the mothers of the wage-earning women.   A working-class mother usually dislikes admitting that she is dependent on her children, or, as she puts it, " a burden " on them, and without wishing to deceive the investigators, she is likely to repudiate the suggestion, being helped in doing so by the fact that very rarely has she worked out even in her own mind a debit and credit account of the contributions and costings of the wage-earning members of her family.   Miss Hogg's estimate was based, like Mr. Rowntree's, on a door-to-door investigation, but as it was undertaken for a purpose which had nothing to do with women's dependants, it was more likely to elude bias. She concluded that 28 per cent. of women workers have partial and 5 per cent. total responsibility for dependants.

It has been sometimes suggested that a system of family allowances should include adult dependants, whether of men or women wage-earners.   But anyone who during the war had experience of the payment of separation allowances to dependants " other than wives and children " will hesitate to advocate such a provision, because of the difficulties of investigation and the temptation to fraud which it would bring with it.   It would certainly increase the expenses and complication of administering the system and make actuarial computation of the cost of allowances much more difficult. It is also open to the objection that a system devised to recognize the value to the community of healthy motherhood and childhood and to assure to these their rightful share of the community's wealth, should not be set in false colours in the public eyes by having mixed up with it provision for meeting exceptional cases of breakdown.   In a well-organized community, the normal needs of old age and sickness would be met out of insurance and savings, and where these were wanting or inadequate the claim is one that might well be left to the affection and self-sacrifice of relatives and friends, helped out whenever necessary by public and private charity. Wages and salaries, even at the minimum level, should not be so exiguous as to allow of no margin to cover exceptional calls. As Mr. Rowntree points out, many of the cases of so-called " dependency " on women wage-earners (and he might have added on men too) are really those of relatives acting as unpaid housekeepers. These would be covered if it were recognized that neither men nor women, married or unmarried, should be expected to do their own house work while giving full time service in the labour market. The Australian proposal that minimum wages should be fixed to cover the normal needs of two adult individuals—if extended to women as well as men —would reasonably meet the case. As in fact the unmarried working-class wage-earner does not usually· absorb the whole time of the woman who looks after him, this would leave a margin which might be devoted, as the worker's disposition and circumstances might prompt, either to saving up a nest egg towards the future home, or meeting the claims of exceptional domestic trouble, or providing (as the bachelor's surplus does now in nine cases out of ten) for such extra luxuries as the unmarried may be thought reasonably to need to compensate them for the forlornness of their single state.

PART II

The Restitution of the Family

CHAPTER V

EXPERIMENTS IN FAMILY ALLOWANCES

It has been the Great War, more than anything else, that has brought the question of direct provision for families into practical politics; first, by providing a great object lesson in its working through the system of separation allowances; secondly, by producing the conditions of economic dislocation and mutual distrust among the nations which have obliged them to take stock, more seriously than ever before, of their national resources in wealth and in population.

But the idea of direct provision did not originate with the war. It has been put forward from time to time tentatively by various observers approaching the question from very different angles. As long ago as 1795, the younger Pitt, speaking in the House of Commons in a debate on Whitbread's Minimum Wage Bill, pointed out that:—

> " there was a difference in the numbers which composed the families of the labouring poor. . . . So that were the minimum fixed upon the standard of a large family, it might operate as an encouragement to idleness on one part of the community; and if it were fixed on the standard of a small family, those would not enjoy the benefit of it for whose relief it was intended. What measures then could be found to supply the defect ? Let us make relief in cases where there are a number of children a matter of right and an honour, instead of a ground for opprobrium and contempt."[1]

As a measure for improving the status of women as well as the welfare of children, the idea was given publicity by Mr. H. G. Wells in the *New Machiavelli* and the name he gave it, " the endowment of motherhood", laid hold of the popular imagination. But even before that it was busying the minds of feminists. It is over twenty years since I wrote for a College society a paper[2] which sketched out many of the arguments used in this book, especially those relating to the social disadvantages of the present system and its bearing on the

---

[1] *Select Documents of English History* (G. Bell & Sons, 1919), p. 562.

[2] Published many years later as a pamphlet on " The Problem of Women's Wages " (Northern Publishing Company, 1912).

relation between men's and women's labour, and concluded that the remedy was for Society to "substitute a system of more direct payment of the costs of its own renewal" for "the arrangement by which the cost of rearing fresh generations is thrown as a rule upon the male parent". The experience of separation allowances gained during the war and the new readiness of the public to consider schemes of social reconstruction made the time seem ripe for a development of this idea and in 1917 a small Committee was formed at my suggestion to draft a scheme for the national endowment of motherhood. Its report,[1] compiled principally by Mr. Emil Burns, attracted little attention; public criticism concentrated itself chiefly on the statement that to provide for all mothers and children up to fourteen on approximately the scale of separation allowances would cost something like £240 million per annum. The mere mention of such a sum proved sufficient to prevent serious consideration of the scheme on the part of the ordinary reader, who persisted in regarding the cost as though it implied a wholly new burden on national resources instead of a new way of meeting an existing charge.[2]

The investigations of the War Cabinet Committee on women in industry served to draw further attention to the subject and the minority report, drawn up by Mrs. Sidney Webb, is notable as containing the first full statement, so far as I am aware, by a leading member of the Labour Party of the disadvantages of providing for families through wages based on the fiction of the uniform standard family and also the first suggestion of the possibility of dealing with the matter through the industrial pool system. She says:—

"It has been suggested that this charge might be thrown, at any rate in part, upon employers of labour by a weekly stamp duty analogous to the charge under the National Insurance Acts, of an identical sum for each person employed, of whatever age or sex. The proceeds, including possibly a Government subvention sufficient to cover the average periods of unemployment, sickness or other " lost

---

[1] *Equal Pay and the Family*, by K. D. Courtney, N. Noel Brailsford, E. F. Rathbone, A. Maude Royden, Mary Stocks, Elinor Burns and Emil Burns (Headley Bros., 1918). 1s.

[2] The Committee nevertheless proceeded to enlarge its membership and to turn itself into a Family Endowment Council, which has continued to work at the subject, collecting statistics and information relating to foreign experiments and making these public through the usual media of the press, leaflets, pamphlets, lectures and conferences. Its members now include Lord Askwith, Mr. Ramsay Muir, M.P., Mr. C. Dampier Whetham, Mrs. Barbara Drake and others. None of them are committed to any special scheme of family endowment, nor to any of the views expressed in the publications of the Council—merely to a desire to promote further study of the subject.

time "—seeing that there must obviously be no corresponding interruption in the children's maintenance—could then be distributed, subject to the necessary conditions, at the rate of so much per week per child, through the local health or local education authorities, to all mothers of children under the prescribed age.

" Such a method of raising the funds would, however, have various economic drawbacks, and would probably be resented by organized labour no less than by the employers. It would, I think, be better for the Children's Fund—the 'bairns' part' in the national income—to be provided from the Exchequer (that is to say, by taxation) like any other obligation of the community."[1]

Another scheme of national provision which attained considerable publicity was that of Mr. and Mrs. Dennis Milner. They proposed that to every man, woman and child should be secured as an inalienable right a State Bonus, "just sufficient to maintain life and liberty if all else failed."[2] They estimated the sum necessary as 5s. per head per week (pre-war value), to be adjusted periodically to changes in the cost of living; to cost approximately £470 million per annum, or £400 million after deducting savings on relief, etc., and to be raised by a tax on all incomes, deducted at source.

(a) Australia

(i) THE AUSTRALIAN COMMONWEALTH

The first step actually taken by any nation towards giving the family its rightful economic status was in Australia, where the experiment began, not of establishing family allowances, but, in effect, of clearing the way for them, by reducing to the absurd the present method of providing for the family through men's wages. The experiment of the universal legalized minimum wage, based on the needs of a family, which was destined to provide this *reductio ad absurdum*, was not entered on consciously, deliberately and formally, as it probably would have been if Australia had happened to be colonized by a Latin instead of an Anglo-Saxon race. It grew up, in a haphazard fashion which reminds one that Australia is indeed Great Britain's own daughter, out of a bit of case law. In 1900, a Commonwealth Constitution Act was passed. It was framed by a Convention of which one Mr. H. B. Higgins was a member and it contained a clause (Section 51, sub-section 35) suggested by him which conferred upon the Federal Parliament legislative power with regard to " conciliation and arbitration for the prevention and settlement of industrial disputes extending beyond the limits of any one State." Under this clause and

[1] Report of the War Cabinet Committee on Women in Industry, Cmd. 135, p. 307; *see* also p. 306 of same report.
[2] *Scheme for a State Bonus* (Simpkin, Marshall, Hamilton, Kent & Co., 1918), 3d.

two subsequent Acts a Commonwealth Arbitration Court was set up and in 1907 it had to adjudicate in a case brought by a manufacturer of reaping machines to obtain a declaration (necessary to secure certain exemptions under the Excise Tariff Act) that his conditions of remuneration were " fair and reasonable". Mr. H. B. Higgins—by then Mr. Justice Higgins—was President of the Court. The " Harvester Case", as it was called, occupied nineteen days and in his finding the Judge laid it down that, by " fair and reasonable " conditions of remuneration, Parliament had clearly not meant merely such conditions as might be obtained through the ordinary higgling of the market.

" The standard of ' fair and reasonable ' must therefore be something else; and I cannot think of any other standard appropriate than the normal needs of the average employee regarded as a human being living in a civilized community."

And he goes on to define the standard as wages sufficient to provide food and shelter and clothing and " a condition of frugal comfort estimated by current human standards".[1]

He then summarized the evidence he had taken to ascertain what such a standard would involve and announced the decision he had arrived at.

" I have tried to ascertain the cost of living—the amount which has to be paid for food, shelter, clothing, for an average labourer with normal wants, and under normal conditions. Some very interesting evidence has been given, by working men's wives and others; and the evidence has been absolutely undisputed. I allowed Mr. Schutt, the applicant's counsel, an opportunity to call evidence upon this subject even after his case had been closed; but notwithstanding the fortnight or more allowed him for investigation, he admitted that he could produce no specific evidence in contradiction. He also admitted that the evidence given by a land agent, Mr. Aumont, as to the rents, and by a butcher as to meat, could not be contradicted. There is no doubt that there has been, during the last year or two, a progressive rise in rents, and in the price of meat, and in the price of many of the modest requirements of the worker's household. The usual rent paid by a labourer, as distinguished from an artisan, appears to be 7s.; and, taking the rent at 7s., the necessary average weekly expenditure for a labourer's home of about five persons would seem to be about £1 12s. 5d. The lists of expenditure submitted to me vary not only in amounts, but in basis of computation. But I have confined the figures to rent, groceries, bread, meat, milk, fuel, vegetables, and fruit; and the average of the list of nine housekeeping women is £1 12s. 5d. This expenditure does not cover light (some of the lists omitted light), clothes, boots, furniture, utensils (being casual, not weekly expenditure), rates, life insurance, savings, accident or benefit societies, loss of employment, Union pay, books and newspapers, tram and train fares, sewing machine, mangle, school requisites, amusements and holidays, intoxicating liquors, tobacco, sickness and death, domestic help, or any expenditure for unusual contingencies, religion, or charity. If the wages are 36s. per week, the amount left to pay for all these things is only 3s. 7d.; and the area is rather large for 3s. 7d. to cover—even in the case of total abstainers and non-smokers—the case of most of the men in question. One witness, the wife of one who was formerly a vatman in a candle works, says that in the days when her husband was working at the vat at 36s. per week, she was unable to provide meat

[1] *The Next Step: A Family Basic Income*, by A. B. Piddington, K.C. (Macmillan & Co., Melbourne, 1921), pp. 3-4.

for him on about three days in the week. This inability to procure sustaining food
—whatever kind may be selected—is certainly not conducive to the maintenance
of the worker in industrial efficiency. Then, on looking at the rates ruling elsewhere, I find that the public bodies which do not aim at profit, but which are
responsible to electors or others for economy, very generally pay 7s. The Metropolitan Board has 7s. for a minimum; the Melbourne City Council also. Of
seventeen municipal councils in Victoria, thirteen pay 7s. as a minimum; and only
two pay a man so low as 6s. 6d. The Woodworkers Wages Board, 24th July,
1907, fixed 7s. In the agreement made in Adelaide between employers and
employees, in this very industry, the minimum is 7s. 6d. On the other hand,
the rate in the Victorian Railway Workshops is 6s. 6d. But the Victorian Railway
Commissioners, do, I presume, aim at a profit, and as we were told in the evidence,
the officials keep their fingers on the pulse of external labour conditions, and
endeavour to pay not more than the external trade minimum. My hesitation has
been chiefly between 7s. and 7s. 6d. ; but I put the minimum at 7s. as I do not
think that I could refuse to declare an employer's remuneration to be fair and
reasonable, if I find him paying 7s. Under the circumstances, I cannot declare that
the applicant's conditions of remuneration are fair and reasonable as to his
labourers."[1]

This celebrated judgment was not only held to have established the principle of " the living wage " based on family
needs as a principle of Australian law, but the actual figure
of 7s. a day, arrived at after the perfunctory enquiry described
in the above quotation, has remained the basis of the awards
of the Commonwealth Arbitration Courts ever since, the figure
being from time to time adjusted to changes in the cost of living
according to figures supplied by the Commonwealth's statisticians. The decisions of this Court only affect actual disputants
in cases coming within its jurisdiction. They are not a common
rule for industry; the conditions of labour in most industries
being left to be regulated by the laws of the different States.
But it is said that the influence of the Court extends much beyond its jurisdiction and that the standard it has set up is
usually followed by the State Courts and by those employers
who adjust their relations with their employees without coming
into Court.

The laws of the different States vary, but all recognize in
some form the principle of legal regulation of wages. In two
of them tribunals exist—the Industrial Arbitration Court of
Queensland and the Board of Trade of New South Wales—
which have the power to fix a general basic wage. Victoria has
160 separate Wage Boards which fix wages in each industry
without any defined relation to each other or to the supposed
cost of living of a family. The rest have Courts which lay down
minimum wages in cases of disputes and all these have adopted,
with modifications, the supposed needs of the five-member
family according to the Harvester judgement as the basis of

their decisions. In New South Wales a four-member family is adopted as the unit, in accordance with a decision made in 1914 by Judge Heydon, who pointed out that the average number of children in married workers' families was a little less than two.

During the years of war, when prices were rising steadily, there began to be increasing dissatisfaction all over Australia with the rates of wages then laid down, and in a speech on October 30, 1919, at the eve of the General Election, the Prime Minister of the Federal Government, the Rt. Hon. W. M. Hughes, made the following announcement:—

" If we are to have industrial peace we must be prepared to pay the price, and that price is justice to the worker.   Nothing less will serve.   We have long ago adopted in Australia the principles of compulsory arbitration for the settlement of industrial disputes and of the minimum wage.   The cause of much of the industrial unrest, which is like fuel to the fires of Bolshevism and direct action, arises with the real wage of the worker—that is to say, the things he can buy with the money he receives. This real wage decreases with an increase in the cost of living. Now, once it is admitted that it is in the interests of the community that such a wage should be paid as will enable a man to marry and bring up children in decent, wholesome conditions—and that point has been settled long ago—it seems obvious that we must devise better machinery for insuring the payment of such a wage than at present exists.   Means must be found which will insure that the minimum wage shall be adjusted automatically, or almost automatically, with the cost of living, so that within the limits of the minimum wage at least the sovereign shall always purchase the same amount of the necessaries of life. The Government is, therefore, appointing a Royal Commission to inquire into the cost of living in relation to the minimum or basic wage.   The Commission will be fully clothed with power to ascertain what is a fair basic wage and how much the purchasing power of the sovereign has been depreciated during the war ; also how the basic wage may be adjusted to the present purchasing power of the sovereign, and the best means when once so adjusted of automatically adjusting itself to the rise and fall of the sovereign. The Government will at the earliest date possible create effective machinery to give effect to these principles.   Labour is entitled to a fair share of the wealth it produces. The fundamental question of the basic wage having been thus satisfactorily—because permanently—settled, there remain other causes of industrial unrest which must be dealt with if we are to have industrial peace." [1]

The Commission appointed in accordance with this promise represents the first attempt ever made (so far as I can ascertain) by the Government of any nation to put a real content into the empty phrase " a living wage", and its work deserves full consideration; not because of its immediate legislative results, which were mediocre, but because it afforded a smashing demonstration of the futility of the conception of a " living wage " based on the fiction of the uniform typical family.

The Commission consisted of three representatives of employers, nominated respectively by the Associated Chambers of Commerce of Australia, the Associated Chambers of

[1] Report of the Royal Commission on the Basic Wage, 1920, pp. 7-8.

Manufacturers of Australia and the Central Council of Employers of Australia, and three representatives of employees, nominated by the Conference of Federated Unions of Australia. These six agreed upon as Chairman a distinguished lawyer, Mr. A. B. Piddington, K.C., Chief Commissioner of the Inter-State Commission, and he was duly appointed by the Governor. Both sides were represented by Counsel and the Commission had placed at its disposal the services of the Commonwealth statistician, Mr. Sutcliffe.[1]   Considering the object of the Commission, it seems strange that it did not include a single woman. Had such a body been appointed in this country the Government would doubtless have selected some one of that panel of about a dozen women, mostly near relatives of promi-nent politicians, who for the last ten years since women became formidable have almost invariably served to represent their sex on Government committees or commissions closely affecting women's affairs.

The reference given to the Commission was to enquire into the following matters[2]:

1. The actual cost of living at the present time, according to reasonable standards of comfort, including all matters comprised in the ordinary expenditure of a household, for a man with a wife and three children under fourteen years of age, and the several items and amounts which make up that cost ;
2. The actual corresponding cost of living during each of the last five years ;
3. How the basic wage may be automatically adjusted to the rise and fall from time to time of the purchasing power of the sovereign.

Their labours extended over nearly a year and included 115 public sittings and 69 private deliberations. They exam-ined 796 witnesses and inspected 580 exhibits; making a sepa-rate enquiry and a separate finding as to the cost of living for the capital cities of each of the six States of Australia. They decided to leave the cost of living in the country districts and towns to be worked out subsequently on the basis of their figures by a Bureau of Labour Statistics, which they recom-mended to be established for the purpose of carrying out the periodic automatic adjustment of the basic wage suggested in Clause 3 of the reference to the Commission.[3]

The most important part of their task was obviously that indicated in Clause 1. They found that the actual cost of living at the time of the enquiry varied in the different States from £5 17s. in Sydney to £5 6s. 2d. in Brisbane.[4]   This included all matters comprised in the ordinary expenditure of a house-

[1] Ibid., pp. 8, 14.   [2] Ibid., p. 7.
[3] Ibid., pp. 13-14, 18-19   [4] Ibid., pp. 58-9.

hold, for a man with a wife and three children under fourteen years of age, according to reasonable standards of comfort. The items making up the expenditure were as follows, the figures given being those for Melbourne:—

	Melbourne.
	£ s. d.
Rent	1 0 0
Clothing—Man	8 5
„ Woman	10 9
„ Boy (10½)	4 6
„ Girl (7)	3 5
„ Boy (3½)	1 11
Food	2 6 1½
Fuel and light	4 9
Groceries (not food)	1 6
Renewal of household utensils, drapery and crockery	2 7½
Union and Lodge dues	1 9
Medicine, dentist, &c.	9
Domestic assistance	1 6
Newspapers, stationery and stamps	1 0
Recreation, amusements and library	2 0
Smoking	2 0
Barber	3
Fares	2 6
School requisites	3
	£5 16 0

It should interest the British reader to compare this finding with Mr. Rowntree's estimates of the " cost of living " of a five-member family in *The Human Needs of Labour*. This it will be remembered he worked out on the basis of July 1914 prices as 35*s*. 3*d*., viz.:—[1]

	s. d.
Food	15 1
Rent	6 0
Clothes	5 0
Fuel	2 6
Sundries :—	
Household	1 8
Personal	5 0
Total	35 3

which at the price level of 1920 (the date of the Australian Commission's Report) would be equivalent to £4 14*s*. 10*d*. Neither of these estimates, it should be remembered, purport to be estimates of the lowest amounts on which the families considered could exist in health and decency. [2] The Australian Commission expressly rejected the suggestion that it should take as its standard the physiological minimum necessary for bare existence or that it should consider only the actual

[1] *The Human Needs of Labour*, p. 129.
[2] Mr. Rowntree had worked out a lower minimum in his earlier book on " Poverty."

expenditure of " the humblest type of worker". They considered it to be " the main principle of the modern regulation of wages in Australia . . . that even the humblest worker ought to receive a wage which will afford him ' reasonable standards of comfort ' in regard to ' all matters comprised in the ordinary expenditure of a household ' " and therefore set themselves to determine what these reasonable standards of comfort were " not by reference to any one type or group of employees, but by reference to the needs which are common to all employees, following the accepted principle that there is a standard of living below which no employee should be asked to live".[1]

There is nothing new in the verbal assertion of this principle. What is new is the attempt to give it content and validity by working out in full detail the kind of family budget which such a standard of living would require. The result will interest at least women readers:—

Items contained in the model budget of the Report o the Australian Royal Basic Wage Commission.[2]

HOUSING.

Rental ordinarily paid by the tenant of a five-roomed house in sound tenantable condition; not actually cramped as to allotment; situated in decent surroundings ; and provided with bath, copper and tubs. The rent of such a house in Melbourne was in November, 1920, found to be £1 0s. 0d. per week.

CLOTHING.

Husband.—Suits, 2 to last 3 years; hat, 1 a year; socks, 6 a year ; ties, 2 a year; braces, 1 best to last 3 years, and another to last 1 year ; shirts, 4 working to last 1 year, and 5 best to last 3 years; flannels, 2 a year ; underpants, 2 a year ; collars, 6 a year ; handerchiefs, 6 a year ; pyjamas 3 to last 2 years ; working trousers, 2 a year ; overcoat, 1 to last 4 years ; umbrella, 1 to last 3 years ; boots, 1 best to last 2 years, and 3 working to last 2 years;   shoes 1 to last 2 years ; boot repairs, 3 a year ; sundries. The cost at November prices was 8s. 5d. per week.

Wife.—Hats, best, 2 to last 2 years, and another to last a year; costume, winter, 1 to last 3 years, and summer, 1 to last 3 years; skirt, blue serge, 1 to last 3 years, tweed, 1 to last 2 years; blouse, silk, 1 to last 2 years, voile, 1 a year, cambric, 3 to last 2 years, winceyette, 3 to last 2 years; camisoles, 4 a year; combinations, 4 to last 2 years; undervests, woollen, 1 to last 2 years, cotton, 3 to last 2 years; bloomers, winter, 2 to last 2 years; nightdresses, 4 to last 2 years; underskirts, white, 1 to last 3 years, moreen, 1 to last 3 years; corsets, best, 1 to last 2 years, and another to last a year; dressing gown, 1 to last 3 years; aprons, 4 a year; stockings, cashmere, 3 a year, cotton, 3 a year; handkerchiefs, 6 a year; gossamer, 1 a year; veil, 1 a year; gloves, silk, 1 a year, cotton, 1 a year; top coat, 1 to last 4 years; golfer, 1 to last 3 years; umbrella, 1 to last 3 years; shoes, best, 1 a year, second, 1 a year; slippers, 1 a year; repairs, best 1 a year, second 1 a year ; sundries. The cost at November prices was 10s. 9d. per week.

---

[1] Report of the Royal Commission on the Basic Wage, p. 17.
[2] List taken from Piddington's *The Next Step* (pp.7-9); costs as in Melbourne. The full lists with items priced for each city separately are in the Commission's Report; also the lists claimed by the representatives of the Employers and the Unions respectively.

Boy, 10½ years.—Overcoat, 1 to last 3 years; suits, 2 to last 2 years; pants, 4 to last 2 years; jersey, 1 to last 2 years; summer coat, 2 to last 2 years; shirts, 4 a year; stockings, 4 a year; caps, 1 a year; straw hat, 1 to last 2 years; soft hat, 1 a year; handkerchiefs, 6 a year; braces, 1 a year; ties, 2 a year; singlets, 4 to last 2 years; pyjamas, 3 to last 2 years; boots, best 1 a year, school 2 a year; repairs, 2 a year; collars, 3 a year. The cost at November prices was 4s. 6d. per week.

Girl, 7 years.—Singlets, 2 to last 2 years; stays, 2 a year; bloomers, cotton, 2 a year, woollen, 1 to last 2 years; petticoats, 2 to last 2 years; dresses, best, 1 a year, voile, 1 a year, print, 2 a year; jersey, 1 to last 2 years; hats, 2 a year; cap, 1 a year; pyjamas, 2 to last 3 years; socks, 4 a year; handkerchiefs, 6 a year; top coat, 1 to last 3 years; boots, best, 2 to last 3 years, school, 3 to last 2 years; repairs, 2 a year; sundries. The cost at November prices was 3s. 5d. per week.

Boy, 3½ years.—Overcoat, 1 to last 3 years; suits, light, 1 to last 2 years, heavy, 1 to last 2 years; pants, 1 a year; jersey, 1 to last 2 years; blouse coat, 2 to last 2 years; shirts, 2 a year; stockings, 4 a year; cap, 1 to last 1½ years; handkerchiefs, 3 a year; braces, 1 a year; singlets, 2 a year; nightshirts, 2 a year; boots, best, 1 a year; shoes, 2 a year; collars, 2 a year; boot repairs, 1 a year. The cost at November prices was 1s. 11d. per week.

FOOD.

Husband, Wife, Boy (10½ years), Girl (7 years), and Boy (3½ years).—Per week.— Bread 20 lbs., flour 3 lbs., oatmeal 1½ lbs., rice ½ lb., sago and cornflour ½ lb., eggs 1 doz., milk 7 qts., sugar 5½ lbs., jam 2 lbs., treacle ½ lb., butter 2 lbs., beef 8 lbs., mutton 4 lbs., fish 2 lbs., bacon ½ lb., fruit (fresh) 8 lbs., raisins ¼ lb., currants ¼ lb., potatoes 11 lbs., onions 1½ lbs., vegetables 8 lbs., tea ½ lb., coffee ¼ lb. The cost at November prices was £2 6s. 1¼d. per week.

MISCELLANEOUS ITEMS.

Husband, Wife, Boy (10½ years), Girl (7 years), and Boy (3½ years).—Per week.— Fuel, 1¼ cwt. wood; lighting, 1s.; groceries (not food), 1s. 6d.; renewals of household utensils (general and cooking), 6d.; renewals of household drapery, etc.: 1 pair D.B. blankets, to last 15 years; 2 pairs S.B. blankets, to last 15 years; 1 D.B. quilt, to last 15 years; 2 S.B. quilt, to last 10 years; 1 pair D.B. sheets to last 2 years; 2 pairs S.B. sheets, to last 2 years; 5 pillow slips a year; 3 towels a year; 1 tablecloth, to last 5 years; 5 serviettes, to last 5 years; 2 pairs window curtains, to last 4 years; renewal of household crockery, glassware and cutlery, 4½d.; union dues, 6d.; lodge dues, 1s. 3d.; medicine, dentist, etc., 9d.; domestic assistance, 1s. 6d.; newspapers, stationery and stamps, 1s.; recreation, amusements and library, 2s.; smoking, 2s.; barber, 3d.; fares 2s. 6d.; school requisites, 3d. The cost at November prices was £1 0s. 10½d. per week.

Total Cost of Living, Melbourne, November, 1920:—

	£	s.	d.
Rent	1	0	0
Food	2	6	1½
Clothing	1	9	0
Miscellaneous	1	0	10½
	£5	16	0

In studying this mass of detail, it is impossible I think for the observer, especially perhaps for the woman observer, not to be struck with two things: first the immense pains expended by the Commission in carrying out their task as thoroughly and impartially as possible; secondly, the extraordinary artificiality and futility of the uniform family standard as shewn up by their findings. It is really touching to think of those seven men—the three representatives of the great bodies of employers in Australia and the three representatives of its federated unions and the distinguished lawyer who presided—considering whether the supposititious wife of the typical Australian workman should be allowed six blouses a year (two silk, two voile, and two cambric or winceyette) as claimed by the Federated Unions; or only three (one silk, one voile, one cambric or winceyette) as suggested by the Employers; and finally deciding on a just compromise which allows to the garment of each material its appropriate length of service, and so on through all the innumerable articles of clothing, diet and utensils required for every member of the imaginary household. We even find them collecting statistics as to the proportion of clothing that is bought at sale time and deciding on a reduction of 3 per cent. on the itemized cost list to allow for the advantages of sale time purchasing; while a further reduction of 5 per cent. is allowed to cover the saving made by thrifty housewives in cutting down the garments of the older members of the family to fit the younger.[1] As to this they remark:—

"With regard to infants' clothing the difficulty arises that *while the typical family maintains its structure* (i.e., contains three children and no more under fourteen) the question of carry-over or replacement of infants' clothing is almost an insoluble one."[2]

Exactly so; but if only all workmen had families, and all families were typical families "retaining their structure" and including invariably just three children (boy $10\frac{1}{2}$; girl 7; boy $3\frac{1}{2}$) how much easier of solution the problem of the living wage would be! If the findings of the Commission had in fact been made the basis of a legalized minimum wage in Australia and the details of the findings had obtained the publicity they deserve, one can imagine the Australian youth of twenty-one planning the purchase of a motor-bicycle and reflecting that he could devote to it the whole of the £12 10s. 3d., the £9 13s. 11d. and the £5 10s. 9d. secured to him by a paternal government to pay for the clothing of his three supposititious children. Or one can imagine him backing his favourite at the races with the price of his supposititious wife's "one gossamer 5s. 6d." or "two winter bloomers 8s."[3]

But the Commission's findings have not been made the basis of a new legalized minimum wage, and it is clear that

[1] Report of Royal Commission on the Basic Wage, pp. 32-3.
[2] *Ibid.*, p. 25. The italics are mine.
[3] *Ibid.*, pp. 30-2.

they never will be, at least in the form of a uniform five-member family wage. It is further clear that at least one member of the Commission—its chairman—saw plainly the real bearing of the evidence laid before him and the conclusions to which it pointed.

The Commission printed its Report on November 19, 1920, and it is significant that it was a unanimous report, so far as concerns its main findings as to the actual cost of living, according to reasonable standards of comfort.[1] The Prime Minister immediately called upon the Commonwealth Statistician, Mr. G. H. Knibbs, C.M.G., to pronounce as to the feasibility of paying to all adult male employees a wage based on the Commission's findings, i.e., a wage of not less than £5 16s. a week. His reply came promptly. It is to the effect that:

" Such a wage cannot be paid to all adult employees because the whole produced wealth of the country, including all that portion of produced wealth which now goes in the shape of profit to employers would not, if divided up equally amongst employees, yield the necessary weekly amount ". [2]

The Prime Minister then consulted the Chairman of the Commission, Mr. A. B. Piddington, who submitted to him the following Memorandum.[3] I have reproduced it nearly in full, because it seems to me to sum up with admirable brevity and lucidity the case against the fiction of the uniform family wage. Those who have followed the arguments of Chapter II—arguments which I and others have been urging on the British public in articles, letters to the press and speeches for the last five years—will notice how closely similar are the conclusions arrived at quite independently and from different data by this Australian jurist and statesman, as to the failure of the uniform family wage theory to fit the facts, the impossibility of realizing it out of existing national resources, the vast waste of resources on mythical children and the cruelty to real mothers and children which it involves. What however we have not attempted here is the striking demonstration contained in the table headed " Rise in Money Wages " and the preceding paragraph on the race between

[1] A Minority Report by two of the employers'. representatives merely dissents rom any expression in the Report which seems to imply that its findings must necessarily become the basic wage, and further dissents from any impression which implied that the basic wage of 1914 was too low.

[2] *The Next Step*, by A. B. Piddington, p. 22.

[3] Report of the Royal Commission on the Basic Wage, pp. 89-93.

wages and prices which would ensue from an attempt to place wages compulsorily upon this unreal basis.

. . . . . .

MEMORANDUM

1. The True Incidence of the Cost of Living.

The present basic wage purports to provide:—

(a) In New South Wales Awards the actual cost of living of a man, wife and two dependent children.

(b) Elsewhere in the Commonwealth the same, but with three children (henceforth called the typical family).

So many employees in New South Wales are under the Commonwealth Awards that I shall assume the Commonwealth Court's family throughout.

It is self-evident that while this wage system is based on the theory that the minimum of wages is that which will enable employees to live in comfort, it does not follow that system. Assuming that the basic wage does provide the actual cost of living of the typical family,

1. All families with more than *three* dependent children suffer privation.

2. All families with less than *three* children receive more than is necessary for the living wage.

3. All unmarried men receive what would support a wife and also *three* children.

[Here figures are given shewing population of male wage-earners with their condition as to marriage and number of children under 14.]

From this it appears:—

1. That at present the industries of the Commonwealth pay as if the children in the Commonwealth were 3,000,000 (i.e., three children for each of 1,000,000 employees). In point of fact the children of employees in the Commonwealth number 900,000.

2. Thus industries now pay for—

    450,000 non-existent wives.

    2,100,000 non-existent children.

There is little doubt that the present quasi-submergence of employees with families is due to ignoring the true incidence of the actual cost of living. From the produced wealth of the country, its children have less than enough in order that the unmarried childless may have more than enough.

2. How the Findings of the Commission as to Cost of Living may be distributed between (1) man and wife ; (2) each of three dependent children.

The work of the Commission enables the cost of each child in the typical family to be ascertained precisely, except as to its share in the sections—Rent and Miscellaneous requirements. A careful estimate as to these two sections renders results upon which the following may be taken to be a fair distribution of the actual cost of living:—

	Per week. £ s. d.	
(a) Man and wife . . .	4 0 0	
(b) Three dependent children . .	1 16 0	(=an average 12s. each per week.)
	£5 16 0	

3. How the said finding of the Commission can be made effective so as to secure for every employee the actual cost of living according to its true incidence, accepting the finding of £5 16s. 0d. as the actual cost of living for a man, wife and three children.

(a) To secure the actual cost of living for each employee according to its true incidence, it is desirable that every employee should receive enough to keep a man and wife,

  (1) because during bachelorhood, which ends, on the average for the whole Commonwealth, at the age of 29, ample opportunity should be provided to save up for equipping the home.

  (2) because a man should be able to marry and support a wife at an early age. The figures as to 450,000 non-existent wives may therefore be disregarded.

(b) Every employee must be paid the same amount of wages; otherwise married men with children will be at a disadvantage. There is, indeed, no conceivable reason, either on economic or humane grounds, why an employer's obligation to each individual employee should vary with the number of that employee's children.

(c) There is, however, every reason why employers as a whole throughout the Commonwealth should pay for the living needs of their employees as a whole. Indeed, that they should do so is the basis of the whole theory of the living wage. The proposal below for a tax upon employers as a whole is based upon this consideration.

(d) The desired result can be secured by a basic wage of £4 per week paid by the employer to the employee, and the payment of an endowment for all dependent children, whether *three*, or less, or more, in the family at the rate of 12s. per week.

[The Memorandum proceeds to shew that under the then existing basic rate of £3 17s., 38·6 per cent. of all men employees of the Commonwealth, or 70 per cent. of all married employees were getting less than enough to provide a reasonable standard.]

4. The effect upon industry, domestic and for foreign countries, of making a basic wage for all employees of £5 16s. 0d.

The increased burden of industry from raising a present basic wage of say £4 to £5 16s. would be for 1,000,000 employees the sum of £93,000,000 per annum. The latest figures (1918) of the total production of the Commonwealth shewed it was valued at £298,000,000. Thus the increased burden upon industry would amount to 31 per cent. of the production in 1918, but as prices of things produced have universally risen since, this percentage would be somewhat reduced. It may fairly be taken that the labour cost of things produced, carried out to the last analysis, equals 50 per cent. of their value as produced, so that the increased burden on industry would make the labour cost of things produced 62 per cent. higher than it is, less whatever deduction should be allowed as above suggested. If it could be supposed that the whole of the additional £93,000,000 labour cost could be passed on to the community, the increase in prices would altogether outstrip the purchasing power of employees having a basic wage of £5 16s. (*see below*). But of the £298,000,000 in 1918, £113,000,000, or about 38 per cent., was exported. Whether the increased wage cost of 62 per cent. could be added to the prices asked for the 38 per cent. of our products, would depend upon world prices, that is, upon outside competition with all countries in the markets of the world. I have not had time to go into details with regard to our individual export industries, but it seems certain that, as far as manufacturing industries for export are concerned, they would be ruined. With regard to primary industries, the percentage of labour cost in them is below the percentage of labour cost (carried to the last analysis) in the industries of the Commonwealth as a whole, and moreover wool, and (at present) wheat enjoy a favourable position in outside markets compared with other countries. Still, the increase in the price even of the products of our primary industries would before long be a formidable drawback to their development, and possibly to their continuance. The total obligations, under the new proposal, of employers of about £4 10s. per week would not, as far as I can judge, have any injurious effect upon our primary industries, as it is not so much above the level of wages in other countries as to countervail our natural superiority of opportunity. Nor would other industries, in my opinion, be adversely affected.

Another result of adding to the cost of production of goods for domestic consumption (which was 62 per cent. of the total production of 1918) the additional wages cost (£1 16s.) would be to so raise prices for such goods that all secondary industries would be liable to be ruined by importations unless the Tariff was very substantially increased.

Increased Wages Bill of Commonwealth.

Assuming the existing basic wage to be £4 per week, we have the following figures:—

If 1,000,000 employees receive £1 16s. increase . . £93,000,000
If 1,000,000 employees receive £4 per week, there would
   need to be added 12s. per week for 900,000 children . £28,080,000
   Saving for industry £64,920,000

This saving would be due to the fact that the extension of the cost of living of the typical family into the basic wage of every employee would involve employers as a whole paying for 2,100,000 non-existent children.

5. The effect of paying £5 16s. 0d. per week to all employees upon prices and upon the actual realization of the desired standard of comfort.

If £5 16s. is paid to all employees, it is demonstrably impossible ever to provide for the family with three children the standard of comfort determined by the Commission, and now procurable for the amount of £5 16s. This is because of the resultant rise in prices. There may, of course, be modifying influences, or other economic factors, such as a general drop in world prices, but this must be laid out of consideration in order to perceive clearly the effect which must follow from the cause to be presumed. Omitting, therefore, all other influences on prices in order to isolate the issue and shew what the wage rise from £4 to £5 16s. —about 45 per cent.—would do in bringing about increased prices, the table printed in Knibbs' Labour Report, No. 6, p. 183, shews that it will be impossible for the worker ever to catch up to the standard of comfort now purchasable for £5 16s. after all necessary adjustment of prices and readjustment of wages take place. Thus, with quarterly automatic adjustment of wages to prices, assuming labour-cost to be 50 per cent. production value or price, then if a present wage of £4 were increased to £5 16s. the following table shews what would be the course of events :—

	Rise in Money Wages.		Percentage Increase.	Resulting Effect on Prices, percentage.
	From—	To—		
	£ s. d.	£ s. d.		
November, 1920 .	4 0 0	5 16 6	45	22½
February, 1921 . .	5 16 6	7 3 0	22½	11¼
May, 1921 . . .	7 3 0	7 19 0	11¼	5½
August, 1921 . .	7 19 0	8 7 9	5½	2¾
November, 1921 . .	8 7 9	8 12 4	2¾	1¾ [1]

It will be seen that taking the adjusted wage in the second column and the wage from which it will have been adjusted in the first column and comparing them, the worker will every quarter be getting a less wage than is necessary for the standard of comfort for the typical family.

Comparison of Alternative Scheme.

An alternative scheme enabling every employee to have the standard of comfort prescribed by the Commission could be prepared on these lines.

[1] Continuable indefinitely.

If employers were to pay £4 to each employee, and a tax of £27 18s. per year—10s. 9d. per week per employee—the latter would bring in the necessary £27,900,000 a year for the endowment of the 900,000 children. The Commonwealth could then pay to the mothers of families 12s. a week for each child.

The total obligation of the employer would be £4 10s. 9d. (wage and tax) per week.

EFFECT AS TO EMPLOYEES.

1. Every employee would receive enough for a man and wife. He could marry or save for marriage as soon as he earns a man's wage.

2. Every worker's family would receive its cost of living, no matter how many children there were.

3. There would be an effect on prices only if the employer passed on the full amount of the tax. The effect on prices would be about 6 per cent. increase instead of 22½ per cent.

On the day following his receipt of this Memorandum the Prime Minister read to the House of Representatives the opinion expressed by the Government Statistician as to the impracticability of putting into force a basic wage of £5 16s. and announced that the Government absolutely refused to attempt it. He also read to them the alternative proposals made by Mr. Piddington, but reserved his decision as to carrying them out. Three weeks later, he made a further announcement with regard to employees in the public services of the Commonwealth, who for some time had been agitating for an increase of wages. There would, he said, be a minimum wage of £4 a week for married men (this being the proportion of the Commission's finding of £5 16s. allocated to man and wife in Mr. Piddington's memorandum) with an additional allowance of 5s. a week for each child (instead of the 12s. a week proposed in the memorandum). Single men were to have their salaries increased by the same sum as married men, viz., £12 per annum.[1]

So far this appears to have been the full extent of the effect given to the Commission's findings. Mr. Hughes not long afterwards departed for this country to attend the meeting of Prime Ministers of British Dominions and, so far as I have been able to ascertain, no further action has been taken in the Federal Parliament.

The All-Australian National Congress of Trade Unions, held at Melbourne in the following June, resolved:—

" 'That this Congress adopts the findings of the Federal Basic Wage Commission in their entirety, and calls upon the Prime Minister, the Federal Government, and the State Governments, to take action to give all workers the benefit of the wage prescribed by the Commission.' Another motion was carried unanimously ' To endorse the principle of the endowment of motherhood and childhood. . . such payment to be a charge on the whole community and to be recognized as

[1] *The Next Step*, pp. 26-7.

an individual right, and not associated in any way with the economic circumstances of the husband or father.' No resolution was carried as to finance in either connection".[1]

A test case to secure the adoption of the finding of £5 16s. per week as the basic minimum wage for men was subsequently brought before the Commonwealth Arbitration Court at the instance of the Trade Unions. The President, Mr. Justice Powers, refused the application, chiefly on the ground that the standard proposed was "not practicable at the present time as a flat rate". But his judgment made it clear that in adhering to the old standard he felt strongly its inadequacy to meet the needs of families and that he endorsed Mr. Piddington's conclusions. He said:—

" The families cannot be really benefited by simply increasing the basic wage to all, including the young married man, and married man without children, by the amount asked for by the Unions. The result would be that prices would immediately go up, and they would be at the same disadvantage as before.
" I am satisfied from the inquiries I have made myself that it (i.e., the proposal for a Family Basic Income on the lines here suggested) is practicable, and that it would do more to make the people who are now in an intolerable position more satisfied than they would be by any other method that has been suggested. Pending legislation, however, the present basic wage must be continued".[2]

(ii) NEW SOUTH WALES

While all these investigations and discussions were going on among those concerned in the federal administration of Australia, parallel action was being taken in the separate States, which, as already explained, have also jurisdiction in questions of wages. New South Wales had been specially active. As long ago as September 1916 Dr. Richard Arthur had moved in the Legislative Assembly of that State a resolution calling attention to the hardship imposed on large families by the flat rate minimum wage and proposing that

" a separate income tax should be imposed on all net income of over £2 a week, single persons to pay double the tax that married persons do. From the revenue so obtained an endowment should be paid to the mother of every child after the first until the age of fourteen years".

But he admitted that his object was propaganda and that at the moment the matter must be regarded as one of academic interest. He repeated his motion in 1917, and also brought a proposal for child endowment before the annual conference of the National Party of which he was a member and which had recently come into power. It was laughed

[1] *Ibid.*, pp. 65-6.   [2] *Ibid.*, p. 67.

out of Court on that occasion, but two years later, in 1919, it was carried unanimously and placed on the programme of the party.[1]   During the same year, as a result of the rise in prices, an agitation arose for an increase in wages, which were then being fixed by the State Industrial Arbitration Courts for industries within their jurisdiction on the basis of the minimum of £3 declared by the Board of Trade in 1917.   The Board in October gave notice of its intention to raise the minimum to £3 17s.   This was greeted by an outcry from employers, who declared that the industries of the State could not bear such an increase; that foreign trade would be paralysed and domestic trade driven over the border into States which had a lower minimum.   The Prime Minister, Mr. Holman, embarrassed by the outcry and under continual pressure from the indefatigable Dr. Arthur to carry out the principle to which his party was committed, introduced a hastily drawn up measure designed to serve the double purpose of reducing the proposed burden on industry and securing the promised relief to wage-earners with families.   It was called the Maintenance of Children Bill and the chief provisions were to the following effect:—

The basic minimum just declared by the Board of Trade was to be withdrawn and any awards already based on it were to be declared void.   Immediately and for the future, the minimum was to be based on the needs of man and wife. Children were to be provided for by allowances paid to the mother or female guardian out of a fund under the control of the Treasury.   In order to form this fund, the Government Statistician was to ascertain annually, (a) the cost of maintaining a child, adjusted to the current cost of living, (b) the number of children of employees to be provided for. These were to be arranged in twelve groups, according to the wages received by their parent, and only the children of employees earning less than 5s. above the minimum were to receive the full cost-of-living allowance; the allowances paid to the others being graduated on a sliding scale.   A separate account was to be kept of the children of male employees and those of female employees, children whose father and mother both worked being credited to the former.   The amount required, having been calculated from these figures, was to be raised by a levy on the employers, each paying

[1] N.S.W. Parliamentary Debates, December 22, 1920, p. 4094.

to the men's fund in proportion to the number of his male employees and to the women's fund in proportion to his female employees.

By this curious device the Bill, it will be noticed, carefully preserves to the employer of female labour his existing privilege of shirking his full share of the cost of labour recruitment; while it guards against the risk that the employer of male labour will also shirk this duty by avoiding the employment of married men.

It was estimated by the Government Statistician that if this Bill were put into operation, the number of children to be provided for would be 337,000 and the cost of full maintenance per child 7s. 6d. He reckoned that, taking increase of wages and cost of children's allowances together, the additional burden on industry would be £6,520,000 whereas the additional burden on industry imposed by the increase of the basic minimum would be £11,930,000. Thus the Bill would mean a saving of nearly 5½ millions sterling per annum.

But it came too late. While it was being discussed in the Lower House, the Industrial Arbitration Courts were actually making awards on the basis of the £3 17s. minimum. The Trade Unions regarded the Bill as an attempt to filch from them an overdue advance to which the Government was practically pledged, and to keep in the employers' pockets 5½ millions sterling which rightfully belonged to the men. There were other features of the Bill that strengthened their suspicions that it was a pro-capitalist measure. It expressly enacted that no allowance should be paid to the child of any employee in respect of any period during which the employee had been on strike, and it followed implicitly from the basis on which the employers' contributions to the fund were levied—in respect of persons actually at work —that no allowances would be payable during periods of unemployment. For these reasons the Bill was vigorously opposed by the Labour Party, led in the House by Mr. Storey. Nor was it generally welcomed by the representatives of the employing classes. The more Conservative section, in spite of the evidence of the Government Statistician, evidently could not believe that a measure for the direct maintenance of children could be anything but socialistic and, with better reason, feared that the Labour Party, if it came into power, would insist on the children's allowances being super-

imposed on the higher basic minimum. There were also some
real difficulties such as are incidental to any pioneer measure,
which sufficed to daunt the more timid minds of all parties.
There was in especial the inconvenience of placing the workers
in State-controlled industries under a system of remuneration
quite different from that of workers under Federal awards,
the latter numbering about 71,000 out of a wage-earning
population of just under half a million. Had the Bill come into
effect, it is probable that this difficulty would never have
materialized, for the example of New South Wales would
have sufficed to give the needed impetus to the proposals made by
the Chairman of the Basic Wage Commission just a year later.

But the forces of opposition were too strong, and though
the Bill struggled successfully through the Legislative Assembly
(the Lower House) it perished in the Legislative Council
(the Upper House) and the Government made no further effort
to revive it. The new basic wage of £3 17s. came into effect
and was followed by a further rise in the cost of living so
considerable that the basic minimum had to be raised again
next year to £4 5s.; even this being admittedly less than sufficient to cover the increase in the cost of living.

Soon after the defeat of the Bill a General Election took
place. The National Party went out of power and was
succeeded by a Labour Government with Mr. Storey at its
head. Mr. Storey had led the opposition of his party to
the Maintenance of Children Bill, but in doing so had
repeatedly insisted that it was only the lowering of the basic
minimum and the endowment of children through industry
that his party objected to; they were strongly in favour of
State endowment of motherhood and childhood and urged
that " the whole community should pay in order to meet
the responsibilities of those who are rearing families". At
the polls his party made a strong bid for the women's votes
by promising immediate legislation on these lines and according to Dr. Arthur they obtained a great deal of support by
doing so. He told the House that when, during the winter
of 1919-20, the Lady Mayoress organized a clothing fund
to help necessitous families, the Labour members of the
Committee assured every recipient mother that it was the
last time such charity would be needed, as before next winter
the promised Motherhood Endowment Bill would be made law.[1]

---

[1] N.S.W. Parliamentary Debates, December 22, 1920, pp. 4098-9.

Nothing was done however during the first Session of the new Parliament and it was not until December 22, within a few days of the adjournment, that the Minister of Health, Mr. McGirr, pricked by the repeated taunts of Dr. Arthur, apologized to the House for the delay—due, he explained, to the financial difficulties in which the Government had been left by its predecessors—and announced his intention to bring forward next Session a Motherhood Endowment Bill to provide an allowance of 6s. a week for each child in excess of two in families where the income did not exceed the basic wage by more than the amount that would be payable. Thus a mother with four children and an income of 6s. above the minimum would receive an allowance only for the fourth child, and so on. Mr. McGirr was mysterious as to where the money was to come from, but assured the House that the Government had a plan and repeated several times in varying phrases the promise that

" by the time we wind up the next Session of Parliament the child of every worker in the State will be receiving the endowment which I promised, and to give which I pledge my existence as a Cabinet Minister on the floor of the House this afternoon. . . . I say that before we leave Parliament House next session it will be the law of the land".[1]

In the following May (1921) Mr. McGirr announced that the Bill was ready for introduction and described its provisions, which included, besides allowances for children, pensions for widows and deserted wives and wives of invalids and prisoners. The Bill received what is called " a great press " all over the world. Its author claimed for it that it was the first Bill of its kind in history and that other nations would quickly follow his example when its beneficent results were seen. He estimated that its annual cost would be £1,600,000 and indicated that of this £500,000 would be diverted from sums spent in relief by other departments and £300,000 raised by means of a State lottery. He did not explain how the rest would be provided.

The Bill was not introduced till the end of September. On November 22 it passed through its final stages in the Legislative Assembly and on December 6 it received a second reading in the Legislative Council and was sent to Committee. Parliament was dissolved early in the following session and the Labour Party went out of office. Its critics loudly declared that the Government had never been in earnest about the

[1] N.S.W. Parliamentary Debates, December 22, 1920, p. 4090.

Motherhood Endowment Bill and pointed out that the Treasurer had not even mentioned it when forecasting his budget in December, although the plan of financing the Bill by a lottery had been abandoned in deference to the strong opposition it had aroused.

Without impugning the sincerity of their intentions it is probable that the Government were in fact daunted by the difficulty of finding the money. If the Commonwealth could not afford to pay adequate wages even on the uniform family basis, it is unlikely that New South Wales could afford to superimpose on that basis provision for surplus children.

Thus for the present, the cause of direct provision for children in Australia is marking time. It has able adherents in all parties who do not let it sleep, but so far no party has made the question really their own. Even more in Australia than in other countries, it is plain that the real impediment is the cupidity of those who have, or think they have, something to gain from the ambiguities and inequities of the present system. For an Australian cannot deceive himself or others into thinking that he fears to provide adequately for children lest it may lead to a higher birth-rate. He urgently wants a higher birth-rate so as to maintain the predominance of white races. Nor is he clinging to the creed of a purely " supply and demand " wage. For fifteen years he has been accustomed to see the lower limit of wages based professedly on living needs and he knows that the doctrine has come to stay. But—if an employer—he secretly fears that he may have to pay more when the fog that has clung about the whole subject has been blown away and he is faced not with perfunctory estimates based on the supposed needs of a mythical standard family, but with the real needs of actually existent human beings. If a childless workman, he is reluctant to part with the profit which this myth of a standard family has brought him.

The influence which these two motives have exercised will be appreciated if we remember the history of the Harvester case. This, as we have seen, based the cost of living on an enquiry into the actual expenditure of nine housewives in one suburb of Melbourne, supplemented by the evidence of one house agent as to rents and one butcher as to meat, and checked by comparison with wages paid in the public service of several States. The exhaustive enquiries of the Basic

Wage Commission shewed the estimate so arrived at to have been far too low. Yet for ten years it held its place practically unchallenged, as the basis of the wage-rates of an entire continent.

For a parallel to this, let us imagine that the price of pork was legally determinable in this country and that year after year it was adjusted by the Court to a standard originally based on the costing, as estimated by nine farmers selected at haphazard, of nine litters of Berkshire pigs. A human child may be " of more value than many sparrows," but incomparably less scientific study has been devoted to the problem of its " costs of production " and the economic arrangements for meeting them, than to those of any other product, animate or inanimate, that has a market value.

I say this not in criticism of Australia, for indeed it has led the way in at least recognizing that such a problem does exist not only for individual parents but for economists and statesmen.

(b) France[1]

Meantime, far away in Europe, two countries on every other subject opposed to each other were quietly and independently —so far as I know, without knowledge either of each other's action or of the theorizing on the subject going on in Australia and Great Britain—putting into practice the principle of child endowment. Both in France and Germany the experiment began not in response to a popular demand but through the initiative of employers, singly or in groups, impelled thereto by a combination of patriotic, humane and self-interested motives. In both lands it spread with marvellous rapidity, not without some opposition and a good deal of discussion, but of an inconspicuous kind which has attracted next to no attention except in those circles inside the country and in the

---

[1] The following account of family allowances in France is based mainly on M. Victor Guesdon's *Le Mouvement de Création et d'Extension des Caisses d'Allocations Familiales* (Paris, 1922) and on information obtained by correspondence with various trade unions. The following articles and pamphlets have also been consulted (amongst others):—Articles in *Bulletin du Ministère du Travail*, March to December 1920 ; various articles in *L'Information Sociale* ; " Les Allocations Familiales'," by E. Romanet, in *Chronique Sociale de France*, May 1922 ; Report of M. Fouquet on the work of the *Caisses de Compensation* in *La Revue Philanthropique*, May 15, 1922 ; *Salaires, Allocations Familiales et Caisses de Compensation* by René Hubert (*Société d'Études et d'Informations Economiques*, Paris, 1921) : *L'Effort du Patronat Français*, pamphlets containing speeches made at the opening of the hundredth *Caisse de Compensation* (*La Journée Industrielle*, Paris, 1922); " The Family Wage System Abroad," in *Labour Gazette*, March 1923.

neighbouring countries which were immediately interested. I have within the last few months met intelligent French-women, active in the women's movement in France, who knew that in some industries *allocations familiales* were paid, but regarded them as of no great importance and opened their eyes in astonishment when I suggested that there perhaps was the beginning of a movement destined to make more difference to the status of women and the welfare of children than anything that has happened in the world since the beginning of Christianity.

Family allowances in an extremely rudimentary form were started in France in 1890 by the Railway Companies, followed soon after by the Mining Companies. But they consisted merely of a grant of 24 francs a year, paid on behalf of the fourth and each subsequent child and then only if his parent's wages did not exceed 2,000 francs a year. In 1917, the State also introduced allowances for the children of its lesser-paid employees, on a scale fixed in October 1919 at 330 francs per annum for the first and second child respectively and 480 francs for each subsequent child, to cease at the age of sixteen.

But the first to give a real impetus to the movement in France was M. Romanet, managing director of Etablissements Joya of Grenoble, a large firm of manufacturers of heavy iron, copper and other metal work. M. Romanet is a Roman Catholic, a man of fervent piety, sensitive conscience, immense energy and large vision. Under his influence Maison Joya has been a centre of experiments in industrial welfare since 1905, when he received his inspiration from a series of lectures given at Grenoble by l'Abbé Cetty of Mulhouse. The following year, the workmen belonging to Maison Joya took the initiative in breaking up a strike which had paralysed Grenoble for a month. M. Joya promised to shew his gratitude and did so by forming a kind of Works' Council (*Conseil d'Usines*) composed of all employees of over twenty years' standing in the firm, with consultative powers on questions of pay, health, discipline, etc. Other enterprises followed, many of them being copied by other firms in Grenoble and sometimes extended into a general scheme for the district. These included a number of social insurance schemes for sickness (including medical attendance and home nursing), unemployment, old age pensions (supplementary to the State pensions) and payments at death; compulsory training courses for apprentices; technical committees for suggesting improvements in processes; and an elaborate scheme of profit-sharing.

But the most original and far-reaching of these experiments was the scheme of family allowances (*allocations familiales*). This began in May 1916. There is at Grenoble a certain Society with a religious basis, *La Ruche populaire de St. Bruno*, which aims at uniting workers of all classes in the study of social questions, much after the manner apparently of our Christian Social Union. At one of its discussions during the war, several workmen employed by Maison Joya complained of the burden weighing on parents of large families and the difficulty they had in making both ends meet. Enquiries were therefore made into the households of eight workmen employed by M. Joya, all exceptionally hard-working, with families of various sizes. They comprised (1) a single workman; (2) a married couple without family; (3) a widow with son and daughter both working; (4) parents with two boys of ten and five; (5) parents with four small children and another expected; (6) parents with four small children; (7) parents with four girls, three working; (8) parents with five small children.

The result shewed that No. 1 was comfortably off, and saving regularly; but was *égoïste*, without ambition or attachment to his firm or his town. No. 2 were comfortable and saving. No. 3 were suffering visibly from under-feeding but just balanced their budget. No. 4 were comfortable; because the wife was free to work and did so. No. 5 were harassed and in debt; they could only afford one litre of wine and a franc's worth of horseflesh a day. No. 6 were always in debt, but just managed to exist with the help of parcels from parents in the country. No. 7 just balanced their budget. No. 8, buying nothing but the barest necessaries, were always short by nearly 100 francs a month.

Satisfied by this demonstration that the position of the families with children was one of real hardship, M. Romanet considered how it could be ameliorated. He argued that a rise in wages, apart from its cost to industry, would not meet the case. Previous rises had been followed by an increase in the cost of living, which for the man with wife and family to feed and clothe had more than swallowed up the value of the rise, though it left the bachelor with a substantial margin.

He concluded that allowances for children were the right
solution and persuaded M. Joya to introduce them. The scale
first adopted was very low:—

For one child under 13	7·50	francs per month
„ two children under 13	18·0	„ „ „
„ three children under 13 . . . ·	31·50	„ „ „
„ four children under 13	48·0	„ „ „
and 12 francs for each subsequent child.		

This caused some stir in Grenoble. Employees of other
firms in the same industry began to agitate for similar privileges, and after various conferences at which M. Romanet
expounded his views, all the firms belonging to the metal-
working and engineering industry of the district agreed to pay
family allowances on an agreed scale. This was several times
raised and in 1921 stood at 20 francs per month for the first,
25 francs for the second and 30 francs for subsequent children.
It was soon however seen that employers would be under a
considerable temptation to economize by avoiding the employment of men with families and the system might injure just
those whom it was intended to benefit. To avoid this, M.
Romanet hit on the device of pooling the cost of allowances
among the employers joining in the agreement by the formation of a compensation fund for family allowances (*Caisse de
compensation pour allocations familiales*, at first called *sursalaires
familiales*). The principle of this is quite simple, though there
are many varieties in form and method. The allowances are
paid monthly for the benefit of the dependent children below
a certain age of all the employees of firms belonging to the
Caisse and the cost is divided up among the firms according to
some agreed principle—usually either in proportion to the
total number of their employees, men or women, married or
single, or in proportion to the total amount of their wages bill.
In addition, some of the *Caisses* pay one or both of the following
benefits:—a lump sum at the birth of a child (*prime de naissance*);
an allowance to the mother while nursing (*prime d'allaitement*).

   The *Caisse* initiated by M. Romanet for the metal-working
and engineering industry of Grenoble began its operations in
May 1918. But meantime the idea had either penetrated or
arisen by spontaneous generation elsewhere, and he was anticipated by the formation in the previous January of a *Caisse*
at Lorient, initiated by M. Marèche, the President of the
Chamber of Commerce, under the control of the Alliance of
Industry and Commerce. This was done in response to an

agitation by the workers of the port for an increase in wages, and though the workers at first opposed this form of increase, the *Caisse* flourished from the start. The scale of allowances, beginning at 25 centimes a day for the first child and 50 centimes for each subsequent child, was doubled at the end of the first year. In 1918, the *Caisse* distributed 28,633 francs in allowances; in 1919, 92,417 francs and in 1920, 64,053 francs.

From that time, *Caisses de Compensation* sprang up rapidly all over France. In some cases they originated with the associations (*syndicats*) or federations (*consortiums*) of employers, and where this was so they were generally on an occupational basis. For example, at Grenoble, and the department of Isère to which it belongs, following the example of the metal-working and engineering industry six other *Caisses* were started for different sections of industry, all centred in the Chamber of Commerce. Another important *Caisse* on an occupational basis was started in June 1919 by the federation of employers in the textile industry of Normandy, and yet another, perhaps the most enterprising and flourishing of all, was the *Caisse* started by the *Consortium du Textile de Roubaix Tourcoing* in March 1920. This distributed in its first two years over 20 million francs in allowances among 20,000 children. In other towns, the movement came from the Chambers of Commerce themselves, the *Caisses* being on a regional basis and including all branches of trade and industry willing to join. An instance of this is the *Caisse Regionale des institutions familiales ouvrières* founded at Nantes in December 1919, and another, the important Parisian *Caisse Regionale* started in March 1920 with 500 adherent firms, employing 120,000 workmen, and distributing in its first eighteen months over $21\frac{1}{2}$ million francs in allowances.

One reason for the rapid spread of the movement was the missionary zeal of the promoters. From the first they preached family allowances with the enthusiasm of converts to a new gospel. Opportunities for propaganda were found at various conferences, such as the annual meeting of the *Congrès de Natalité*. But in December 1920, at the invitation of the *Consortium de Roubaix Tourcoing*, a Congress was called of the *Caisses pour allocations familiales*. There were by that time thirty of them. They decided to form a central committee and a *Bureau d'étude et de propagande* with an office at 7 Rue de

284 EXPERIMENTS IN FAMILY ALLOWANCES

Madrid, Paris. The Committee was composed of one representative of each of the twelve important industrial districts of
France. This Bureau, besides acting as a general clearing house
of information for employers on all subjects relating to the
formation and management of *Caisses*, pursues researches,
arranges conferences and meetings and issues pamphlets and
leaflets.

Under the influence of this propaganda, such rapid progress
was made that at the third annual congress of the *Caisses*,
held at Nantes in June 1923, the President, M. Mathon,
claimed that there were affiliated to the Committee 120
Caisses, including 7,600 firms and distributing in family allowances over 92 million francs annually for the direct or indirect
benefit of 880,000 wage-earners. Including the great public
and private bodies which administer allowances individually,
he reckoned that the allowances paid amount to over 300
million francs annually and affect over $2\frac{1}{2}$ million wage-
earners. According to M. Partiot, Vice-President of the
Syndicat des Mécaniciens, Chaudronniers et Fondeurs de France,
there are in France only about 8 million wage-earners eligible
to come under social insurance, of whom $3\frac{1}{2}$ millions are engaged in agriculture. He therefore calculates that the system
of family allowances already covers about half the industrial
wage-earners of France.

This is a remarkable achievement for a movement as yet
barely five years old. Its success is due no doubt largely to
the circumstances amid which it was born, just at the end of
the war when the minds of patriotic Frenchmen and far-seeing
employers were filled with a mixture of motives—with gratitude to the men who had saved their country; with anticipation
of great industrial and social developments and uneasiness
lest industrial unrest should prevent them taking full advantage
of these new opportunities; above all with grave alarm at the
long, steady and rapid decline of the French birth-rate and
the diminution of the population of France in respect to other
great Powers. Although the motives that have led so many
employers to adopt the system of family allowances have been
partly humane and partly economic, there is no doubt that
the hope of increasing the birth-rate and the survival-rate have
played a great part; perhaps the chief part. But before asking
whether this hope has so far been justified, what other results
have been obtained from the movement, how it has been re-

ceived by the workers themselves and what are its future prospects, I propose to describe in some detail how the system is worked:—

It is not a uniform system. As already explained, some of the *Caisses* are on an occupational and some on a regional basis. Those of the regional type are much the more numerous, this system being preferred on the ground that cost of living varies with districts rather than with trades and that the benefits ought to be adjusted accordingly.

The most important difference concerns the benefits conferred. Owing to fluctuations in the value of the French franc and the difference both in cost and standards of living between France and Great Britain, it is difficult for the English reader to form a very clear idea of what the allowances are really worth as a contribution to family maintenance. From the glowing speeches made by employers at congresses and banquets, one might imagine that they lifted the burden of *la famille nombreuse* entirely off the shoulders of the harassed parents and made *la fécondité* economically possible to them. But the same speeches generally dwell with satisfaction on the fact that the charge on employers usually amounts to a little less than 2 per cent. of the wage bill, and this, even in a country where the number of dependent children per married employee is estimated at only 1·66, seems a very low rate. It may be compared with Mr. Piddington's calculation that the tax on employers necessary to produce an allowance of 12s. a week per child would be 10s. 9d. per employee per week.[1] M. Romanet of Grenoble calculates that the allowances paid by his *Caisse* represent about one-third of the cost of child maintenance, and he defends this by saying that the benefit of children is shared between parents, employers and the State.

The chief allowance is the monthly payment per child, paid by all *Caisses*, but with great differences in scale and other conditions. Most *Caisses* pay allowances to weekly wage-earners and salaried workers alike, but only to those earning below a certain sum. The income limit varies from 8,000 francs to 15,000 francs. The following are the monthly allowances paid by some of the most important *Caisses*, arranged in order of the total amount annually expended:—

[1] Report of the Royal Commission on the Basic Wage (Australia), 1920, p.92.

Roubaix Tourcoing (textile)	1st child, 50 frs.; for each subsequent child, 75 frs.
Paris (regional)	1st child, 10 frs.; 2nd child, 20 frs.; each subsequent child, 30 frs.
Mulhouse	25 frs. for each child.
Lyons (3 *Caisses*)	1st child, 15 frs.; 2nd child, 25 frs.; each subsequent child, 30 frs.
Paris (building trades) ..	1st child, 15 frs.; 2nd child, 30 frs.; each subsequent child, 40 frs.
Strasbourg	25 frs. for each child.
Rouen (3 *Caisses*)	Textiles and Building: 1st child, 15 frs.; 2nd child, 20 frs.; 3rd child, 25 frs.; each subsequent child, 30 frs.
	Port: 1st child, 10 frs.; 2nd child, 15 frs.; 3rd child, 20 frs.; each subsequent child, 25 frs.
Lille (3 *Caisses*)	Textiles and Metallurgy, Metalworking and Engineering: 1st child, nil; 2nd and 3rd child, 30 frs.; each subsequent child, 40 frs.
	Building: 25 frs. each child.
Valenciennes	15 frs. for each child.
Nantes	12·50 frs. for each child.
Troyes	1st child, 20 frs.; 2nd and 3rd child, 25 frs.; each subsequent child, 30 frs.
Elbœuf	1st, 2nd and 3rd child, 40 frs. each; each subsequent child, 50 frs.

The age up to which allowances are paid varies from thirteen (e.g., at Roubaix, Rouen, Bordeaux) up to sixteen (only at Le Havre); the most usual age being fourteen.

Some of the above (e.g., Roubaix, Mulhouse, Strasbourg) reckon the allowance not per month but per working day of eight hours.

Eleven *Caisses* pay no allowance for the first child and of these three pay none for the second either. Only one (Le

Havre; port workers), with the minute allowance of 10 francs for the first and 5 francs for each subsequent child, follows the plan which separation allowances made so familiar to us in this country, of giving more for the first than for later children. Any system which aimed at providing adequately and systematically for child maintenance would naturally recognize in this way the fact that cost diminishes as the number of children increases; but the French plan reflects the predominant motive of the scheme—to encourage large families—and is also economical, as families with only one child outnumber all the rest. This is shewn by the following details of the families assisted at Roubaix:—

Number of families with	1 child (allowance 1 franc per working day),	7,559
„ „ „ „	2 children („ 5 francs „ „ „),	2,987
„ „ „ „	3 „ („ 8 „ „ „ „),	1,143
„ „ „ „	4 „ („ 12 „ „ „ „),	543
„ „ „ „	5 „ („ 15 „ „ „ „),	194
„ „ „ „	6 „ („ 18 „ „ „ „),	74
„ „ „ „	7 „ („ 21 „ „ „ „),	14
„ „ „ „	8 „ („ 24 „ „ „ „),	4
„ „ „ „	9 „ („ 27 „ „ „ „),	1

We are told by M. Victor Guesdon that the scale at Roubaix, being so much higher than that of other *Caisses*, is much criticized by employers elsewhere. The enterprising management of the same *Caisse* have introduced another innovation into their system of payment which has attracted much attention. At first like all other *Caisses* they recognized as entitled to benefit only those employees who were heads of dependent families—fathers, widowed mothers, the eldest of a family of orphans, etc. But under this system the firms engaged in processes employing chiefly female and juvenile labour paid into the *Caisse* much more than they drew out in allowances; while those employing chiefly male labour benefited more than they contributed. To rectify this, they decided from July 1922 to treat every employee over thirteen who was a member of a household containing children under thirteen as though he or she was equally responsible with the other members of the household for the maintenance of the children. The only members not recognized as sharing in the responsibility were wives exclusively engaged in household duties and men on military service. Thus if the household consisted of a man and a son and a daughter, all three working for firms adhering to the *Caisse*, each would draw a third of the allowance to which the younger children of the household were entitled;

if the daughter stayed at home or worked for a non-adherent firm, only two-thirds of the allowance would be paid. It is claimed that this has had an excellent effect on the prosperity of the *Caisse* by equalizing the burden of the charges on the firms.

A question which has been much discussed and is recognized, M. Victor Guesdon tells us, as *des plus délicates* is whether the allowance shall be paid to the wage-earner or the children's mother. In Australia, as we have seen, all the plans put forward have taken it as a matter of course that the payment goes to the mother. Both the New South Wales Bills, that introduced by Mr. Holman's National Party Government and that of the Labour Government, proposed this and in the debates in Parliament it was practically unchallenged. But in France the tradition established by the Napoleonic code is very strong and the subordination of wives still prevails at least in theory. Hence the founders of the earliest *Caisses*—Grenoble and Lorient—arranged without question for the payment of the allowances to the wage-earner and this I gather is still the practice of the majority, including Roubaix, Mulhouse, and Nantes. M. Dupont, speaking on behalf of these at the Congress of *Caisses* at Paris in 1921, declared *que l'ouvrier, très susceptible, verrait d'un mauvais œil le versement à la mère de famille. Ce serait, vis-a-vis du chef du famille, une marque de défiance qui ne serait pas acceptée"* [1] Fortunately however there are arguments pointing in the other direction which appeal strongly even to Frenchmen who do not question the sacred rights of the *chef du famille*, and these have induced the powerful Parisian *Caisse régionale* and a number of others, including Lille (metal-working and engineering and textile industries), Amiens, Dijon, and Tours, to institute payment direct to the mother. These believe that this is the best way of insuring that the money will be used exclusively for the benefit of the children for whom it is intended and will thus better promote one of the main objects of the system —a higher survival rate and healthy children. Even if paid to the father it would normally be expended by the mother and in passing through the hands of both parents the chances of possible leakage are doubled. Further, pay-

[1] In the same spirit, when Mr. Lloyd George's Health Insurance Act was being debated in the House, there were speakers who declared that working men would regard as an insult the proposed payment of the 30s. maternity allowance direct to the woman for whom it was intended.

ment to the mother emphasizes the fact on which great stress is laid by the promoters of the system, viz., that the payment is not part of wages and is not therefore a departure (as sometimes alleged by its opponents) from the principle *au travail égal, salaire égal.* M. Victor Guesdon notes that it has been found much easier to establish the custom of payment to the mother in those districts where the allowances are paid directly by the *Caisses*, than in those where the employers pay and the *Caisse* merely adjusts the cost subsequently. When the latter is the custom, even if the allowances are put in a separate envelope and paid in a separate office, the workman tends to regard it as a sort of bonus on his wages, which he has a right to receive himself and spend as he pleases. Further the whole transaction comes much more under the eye of the childless worker and is more likely to excite his jealousy than where the allowance is paid through a separate organization and directly to the mother.

Another *question délicate,* on which there are conflicting views, concerns the payment of allowances to unmarried mothers. The managing committees of some *Caisses* take the view that as their object is to recognize parenthood as a social institution, women who have brought children into the world irregularly, outside the bonds of the family, ought not to receive the benefits of the system. Others point out that the child is the real beneficiary and should not be made to suffer for the mother's fault. Those who take the latter view appear to be in the majority, but some of them make a distinction between children who are the offspring of more or less permanent and acknowledged though irregular unions and " chance children " and accept only the former.

The great majority of *Caisses*, in addition to the monthly children's allowances, give a lump sum at the birth (*prime de naissance*) and a minority of these grant in addition a sum towards the cost of nursing, usually restricted to children fed at the breast (*prime d'allaitement*). Thus among the most generous is Blois, which gives 300 francs at the birth of the first child, 100 for each subsequent child and 30 francs a month for ten months. Paris (regional) gives 250 francs for the first child, 150 for subsequent children and 30 francs a month for ten months. Others merely give a lump sum at each birth, 100 or 200 francs being the most usual amounts. These *primes de naissance* did not originate with the *Caisses*. The nervous anxiety for an increased birth-rate, which has existed in French official circles for many years, was intensified by the war, and in June 1918 Parliament voted credits to assist local authorities in schemes for the encouragement of maternity. In most of the departments of France the *Conseils Généraux* give *primes de naissance* of varying amounts and under varying conditions ; 300 francs for the fourth living child and its successors is perhaps the commonest figure ; but some departments start with the third child and some increase the sum for each successive child. Often half the sum is paid at birth and half when the child reaches twelve months ; some pay nothing till this term is safely reached. Many municipal authorities also pay " primes " to their employees at the time of marriage.

A few *Caisses* only, including Lyons, Vienne, Nantes, Lorient and Dijon, grant allowances to wage-earners on behalf of aged or invalid parents dependent on them.

The organization and financial arrangements of the *Caisses* vary as much as their schemes of benefits. As already indicated, in some *Caisses* the constituent firms themselves pay the allowances due to their employees, the *Caisses* merely fulfilling the function of " compensation", i.e., adjusting the charges ; in others, the *Caisse* itself acts as distributor. Under either system, the duty of the *Caisse* is to reckon up at fixed periods (*a*) the total amount that has been distributed, (*b*) the proportion of it payable by each firm according to the basis of assessment agreed on. If the firms have been the original paymasters, the *Caisse* then repays the amount due to those who have spent more than their share (called *cotisation*) and collects from those who have paid less than their share. If the *Caisse* has itself made the payments, then its duty is merely one of collection.

The basis of the assessment (called the *taux de compensation*) is most commonly the wage bills of the constituent firms ; those wages and salaries being generally excluded from the reckoning which are above the limit up to which employees are entitled to allowances (a limit varying, it will be remembered, from 8,000 to 15,000 francs). This basis of course obliges the firms to reveal the secrets of their wage bills to the officer of the *Caisse*. Some firms shrink from this ; partly for fear of indiscretion ; partly lest the *Caisses* may be compelled some time or other to yield up their secrets to the tax-collecting authorities. On the other hand, it is pointed out that firms already have to make returns of their wage bills to insurance companies for purposes of accident insurance, etc., and very little extra trouble or risk is involved in duplicating the return. Great stress is laid on the confidential nature of the records kept by the *Caisse* and their privacy is carefully guarded.

When this basis is adopted, the officers of the *Caisse* have merely to divide the total amount of the allowances paid for the period in question by the total amount of the wages paid, in order to find the unit of assessment. This multiplied by the wage bill of each constitutent firm gives the amount of the contribution due. For example, if the allowances paid have been 40,000 francs and the wages paid 2,000,000, the unit of assessment would be ·02 and the share of a firm with a wage bill of 50,000 francs would be 1,000.

Some *Caisses* have introduced a variation on this plan in order to conciliate those of their constituent firms which belong to industries employing chiefly women or young persons. It was found that these resented being asked to pay at the same rate as firms employing large numbers of men with families. Accordingly the firms belonging to the *Caisses* are arranged in trade groups, roughly in accordance with their usual measure of family responsibility, and each group receives a different " coefficient " indicating the proportionate contribution. Thus the coefficient of the metalworking and engineering group may be 3 and that of the textiles, with their numerous women workers, 1·50.

Other *Caisses* adopt a different basis altogether and assess firms (as the New South Wales Maintenance of Children's Bill proposed to do) according to the number of their employees ; some of them (again as in the New South Wales Bill) reckoning men and women and the allowances paid on behalf of their respective dependants in quite separate groups ; others dealing with them together, but allowing a percentage reduction for women and young persons. The *Caisse Régionale* of Lyons and the *Caisse* of the metal-working and engineering industry at Grenoble are the two most important of those employing this system, which is said to be more troublesome to carry out than the wage-bill basis, because the fluctuations in the numbers employed involve frequent adjustment. A few *Caisses* to avoid this difficulty take as the basis not the number of employees but the number of hours worked.

Finally there is the basis chosen by two *Caisses* for agricultural workers (Paris and Tours), which assess their members according to the number of *hectares* (i.e., a little over 2 acres) of land they own. The third agricultural *Caisse* (Bordeaux) has chosen the number of employees as its basis. Another scheme for an agricultural *Caisse*, proposed by M. Pinat of Grenoble but not yet in operation, is devised to meet the difficulty that in France the majority of agriculturists are peasant proprietors, employing few if any hands outside the members of their own families. It is on a mutual insurance basis and proposes that the fund for allowances should be provided by :

(a) Contributions payable by every head of a family joining the *Caisse*, in proportion to the extent of his land.

(b) An additional contribution payable for each employee over 16 not belonging to the member's own family.

(c) Annual subscriptions of fixed amounts from founders and honorary members.

(d) Annual contributions (not compulsory) from each commune in the district in proportion to the number of households ; such contributions to entitle the municipal council of the Commune to nominate a certain number of poor children to receive allowances, supplementary to those to which they are entitled if members of the *Caisse*.

In view of the great proportion of the French population engaged in agriculture, the problem of how effectively to apply the system of allowances to them is one that engages much attention, but hitherto not much progress seems to have been made.

On whatever basis the contributions of members of the *Caisses* are calculated, the charge varies of course with the scale of benefits adopted, but it seems rarely to exceed 2 per cent. of the wage bill paid. The *Caisse* at Roubaix is an exception. The benefits paid being more than double the average elsewhere, the employer's *cotisation* is about 5 per cent. of his wage bill.

The costs of administration of the *Caisses* are extremely low, varying from 1·25 to 1·75 francs per 1,000 francs of the wage bills of the constituent firms. When the *Caisse* merely adjusts the burden of allowances paid by the employers, very little personnel is required—sometimes for small *Caisses* only the part-time services of a single official. On the other hand some *Caisses* have developed a considerable organization, which not merely pays the stipulated benefits, but engages in all kinds of supplementary work of a quasi-benevolent character, with the object of influencing not only the birthrate but the survival-rate.

In France, as in this country, there has been of recent years and especially since the war a great outgrowth of child-welfare schemes ; some under local authorities and some supported by private effort—health visitors, pre-natal and post-natal clinics, crèches, *gouttes de lait* (depots for supplying milk free or at reduced price to necessitous mothers), *mutualités maternelles* (insurance for confinement), holiday homes, sanatoria, etc. The *Caisses* have become an important channel for such schemes, some of them running enterprises of their own, others co-operating with those existing already, aiding them with grants and acting as a link between them and the bene-ficiaries of allowances. Thus the Director of the Paris *Caisse Régionale* has divided his area into six sections and established in each a number of health visitors (*dames visiteuses*), thirty-two in all, to keep in touch with the mothers in receipt of allow-ances, advise them about feeding, arrange hospital and con-valescent treatment and so forth. In Lyons, we are told by the director of the *Caisse Régionale*, M. Berrane, that he was led to establish a child-welfare service by observing the excellent results achieved by the one established by the *Caisse de Textile*. Although the workers were living under the same conditions as those under his own supervision, their infant mortality was far less, having fallen 56 per cent. after nine months' work. A joint service was subsequently established for the two *Caisses*, under a committee of the principal medical men of the city. Here as in Paris much importance is attached to the services of health visitors. At Nancy the *Caisse* main-tains six free beds at the Sanatorium for its beneficiaries. Nearly everywhere, says M. Victor Guesdon, the firms be-longing to *Caisses* arrange at their factories infant consultations, where the babies are examined and weighed and records kept of their progress. Some *Caisses* make a separate levy of small amount on their members to cover the cost of these activities. Great stress is laid by some of the chief promoters of the *Caisses* on the value of such efforts and of the whole mechanism, not only in achieving their immediate object—the care of child life—but in stabilizing the personnel of the constituent firms by improving the relationship between employers and em-ployed, bringing them into closer touch with one another and establishing a feeling of mutual understanding and confidence. Thus M. Mathon of Roubaix says that at the office of his *Caisse* an average of 150 signed letters from workers are received daily, containing all manner of claims, requests, complaints, and every week about 400 workmen and work-women call personally to make their wants known "without reticence and without fear".

One gathers from this and similar descriptions that the *Caisse pour allocations familiales* is tending in many places to become a kind of general welfare department, performing many of the functions of a Welfare Manager in a British factory, but differing in that it is common to the whole industry or district.   There are other more questionable ways in which the system is being used by employers to " stabilize their personnel".   In some *Caisses* it is the rule that workers do not begin to become entitled to family allow-ances until they have been a certain period in the employ of the firm.   Generally the period is a month, but occasionally it is as much as a year.   Further, in some the allowance is not paid for any seriously broken month, unless the break is due to some cause beyond the worker's control.   For example, at Roubaix, the allowance although calculated per day of eight hours is by rule not payable for any month if the worker quits his employment during the course of it, or is absent for more than four days without medical certificate, or is on strike for any part of it.   A particularly oppressive application of this rule which is widely quoted by the opponents of the system concerned a one-day's general strike in which the Roubaix workers took part, to shew sympathy with the workers killed at Le Havre in an industrial disturbance.   The children's allow-ances of the strikers were forfeited for the whole month !   If the break is caused by a lock-out, or by dismissal, or involuntary short time, the allowances are payable only for the period worked.

These incidental uses made of the system of family allow-ances to strengthen the position of employers are obviously not essential to it.   The one just described is plainly even injurious to its main object—the fostering of child life.   To dock the children's food in order to punish the fathers for striking or absenting themselves from work is hardly consistent with the principle on which the promoters so often insist, that the allowances are not part of wages, but are a recognition of the future value of children to the State and to industry. But these inconsistencies go far to explain two things—the attitude of organized labour towards the system and the attitude of the employers towards State intervention.

The Trade Unions—which it must be remembered are less powerful and represent a smaller proportion of the workers than those in this country—appear to have considerably modified their views during the three or four years that the system has been in operation. The employers in their earlier descriptions of the scheme generally allude to them, when they mention them at all, as hostile. But their hostility does not seem to have manifested itself in any attempt to interfere actively with the *Caisses*, or to penalize firms who joined or workers who benefited by them. Their attitude even at this early stage is described by *Le Peuple*, the organ of the *Confédération Générale du Travail*, as one of indifference rather than hostility.

Recent pronouncements shew that both the Socialist Trade Unions of the *Confédération Générale du Travail* and the Catholic Trade Unions of the *Fédération Française des Syndicats d'Employés Catholiques* have now definitely accepted the principle of family allowances and place them among the reforms they demand ; but there is a difference between the two groups. Both want the system made compulsory and universal, but the Socialist Unions give no credit to the existing *Caisses* and resent their subjection to the employers ; while the Catholics recognize as an " *effort louable* " what has already been done, but point to the large number of firms which still hold aloof as a proof of the necessity of compulsion. They would like to see the existing *Caisses* recognized, but administered by Committees elected by the Employers' Associations and Trade Unions and with conditions and scale of benefits regulated and standardized by the State. A resolution to this effect was recently passed by their Federation. Much the same view is held by the *Confédération française de Travailleurs chrétiens* ; by the *Conseil professionnel de Législation sociale et du Travail* ; and the *Fédération française des Unions de Syndicats professionnels feminins*. The only group of Trade Unionists which refuses to give any sort of benediction to family allowances is the *Confédération Générale du Travail Unitaire*,[1] representing the extreme left wing of opinion. Their organization, in the words of one of their secretaries,

" is constituted on the basis of the class war to recognize no immediate object but the raising of wages and no ultimate object but the disappearance of classes and the installation of a society in which the producer shall be the master".

[1] This is the Communist organization, not to be confused with the *Confédération Générale du Travail*.

Much the most important of all these bodies is the *Confédération Générale du Travail*. At its Annual Congress in January 1923, on the motion of one of its secretaries, M. Georges Buisson, a long resolution was passed declaring that the service of family allowances, premiums at birth, and allowances to nursing mothers should be under the control of the State (*la collectivité*), managed by officially appointed committees, including representatives of the various interests concerned, and financed by compulsory contributions from employers and by subsidies from the public purse. The allowances should be completely separated from the question of labour, and should not be affected by its fluctuations, or by unemployment or illness. The present system is denounced on the ground that, if the allowances are paid by individual employers, there is a risk of discrimination against married workers ; if by the *Caisse*, this gives the employing class an unwarrantable power of interference in the workman's household, and enables them by means of objectionable regulations to keep the workers in tutelage and to counteract their efforts of emancipation.

An article in *l'Information Sociale* (1923), reviewing the opinion of leading French Trade Unionists on family allowances, gives evidence that this resolution accurately represents the general attitude. For example, the three secretaries of the workers' federation for the building trades (*Fédération de Bâtiment*) are quoted as approving the principle of family allowances but thinking it ought to be *generalisée par la sociète*. M. Lapierre, one of the secretaries of the C.G.T., expounding the same view before a meeting specially convened to consider the subject at the request of the *Union des Syndicats du Nord*, had said :

" Two million workers are benefited by the advantages accorded by the *Caisses* managed by the employers or the public authorities. It would be impossible to persuade these wage-earners that they should refuse to accept the special grants made to fathers of families.

" I am in favour of making the system general because it is inadmissible that there should be in the same department or town unimaginable differences in the treatment of workmen with children according to whether they happen to be employed by a firm affiliated to a *Caisse de Compensation* or to one which holds aloof !

" I demand the immediate transformation of the present system, because I consider it to be a grave danger to the organizations of workers and their beneficiaries. In its existing form, the institution of family allowances is aimed at undermining the freedom of the workers".

Much the same feeling had been expressed by M. Lenoir, one of the secretaries of the workers' federation for the metal-working and engineering industries (*Fédération ouvrière des*

Metaux). His organization as early as 1919 had issued a manifesto passionately protesting against the whole growing system of welfare work as practised by employers. They were taking upon themselves, the manifesto declared, *les missions les plus délicates* towards the worker and his family— maternity and family allowances, schools, trade classes— " a whole system adapted for the exploitation of man by man". Nothing required or qualified the employers to undertake such functions, which belonged properly to the community as a whole (*la collectivité*). The worker's child was not the thing of the manufacturers (*la chose des industriels*). It was a human being with a value for the future which belonged to the community. All this structure of social welfare work was but a crafty device to disguise the real greed and violence of the present system. M. Lenoir had made it clear that he was still of the same opinion, but

" To-day we are face to face with a considerable edifice. It could not be destroyed without inconvenience, without difficulty. Only one course remains open : to transform it by amending and perfecting it".

Hence he had come to the conclusion that the affiliation of employers to a *Caisse d'allocations familiales* ought to be made compulsory without delay and the State ought effectively to control the administration. The continued payment of family allowances during periods of unemployment and strikes should be assured. This would necessarily mean that the community would participate in the financial burden, but that would bring with it participation in management.

M. Vandeputte, secretary of the workers' federation for the textile industries, is quoted as proposing that the employers should be deposed from the *Caisses de compensation* and that the community should take charge. To illustrate the need for this, he cited the incident already mentioned of the one-day strike at Roubaix and declared that the mothers of families had been warned by circular and by visitors of the consequences to the family if the wage-earners quitted work.

The writer of the article points out that these opinions come from leaders in industries where the system is most strongly developed—building, metals, textiles (the textile industry is described as *la citadelle des allocations familiales*). He notes that leaders in industries which have less actual experience of the system are rather colder and more hesitating in their acceptance of the principle. Nevertheless they do accept it and their policy is exactly the same as those already cited—viz., State control and the allowances to be made independent of industrial vicissitudes. Thus the Annual Congress of workers in the leather and hides industry (*cuirs et peaux*), where the system had been adopted in only a few districts, had expressed an opinion hostile to *sursalaires familiales* but left the branches free to take their own line. The secretary for the book industry, M. Liochon, explained that every time the employers had proposed an amelioration in the form of aid to fathers of families, they had replied that that was not within the province of the federation ; their sole object was to secure fair time rates (*un tarif horaire*) corresponding to the cost of living.

Reading between the lines of these various opinions, it is easy to see that the hostility they express towards the present management of the *Caisses* is very largely founded on the same general grounds as the dislike felt by most English trade union leaders for systems of profit-sharing, premium bonus, factory welfare work, etc. These are regarded as likely to weaken the solidarity of the workers by making them more content with their present position and by lessening their zeal for the main objectives of higher wages, shorter hours, more control and finally socialization of industry. In addition, the French workers resent their complete exclusion from the management of an organization which so intimately affects them and they are naturally made angry and uneasy by such a lesson as the incident of the one-day strike at Roubaix affords of the potential use of the allowances to strengthen the hold of the employer on the worker. But neither in these opinions nor elsewhere have I found any evidence or suggestion that the introduction of *allocations familiales* has in fact led to any of the evil results sometimes anticipated ; that there have been attempts on the part of the employers to lessen the cost by discriminating against married men ; or that the system has had the effect of lowering wages, except in the sense that when a rise has been demanded the employers have sometimes proposed the introduction of family allowances as a substitute. An instance of this occurred at Roubaix, where the allowances were first introduced in lieu of a portion of a rise of wages due under a sliding scale. On the other hand it may be noted that though family allowances at Roubaix are nearly double those paid anywhere else, the rate of wages of textile workers in this district has, since the introduction of allowances, not only maintained but increased its superiority to the general average for the whole country.[1]

As to the attitude of the unmarried men, M. Bonvoisin remarks that they appear generally to have recognized that their fellow workers with families merited special treatment, but that in the beginning it was probably due to their predominating influence that the Trade Unions pronounced against the system.

In proportion as the Trade Unions have become bent on securing State control of the system of *allocations familiales*, the opinion of the employers has crystallized more solidly against control. In the early stages of the movement some of the most influential among them were disposed to advocate making payment of allowances and adhesion to a *Caisse* legally compulsory, because they felt they were being put at an unfair disadvantage in competing with employers who refused to pay allowances and so saved approximately 2 per cent. on their cost of production. This view was put forward on several occasions by representatives of the building and metal-working and engineering industries and by the textiles at Roubaix. But they seem to have changed their view when they saw that State compulsion would inevitably strengthen the demand for State control in matters of administration and finance. As early as February 1920, a Bill was brought before the Chamber of Deputies by M. Bokanouski, which proposed that everyone employing regularly even one worker should be compelled to join a *Caisse* and to pay monthly allowances, allowances to pregnant and nursing mothers and bonuses at birth—these on a scale proportionate to the earnings of the worker and much higher than any scale (except that at Roubaix) actually being paid ; the levy on employers to be at least 5 per cent. of their wages bill. The proposal was not met with much favour by anyone, not even by the Trade Unions, who had not at that time accepted the principle of family allowances. It was referred to the Committee for social insurance (*Commission d'assurance et de prévoyance sociale*) and emerged in a considerably

---

[1] Thus, while the wages of textile weavers at Roubaix were on an average 3.6 francs per day in 1911 as compared with an average for the whole country of 3.32, they had risen by 1921 to 21.2 francs, an increase of 489 per cent, as against a general average of 14.33 francs, an increase of only 332 per cent. (*Wage Changes in Various Countries*, published by the International Labour Office, and taken from the *Bulletin de la Statistique Générale de France*).

modified form as readjusted by M. Victor Jeans. His scheme
reduced the scale of benefits ; proposed to apply compulsion
only to employers of at least ten persons ; but identified the
system with the State even more completely than the original
proposal, since the private *Caisses* were to be swept away and
replaced by State organization. But by that time employers
had made up their minds steadily against any form of State
intervention, on the ground that it would inevitably lead to
higher rates of contribution and increased cost of administration, that it would be an interference with the rights and
liberties of employers, and that the rigidity of a legalized system
was unsuitable to a form of organization which was still in the
experimental stage. On the last point they referred with some
justice to the great variety of experiments, adjusted to the
needs of different districts and industries, that had developed
under the voluntary system.

In one respect only has the assistance of the State been
successfully invoked. The *Caisse professionnelle* for the building
trade of Paris and the Union of Public Contractors (*Syndicat
des Entrepreneurs des Travaux Publics*), finding that their members
were being undercut by firms which economized by not paying
allowances, applied to the Ministry of Public Works to make
such payment essential for those tendering for work under his
department. This was carried into effect. But even that
modest measure of State intervention is looked askance at by
some of the purists for unrestricted private enterprise.

One must not however allow oneself to forget that the movement, in its national developments, is as yet barely five years
old. Hitherto its growth has been rapid enough to encourage
its advocates to rely on its native force and their own powers
of persuasion to secure its complete triumph. But if that
expectation is disappointed and the adherents of *Caisses* find
themselves seriously harassed by the action of the employers
who remain outside, they may change their minds about
compulsion.

So far those committed to the system seem thoroughly
satisfied with the results on their relations with their employees and the quality of their work. The third Congress
of *Caisses* held at Nantes in June 1923 was marked by the
same note of enthusiasm as its predecessors. One claim
however which might have been expected does not seem to
have been made. We hear nothing of any actual increase

in the birth-rate among the beneficiaries. Possibly it is too early to draw any definite conclusions, but it is significant that M. Glorieux, writing in *la Vie*, the monthly organ of the *Ligue pour le Relèvement de la Natalité française*, declares that at Roubaix Tourcoing, " after the experiment has been vigorously pushed for three years and forty million francs spent in family allowances", the birth-rate has actually fallen from 1·18 to 0·78. If that is disappointing from the French point of view, it may help to reassure those who fear the application of the system to this country on the ground that it may lead to over-population.

(c) **Germany**

Considering the relative positions of France and Germany, it is curious to find how closely similar has been the development of the movement for family allowances in the two countries. There are points of difference arising out of their different circumstances, but the points of resemblance are much more numerous. This being so, I will not repeat myself by describing the German movement at great length. Those who wish for further detail can easily obtain it, for the literature on the subject in Germany as in France is already fairly voluminous.[1]

As in France the beginnings of the system were pre-war. For a good many years it had been usual for employees of the German State and local authorities to receive allowances for their families in addition to wages, and the same plan was adopted by some large monopolistic undertakings, such as the Zeiss optical works. Agricultural workers also received (and still receive) similar allowances, usually paid in kind. During the war the practice was widely extended to private firms, especially those engaged in Government work. For example it was adopted by Krupp's in 1916. The change was facilitated by the fact that the Government usually allowed

---

[1] Most of the facts which follow are taken from an article by Dr. Edouard Heimann, of the University of Freiburg, translated by (Mrs.) M. L. Stocks in the *Economic Journal*, December 1923 ; from *Der Soziallohn*, by Gerard Braun ; and from two articles by Dr. Alice Salomon in the *Woman's Leader*, May 4 and 11, 1923. From the first-named source I gather that articles for and against family allowances are as follows: For.—In *Soziale Praxis*, 1921, by Kulemann, Col. 414; Potthof, Col. 530; Meehs, Col. 803; in the *Zentralblatt*, 1921, Nos. 1 *et seq.* (organ of the Christian Unions); in *Bericht der Vereinigung der Deutschen Arbeitgeberverbände*, article of Klaue. Against.—In *Soziale Praxis*, 1922, by Georg, Col. 550, and Brauer, Col. 1234; in *Deutsche Bergwerkszeitung*, 1921, No. 142. See also *Labour Gazette*, March 1923.

such firms their full cost of production, plus 10 per cent. profit. For this reason and also because of the great demand for workers, the employers were under no temptation to discriminate against married men. The Trade Unions however have always looked askance at the payment of allowances by individual employers, in spite of the growing popularity of the cry " to each according to his need", and after the revolution they were in most cases formally abandoned. Very soon however, the growing economic tension led to their re-introduction and since then most collective agreements relating to wages have provided for family allowances in some form. The system has spread much more in some industries than others. Thus an analysis of collective agreements, made early in 1923 by the German Ministry of Labour, divides these into three groups :—(1) those where family allowances are universally recognized (coal-mining, mechanical engineering, the textiles, paper and cardboard) ; (2) those about equally divided between acceptance and non-acceptance of the new system (printing, the food, drink and tobacco trades, pottery and glass, commercial employment) ; (3) those where it is rarely found (building and wood-working, the clothing trades, hotel and restaurant service).

In most cases the allowance is still paid by the individual firms, compensation funds on the pool system being a comparatively late introduction. The first such fund was instituted in January 1920 by the Union of Berlin Metal Industries, one of the largest and most powerful industrial groups in the country. Their example was followed by the chemical industry of Cologne, the employers' federation of the fine pottery industry, the employers' federation in the Berg industrial district, the Munster textile industry and many others. As in France some of the pools are confined to a single industry, others embrace a number of industries within a given locality, opinions differing as to which plan is preferable. The basis of assessment for the pool of the Berlin metal industry and also the fine pottery industry is a percentage of the wages bill ; the alternative plan of a payment according to numbers employed was tried and rejected by both as unsatisfactory. The dependants of male and female employees are sometimes reckoned separately and paid for out of separate pools, sometimes all together.

Allowances in Germany are not always confined to children,

but are in some occupations extended to other dependants of employees. Thus among the Berlin metal workers, the employee may claim on behalf of a wife, or woman taking the place of a wife ; on behalf of children, legitimate or illegitimate, under fourteen or physically incapacitated ; and on behalf of any other relatives who are members of the claimant's household and incapable of self-support. In some occupations, especially those of higher status, the allowance is continued for sons and daughters receiving education at secondary schools or even at universities. The amounts granted are very small—never sufficient for full support. In most industries, the allowances are the same for each child ; but in some they are increased and in some lowered for younger children. A few make the allowance a percentage of the parent's wage.

The new system is the subject of much controversy in Germany. The arguments used on both sides closely resemble those we have already heard echoed from other lands, except that desire to increase the birth-rate is not one of them. On the contrary, when Knust—the chief opponent of the scheme on the employers' side—objects that it may have this effect, he is answered that the low scale of the allowance makes it unlikely. The main argument for the scheme is the familiar one—which has special force under the special circumstances of Germany—that it enables the needs of the family to be adequately met without imposing an intolerable burden on industry. The main arguments against it are the supposed fear of discrimination against married men and the supposed injustice to those without dependants. As to the first point, in spite of the widespread payment of allowances by individual firms, it does not seem to be alleged that married men have so far actually suffered.[1] Dr. Heimann points out that they are usually the steadier and more valuable workers. Further, under the system introduced since the revolution, men are taken on and dismissed not by the employer, but by the workers' representatives. But it is acknowledged that in times of depressed trade and so long as the system is not universal this is a danger, and the pool system was introduced to meet it. It is evident however that the chief obstacle the system has to meet is the jealousy of the unmarried men. Increased weight is given to this in Germany

[1] i.e., up to the date of my information, late in 1923.

by two facts.   First, the unfortunate name given to the
system of " Social Wages " or " Family Wages " (*Soziallohn* or
Familienlohn) gives colour to the view that it infringes the
principle of payment according to value of work done.   We
have already seen how French employers try to meet this.[1]
Secondly, Dr. Heimann explains that the separation of the
workers into rival groups of Unions, differing in their political
and ethical views, leads to keen competition for recruits and
consequently to a strong desire to please the younger workers,
from whom these recruits are naturally drawn.   All the more
credit, he thinks, is due to the German Federation of Christian
Unions for the strong stand they have made on behalf of the
family wage.   The Socialist Unions, on the other hand, have
been in theory steadily opposed to it, though it does not
appear that their opposition has taken an active form, since
it has not prevented the inclusion of family allowances in
collective wage-agreements to the wide extent already described.   Their leader, Leipart, has proposed as an alternative
an extension of communal services for children—free schooling,
books, meals and clothing.   Knust has declared that the
resentment of the younger men at the family wage led to a
falling-off in production.   As a result, a questionnaire was
sent out by the Federation of German Employers' Unions
(*Vereinigung der deutschen Arbeitgeberverbände*) asking whether this
was the case.   The replies received unanimously affirmed that
no such result had followed.   On the other hand the Chairman
of the National Mining Union[2] complains that the relatively
high earnings of the younger men lead them to slack off and
absent themselves and Heimann points out that they manage
to lead a fairly luxurious life on their wages and enjoy tobacco,
alcohol, cinemas and expensive sweethearts.[3]   So little does
human nature differ in victorious France and England and
ruined Germany !

(d) Belgium

In Belgium [4] the system of family allowances closely
resembles that of France, but its development has been less

[1] *See* p. 163.   [2] *Bergwerkzeitung*, July 19, 1921.   [3] Cp. above, pp. 32-3, 39
[4] For the following account I am indebted to the pamphlet by M. Bondas.
Joint Secretary of the *Commission Syndicale*, on *Le Sursalaire et les Allocations,
Familiales* (Brussels, 1922);   to correspondence received by the Family Endowment Council from the *Comité d'Etudes des Allocations Familiales* and the *Confédération Générale des Syndicats chrétiens et libres de Belgique;* and to various issues
of *Labour Overseas.*

rapid, probably because the strong incentive of desire for an increased birth-rate is lacking. It was first introduced in 1915 in the region of Charleroi, but does not seem to have made much progress till after the war, when a number of *Caisses* were formed, chiefly in the mining districts. We are told that the employers were induced to take this step " to counteract the attraction of Belgian labour into France by the higher wages obtainable in undertakings where family allowances are paid in that country".[1]

But the most important *Caisse* instituted has been that of Liège, founded in December 1922. It is on a regional basis, open to all industrial and commercial undertakings in the three provinces of Liège, Limbourg and Luxembourg, but judging from the list of its original members, most of its adherents belong to the metal-working and engineering industries. Its chief features are the following :—Allowances are granted only on behalf of children under fourteen, legally or actually dependent on the employee. They are apparently not confined to employees below a certain wage or salary limit. The amounts are graded from 10 francs a month for the first child to 40 francs for fourth and subsequent children. In addition there are *primes de naissance* of 250 francs at the birth of the first child and 150 francs at that of subsequent children. Both allowances and *primes* are paid through the post to the mother or female guardian. The *cotisation* on employers is based on their wages and salaries bill and may not exceed 5 per cent of this.

In other Belgian funds of which I have particulars the amounts are smaller and sometimes begin only with the third or fourth child.

Employees of the State (with the exception of the fighting services) receive allowances for dependent children up to the age of twenty-one. These were fixed by a decree of July 1920 at a flat rate of 50 centimes a day or 182·50 francs per annum.

The attitude of the Trade Unions appears to be much the same as in France and Germany. The Christian or " free " Unions are altogether cordial. The Socialist Unions dislike the *Caisse* system, but approve in principle of assistance to the family, provided it is given by the State. But neither their dislike nor their advocacy appears to have taken an

[1] *Labour Gazette*, March 1923.

active fighting form.   A resolution passed by the *Comité Nationale de la Commission Syndicale de Belgique* on February 6, 1923, is significant of their attitude.   It begins by affirming that " to each according to his need " is a fundamental principle of Socialism and that this has been recognized by the inclusion of family allowances in trade-union benefits for unemployment, etc.   It asserts the necessity of assistance for large families.   It declares allowances for maternity and nursing mothers to be an inalienable human right, which should be included in a general scheme of social insurance independent of all questions of employment.   But it repudiates what it considers the false philanthropy and degrading charity of employers, who aim only at the further enslavement of the workers.   All this, it will be noticed, eludes the question of whether family allowances for the normal family are desired even from the State.   Reading between the lines of this and of M. Bondas' pamphlet one gathers that though he himself is a thorough convert to direct provision for families through the State, his organization is still hesitating to commit itself to a hearty advocacy because like the workers of other nations its hopes are still set on the " fool's paradise " of the uniform family wage.

(e) Holland[1]

The custom of making direct provision for families began during the war in some departments of State employment and a few private enterprises, and it has grown during subsequent years.   It has sometimes taken the form of fixing special rates for married employees, irrespective of whether they had families or not.   For example, when the salaries of elementary school teachers were fixed in 1919, the three latest periodic increments were confined to the married.   In 1920 the consultative body of representatives of the Government and the Trade Unions recommended an increase of five per cent. on the salaries of the married and the establishment of minimum rates which did not apply to the unmarried.   The latter part of the suggestion was adopted, but instead of the five per cent. increase, children's allowances were granted

---

[1] Information has been kindly supplied me by Mme. Ramondt Hirschman of Amsterdam, supplemented by notes in *Labour Gazette*, March 1923, and in various issues of *Labour Overseas*.

to all State employees, including postmen, railway workers, the fighting services and teachers, varying from 50 francs to 200 francs per child per annum, the allowances for children of civil servants being continued up till eighteen. This example was followed by the authorities of all provinces except North Holland, and by the municipal authorities of several towns ; some of which formed a children's fund on the pool system. Some private manufacturing and commercial firms also adopted children's allowances individually or on the pool system. Up till January 1920, there had been concluded twenty-two collective agreements affecting 756 establishments with 34,000 workers, which contained provisions as to family allowances. Grants were made in respect of children up to ages varying from thirteen to sixteen, and the allowances ranged from 0·20 to 1·30 florins weekly for each child. In some cases grants began only with the third or fourth child. As in other countries, the strongest support comes from the Roman Catholic or " Orthodox Protestant " sections of opinion. In 1920, a committee was formed to oppose the system, and found great support in the Democratic and Social Democratic parties; also among the feminist organizations. The latter adhere tenaciously to the principle of " equal pay for equal work " and succeeded in 1918 in getting Parliament to endorse this principle, which they consider infringed by children's allowances. The policy advocated by these and by the Social Democrats is that of " absolute family wages", i.e., the uniform living wage. These they consider should be sufficient to allow comfortable maintenance for a family of four or five children, while admitting that this would mean comparative luxury for the childless worker.

(f) Other Countries

In Austria, the employers in some industries, especially metal working and engineering, paid children's allowances to their workers for some years before an Act of December 1921 made the practice compulsory, by requiring bonuses proportioned to the price of bread to be paid to the workers for themselves, their wives and children. The provision was to continue in force until a Children's Insurance Act should be passed. According to *Industrial and Labour Information* for February 16, 1923, the Social Democratic Party has prepared such a Bill. In order to equalize the burden on employers, a number of *Caisses* have been established.[1]

In Czecho-Slovakia recognition of the claims of the family is a characteristic feature of the wage system. But only in the case of non-manual workers does it take the form of allowances varying with the number of children. For the manual workers the usual provision is that of a cost-of-living allowance—or sometimes actual board and lodging or allowances in kind—either restricted to married workers, or (more often) at a higher scale for the married than for the single workman. Often widowers and widows, sometimes single men with dependants, rank with the married in this respect. Children are not usually mentioned. A memorandum issued in February 1923, by the International Labour Office of the League of Nations, gives as examples of the practice of the country particulars of thirteen collective agreements, mostly concluded in 1920 or 1921, in eleven of which the provision made is on the above lines. They include the glass industry, the brewing industry, the malt industry, agricultural workers (Northern Moravia and Silesia), the milling workers (Prague) the textile workers (Eastern Bohemia). In one agreement (alcohol distilleries) allowances for wives and children are mentioned, and in one (commercial employees at Prague) the married workers receive a supplement of 10 per cent. on their salaries over the unmarried.

In Switzerland, the Roman Catholic employers at Geneva have taken up the proposal for family allowances with enthusiasm, and a number of them have introduced it and applied it to their own employees. One of these employers, M. Chamay, informs me that the system gives great satisfaction both to the employers and workmen and that his colleagues in manufacturing firms have found it to have an excellent effect on output. The cost is about $2\frac{1}{2}$ per cent. on the wage bill. A scheme for a compensation fund on the French model was drawn up in 1921 by the *Union Sociale des Patrons Catholiques*, but, owing to the crisis of trade depression in Switzerland, its realization has been deferred.

In Denmark, " equal pay " for men and women, married and unmarried, prevails in State employment and in the employment of many municipalities. But the extra allowance granted since the war to meet the high cost of living is higher

[1] *See Labour Gazette*, March 1923.

by one-third for married than unmarried workers. Denmark has a system of pensions for all widows having dependent children,[1] and with incomes below a certain limit.

In Sweden, by an agreement of June 1919, the Railway Companies pay cost of living allowances to salaried employees for their wives and children under fifteen.[2]

In Spain, a conference of the Employers' Association at Vigo in June 1921 declared itself in favour of the " family wage " and decided to establish funds under the direction of the employers, from which payment should be made of an allowance for each child under thirteen.[3]

In New Zealand, a Bill on lines similar to Mr. McGirr's Bill in New South Wales was introduced in 1922 by the Labour Party into the House of Representatives; but got no further. There is a universal system of pensions for widows with children under fourteen, the widow receiving 7s. 6d. for herself and 7s. 6d. for each child.

Finally, in Japan, the Government is said to be considering a number of measures to encourage fatherhood by exempting fathers of more than three from the tax on earned incomes, by taxing childless men and by instituting an " Order of Many Human Treasures."

POSTSCRIPT.

February 1924. Since this book went to press, the following developments in the system of family allowances have been recorded:

In France, the promised extension of the system to all public works has taken shape in three Presidential Decrees. The effect of these, taken together, is to make compulsory the insertion in all tenders for Government work of a clause obliging the contractor to pay family allowances and—unless he employs at least 2,000 persons and has his own approved scheme—to belong to a *Caisse* approved by the Minister of Labour. With regard to works carried out for the Departments and the Communes, it is left to these local authorities to decide whether this compulsory clause shall be inserted in the forms of tender or not. The rates of allowances to be paid and the other conditions imposed are laid down by the Minister of Labour and vary for the different Departments.

[1] I am indebted for this information to Fru Neergaard, of Copenhagen.
[2] *Labour Gazette*, March 1923. [3] *Ibid.*

In Belgium, the system made rapid strides during the latter part of 1923. A report by M. Paul Goldschmidt, secretary of the *Comité d'Études des Allocations Familiales* at Brussels, shewed that up to November 1923, the number of workers covered by the system was over 254,000. This is estimated to be about 18 per cent. of the total number of workers employed in Belgium in private industry. The following industries—mining; certain metals (zinc, copper, lead, nickel, etc.); building and public works; plate glass—have their own schemes for family allowances. That for mining covers the whole industry, numbering over 152,000 workers. Other industries are grouped in regional *caisses*. Discussing the attitude of employers and workers to the system, M. Goldschmidt declares that the employers find themselves amply repaid for the cost of the scheme by the good spirit it engenders among the workers. This constitutes " a powerful lever towards production". He says that the Socialist trade unions, after opposing the system as an infringement of the principle of " equal pay for equal work", are now reassured in this respect by the strict separation of the allowances from the question of wages. Their leaders, while remaining bitterly opposed to the control of the system by the employers, have accepted the principle of family allowances and have announced their intention of framing a Bill to make the system obligatory and to place it under State control.

In Austria, the projected Children's Insurance Bill has been introduced by the Government. It provides for the inclusion in all collective agreements, except for those employed in agriculture and forestry, of provisions for the payment of family allowances, at rates to be laid down by the agreement. If the agreement covers a number of employers, it must contain provisions for establishing a compensation pool, to be controlled by a committee composed of equal numbers of representatives of employers and workers.

See the Appendix, p. 317 for later developments.

CHAPTER VI

THE CASE OF THE OPPOSITION

Everything that I have to say in reply to the opponents or critics of family allowances must be considered in conjunction with what has been said in previous Chapters as to the financial difficulties and social defects of the present way of providing for families. I do not believe in the method so often adopted by advocates of a reform, of denying that it presents any difficulties, involves any risks, would entail any disadvantages —or if denial is impossible of whittling down and belittling these things. In order to establish the case for a reform, it is not necessary to prove that nothing, or next to nothing, can justifiably be said against it. It is enough if it can be shewn that the benefits which may reasonably be expected far outweigh the disadvantages that may be reasonably feared.

So far as it has been formulated, the case against family allowances appears to fall under four headings :—

(a) The fear of over-population or mal-population.

(b) The fear of weakening parental responsibility.

(c) The fear of lowering wages or preventing their rise; and conversely—

(d) The fear of increasing the charges on industry or on the taxpayer.

There is a fifth objection, never plainly formulated, but underlying the others in very many minds. I will call it

(e) The Turk complex.

I· will discuss these in order:—

(a) The Fear of Over-population or Mal-population

What effect may direct provision for families reasonably be expected to have on the birth-rate and on the quality of the children born ? The answer will obviously be affected by the form in which the provision is made—whether it is universal or subject to an income limit and if so what limit; whether it is at a flat rate for all classes entitled to it, or graded so as to represent approximately the same value to families with a differing standard of life; whether it is on a flat rate for all the children of a family or is on an ascending or descending scale; whether it is given unconditionally or subject to conditions, and if so what conditions.

Conversely, the answer should affect the form in which the provision is made. If there is reason to suppose that a certain form of provision would influence the birth-rate in a way that is undesirable from a eugenic or economic or moral point of view, that is a reason for changing the form; not necessarily for abandoning the provision. Opponents of direct provision cannot dispose of it by setting up a proposal endowed with every conceivable dysgenic, uneconomic and demoralizing attribute and then knocking that down. They must be prepared to show that these maleficent attributes are of the essence of direct provision, or at least practically inseparable from it.

Public opinion oscillates at different periods, and during the same period under the influence of thinkers of different schools, between fear of a declining birth-rate and fear of over-population. When the former fear is uppermost, the grounds for it are usually political. Those who feel it are either " thinking imperially " and have visions of a world more and more peopled and dominated by the Anglo-Saxon race; or they are obsessed by the thought of other nations with imperial aspirations, believed to be casting longing eyes at the rich possessions and imperfectly occupied spaces of the British Dominions. They want more children both as colonists and as future defenders; as pacifist labour speakers crudely and rudely put it, they want them as " cannon fodder".

The dread of over-population has always an economic basis. Those who feel it are possessed by the idea of a Society whose need and desire to consume has outstripped its capacity to produce. When they " think internationally " they see a Europe disorganized and exhausted by the war, accustomed to draw its raw materials from the New World and to pay for them in goods which the New World during the war has learnt to manufacture for itself. When they look at home, the working-class seems to them like a headstrong boy, conscious of its strength, insistent in its appetites, and bent on gobbling up the reserves and sweeping away the safeguards which previous generations have respected.

At present the opinion of experts seems divided between the two fears. Mr. Carr-Saunders, in the comprehensive book on Population which is the last word on the subject, quotes as " in conformity with the opinion of the great majority of economists " Mr. J. A. Hobson's saying that

"there is no evidence that the world's population is outrunning its natural resources; but on the contrary the presumption is that for their fuller utilization a larger population is necessary and thereby could be maintained with a higher standard of living " (*The Declining Birth-rate*, p. 75.) [1]

On the other hand, the brilliant group of younger Liberals led by Mr. Keynes are of a different opinion and their organ, the *Nation*, is popularly supposed to have for its watchwords, " Capitalism and Contraception". None of these leaders of opinion have as yet condescended to take the proposal for direct provision very seriously or discuss it thoroughly, but when any of them have cast a careless glance at it, I fancy it has seemed to them just another of the many schemes suggested by well-meaning sentimentalists for encouraging the propagation of the unfit and making it easier for the lazy or inefficient to maintain themselves without much work. [2]

Professor Pigou in a recent Galton lecture [3] devotes to the subject a few paragraphs which make it clear, I think, that he has by no means finished thinking the matter out. He alludes to the spread of " social wages " in Germany and to the proposal of the Chairman of the Royal Commission on the Basic Wage in Australia as examples of a tendency which must cause disquietude to eugenists, and at first suggests that a bounty to the families of wage-earners in proportion to the number of their children " can hardly fail to produce large families among the people to whom the prospect of it is held out." But immediately after he modifies this by a paragraph which dives into the heart of the subject:—

" Even here, however, it would be rash, on the basis of existing knowledge, to speak with any assurance. It must be remembered that, as things are at present, members of the very lowest economic class do not regulate the size of their families by economic considerations, and that their children, if they cannot themselves support them, are in fact supported at the public expense. Hence a bounty, based on the size of families, among manual wage earners generally would not cause the lowest type of wage earner to have more children than he has now. It would, however, affect in this way the higher types of wage earners. These higher types of wage earners would thus come to have larger families than before relatively to the lowest type of wage earners as well as, perhaps, relatively to the

[1] *The Population Problem*, by A. M. Carr-Saunders (Clarendon Press, 1922), p. 309.
[2] Professor Edgeworth has dealt shortly with the subject in his papers to the British Association in 1922 and 1923, but only in relation to the subject of Women's Wages.   [3] *Eugenics Review*, April 1923.

professional classes. The expansion of the middle section, being thus at the expense of both extremes, cannot, on any assumption about the relation between economic status and racial quality, be condemned *a priori* as injurious on the whole. The issue is one that could only be settled, if it can be settled at all, on the basis of a very laborious enquiry in which Eugenists, Economists and Statisticians would all need to play a part".[1]

It would indeed be " rash to speak with any assurance " as to how the birth-rate will react to any social change; for hitherto it has shown a very human and provoking perversity —cynics might say because women have so much to do with it—in belying nearly every prediction that has been made about it. But there are certain considerations which seem to indicate (I will try to emulate Professor Pigou's cautious manner of statement) that the careful enquiry he suggests would result in reassuring eugenists as to the probable effect of family endowment.

After all, as he indicates,[2] the question that causes the most immediate anxiety to eugenists is not the quantity of the population but its quality. The most significant facts bearing on this are those concerning the relative fertility of different social classes and occupations and the changes in their relative fertility. The late Registrar-General for England and Wales, Dr. Stevenson, analysed the births during 1911 according to the occupation of the father and arranged them in five groups according to social status.[3] His summary shews that the births per 1000 married males aged under 55 years (including retired persons) in the different groups were as follows:—

1. Upper and middle class 119
2. Intermediate 132
3. Skilled workmen 153
4. Intermediate 158
5. Unskilled workmen 213

Comparing these results with a similar analysis of births in decennial periods down to 1851-61 he comes to the conclusion that the steady decline of fertility downwards through the social scale is, broadly speaking, a new phenomenon. As he went backwards the birth-rate of different classes tended to approximate so much, that if the analysis could have been carried twenty years further back (which was not possible owing to the inadequacy of the earlier returns) " a period of

[1] *Ibid.*, p. 312.   [2] *Ibid.*, p. 311.

[3] Evidence of Dr. Stevenson in *The Declining Birth-rate*, published by the National Council of Public Morals (Chapman & Hall, 1916), pp. 9, 353.

substantial equality between all classes might possibly have been met with".[1]

It is generally agreed that these facts are very disquieting. They indicate that the community has been recruiting itself in a steadily increasing proportion from those strata of its population who are least likely to pass on to their children a satisfactory heritage of physical and mental attributes, or to give them when born the best kind of environment and education. To say this is not to imply that—to put it bluntly—unskilled labourers are uniformly worse stock to breed from than skilled artisans, or skilled artisans than professional men. Undoubtedly there is much good and much bad stock in all classes. There may be some men and women among the very well-to-do who are as unfitted for healthy parentage by vice, or by generations of too good living, or by in-breeding, as most slum dwellers. Chance and circumstances prevent many children of exceptional capacity from rising out of the class in which they were born and the qualities which assist others to rise are not necessarily the highest.

But allowing for all this, a certain selective process does go on and it is most effective between the four lowest of Dr. Stevenson's five classes. Owing to the long and expensive training necessary for the professions and their different social habits, and owing to the capital necessary for the upper grades of business, it is much harder for ambitious boys belonging to the artisan and lower middle classes to rise into Class I than for the clever sons of labourers to get apprenticed to a trade or a footing on the lowest rungs of business. Also when there is a question of sinking not rising, there is a barrier between the upper and middle classes and those immediately below them. If the son of a lawyer or doctor is a duffer or a slacker, he will almost certainly not become a skilled artisan. He will be sent to the Colonies or put, through influence, to some minor routine job in business. If he is a rotter as well, he may sink into the casual labourer class, which serves as a refuse heap for all the rest.

For these reasons and also because the numbers included in the lower groups are much larger than in the higher, I

---

[1] " The Fertility of Various Social Classes in England and Wales from the Middle of the Nineteenth Century to 1911", by Dr. Stevenson, in *Journal of the Royal Statistical Society*, 1920, p. 417. On the other hand Adam Smith (*Wealth of Nations*, Book I, Chap. VIII) refers to the higher birth-rate of the poorer classes as a matter of common knowledge.

suggest to Professor Pigou that there is more reason to be alarmed at the contrast between a birth-rate of 213 per 1000 in the lowest ranks of workers and 153 among skilled workers than at the latter figure contrasted with the 119 births per 1000 at the top of the scale.[1]

But in any case there is no need to assume as he does that a system of direct provision for children would be confined to weekly wage-earners. Indeed the easiest of all occupations to begin with would be the Civil Service and the Local Government service, including the teachers, and when the system became general, whether it was on an occupational basis or took the form of a single State scheme, there would be no insuperable difficulty, as I shall later try to shew, in grading the burden and the benefits so as to meet the needs of different ranks of workers.

But the immediate problem for our consideration is the explanation of these disquieting figures as to the distribution of the birth-rate. It is usually assumed that the inequality of the distribution and the newness of the inequality prove it to be due, largely if not wholly, to deliberate limitation of families. Some think this exaggerated and suggest that population is subject to natural fluctuations due to either physiological or unconscious psychological causes.[2] However this may be, I do not think any woman who is in close touch with large numbers of women can doubt that deliberate limitation—however brought about—plays a great part.

What are the motives that lead to limitation and why do they influence most those who apparently could best afford to have large families? To say with Mombert, Brentano and others that " fertility decreases as prosperity increases " is true, but it seems to me misleading. It suggests a directly casual relation between the two facts. But what seems really to lead to limitation is not prosperity but rather the reverse, viz., disparity between the standard of life and the means of gratifying it. This becomes plain when we study some of the occupational figures given by Dr. Stevenson.[3] For instance, the comparative birth-rate in eleven occupations is as follows

[1] To follow out the above argument effectively, it would be necessary to ascertain exactly how Dr. Stevenson's five groups were made up and what numbers were represented by each.
[2] See J. G. Udny Yule's pamphlet, The Fall of the Birthrate (Cambridge) University Press, 1920), and Dr. Brownlee's evidence in The Declining Birth-rate (Chapman & Hall, 1916).
[3] Evidence of Dr. Stevenson, in The Declining Birth-rate, pp. 357-8, and pp. 14-15.

(the birth-rate for the general population being taken as 100):—

Coal-miners	126.4
Agricultural labourers	113.4
Boiler-makers	110.1
Farmers	100.5
Carpenters	95.3
Cotton-spinners	91.9
Cotton-weavers	81.2
Nonconformist ministers	79.8
Clergymen (C. of E.)	72.0
Teachers	70.3
Doctors	64.7

Would anyone say that the lower fertility of the clergyman as compared to that of the miner or boiler-maker is due to his greater prosperity? " Prosperity " is relative to need. A clergyman with £300 or £400 a year probably feels himself poorer than a miner or boiler-maker with £4 or £5 a week. He and his wife will certainly be less well able to live up to the standard of life of their friends and relatives of the same social status and to give their children the same educational advantages.

Other factors likely to affect the conduct of married couples of differing social status, or of the same social status but differing mental and moral calibre, are the relative satisfaction they take in sexual enjoyment compared to the other pleasures and interests of life; the relative degrees of their imagination, foresight, prudence, ambition, self-control. The paradox of the present system of child maintenance is that under it, broadly speaking, the more fitted married couples are in all the above respects for the responsibilities of parenthood, the less likely they are to incur them, except to the extent of the one, two or three children to whom they think their means will allow them to do full justice. This is perhaps only doubtfully and partially true of the upper social grades. The standard of life in these grades, though the experience of the war and the scarcity of domestic servants have had a wholesomely simplifying influence, is still no doubt higher than is necessary for full and healthy living, and many parents who restrict their families are influenced, so far as their motives are economic at all, by snobbish or self-indulgent reasons. But who can blame the labourers, the mechanics, the clerks, the shop assistants, the struggling professional and business men without influence or capital to back them who refuse to have more than one or two children, because they know that every additional one would deprive its elders of something they really need if they are to have " a good chance", and would besides add to demands on the wife's time and strength which are already sufficiently heavy ?

I do not believe that anyone who has been in touch with the facts can doubt that on the whole the elements in the working classes who are restricting their families (in whatever way they do it) represent the cream and those who are not practising restriction represent the dregs. Of course there are many individual exceptions—parents whose love of children is so great that they want as many as possible, or who are prevented by their religious opinions from using contraceptive measures and by the strength of their feelings from practising abstinence. But they are a declining minority.

The figures that were earliest quoted to prove this are still I think the most convincing. In 1897, Mr. and Mrs. Webb drew attention to the table of lying-in benefit claims in the Hearts of Oak Benefit Society. This had then over 200,000 members, who must by the rules of admission be of good character and in regular employment and who were drawn chiefly from the artisan and skilled operative class, with an admixture of small shop keepers. In this large and highly select group of specially thrifty families, the reduction in the birth-rate between 1880 and 1896 had been more than twice that in the community as a whole.[1] Since then, a great deal of fresh evidence has been collected, pointing almost without exception the same way. I have not space here to examine it thoroughly, but the following quotations from Miss Elderton's careful investigations are typical and significant for our purpose:—

" We have increasing evidence from the material provided by medical officers of health in the North of England that within each district it is the less healthy parents, the men and women with the worst habits, and the fathers with the lowest wages who have the largest families".[2]

" Data have already been published by the Galton Library which prove that in Blackburn, Preston and Salford the more desirable members of the working class population of those towns have a smaller birthrate".[3]

In Bradford (where a specially elaborate enquiry was carried out with the help of the Medical Officer of Health), " it is the more desirable parents who are having the fewer children. . . . There is a quite significant correlation between bad health of the mother and a large gross family and between bad habits of both parents and a large gross family. . . . . Well-ventilated and clean homes have fewer children in them and the results are remarkably uniform".[4]

[1] *Industrial Democracy,* 1902 edition, pp. 637-8.

[2] *Report on the English Birthrate,* by Ethel M. Elderton, published on behalf of the Galton Laboratory (Dulau & Co., 1914), 223.

[3] *Ibid.,* pp. 223-4.   [4] *Ibid.,* pp. 226, 231.

" Data similar to these from Bradford for the upper and middle classes in England are not at present available, but all the evidence we have points to a differential birthrate within those classes as in the working classes themselves ; the healthy, careful and thrifty are having smaller families than the unhealthy, careless and thriftless".[1]

One very significant fact brought out by these and other investigators concerned the connection between overcrowding and indiscriminate child-bearing. The census of 1911 shews that

" Fertility decreases regularly as the size of the tenement increases till six or seven rooms are reached, and thereafter remains constant. (This holds good for duration of marriage 0-2 years, but not for duration 15-20 years, in the case of which fertility falls throughout as the size of tenement increases).
" Infant mortality decreases regularly as the size of tenement increases, being for tenements of ten rooms or more, less than half the average and less than one-third of that in one-room tenements."[2]

Miss Elderton found that in Lancashire the birth-rate had fallen the most where there were the best housing conditions.[3]

What is the explanation of this association between a high birth-rate and bad housing conditions ? Obviously it is largely that the parents of big families cannot spare much money for rent. What they have is needed for the elementary necessaries of food and clothing. Under the present system of providing for families, the greater the wage-earner's need for a roomy and well-equipped house, the less likely he is to be able to afford it.[4]   But that is not the whole explanation. There is much reason for thinking that overcrowding is partly the cause as well as largely the effect of a high birth-rate. It acts on the birth-rate no doubt partly by lowering the general standard of life. Families that are herded together like animals tend to become like animals—to lose hope, and ambition, and self-control. Lack of privacy and of sufficient bedding increases the difficulty of practising either contraception or continence.

Whatever the explanation, we are faced with the deadly fact, which stands for a greater amount of suffering, inefficiency and waste than the imagination can easily grasp, that the unfittest parents and homes are receiving the largest numbers of children.

[1] *Ibid.,* pp. 231-2.

[2] *The Declining Birth-rate,* Dr. Stevenson's evidence, p. 355.

[3] Elderton, *op. cit.,* pp. 218-9.

[4] Owing to this cause, the 200,000 houses built under the Addison Act, at a vast cost of public money, expressly to provide " homes for heroes," have in fact been filled largely with middle-class people or newly-married couples with one child, while the returned " heroes " are still herded with their wives and families into grossly overcrowded and insanitary slums.

What effect would direct provision have on this ? As Professor Pigou admits, our present experience gives no warrant for supposing that it would cause the lowest class of wage-earners to have more children. All the facts shew how little influenced they are by prudential considerations, and the probability is that they already have as many as nature permits. The highest birth-rate of all is found among the casually employed workers of seaports. But it may be said that present experience is not conclusive, since the effect of a direct payment for each child has not been tried. That is true, and my own social experience leads me to believe that among the present generation of such wage-earners there are some whom the prospect of a payment would induce to increase their physical demands on their wives in the hope (which for the above reason would probably not be justified) that it would lead to more children. Even if the payment were made to the mother in trust for the children and were legally the property of the latter (as would be the case in any well-contrived system) there are some fathers who would commandeer it and some mothers who would misappropriate it. But I do not think the number would be large and unless the parents did this they would have no pecuniary interest in propagation. Their attitude would be that of the French workman who, when asked if he thought that family allowances would increase the birth-rate, replied, " Croyez-vous qu'un ouvrier fasse un enfant pour 90 francs ? " I have heard Englishwomen, remembering the experiences of pregnancy and child-birth and what it means to rear a child, put the question even more crudely.

But set against the possible effect of family allowances on the birth-rate of this minority of really brutal husbands, their effect on the standard of living in the whole class of poor wage-earners to whom they belong. Remember the facts cited above as to the close connection of a high birth-rate with poverty, overcrowding and bad social habits. Next, turn your mind back to the argument set forth in Chapter III as to the effect on standards of living and social habits of the " cycle of prosperity " which inevitably results for the average workman from the present system of providing for families through wages—his childhood spent and habits formed in a home which is poor and overcrowded just because the household is passing through a period of " maximum dependency "; the abundant pocket-money of the early years of wage-earning, when the " living wage " claimed in the name of an imaginary family may be spent in acquiring habits of drink and betting ; then marriage and the period of maximum dependency repeating itself in his own case. Lastly, remember the experience of the war and the excellent results of separation allowances on child welfare and on the conditions of the homes into which they went.

Does it not all point irresistibly to the conclusion that direct provision paid to the mother would raise the standard of life of the poorer wage-earners and that an orderly and self-respecting living is the best cure for indiscriminate and dysgenic breeding ?

But what would its effect be on the classes who are already restricting their numbers ? Would it cause them to have more children ? So far as the motives that restrain them now are economic, it seems almost certain that it would tend that way. The child-loving but prudent parents would feel that they could safely venture on a larger family than they dare have now. But anyone who imagines that there would be a general return to the families of eight, twelve or fourteen children that were so common in the sixties and the seventies must know singularly little of the modern woman. Not that she cares a whit less for children than her grandmother did—I am inclined to think that on the average she cares more, because her affection has not been dulled by satiety—but she has considerably more regard for her own health; very definitely wants room in her life for something else besides motherhood ; honestly believes that in the long run a fully developed human being will make the best parent ; and—most important of all—she knows about contraception. The Dame Partingtons who try to prevent the tide of that knowledge from spreading to those classes who are last reached by every new form of knowledge, would be more fruitfully occupied in explaining to those women who already have it, why their use of it is under present conditions a national danger, since it is resulting in exactly the wrong sort of selection. The appeal would not be resented ; for no class resents being told that the nation needs more of its children and grandchildren, but it is doubtful whether it would have much practical effect, until the bread-and-butter argument has been disposed of by direct provison.

Through a more subtle motive than the bread-and-butter

one, direct provision might influence the problem of selection. There is no doubt that what tends to deter the abler and more thoughtful women from child-bearing, or at least induces them to bring it to an end at an early age, is not only the material consequences of the present system.   They resent the complete dependency it involves for themselves on the husband's wage and the consequent inferiority (in a community dominated as ours is by money values) of their status to his; all the public opinion in short that expresses itself in the sayings, " a man should be master in his own house"; " he who pays the piper should call the tune".   This point has been fully dealt with in Chapter III, Section (*d*). I only refer to it here to point the moral for the eugenist.   The more energetic and capable the woman is, the more likely she is to seek escape from this dependency by returning as soon as possible to her profession or trade.[1]

Mr. and Mrs. Sidney Webb as early as 1897 pointed out this cause of the falling birth-rate among the aristocracy of the working classes :—

" We attribute this adoption of Neo-Malthusian devices to prevent the burden of a large family. . .chiefly to the spread of education among working-class women, to their discontent with a life of constant ill-health and domestic worry under narrow circumstances and to the growth among them of aspirations for a fuller and more independent existence of their own.   This change implies, on the part of both husband and wife, a large measure of foresight, deliberateness and self-control which is out of the reach of the less intelligent and more self-indulgent classes, and difficult for the very poor, especially for the occupants of one-roomed houses".[2]

The same tendency is even stronger in the professional classes.   The more successful a woman has been in her calling before marriage, the more she feels both the actual loss of income and the loss of independence involved in marriage. She is much less likely to marry unless " bowled off her feet " and much more likely to cling to her profession after marriage than a sister who has been less successful or has stayed at home on an allowance from her parent.

[1] The most salient example of this is to be seen in the Lancashire cotton-weaving industry, which includes perhaps the most intelligent and highly-organized body of women wage-earners in England, and has a birth-rate nearly as low as the learned professions (*see p.* 191).   It is a symptom of their quality that these women, in spite of carrying on two occupations at once, have as good health and keep their homes nearly as clean as and better ventilated than those of non-wage-earning mothers of the same class and district (*see* Miss Elderton's *Report on the English Birth-rate.*)   Mrs. J. L. Stocks, in speaking of family endowment to an audience including many Lancashire factory women, found they were opposed to it for the unusual reason that "it would tend to keep married women in the home, whereas their proper place was the factory".

[2] *Industrial Democracy*, 1902 edition, p. 638.

The anti-feminist who is also a eugenist must have a grudge against Nature for not arranging that sons should inherit their qualities solely from their father and daughters solely from their mother. If that were so, he could console himself for the distasteful facts I have been setting out by reflecting that after all the women who have these " disloyal " feelings would not make the best wives and mothers and that there are a good many women still left of a more docile type, who accept their dependency as divinely ordained. But as things are, he must admit that a race which has, rightly or wrongly, assumed to itself the place in the world which the Anglo-Saxon race now occupies, is not safe if it breeds its sons chiefly from the docile, sheep-like type of woman. If it is true, as many eugenists believe, that the little finger of heredity is thicker than the loins of education and environment, it may quite well be that a man who gives his children a stupid, sheep-like mother may be doing a greater injury to them and to the race, than if he mates with a Mrs. Jellyby or a Becky Sharp.

Previous generations believed in docile women, but they did not suffer eugenically for their belief, because there were no other openings for women but marriage and when married no way was known to them to escape bearing as many children as nature made possible. The anti-feminist would like to return to this condition of things, but it is too late. So long as the battle for the suffrage and for women's education hung in the balance we feminists were very careful what we said and in whose presence we spoke when treating of these matters. But now that those irrevocable gifts have been given, we can afford to speak our minds. But we have nothing to say that need make the eugenist who is not an anti-feminist unhappy. After all, the work that a woman does in her own home in bearing and rearing children is not only so much more important to society, but so much more skilled, varied and interesting than nine out of ten of the jobs done by working women, or for the matter of that by working men, that only crass bad management on the part of society has made it seem more distasteful than tending a loom or punching a tram ticket. Divorce maternity from the economic conditions of a glorified serfdom and there will be no danger that the majority of capable women will shirk their fair share of it.

To sum up: I conclude that, judging from the evidence

as to the causes that affect the birth-rate, direct provision for children, by raising the standard of life of the poorer wage-earning classes, will substantially lower their birth-rate as a whole, though it may possibly raise slightly that of a small and diminishing minority of specially low families. It will probably raise, but not to a large extent, the birth-rate of the artisan, lower middle and struggling professional classes. It will not affect the birth-rate of the well-to-do, except that by raising the status of marriage and motherhood it may slightly increase the number of children born in these classes from the abler mothers. It should be noted that the stimulating effect of direct provision on the birth-rate will probably take place at once; the restrictive effect will need at least a generation to make itself felt.

Let me leave with the eugenist one parting reflection. When society has taken upon itself the direct maintenance of children, whether it does it through the State or through the machinery of industry, it will have its hand for the first time on the tiller of maternity. Without any fussy interference or prying inquisitiveness into the privacy of individual families, through the impartial, impersonal action of the economic check or the economic stimulus, it can do something at least to control the quality and quantity of population by methods less wasteful and ruthless than those of starvation, war, pestilence and the struggle for survival. It can do this by manipulating the amount, incidence and conditions of family allowances. These will be discussed in a future chapter.

(b) The Fear of Weakening Parental Responsibility

The most frequently used and perhaps, as far as well-to-do people are concerned, the most effective argument against any change in the present system of providing for families consists in a rather vague invocation of the sanctity of family relationships and of the principle of parental responsibility. It is assumed in these appeals that the beauty of the tie between husband and wife, father and child, will be impaired, and its strength weakened, if there is anything less than complete financial dependency. It is further assumed that the father's motive to industry will be undermined if he no longer feels that he stands between his children and starvation. The case is not of course put so crudely as this, but stripped of the phraseology of sentiment, this appears to be the substance of it. A moral injury to the family and an economic injury to society are predicted if direct provision for children is adopted.

The first thing to note about these predictions is that they are applied by well-to-do people to working-class people; never by well-to-do people to the members of their own class. The prosperous middle and upper class has its own custom of marriage settlements which mitigates, to at least as great an extent as family allowances would do, the financial dependency of wives and children on husbands and fathers. Yet I have never heard the custom denounced by well-to-do critics. A prosperous man of business, however conservative his views on the women's question, does not if he can help it allow his daughter to go quite empty-handed to her new home, nor is he thought to show an unworthy distrust of his future son-in-law if he ties up the money tightly on the daughter and her children. Few people will suggest in such a case that the young man's sense of responsibility will be weakened, or that he will be tempted to idle ways, because he knows that whether he succeeds or fails, a pittance sufficient to secure them from actual want has been secured to his wife and children. Few people would think it disloyal of the wife, if she confessed to a desire to possess a little money absolutely her own. Few people, most certainly of all, would make the suggestion (so clearly ludicrous when applied to one's own class!) that the spiritual side of family life was endangered by the custom of marriage settlements. Most well-to-do parents indeed would be aghast at the idea of a cherished daughter running such a risk as is undertaken by nearly every working woman who marries within her own class. Such a woman knows that her future and that of her babies will depend absolutely on her husband's life and on his continued good health, good character, and success in finding and keeping employment, and that if any one of these factors fails for more than a few weeks or months it means for the whole family destitution, mitigated only by such earnings as are possible to a woman cumbered with young children, or by the dire humiliation of poor-relief or charity. Young couples take the risk (for of course it is his risk as well as hers) as a matter of course, and cultivate instinctively the habit of ignoring danger which is the most usual form of courage. If the risk were inevitable, this would be the right attitude. But if it is not inevitable, has the husband a right to take it for his wife, or the wife for her children ?

Does parental reponsibility require that parents shall assume themselves invincible ? Does it not rather require that they should, in their capacities as citizens who are partly responsible for the arrangements of the society in which they live, strive to remould¦ those arrangements, so that they may afford to the young a reasonable measure of protection from the slings and arrows of outrageous fortune ? There is something surely a little contemptible about the complacent attitude of some middle-class people who, sheltered themselves and able to shelter those they care for from the certitude of hardship and the heavy risk of disaster inherent in an ordinary working-class marriage, oppose the erection of a bulwark for the protection of others, on the ground that hardship is strengthening for the character and parental self-sacrifice a beautiful thing. It reminds one of the non-combatants in the early days of the war who used to stick white feathers on to young men's coats, or the elderly clubmen who think war necessary for the maintenance of a virile race.

It must be admitted, however, that those who feel the objection I am discussing are not all of this complacent type. Some of them are social workers whose fears are grounded not on sentiment but on a long experience of the weaker side of human nature. Nor can one dispose of the argument merely by shewing that those who use it do not apply it to the circumstances of their own class. It may be said that in the working-class family, the supply of primary human needs bulks so much larger than in the fuller, richer lives of the well-to-do that in removing the burden of providing part of them from the male wage-earner one runs a greater risk of weakening his motive to exert himself. This is probably true, but the argument is significant. It shews that the objection assumes the existence of a number of wage-earners with a standard of living so low, that they would rather subsist on the share of their children's allowances which they can coax or coerce out of their wives, than work to secure for themselves and for the whole family something better than the primary needs of the body. No one will deny that there are such men. I believe there are more of them than the accredited spokesmen of Labour are willing to admit; and they are of various grades. Some of them are " born lazy " or utterly selfish. They do not support their wives at present, but either do nothing and make their wives work for them, or spend everything or nearly everything they earn on themselves.   Direct provision could not make them any worse than they are at present, but it would mitigate the suffering of their families.   Others have the normal family affections, but are indolent in body and weak in will.   They dislike work and are kept at it largely by the nagging of their wives and the fear of seeing their children suffer.   I grant that the immediate effect on them of family allowances would probably be bad ; though not worse than the policy of giving outdoor relief and unemployment insurance to unemployed men with families, which has rooted itself firmly during the last few years and with all its disadvantages has done so much to preserve the standard of the people from deterioration.[1]

But such men are a minority even now, even in the casual labouring class in which they mostly congregate.   And again I must repeat, they are to a great extent the product of the very system which family endowment is intended to supersede. Of course this is not universally true.   There are lazy and weak-willed and selfish people in every class of society.   There will continue to be some such people under any system of provision for children, and possibly direct provision may make the way of the sluggard a trifle easier for them.   But to keep the present system in existence for the sake of coercing them—the present system with the colossal waste and maladjustment of national resources which it involves, the suffering of children and the enslavement of women—that indeed is a policy on the level of the statesmanship which thinks to get vast sums of reparations out of Germany by hamstringing its industries and paralysing the trade of Europe.   Or it is like the Chinaman's device for securing a dinner of roast pork by burning down his house.

But for the benefit of those who are obsessed by this particular objection to direct provision for families, I suggest that it is open to them to press for safeguards which would almost completely meet it. As we have seen from Chapter V, all those countries which have so far experimented in family allowances have made them contingent on the wage-earners' employment.   This was also proposed in the New South Wales Maintenance of Children Bill.   The allowances cease when the wage-earner is out of work or on strike.   In France they are manipulated so as to offer a direct inducement to

[1] See pp. 49 seq.

men to remain in the same employment and to turn up to work regularly, and they are believed by employers to have that effect.

I do not myself approve of these arrangements for making the suffering of children a lash for their fathers' backs. But I mention them to shew those who prefer in this matter the spirit of the Old Testament to that of the New, that their doctrine is not necessarily incompatible with direct provision. I admit however that I think they have a lost cause in the England of to-day.   The whole trend of public opinion, especially in the working classes and among women of all classes, is against visiting the sins of the fathers on the children— even as a method of disciplining the fathers.   It is not only tender-heartedness that makes us refrain, but the consciousness that if we do it the effects will indeed prolong themselves unto the third and fourth generation, and that the whole community will pay the price.

Turn for one moment to the other side.   Let those who think that family life is strengthened by the complete dependency of wives and children, put themselves in the place of the women whose legal and economic conditions were described in Chapter III.   It is not necessary to select the victims of idle or bad husbands.   Take the case of a woman who has married in youth the man of her choice and has found in him a partner neither better nor worse than the average run of men —fairly industrious and efficient, affectionate, well-meaning, capable when the stimulus is strong enough of great heroism and self-sacrifice ; but in ordinary life ordinarily self-centred and self-indulgent, a creature of the habits acquired in his care-free youth, slow-witted and unimaginative about needs and feelings he has never experienced.   The finer and more sensitive such a woman is, the more proficient in womanly ways, the better a housekeeper, the more devoted and ambitious a mother, the more likely she is to be chafed and irked by her dependency and the consequences—the expanding family and unexpanding income, the ill-equipped, overcrowded home, the lack of privacy and space, the inability to provide her children with the things they need.   In her sore mind there forms a little festering pool of bitterness against her husband.   She may be too loyal to give it expression, but it gradually changes the relation between them, stopping free speech and causing affection to cool into a half maternal and protective, half contemptuous tolerance. As for the actively unhappy marriages, it is probably safe to say that in the large majority the rift has begun in quarrels about money, in the husband's inability to earn, or refusal to give, enough for the support of the home, or (more rarely) in the wife's failure to spend it well.[1]

As for the children, what proportion of them, if compelled in later life to formulate their filial memories, would have to set down among them that, while they and mother had generally gone ill-clad and ill-fed, father had seldom if ever forgone his hearty meals and little luxuries.[2]

Does anyone think that these things make for the strengthening of family ties, and is it wise to subject poor human nature to such unnecessary strains? Granted that poverty and dependency, like war, do often call out what is finest in human nature—its capacity for endurance and self-sacrifice, the triumph of the spiritual over the material—do they not also call out what is basest? And are they necessary to the full manifestation of these finer things? Do not the unalterable facts of human life—the miracles of marriage and birth, the helplessness of infancy, sickness and old age, the infirmities of character which make us all such a trial to our nearest—do not these give to human nature ample room and occasion to rise to the full measure of its stature? It would be a poor look-out for the institution of the family if it were really held together by the bond of £ s. d. But it is held together by something much stronger—by the call of the blood ; by the memory of experiences enjoyed or endured together ; above all by Nature herself, who makes the man need the woman, the woman the man and both the child.

(c) The Fear of Lowering Wages

(d) The Fear of Increasing the Burden on Industry

These two objections can best be discussed together ; for they are concerned with the same issues, namely, the cost of family allowances and who is to bear it.

---

[1] Lest these seem rash generalizations, I had better explain that throughout the war I had to investigate and report to the War Office (afterwards the Ministry of Pensions) on practically every case in which a Liverpool soldier deserted his wife or brought charges against her. In this way, I learnt the inner history of several hundred cases of matrimonial breakdown. In addition, the pre-war experiences described on p. 58n. have let one into the domestic secrets of large numbers of homes.

[2] *See* the facts and figures on pp. 43-4.

We may picture the national income as a heap of wealth which has hitherto been shared out among a number of claimants—landowners, capitalists, employers, and wage-earners. There is a fifth claimant—the State—which exacts from the rest a varying proportion of their takings. The advocates of family allowances now appear to put in a claim for a direct share of the heap. The claim does not really involve an additional charge on it, for the wives and children have had to be kept somehow out of the shares of the rest. But obviously it involves some redistribution of the other shares—at least one or more of them. If the State provides the allowances, all the four other claimants, but especially the three more prosperous of them, will have to pay more in taxes. On the other hand some other claims on their incomes will be diminished, but not necessarily in the same respective proportions as their payments. If the allowances are paid out of an occupational pool, as in France and Germany, those immediately concerned are the employers and the wage-earners, though the rest may be indirectly affected through the raising or lowering of the costs of production and consequently of prices.

All concerned are perplexed and embarrassed by the claim, and uncertain whether they stand to gain or lose more by it. The wage-earners who ostensibly stand to gain by far the most, since it is their wives and children who are the chief sufferers under the inequalities of the present system, are perhaps the most anxious ; first, because they can least afford to take risks ; secondly, because a large proportion of them have not, at any one time, dependent children ; and thirdly, because they are doubtful as to how the grant of family allowances will affect their bargaining power and a chance of securing an increasing share of the heap. The employers, if they consider the facts set out in Chapter II and Chapter III, cannot fail to be struck with the immense wastefulness of the present system and its demoralizing effects on many of the wage-earners. But they have not much hope that the change asked for will diminish the total share that falls to the wage-earning class and unless it does that they do not stand to gain very much directly[1] by its more economical distribution and are not all of them far-sighted enough to see how much they may stand to gain indirectly through increased

[1] Except of course in their consciences and as " members of one another".

efficiency. On the other hand, they are fearful lest the change may take a form which will actually diminish their own share, or increase the proportion of it claimed by the tax-collector or, worst of all, for the reason discussed in the last section, cause the heap itself to shrink.

Obviously no completely conclusive answer can be given to these doubts and fears. The answer must depend largely on the form in which direct provision is made ; and even if that were determined, the economic and psychological consequences of such a far-reaching change are not matters for cocksureness. I can only offer for the comfort of the doubters the following reflections which (I repeat) must be taken in conjunction with all that has gone before as to the evils of the present system and the experience by foreign countries of the new.

It is difficult to speak of the objections of " the workers " as a class without falling into the common error of forgetting that they are distributed into as many political parties as the rest of the community. Those of them who belong to the older parties are for the most part following leaders who do not belong to their own class or think in terms of its class interests. The difficulties they feel with regard to direct provision for families are mainly those dealt with in the other sections of this chapter. The members of the Labour Party and of the Trade Unions who are guided by it in questions of industrial politics can logically have no objection in principle to direct provision. Most of them are committed to maxims such as " to each according to his need " and " no cake for anybody until everybody has enough bread", which are clearly irreconcilable with the system of providing for families through a uniform " living wage". But they have hitherto thought of these maxims almost entirely in reference to the problems of vertical distribution of wealth between members of different classes. When asked to apply them to the problem of horizontal distribution between families within the same class, many of them are disposed, at least at first sight, to resent the suggestion, for one or more of the following reasons :—

First ; there is the secret complex discussed in the next section, which makes some men of all ranks dislike the recognition of their wives and children as separate person-alities with claims equivalent to their own. There is also the tradition which enables them to dress up this feeling in a guise acceptable to their consciences.

Secondly ; there is the belief that the whole energies of
the workers need to be concentrated on the contest between
capital and labour and the dislike of any proposed reform,
not necessarily part of this contest, which threatens not only
to distract time and attention from it but possibly to weaken
the springs of effort by making the present economic system
seem less intolerable.

Thirdly ; in the day-to-day tactics of wage-negotiations,
" our wives and children " has been found a useful cry,
which could be no longer used, at least with the same effect,
if provision for families was made separate from wages.

Fourthly ; there is the fear (closely associated with that
last mentioned) that the employers would find means of
pocketing for themselves the economy on the wage-bill made
theoretically possible by its more efficient distribution.

Fifthly ; there is the point of view of the men without
dependants who, whether the last-named fears were realized
or not, foresee that under the new system they would no
longer enjoy the same comfortable surplus over their married
comrades and who cannot see why they should " help to
pay for other men's children".

The only way of dealing with the first of these obstacles is to
drag it up to the surface and strip it of its wrappings and then
hope that, like the mummy of a dead tyrant, it will shrivel
up and crumble when exposed to air and sunshine.

The answer to the second objection has been anticipated
in Chapter II, Section 3. So far as I am aware, no reasoned
attempt has yet been made by the recognized thinkers of
the Labour Party to refute the calculations made by Dr.
Bowley and Sir Josiah Stamp which prove that, even if
vertical redistribution of wealth could be carried out on
lines more drastic than the most extreme Socialist desires,
the amount would be barely sufficient to bring up the wages
of the less well-paid workers to a standard of present-day
recognized working-class comfort. It would fall far indeed
below the amount required to achieve for everybody such
a standard as even the more frugal and unostentatious of
professional men think necessary for their own families if
they are to live a really full life, including such factors as
provision for privacy and space in their homes, regular and
fairly frequent country holidays, some foreign travel and
so forth. If this is true, is it not cruel to ask the workers to pin

all their faith to the coming of the Socialist State as though it were a Kingdom of Heaven and when found "all these things will be added unto you " ? If prophecy were ever safe, surely it would be safe to predict that if the Socialist State came to-morrow and had the effects on productivity that its reasonable advocates hope rather than those its opponents fear, horizontal redistribution would still be necessary.

But will it delay vertical redistribution, or even give the " haves " the chance to snatch back a little of what the " have nots " have so hardly won ? There can be no doubt that with this cry of " our wives and children " the Trade Unions have hoped to repeat the manœuvre which their predecessors used successfully in the matter of the Factory Acts. A limitation of the hours of labour was then achieved in the name of the women and young persons, which in effect—the labour of the various grades of workers in many kinds of factories being interdependent—secured protection for the men also. Similarly the uniform wage adequate to the needs of a family has been asked for in perfectly good faith, since everyone concerned up till recently believed that to be the only practical way of ensuring provision for families, but not without consciousness that the bachelors would obtain thereby a very substantial perquisite. Direct provision not only threatens to deprive the bachelor of his perquisite, but to weaken the position of the workers at the game they are playing with the employers by filching from them one of the best cards in their hand.

But is it really that ? It may be conceded that the cry of a living wage and the thought of the men's wives and children has had some effect in enlisting the sympathy of the general public on their side in wage-disputes, and this has become important since the workers have come to rely increasingly for the ultimate decision of such disputes on Parliament and on bodies set up by Parliament such as Trade Boards, Joint Industrial Councils and Courts of Arbitration. But has not the strength of this sympathy already been considerably impaired by the ameliorative measures that have been taken, with the full approval of the workers themselves, to blunt the sharp edge of poverty for children—free school meals, free and rate-aided milk and the many charitable funds? Although the whole of these provisions taken together cost a trifling sum in proportion to the child population of the workers and benefit only a small fraction of them, they have created a strong feeling throughout the middle and upper classes, and especially in the great struggling lower-middle class, that "the children of the poor have so much done for them", and this has considerably checked the flow of sympathy with the victims of low wages.

As for the employers, I doubt whether the cry has ever had the potency ascribed to it. Undoubtedly the more humane and enlightened employers desire to pay "a living wage" but unless they control a virtual monopoly they cannot hold out against the forces of competition. One can only judge by results. In 1901 the figures I quoted in Chapter II from Rowntree's *Poverty*, shewing the great proportion of workers' children suffering from privation due to inadequate wages, were first given to the world and they have achieved a very wide publicity. *Poverty* was only one of a considerable group of books pointing out similar facts and illustrating them in different ways from very various points of view. The cry for "a living wage" has never been so much heard as during the last quarter of a century. It has been very generally conceded—in theory. It has had a remarkable *succès d'estime*. But during the nineties real wages, which had risen without a waver from 1880 till then, became nearly stationary and remained so until the War.[1] At present the workers are struggling frantically to save themselves from being driven down below the wage standards of 1914. Must we not confess that the employing classes, though they may be moved to pity by the sufferings of their workers' wives and families, are moved to action in ninety-nine cases out of a hundred only by self-interest, ambition and fear—at least where their business affairs are concerned? They salve their consciences by charitable subscriptions and appeals to the laws of political economy. Let not the workers be too hard on them for that. Have they no beams in their own eyes? The privations of the wives and children come much nearer to them than to the employing class. They know—none better—that children cannot be fed on averages ; that they need three meals apiece every day. Yet they have acquiesced in and encouraged the fiction of the standard or normal family, on the hitherto true excuse that they knew of no other way (again pending the coming of the Socialist millennium) of providing for families. But

[1] *The Change in the Distribution of the National Income*, 1880-1913, by A. L. Bowley (Clarendon Press, 1920), pp. 18-19.

they have certainly not shewn any great anxiety to find another way, and now that it has been found for them and is in operation in other countries, their way of receiving it will afford a test of the relative strength of their interest in the well-being of wives and children and their desire to preserve, even at the cost of that well-being, every shred of a chance of securing for the adult male every advantage he has hitherto enjoyed or hopes to enjoy.

But what of the fourth objection—the fear that if direct provision is brought into operation during the régime of the Capitalist State, the employers will manage so to manipulate it as to cut down the present wage-bill, or at least to prevent an increase that might otherwise take place, so that the wives and children will be no better off than before and the position of the single man considerably worse ? The whole trend of my previous argument as to the wastefulness of the present system, the unnecessary provision which it postulates for over 16 million non-existent children, shews that this is theoretically possible and, assuming the subsistence theory of wages, it is what would happen. I offer the following observations in reply.

First ; no economist of repute now holds the subsistence theory, at least in its original dogmatic and unqualified form, and certainly no Trade Unionists can afford to invoke it; for if true, then is their preaching vain and to no purpose do they die daily in strikes and sacrifices of individual interest, in order to raise the standard of wages of their class above subsistence level. Granted, as all in effect will grant, that the level of wages depends (a) on productivity (the size of the divisible heap) and (b) on bargaining power ;—what effect would direct provision have on these ?

As to productivity, I refer to all I have said in past Chapters of the evil effects of the present system on industrial efficiency ; on the energy and ambition of the young wage-earner ; on the health and hopefulness of the father of a family ; on the health of the child-bearing mother and her progeny, who are the future workers. As to bargaining power, have the same facts no bearing on that ? Does the ease with which the average young wage-earner earns enough to satisfy the low standard of life which he has acquired in his cramped, privation-stricken childhood really tend to make him an active, intelligent, public-spirited Trade Unionist ? If so, how is it that so large a proportion of the leaders of the Labour movement comes from the middle classes or from the aristocracy of the wage-earners ? Imagine that by a miracle, in the twinkling of an eye, the boys and girls between, say, fifteen and twenty-one years old of the professional classes, were transferred to the homes and the occupations of the poorer section of the working class. Imagine further that the facts of their past were blotted out from their minds but that they retained the tastes and instinctive habits of their original class. Apart from all questions of hereditary quality, would not the mere fact of the higher standard they had brought with them into their new sphere make its conditions seem so damnable to them that they would prove the most zealous of Trade Unionists, while their healthier bodies and better trained minds would place them among industry's most efficient workers ?

There are other ways in which direct provision would improve both bargaining power and productivity.

As I have argued in Chapter IV, it would make a thorough application of the principle " equal pay for equal work " for the first time practicable. The competition of women need no longer menace the men's standards of pay, both by actual undercutting and by providing the employer with an ultimate line of defence in wage disputes. Women's labour, neither boycotted nor preferred because of its cheapness, might be allowed to find its natural level and this would promote both maximum and optimum productivity. Further, direct provision would result in withdrawing from the labour market a large proportion of the married women workers, especially those who only entered it because of the inadequacy of their husband's earnings or of what he " turned up " to them. These have always been unsatisfactory to the employers because of their irregularity, and to their fellow-workers, because they are impossible to organize and can easily be forced to take pocket-money wages.

There is another advantage to the wage-earners which might follow from direct provision, though whether it did so or not would depend on the form adopted. If family allowances were paid by the State out of taxation, they would naturally continue throughout periods of unemployment and strikes. If paid out of an occupational pool, this would be a matter for arrangement. It would be reasonable at least to expect their continuance during periods of temporary and involuntary unemployment, since no one can think it right that child-bearing women and children should bear the brunt of these as they do at present. On the other hand a permanently declining industry could not be expected to go on bearing indefinitely the family charges of all its previous adherents, and payment during strikes presents other difficulties. These issues will become clearer later. Meantime, I may point out that the whole theory of direct provision implies the recognition of wives and children as persons whose claims on the community arise out of their own reserve value to it and not out of the husband's and father's contribution to industry. While the family is a unit which must inevitably to some extent suffer together as it prospers together, there is a point beyond which the community cannot afford to let that be carried. A hunger-blockade of the children is not a legitimate weapon of industrial warfare. The conscience of the community would soon assert itself on that point if the mental fog caused by the uniform wage-system were cleared away, and whether the allowances were paid at the expense of the industry affected or of the community in general, they would go far to put the two sides to industrial disputes on a fairer footing than they have ever yet occupied.

But apart altogether from their effect on bargaining power, direct provision would bring with it a certain and great increase in "real wages", not in the conventional but in the *real* meaning of the words. The value of wages to the worker is not the money payment; nor even the amount of goods and services he can buy with the money; but the satisfaction of human needs and additions to human happiness which those goods and services represent. By redistributing a portion of the national income more closely in proportion to needs; by making it certain that a much larger proportion of it would be spent on the essentials of welfare and less on the accessories, horizontal redistribution would ensure a great and immediate increment of well-being throughout the wage-earning and the lesser salaried classes. I do not see how anyone who has considered the facts and figures set out in this book and in other books treating of the conditions of poverty—certainly any member of the Labour Party who knows these conditions at first hand—can seriously dispute this.

But what of those who would be the losers and not the gainers by horizontal redistribution—the man without dependants? It is undeniable that direct provision means some sacrifice on their part, not necessarily of their existing share but of their potential claim on the national income, since the whole object of it is to secure a more equitable adjustment between those with and without dependants. Judging from the opinions that have been expressed to me by the few leaders both on the employers' and the wage-earners' side who have considered the scheme at all, and also by the echoes of foreign experience, this is likely to be in practice the most serious obstacle to its realization. These opinions have related specially to the industrial pool form of provision. One is told that " the younger men will never agree to let men working on the same jobs as themselves, perhaps less efficiently, get higher pay because they have children". When provision by the State is under discussion, this kind of objection is transferred to the taxpayers of both sexes and all classes above income tax limit. It is then they who "cannot see why they should be asked to pay for other people's children". The objection is no less formidable because it is fundamentally selfish, though the objectors partly disguise that from themselves by muddling it up with the other fears I have been discussing. Its potency will depend greatly on the form in which the proposal is made when it first comes up as a concrete proposition for immediate acceptance and the way in which the case is stated by the leaders in whom the respective bodies of objectors trust.

The majority of Englishmen, whatever their class and politics, have intensely conservative minds and are influenced greatly by tradition and the phrases in which tradition has clothed itself. A proposal to which they may take an unconquerable aversion if they first meet it clad in phrases which are repugnant to an already established prejudice may be received with acclamation if it can manage to enlist in its service the particular set of catchwords which happen at the moment to be in favour with the particular set of individuals one is addressing. It is essential to make it plain that family allowances, whether paid out of an industrial pool or out of taxation, are not part of wages—of the worker's remuneration for his toil. If they are anyone's wages they are his wife's; but it is truer and also more expedient to call them a recognition of the special needs and special services of parenthood; or more simply, Society's provision for maternity and childhood as the reserve force of industry and of the State. The French employer has found by practical experience the value, as obviating objections from the unmarried men, of adopting both a nomenclature and a form of administration under which the allowances are kept distinct from wages and paid to the mother.

If by making this point clear, the suspicion of unfairness can be dissipated, it is surely not postulating a very great effort of altruism on the part of the younger men to assume that they can be won over to the scheme. After all, bachelors are not a separate species like ponies, but are rather like colts. The vast majority of them, especially in the wage-earning classes, know that they will marry and marry fairly early. They and their families will be the chief beneficiaries of the scheme. The one legitimate objection to it from their special point of view is that it would lessen their means of saving towards their future home. But, as already pointed out[1] this is not done to anything like the extent of the means available, and for the modest nest-egg which the average young couple usually saves, an equivalent might be provided as one of the benefits of the scheme, on the lines of the " *prime de mariage* " paid by some French companies. This would be more easily arranged if the financing of the scheme were partly on an insurance basis.

Although it is usually the young men who are quoted as the likely opponents, a much more reasonable opposition to direct provision might be expected to come from the older generation—those whose families have passed through the period of dependency without any such assistance and who are now struggling to provide for their old age. For the first generation of the scheme's operation these would lose by it to the extent of any reduction it might cause in the incomes of men without dependants, without any compensatory advantage except that their married sons and wage-earning daughters would be in a better position to help them. But these men are a relatively small minority of their class.[2] Any hardship they

---

[1] *See* pp. 39-40.

[2] In Dr Bowley's study of " Earners and their Dependants " in industrial towns, he found that 38 was the age of maximum responsibility for dependants. But the number of dependent children did not begin to decrease seriously till after 50. Of 7,716 men in the households surveyed, only 1,451 were between 50 and 70, and these had 726 dependent children. The years between the children's leaving school and their marriage are apt to be relatively prosperous owing to the number of wage-earners in the household. (*See Economica*, May 1921, p.10).

incurred would be mitigated by improvements in the old-age pension system; especially a lowering of the age and removal of the income limit—both reforms highly desirable on other grounds.

But those who desire to win over the wage-earners, both those with and those without dependants, to the support of direct provision for families, will make a mistake if they appeal only to self-interested motives, or even to the considerations of a far-sighted and coolly calculated utilitarianism. I have found this myself repeatedly when laying my case before audiences of working-men and women. If the heads of Englishmen are apt to be thick and impervious to new ideas, their hearts are soft, especially where children are concerned. The Tommies who, when they occupied Cologne, could not be dissuaded from sharing their rations with hungry German children, come of a race which could never have deliberately devised an economic system so neglectful of the claims of childhood as the present. It grew up in its present form, as I have tried to shew in the first chapter, out of happenings in the nineteenth century and especially (by a strange irony of fate) out of a movement designed to protect child-life from industrial bondage. Its disadvantages come within the immediate experiences of the wage-earners and do not have to be proved to them by statistics. They are tolerated, because no way out is seen except through vertical redistribution. The idea that there is another way, not incompatible with that, but more immediately achievable and in any case needed to supplement it, has not yet been fully presented to their minds. If this can be done by judicious propaganda, I believe it will take root there because of its appeal to one of the strongest of human instincts, the love of children.

But there is another strong instinct, which impedes its entry:—

(e) The Turk Complex

When the obvious explanation of any part of human behaviour (including our own) seems insufficient, we have learned to look beneath the surface for the hidden motive, unacknowledged and probably unconscious, which may have prompted it.

The reader who has studied the case for direct provision as set out in this book may or may not find it convincing, but

I venture to assert that if capable of weighing evidence, he will not find it negligible. The facts and figures of Chapter II, to say nothing of the social considerations urged in Chapters III and IV, obviously constitute a strong prima facie case against the present system of providing for families. Yet as indicated in Chapter I, the whole problem, and not merely the solution of it discussed in this book, has been almost completely neglected and ignored by economists, statisticians and industrialists. It has been assumed, practically without discussion or question, that the only alternative to the present system or rather lack of system is through a minimum " living wage", based on the needs of a family of a particular size and ladled out to all men whether they have families or not. In spite of all demonstrations of the failure of society to achieve such a wage, the impossibility of achieving it out of present resources and the waste at the one end and suffering at the other which it would entail if achieved, this grotesque conception—apparently with the concurrence of the very sociologists who have supplied the figures for its refutation— continues to be held up before the eyes of the struggling, poverty-stricken masses and their responsible leaders and employers as the economic ideal to strive for. It is as though the portrait of a village idiot were to be enthroned above the altars of all churches, as the symbol of men's hopes and aspirations. Meantime the idea of treating each family as though every man, woman and child in it had a separate stomach to be filled, back to be clothed, individuality to be developed and respected, is either ignored altogether, or brushed aside with some careless allusion to the impossibility of asking employers to proportion wages to the size of a man's family or the danger of encouraging over-population.

What is the explanation of this all but universal attitude ? I do not think we need peer very long into the recesses of the human mind before discerning it.   Among the strongest instincts of human nature is the desire of power, of domination, of being looked up to and admired.   Through all ages and in all countries, with a few insignificant exceptions known to anthropologists, men even the humblest and most oppressed have found scope for the satisfaction of this desire in their power over their own wives and children.   Even the slave was lord in his hut.   His authority rested ultimately on the greater physical strength of the adult male, on the helplessness of infancy and the special needs of maternity. But the instinct of domination, not satisfied with the sanction of physical force, buttressed itself with every other it could devise, with the sanctions of law, of religion, of tradition and custom, of economic dependence. As time went on, other instincts and forces, including the resistance of wives and children against domination and the affection of husbands and fathers which disposed them to yield to this resistance; including also the teaching of Christ (though not of all His accredited exponents) as to the value of every separate individuality, has gradually weakened the *patria potestas*, and deprived it of many of the sanctions by which it was upheld. The instinct of domination, in order to preserve what remained, has been compelled to resort to subterfuge, to assume by a sort of protective mimicry the likeness of more reputable instincts.

The last century has seen the emancipation of women and children from the most oppressive and cruel forms of marital and paternal power, as well as from the economic conditions which bound those of the poorer classes to a kind of industrial slavery. It has given them new rights and opportunities, of education and development; and in the case of women, of citizenship. But as we saw in the first chapter, it has also seen the simultaneous and partly consequent extension of the period of their economic dependency on their male head of the family. Is it fantastic to suggest that in accepting this new burden, the unconscious mind of man was aware that he was also securing a new hold over his dependants, more subtly effective than that which he was forgoing? The privilege of compelling a reluctant wife by physical force to cohabit with him or chastising her (within reason, and provided he used a stick no thicker than his thumb!) was no longer his. Harsh methods of parental control had also gone out of fashion. But instead of these little used or valued sanctions, he had the power of the purse, the knowledge that his wife throughout her married life, his children till adolescence, would have nothing in the world but what he chose to give them. I am not suggesting that men value this power because, in the vast majority of cases, they have any desire to abuse it. It is notorious that the pleasures of virtue are greater than of vice; to give is more blessed than to receive. But it is easy to see what satisfaction the institution of the dependent family gives to all sorts and conditions of men—to the tyrannous man what opportunities of tyranny, to the selfish of self-indulgence, to the generous of preening himself in the sunshine of his own generosity, to the chivalrous of feeling himself the protector of the weak. The very device to which the necessities of the dependent family have led—the device of the uniform family income— ministers to the desire for self-importance, by giving to the man a kind of multiple personality, a five in one and one in five, so that he stands out like the central figure in an Italian picture against a dim richness of angel and Cupid faces.

Further it should be noted that, like all deep-rooted and inherited instincts, this one is independent of the circumstances of the individual case; so that it exists as much in the minds of men who are unmarried or childless, or married to women who have never been economically dependent, as in the minds of fathers of families. It is, in fact, an impersonal instinct, which creates between those who share it a kind of common sex bias which is often stronger even than self-interest or the interests of class.

This being so, it is not surprising that when the idea of direct provision is first presented to men's minds, a large proportion of them find it distasteful, for reasons which they do not care to analyse. Instinctively they clutch at the first objection that comes to their minds—the scheme is socialistic, or it would be burdensome to the taxpayer, or lead to the dismissal of married men. If some intrusive propagandist insists on knocking away these convenient excuses, the mind's next gesture is to turn its back on the obnoxious reform and walk right away from it. Those who have watched the growth of movements which offend a popular prejudice or dominant interest must have noticed that this is what usually befalls them in their earlier stages. Since mediæval times, men have learned better than to persecute the propagandist of unpopular opinions. They retain only one instrument of the Inquisition— the oubliette—and they use it to dispose not of the heretic but of the heresy. Thus when a proposal presents itself which is obnoxious to the hidden Turk in man, he stretches up his hand from his dwelling in the unconscious mind and the proposal disappears from the upper regions of consciousness.

Further, the Turk is a master of the magic of the East and can do wonderful things. He can conjure up an army of phantom children[1] and with their help wring wage advances

[1] See p. 16.

out of close-fisted employers, without their once suspecting the trick which is being played on them. He can persuade hard-headed manufacturers to acquiesce in the fiction that women are incapable of skilled work and it needs the experience of a Great War to shew how much productive capacity has been wasted.[1] He can so befog the minds of learned economists—men who would rather burn off their right hands than knowingly pervert the truth—that when they touch on the subject of the family they commit themselves to statements of a vagueness, an ineptitude, a futility, of which they would be ashamed if they were discussing, say the cost of rearing live-stock, or rationing an army.[2] Strangest of all, he can cast such a spell over devoted husbands and fathers that they see nothing anomalous or unjust in a system which gives their young fellow-workmen as much to waste on beer and football as they spend on the support of their wives and children; nay, that they even think it a divinely ordained arrangement, which it would shake the foundations of society to change.

There are many people—men and women—who have a strong distrust of all reasoned argument, and a belief that there is necessarily something higher and finer in any conclusion based on intuition and instinct. Or even if they allow Reason to dominate their professional and public conduct, they warn it off the doorstep when it approaches their private life and the domain of the domestic affections. Rudyard Kipling, quoted with approval by Mrs. Fawcett and Professor Edgeworth, declares that when the workmen, at the Congress convened by " Imperial Rescript " were invited to adopt Socialist motives " To ease the strong of their burden and help the weak in their need", the English delegate replied "I work for the kids and the missus", and the workers of all countries joined in declaring " We will work for ourselves or a woman for ever and ever". No doubt as they said it, the mind of each delegate shot a glance at his wife and children across the seas; another glance at that self-reflector which everyone carries in his breast, and saw there mirrored the gratifying image of the protecting, self-sacrificing male.

> " And the Devil did grin,
> For his darling sin
> Is selfishness masked as Chivalry." [3]

[1] *See* Chap. IV, Section *b*.
[2] *See* —— But I will leave the reader to supply his own references !
[3] I have taken liberties with these lines from Coleridge's " The Devil's Thoughts ".

I know that in saying all this, I shall irritate many of my readers and few perhaps will bring themselves to take it seriously. But in all seriousness I suggest that to meet the plea for a juster and more effective system of distribution by an appeal to sentiment, even to sentiment that has a healthy human sound, is to encourage a subtle and dangerous form of selfishness. A man has no right to want to keep half the world in purgatory, because he enjoys playing redeemer to his own wife and children.

The verdict of the economists,[1] that the present wealth of the nation, however distributed between classes, is insufficient to supply the " living needs " of families through the machinery of the present wage system, means when translated into terms of flesh and blood that in the future as in the past and the present—barring some uncertain and improbable vast increase of productive capacity—millions of children must be brought up in extreme poverty, the kind of poverty that warps and enfeebles the mind and character as well as the body. If, as the figures indicate,[2] this terrible conclusion can be avoided by direct provision for families, then those leaders of opinion who turn aside from this solution, not on reasoned grounds but because of an instinctive and sentimental distaste, are incurring a great responsibility. It is as though a physician who suspected himself to be on the track of a permanent cure for cancer, should refuse investigation because he finds pleasure and profit in relieving the sufferings of individual patients, or a statesman should obstruct the League of Nations on the ground that war develops unexpected capacities for initiative and heroism.

Even if we suppose the wealth of the world doubled or trebled, it would not afford a standard so high that we can afford to ignore the unfairness of assigning as much to the individual as to the family group. Apart altogether from economic considerations, nothing can justify the subordination of one group of producers—the mothers—to the rest, and their deprivation of all share of their own in the wealth of a community which depends on them for its very existence.

[1] *See* Chap. II, Section *e*.   [2] *See* Chap. VII, Section *g*.

CHAPTER VII

CONDITIONS OF A PRACTICABLE SCHEME

I shall not attempt here to propose an articulated scheme of direct provision, suitable for this country. Such a scheme, if on the lines of the occupational pool, should probably differ slightly for each occupation or group affected, and could only be worked out satisfactorily by those with special knowledge of the conditions concerned. If the proposal were one for universal State provision, the problem would be simpler, but its financial basis would be one for the fiscal expert. Even for those equipped with the necessary knowledge, it would I think be premature to formulate a definite scheme until the general idea of direct provision and the principles involved in it have been sufficiently ventilated for the trend of public opinion to shew itself, so that the proposal may anticipate objections and take the form most likely to secure general support. All I shall attempt here is a brief discussion of the possible alternatives, shewing the considerations which seem likely to determine the lines of a successful scheme.

Most of these considerations have been already indicated in the previous chapters and I must assume that the reader only needs to have them drawn together and presented in their relation to the practical problems and needs of our own time and country.

Judging from the experience of continental nations and the as yet unrealized schemes formulated in Australia, the most probable form of development is that which provides for families out of a pool fed by contributions from the product of industry. From the same sources of experience we may anticipate that the wage-earning classes, at least the more advanced and articulate of them, would much prefer a State scheme paid for out of taxation. It would be unfortunate if —as seems to have happened in Australia—after the leaders of opinion on both sides have been converted in principle to direct provision, a deadlock should ensue, because the employing class wants a provision by voluntary effort through industry and the wage-earners compulsory provision through taxation ; neither side caring enough to force the issue ; or both perhaps even finding in the obstacle a convenient excuse for indulging their secret distaste to a reform which their reason commends.

Both employers and workers are probably mistaken in thinking that the choice between these alternative methods of provision is a class issue. As in the long run the allowances must come out of the product of industry, the question whether they do so directly or are passed through the National Exchequer seems one of method rather than of principle. The method chosen will not necessarily effect the share of the product that comes to capital and labour respectively, though it may do so through its effect on their bargaining power—industrial and also political. No doubt it is the fear of the latter that makes the employing classes shrink from any extension of State action. But the workers might have used their predominant voting strength at any time during the last fifty years to secure extravagant wages by legal enactment for themselves. As they have not done so, why assume that they would extort allowances on an unreasonable scale for their wives and children ? One might suppose that an exaggerated solicitude for these was the last kind of excess to be expected from men of any class, judging from the patience they have shewn over the worst of all the injustices inflicted by the present system—its neglect of the rights of widows and orphans.[1]

Apart from the effect on bargaining power, the two rival methods of direct provision have both certain merits and demerits which are worth discussing. I believe myself, for reasons given later, that in the long run the State method would prove not only the truer expression of the motive idea of the scheme—the value of maternity and childhood independently of all other forms of productive services—but the more economically sound method of distributing national resources. But the occupational plan undeniably has advantages which seem to make it better suited, at least as a first step, to a people so instinctively conservative as the British ; so accustomed to take their reforms in homœopathic doses ; so indifferent, not to say hostile, to logical consistency and

[1] *See* Chap. III, Section *f.*

idealism. It involves a less startling departure from existing practices ; in trying it, we should have the experience of other countries to draw on ; above all, it could be tried tentatively, piecemeal, beginning with the occupations or groupings of people which offer the fewest difficulties, varying the forms and extending the most successful. On the other hand, a piecemeal beginning has the disadvantage that it means the growing up of interests vested in the administration of the separate schemes, which, if the country becomes converted later to the necessity for a State system, may prove an obstacle to its realization. The case for and against the two systems will however become clearer when we have discussed some of the crucial problems which would have to be faced under either system and have seen which lends itself best to their solution. So I will defer my summing up till these have been dealt with.

(a) Possible Occupational Schemes

As already indicated, the most obvious and easily worked scheme to begin with happens to be both an occupational and a State scheme, viz., one applying to the Civil Service and the service of local authorities, including especially the teachers. I have already discussed very fully[1] the conditions which make the introduction of family allowances among these really urgent ; as the only possible way, consistent both with economy and efficiency, of putting an end to a serious conflict of interest between men and women teachers which is injuring the whole profession and the cause of education. The same reason exists in a lesser measure in other departments of the public services. In beginning with these we should be following the precedents of France, Germany and Australia. No pool would here be necessary, but to meet the risk of any economy-loving minor local authorities economizing at the expense of married men, it would be desirable to arrange that the family allowances for employees whose wages come out of the rates, should be paid by the Exchequer.

Of industrial occupations, the easiest to begin with would be those which are highly organized, both on the wage-earners' and the employers' side, and highly specialized. Organization is necessary, because the formation and working of the pool system on lines that would be both economically sound and satisfactory to the wage-earner would require to be planned out between strong bodies representing employers and employed and accustomed to negotiate together on something like equal terms, and both in the planning and on the body entrusted with the execution of the schemes, the workers' wives who are to be the beneficiaries should have ample representation. The paternalism of the French *Caisse*, where everything is done by the employers for the workers without co-operation or even consultation, would be quite unsuited to this country. Specialization is also desirable ; i.e., the industries in which the experiment is begun should be those which normally recruit their employees in early youth and retain them throughout their working life. Otherwise there would be a risk that—so long as the system was confined to a few occupations—workers with dependants would tend to flock into them and the younger workers to move out of them, and if the employers endeavoured to resist the overbalancing of the normal proportion, they would be accused of discrimiating against married men and the reputation of the whole scheme would suffer. It may be noted that in France and Germany, the industries in which family allowances are most widely prevalent and successful possess these characteristics, viz., the textile industries, the metallurgic and mining. On the other hand success is not confined to these. As described in Chapter V, the majority of French *Caisses* are organized on a regional not occupational basis and include a large variety of industries. In some of these industries there must often be, within the same districts, firms adhering to the *Caisse* and others holding aloof.

In this country, the industry which suggests itself as the most suitable from every point of view to begin with is mining. This possesses in a very high degree the requisites just suggested— is highly organized on both sides in great national organizations and is closely specialized. Further the acuteness of the wage difficulty there, the years of fruitless effort that have been spent in trying to find a way out of it, and the conspicuous ability of some of the men's leaders, give reason to hope that any reasonable project for relieving the tension would not fall on entirely deaf ears. Both employers and men have been forced to recognize that the difficulty does not lie in the contumacy of the other side. Both have admitted that the output of the industry during the past few years has been insufficient to yield " a living wage " adequate to the needs of men with families. The men's appeal for a Government subsidy and the request, in which Lancashire owners and men joined, to be allowed to divert the " welfare fund " from its original purpose and use it to subsidize wages, were both based on this admission. Repeatedly, in their desperate search for some way out, the Joint District Boards have been brought very near to the principle of family allowances. For example, when the proposal for diverting the welfare fund was rejected, on the ground among others that if the sum then in the fund was divided among the whole body the amount would be negligible —less than £1 a head—the Lancashire and Cheshire miners countered this by proposing that the distribution should be limited to married men receiving less than a certain wage.

In some of the poorer coalfields, especially those in districts where the Labour Party is strongly represented on the Board of Guardians, the lower-paid men have actually during the recent hard times been receiving poor relief for their families, and the spokesmen of the men in pressing for a subsidy to the industry argued that assistance out of the taxes would cost no more than out of the rates. I do not know whether the obvious retort was made, that this would depend on whether a State subsidy was distributed as relief in proportion to the size of families. But the various experiences of the advantage of this system which the last few years have afforded—through separation allowances, poor relief and unemployment doles—have been preparing the way for the new idea. This experience is not likely to have been thrown away on an industry so conspicuous as coalmining for its large families and the contrasts it affords between the privations of the young families and the affluence of the households where father and three or four sons all draw wages from the pits.

From the employers' side, there are indications that they realize, not only the great importance of finding some way of meeting the allegation that they are not paying a living wage, but also the objections from the point of view of productivity to a system which puts an overstrain on the married men, while it gives every inducement to absenteeism among the young.

In considering what other industries seem specially ripe for direct provision on occupational lines, some light may be gained from two reports recently issued from trade-unionist sources which treat of the in some respects analogous problem of unemployment insurance by industry.[1] The more general of these shews that the opinion of the Trade Unions is greatly divided on this question ; a considerable majority of Unions, representing however a decided minority of members, favouring industrial self-government in the matter of unemployment insurance ; the remainder preferring the State system. Some of the reasons given by the former group are just those already shewn to be applicable to our problem. For example, the United Textile Factory Workers' Association, in enunciating the considerations which make the cotton industry " a peculiarly suitable field for the institution of a system of industrial maintenance", point out that " the force of workers belonging to the industry is very clearly distinct, and the number of workers who shift into and out of the industry is relatively very small indeed". Further " the presence of strong organization on both sides, and the availability of highly efficient Trade Union machinery for administration, greatly simplify the task of introducing into the cotton industry a system of industrial maintenance".   Again, " the fact that both the product and the machinery used in production are highly standardized, and that the calculation of product and productivity on a mathematical basis are familiar to the industry, makes available methods of levying a fund to provide for industrial maintenance such as would be available so readily in most other industries, especially of the manufacturing type".[2] To these factors I may add one which of course does not apply to the unemployment question, but seems very relevant to that of family maintenance, viz., that in the textile industries, almost alone of industrial occupations, there are great numbers of women competing with men on equal terms and receiving the same rates of pay for the same work. Mr. and Mrs. Webb have shewn that in effect this has resulted in a practical segregation of the sexes, the women being " engaged on the comparatively light work paid for at the lower rates" while " a majority of the men will be found practically

---

[1] *Unemployment Insurance by Industry,* published by the National Joint Council of the Trades Union Congress, the Executive Committee of the Labour Party and the Parliamentary Labour Party, 1923 (?), price 6d. *Inquiry into the Cotton Industry,* published by the United Textile Factory Workers' Association 1922 (?) (out of print.)

[2] *Inquiry into the Cotton Industry,* pp. 104-5.

monopolizing the heavy trade, priced at higher rates per yard, and resulting in larger weekly earnings".[1] Thus *on the surface* there is no sex competition. But the fact of there being a great reserve of competent female labour to draw on has resulted in the rates of pay being fixed, apparently without reference to the sex of the worker, but really at rates which represent a kind of compromise between the standard of life of an individual and a family. Hence the woman weaver, if she marries a man of her own occupation, often finds herself obliged to return to the factory in order to supplement her husband's earnings, the two together earning not much more than a male wage-earner in an equally skilled trade such as engineering where women are not employed.[2]

The result of this is seen in the comparatively low birth-rate[3] and high infantile death-rate[4] of the textile districts. A scheme of family allowances would free the mother of young children from the necessity of going into the factory or, if her industrialized habits drew her irresistibly back, would make it possible for her to make adequate provision for the care of the children. Yet it would allow the employers to take as full legitimate advantage as now of the peculiar suitability of women for this industry, without lowering the standard of life of the men and without increasing the costs of production.

All these various factors perhaps explain why the system of family allowances has taken such specially strong hold on the textile industry of France and Germany, while the competition from these countries affords an additional inducement to adopt the same experiment here, possibly as the only means of lightening a pressure of competition which may otherwise end in forcing the workers to lower their standard of life.

The Building Trades have also framed a scheme of unemployment insurance. The liability of this group of trades to seasonal interruptions makes the problem of rescuing the children from the effects of such interruptions especially urgent, but it also makes it more difficult, as does also the frequency of demarcation disputes and the fact that the workers are not as a rule continuously employed by any one

[1] *Industrial Democracy*, 1902 edition, p. 501.
[2] *See* chapter on Women's Wages in *Problems of Modern Industry*, by Sidney and Beatrice Webb, 1920 edition, p. 59.
[3] *See* p. 191.
[4] *See Report on the English Birth Rate* by E. M. Elderton, 1914.

firm. Dock and warehouse labour is another class of occupation which would profit immeasurably by provision for the family. The seasonal variations and the methods of casual employment, which cause the weekly earnings of individual dockers to look when expressed in graphic form like the temperature chart of a pneumonia patient, are economically and morally destructive of a high and sustained standard of family life.[1] No industry lends itself more readily to the shifting in and out of workers, but that has been to some extent and in some ports countered by trade-union action and, if the introduction of family maintenance helped still further to close the industry to the casual outsider, it would be an immense gain to the dockers. The Clearing House system of payment of dock labour existing in Liverpool[2] is in some respects suggestive of the type of co-operation between State and industrial machinery which might be applied to the problem of family maintenance.

Equally urgent for a different reason is the needs of the ill-paid agricultural workers. Here is another industry where there appears to be a genuine and recognized inability to pay a living wage on the old system and it is significant that more inquiries about family allowances have reached me from those interested in this occupation than any other. But there are obvious difficulties owing to the lack of strong organization, and possibly also a danger that young men might drift into the towns and return later as married workers to the land to claim the advantages of the system.

More difficult still would be the problem of the smaller and more scattered or ill-organized occupations—those where the workers are largely either non-Unionists or included in omnibus Unions, such as the National Union of General Workers and the Workers' Union. So far as machinery goes, the example of France, where regional *Caisses* including all manner of industries are more numerous and apparently nearly or quite as strong as those of a more homogeneous kind, shews that there is no insuperable difficulty. The real impediment would probably be the lack of any adequate driving force to secure the adhesion to the scheme of the great

[1] *See* " The Conditions of Labour at the Liverpool Docks " in *Transactions of Liverpool Economic Society*, 1903-4, and *How the Casual Labourer lives* (Northern Publishing Company, Liverpool 1909,) both by the present writer.

[2] *See First Year's Working of the Liverpool Dock Scheme*, by R. Williams (Liverpool Economic Society, 1913).

mass of workers and employers, such as exists in a highly developed and strongly organized trade possessing on both sides able leaders, on the look-out for whatever may improve the prosperity of the industry or the welfare of its workers, and able to overcome the conservatism and timidity of the less enlightened.

Most serious of all would be the problem presented by the workers who have no fixed employers, but are paid by the job, such as navvies, costers, window cleaners at one end of the scale, and at the other doctors, lawyers, journalists, architects. These upper-class professions indeed have strong organizations which could, if they would, administer schemes and collect payments on some system of percentage of earnings. How far the need of such provision exists or is unlikely to make itself felt in these upper grades will be discussed shortly. It is one of a group of questions regarding the form of direct provision which would arise whether the provision were made on occupational lines or through a State system. We will now face these questions :—

(b) Should Family Allowances be Universal or Limited by Occupation or Income

It is obvious that while the gravest evils and injustices resulting from the disinheritance of the family affect chiefly the poorer classes, the general case for family maintenance applies to the whole community. Every occupation or class must recruit itself from the rising generation and must either provide in its cost of production for its share of rearing the future workers or shift that share on to other groups.[1] Within each group it is true that the present system of distribution works out wastefully and unfairly as between those with children and those without and has evil effects on the economic position of the woman worker, on the status of wives and mothers, and on the quality and quantity of the birth-rate. But the emphasis to be laid on these various factors varies with the class. On the one hand, in the more skilled occupations and in direct proportion as they are more skilled, it takes longer for a man to reach his highest occupational value. The remuneration of the professional or commercial man, if he achieves an average amount of success, normally rises until he is well on in the thirties or even beyond them. So normally do his family responsibilities.   Hence there is a rough and approximate grading of income according to needs which does not take place lower down, and in that respect there is less need in these upper-class occupations for direct family maintenance.   On the other hand, from the eugenic point of view, the case for it is strongest in these classes.   It is among them that the birth-rate is lowest and this is undoubtedly explained partly by the greater prevalence of birth-control and partly by their higher age at marriage—both facts directly due to some extent, though not wholly, to the economic penalties which the present system imposes on parenthood.

Professor William McDougall in his book on *National Welfare and National Decay* brings together a mass of evidence indicating that these higher occupations do in fact represent selected hereditary ability as well as better environment and opportunities, and is so strongly persuaded of the urgent necessity, as a measure of national safety, of encouraging the propagation of these better stocks, that he proposes a scheme of family maintenance limited to them alone.   He suggests that :

" every family which has risen above the mean social level (or better still perhaps every family which has any good claim to belong to what may be called ' the selected classes ') should know that the addition of each child should automatically bring with it an increase of income sufficient to meet the expenses normally incurred in the bringing-up of that child. . . This increase of income should I suggest be not less than one-tenth of the earned income and might well be rather more. A family earning an income of £500 a year would then receive for each living child under the age of, say, twenty years, an additional income of £50 a year".[1]

Professor McDougall does not discuss how a legislature elected on a democratic franchise is going to be persuaded to carry into effect this thorough-going application of the principle " to him that hath shall be given".   But I think he has misgivings, for he falls back on the suggestion that the State and Municipalities should begin with their own services and that large employers of skilled labour should be led to follow suit. Apparently he was not aware of the continental developments on these lines.   He further suggests that millionaires should devote their wealth to the same purpose and instead of founding new Universities or Libraries should offer inducements to the professors of those already existing to be fruitful and multiply and replenish the earth.[2]

As a matter of practical politics, in this country at any rate, we are much more likely to see an attempt to restrict direct

[1] *National Welfare and National Decay*, by Prof. Wm. McDougall (Methuen, 1921), p. 197.

[2] *Ibid.*, p. 200.

provision to the lowlier occupations or income levels than the other way round. There are several objections to this besides the eugenic one. Such a restriction would inevitably tend to hamper the free movement of workers from one occupation or grade to another and the promotion of the abler workers. For example ; until nearly the end of the war, no separation allowances were paid to the wives of commissioned officers. This prevented many able non-commissioned officers with large families from accepting commissions, because it would have meant for them a reduction of income.

Under a State scheme, a restriction, if introduced at all, would probably be based not on occupation or salaries but on income. This, as everyone knows who has watched the working of old age pensions or any other form of public assistance with an income limit, is subject to grave evils. It paralyses industry, enterprise and thrift among those near the income limit. It discourages the help of relatives and voluntary agencies. It greatly increases the complexity and expense of administration. Lastly, unless the enquiries made to verify statements of income are so thorough as to be unpleasantly inquisitorial, the restriction is easily evaded and the temptation to evasion put in the way of people of narrow means turns the process into a veritable school of lying and destructor of self-respect.[1]

The usual argument for an income limit in schemes of State assistance is economy. To apply this argument to our proposal is to make the assumption that direct maintenance of families involves the imposition of a wholly new burden on the community, instead of the redistribution of an existing charge. Ignoring for the moment the fallacy of this assumption, which has been dealt with elsewhere, I may point out that even if direct provision were a new burden, wholly or partially, the saving that would be effected in it by limiting the scheme to parents with incomes below £300 a year would be at the very outside 9 per cent[2] of the cost of a universal scheme

[1] I speak here from extensive personal experience. During the war, I had to make or supervise many thousands of such enquiries and I came to the conclusion that their demoralizing influence was very great and very wide-spread.

[2] Taking the average number of persons per family as 4·2 (see Dr. Bowley in *Economica*, May 1921, p. 103), the number of individual households in the United Kingdom is about 11,230,000. According to the latest report of the Commissioner of Inland Revenue (1920-21) the number of incomes over £300 in 1919-20 was 1,026,280. Even if we assume that all these individuals were heads of families, the proportion of parents with incomes over £300 is only 9 per cent, which may therefore be taken as an extreme figure.

and this saving would be at the expense of excluding just the classes who contribute most largely to taxation. If the scheme of allowances were graded according to incomes, the cost of including the higher incomes would of course be greater, but the excess would probably be paid for by the class which benefited by it.[1]

Lastly ; whether the system in view were an occupational or a State system, its extension to all classes would have a considerable psychological value, in reassuring the numerous people in every class who scent in every new proposal a device for exploiting their own order in the interest of others. It would help to convince the wage-earners that the scheme was not a capitalist dodge for lowering wages or securing a cheap supply of " cannon fodder". It would conciliate the struggling middle class, who feel that " everything is done for the working classes " and that, while invariably expected to pay the piper, they are seldom invited to join in the dance. Most important of all, it would immeasurably enhance the status and dignity of the whole conception ; would relieve it from the suspicion of being a sort of glorified Speenhamland system of doles and would place it in the true light of an act of restitution—of recognition of the right of the family to share in the national dividend.

(c) Should Allowances be on a Flat-Rate or Graded ?

(i) ACCORDING TO THE NUMBER OF CHILDREN

We have seen that in France, the children's allowances paid by the *Caisses* are graded upwards ; a trifling sum, or sometimes nothing at all, being paid for the first child and the amount rising for subsequent children ; the object being to encourage large families. The British system of separation allowances for the fighting forces graded in the opposite direction, allowing more for the first than for the second and for the second than for the third or subsequent children. The difference here merely reflects the fact that the expense per head is higher, for housewifely reasons, for a small than for a large family. Whether the plan to be ultimately followed should be on the analogy of the British or French system will depend on whether the community wishes to remain neutral in its attitude towards the population question or to exercise

[1] *See* p. 235.

a restrictive or encouraging influence on it. I merely allude to the subject here to point out that this is one of the ways in which " the devastating torrent of children " might if thought necessary be gently checked or guided ; further, that this might be more effectively done under an occupational than under a State scheme. It is difficult to imagine a Government saying baldly : " We want to encourage University professors to have more children and casual labourers fewer. Therefore we will grade allowances upwards for the families of the former and downwards for those of the latter". But if the provision for each group were separately worked out by those with a knowledge of the problems of their own group, some such adjustment would probably come about quite naturally.

(ii) ACCORDING TO THE INCOME OR OCCUPATION OF THE PARENTS

Here again the answer is very much easier if the scheme in view is an occupational and not a State scheme, though it does not necessarily depend on that. If the system comes about gradually, each occupation or group of occupations making its own arrangements, with or without State assistance, it will probably arise naturally and almost inevitably that the allowances paid will bear some relation to the scale of remuneration and standard of living customary in the occupation or group. If it were not so, the advantages claimed for the scheme in previous chapters would not be obtained or obtained only partially. For example, if the sum fixed were substantially below the actual cost of maintaining a child according to the standard judged reasonable by the group concerned, the family man would feel that he had forgone his claim to " a living wage " on the family basis without obtaining an adequate return ; either the children would be pinched, or he would be unable to obtain the same standard of comfort as his unmarried comrades ; his grievance against his woman competitor and his appeal for preferential treatment would still go on. On the other hand, if the sum fixed were substantially greater than the actual cost, it would be the turn of the childless man and the employers to cry out, since the excess would have to come out of wages or profits or both. Further, the case of those who fear that allowances will act as an incentive to laziness or to over-population would be much strengthened.

The pressure of these counteracting forces would probably result in the allowances being adjusted to allow of a standard of living roughly proportionate to that which the unmarried men of the group would be able to achieve out of their wages. At first, there might be a tendency to fix the scale too low, in order to conciliate the childless men by leaving them as much as possible of their accustomed surplus. But this would probably correct itself as the habit took root of recognizing the separate personalities and needs of wives and children.

The grading would not necessarily go so far as to establish different scales of allowances for the workers belonging to different subdivisions and wage-levels within the same occupational scheme. Whether it did so or not would probably depend partly on whether the subdivision represented merely different stages of promotion of the same set of workers, with roughly the same traditions and standard of living, or whether they were separately recruited from men of different traditions and standards. From the point of view of social justice and democratic sentiment, however, there would be much to be said for recognizing the right of all the children of wage-earners within the same occupational group to the same scale of living, leaving the superior value to the industry of the workers in its higher grades to be remunerated through wages and not through children's allowances. It is probable, I think, that in most occupations this could be done without sacrificing the economic and social advantages of the scheme, since in most cases men belonging to the same occupations (excluding the managerial departments) belong themselves and marry wives who belong roughly speaking to the same social strata, and have approximately the same standards and aspirations for their children, irrespective of the particular rung of the occupational ladder they have reached.

There are some advocates of family allowances who resent the suggestion of any grading at all, either within the same occupation or as between different occupations, on the ground that the service of motherhood and the potential value of all children to the nation is the same, or at least is individual and not dependent on the occupations or incomes of their parents. However true this may be, the fact remains that differences of status exist, and as long as they exist, it is practically impossible, since the lives of children cannot be separated from those of their parents, to secure to all children a uniform standard of living. This fact is recognized by the leaders of trade-unionist opinion in the report already quoted, on the analogous problem of unemployment insurance by industry. They say :

" Industrial schemes would, however, have the advantage over any general scheme that benefits would doubtless be calculated as a percentage of wages ; and the difference in rates of benefit would reflect differences in rates of wages and and in the standards of life which accompany these. Existing differences in the rates of wages in different occupations are indeed illogical and frequently unjustifiable, but so long as they persist there is a case for introducing corresponding differences between the rates of benefit payable in times of unemployment".[1]

The objections which apply to a scale of allowances which took no account of the status of parents under the occupational system, would apply equally to a uniform rate under a State system. If the scale chosen represented a standard of frugal comfort according to current working-class standards, it would not secure the full economic and social benefits of the scheme for any above that level. This might be unimportant as far as concerned the really wealthy, whose standards are largely artificial, but it would be unfortunate as affecting the upper-class artisan and moderately paid professional and commercial classes, for the eugenic and other reasons already mentioned. Yet to fix the scale for everyone at their level might entail a cost greater than the present production of the country could bear, besides raising the usual forebodings as to slackened effort and over-population.

But under a State scheme the difficulty of securing graded benefits would be considerable, though not I think insuperable. The cry would certainly be raised that the State must not stereotype class distinctions or pay higher allowances out of taxation to the children of well-to-do than to those of the manual workers. Plainly it could not be done unless it were not only true in fact but were made unmistakably obvious that the higher rates were paid for by the income groups or occupations which benefited by them.

[1] *Unemployment Insurance by Industry*, p. 11. It should be unnecessary to remind readers who have followed the argument of preceding chapters that to recognize differences of status and standards in this way does not mean that there would be a stereotyping of the present low standard of family maintenance. Assuming that the proportion of the product of industry which went to the workers and their amilies was the same as before, the juster distribution of that proportion according to need would allow of a higher standard all round for the adults of the family as well as their children (*see* p. 211.)   A further rise in standard may be predicted from the greater efficiency and productivity that would result from the system, as soon as its effect had time to tell on the new generation of workers ; and from the saving to the community of the cost of much of its present machinery for salvaging derelicts—workhouses, prisons and all the rest of the machinery of public assistance and penal repression.

A very ingenious scheme for securing this in fact through adjustment of income tax was devised by Mr. Emil Burns and is contained in a booklet issued by a small Committee which in 1916-17 drew up a proposal for the national endowment of motherhood.[1]   It was not endorsed by the majority of the committee, nor I think definitely by its author, but was put forward for consideration.   Mr. Burns pointed out that if the allowances were paid for out of income tax, the amount paid in respect of this tax would of course be higher as the income increased, so that the benefits from the allowance would diminish as the income rose, not only relatively to the standard of life but absolutely in money values.   In order to counteract this for families of moderate income, he proposed to adjust the scale of endowment paid to families in certain income groups in accordance with the special taxation paid by the families in those groups, in such a way that the average net gain (i.e., endowment received less tax paid) should be the same for all income groups below £700 a year.   In this way the individual families receiving endowment within the group (since the endowment but not the taxation would be proportioned to numbers) would draw a benefit which bore a real relation to their standard of life, and thus one of the objects of the scheme would be achieved, viz., that, within each group of incomes, the man with a family should not be in a worse position financially than the childless man, or woman receiving equal pay, within that group.

In principle this plan appears economically sound and just. But it would be difficult to make this clear to the uneducated or sentimental type of voter.   The eleemosynary system of many State benefits, making poverty a condition of receipt, which has been called into being by the exaggerated inequalities of economic distribution, has had a warping effect on public opinion ; accustoming men to think of the State as an almsgiver, or as a doctor only called in to cure pathological conditions, rather than as the regulator of the conditions of normal healthy life.   Hence the suggestion that the State should not merely pay family allowances to the middle classes, but pay them at a higher rate than to the labourer, even when it is explained that this would be done at the expense of the class benefited, is apt to strike the slaves of

[1] *See Equal Pay and the Family,* published by the National Union of Societies for Equal Citzenship (Headley Bros., 1s.), pp. 59 *seq.*

established tradition as an injustice and an anomaly. To meet this unreasonable prejudice, it may be necessary to make the State system a flat-rate one and secure the necessary gradation by supplementary allowances from an occupational pool for all the higher-grade occupations.

(d) Should Direct Provision be made for the Mother, or only for the Children ?

We have seen that in Germany an allowance is frequently made for the wife when she has dependent children, but this is not the case in France or in the Australian schemes. In this country such proposals as have been tentatively made by reformers have generally started with the desire to acknow-ledge the services and establish the economic independence of the wife and mother, and the name by which they are known in popular phraseology is " the endowment of motherhood". It is clear that the hardships in the lot of the married mother and her aspirations after a securer and more honourable status, which have been described in Chapter III, would not be fully met by a form of provision which merely secured to the children the bare minimum necessary for their maintenance and left the mother completely dependent, as she is now, on the will as well as the ability of her husband to support her. A tyrannous or selfish husband could still leave her destitute and force her either into the labour market or, if she found no entry there, into living on the allowances meant for the children. Their tiny incomes might even be an additional temptation to him to do this. Expediency as well as justice require therefore that her position should be made secure, either by including her in the scheme of direct provision, or by strengthening her present claim on her husband's income. There is a good deal to be said for both methods and it is possible that a carefully worked out combination of the two might prove best.

Direct provision for the mother has the moral advantage that it recognizes the value to the community of the function of motherhood, properly discharged. It is unreasonable to deny it this value, merely because there may be too many children for the country's good, or children of the wrong sort. There may be excess or misdirection in every sort of production. I have already given reasons for thinking that both risks are greater under the present system than under direct provision.[1] Logically, provision for the children's needs should include provision for their mother, since her services are indispensable to them, and both should be independent of a possible failure of the husband's income through his misfortune or fault. But this would intensify the objections of those who fear the effect of the scheme on the incentive to industry. If it would be difficult for a wife to refuse to a husband on strike or out of work a share of the children's dinner, it would be still more unlikely she would refuse him her own share.

It has also to be remembered that the functions performed by the working mother do not all arise out of her maternity. She is also her husband's housekeeper ; a service equally needed by the unmarried or childless man, and for which he should be able to pay out of his wages. If she has in addition several quite young children, her work for them may be well worth to the community the value of her keep. But if there are only one or two of school age, it cannot be said that they need all her time and a community bent on economizing might reasonably demur to paying for it ; especially if it remembers that the longer she is kept out of the labour market, the more difficulty she will find in returning to it, if her husband dies or cannot afford the services of a whole-time housekeeper.[2] For these reasons I suggest the the soundest form of direct provision for mothers would not be a flat-rate allowance, such as is paid to a soldier's wife, but a sum on account of each child. It would not greatly matter whether this was merged in the child's own allowance or credited separately to her, as in either case she would have the spending of it. The latter plan would usefully emphasize the fact that the payment was " her bit " but on the other hand it would invite the gibe that she was being " paid for her children " and so set the sentimentalist geese cackling. Except for fear of the same result, it would probably be best to make the sum paid, say, twice as large for a young child as for one of school age. In this way a mother with five or six dependent children might, out of their united allowances and what her husband gave her, be able to pay for the modest amount of domestic help that is

---

[1] *See* Chap. VI, Section *a*.

[2] I do not wish any careless reader to interpret me as suggesting that the work of looking after a house, husband and two school-children, without domestic help, is not amply enough to occupy one woman. My point is that the greater part of her work would be equally needed by a childless man, and therefore does not necessarily form part of the provision for maternal services.

often necessary if she is to do justice to her family without overstraining herself ; while no unnecessary provision would be made for those who could, if required, earn something without neglecting their homes.

The best alternative to direct provision for mothers seems to be, as already suggested, to make minimum wages for men sufficient for the maintenance of two people. If that was secured, it would be difficult to make out a case for an additional payment to mothers, although in fact the unmarried man, at least in the wage-earning classes, has rarely the whole-time services of a woman devoted to him and the newly married wife can and often does pursue her trade till the approach of a child stops her. But the remnant of his surplus which the proposal would leave to the childless man need not be grudged to that hitherto spoiled child of the economic system. It may temper the wind to the shorn lamb. The position of the wife, with or without children, should however be safeguarded, and the various alternative methods of doing this have been discussed in Chapter III, Section e.

(e) Administrative Methods

Some of the points to be borne in mind in framing a concrete scheme have already been dealt with. We have seen, from the experience of foreign countries and from the need for meeting the objections raised in our own, the importance of keeping the system of family allowances—in nomenclature, in the methods of levying and of payment—as distinct as possible from the system of wages, and above all of paying the allowances to the mother.[1]

But in what way and on what conditions should payment be made ? The principle here to be borne in mind is that the men and women of this country are rightly tenacious of the privacy of their homes. Our systems of elementary education, child welfare and public health already involve frequent incursions into the home of an extensive and costly machinery. It is important, and it could easily be arranged, that the new system should not add to that machinery, but where necessary should utilize it. Thus the payment of allowances might be made, in a State scheme, through the post office, as separation allowances are : in an occupational scheme through a body representative of employers, employed

---

[1] *See* Chap. V, pp. 143 *seq.*, 162-3, 168, and Chap. VI, p. 213.

and the mothers. But if the community or the industry undertake direct provision for children, they will probably and reasonably require some evidence that they are getting value for their money. It is true that no such evidence is required from the fathers, through whom indirect provision is made at present. But one of the objects of the new scheme is to improve and not to stereotype existing standards. This need could be met by requiring the mother to produce at stated intervals—possibly quarterly or half-yearly, or oftener in the case of young infants—a certificate from one of a number of constituted authorities, (the school, the infant-welfare centre, the sanitary authority, etc.) that the condition of the child was satisfactory. This would involve merely such a strengthening of existing child-welfare machinery as is recognized to be already desirable. In addition, there would have to be some organization for investigating, on behalf of the authority administering the scheme, cases where the mother failed to get the certificate and complaints of neglect, misapplication of the money, or fraud. When such offences were proved and persisted in, there should be arrangements for transferring the payment to some other guardian or, through the ordinary machinery of the law, removing the children.

None of this need require any interference with the privacy of the home or the responsibility of the parents, except such as is already involved in our whole system of education and public health administration, and it need entail very little additional expense.

It is sometimes suggested that it should be a condition of the payment of family allowances that the mother should not seek wage-earning employment, but stay at home and look after the children. Such a condition would be strongly resented by independent-minded women and would defeat its own end. Some women, including some of those most capable of producing desirable children, are not fitted by temperament for an exclusively domestic life. If they prefer to use part of the allowances to engage domestic help for the care of the children and seek paid work better suited to them, they should be as free to do so as well-to-do women are now, so long as they can shew that their children are properly provided for.

Later on, it may be found desirable to introduce provisions for checking the marriage of the mentally deficient or diseased, by requiring a certificate of health on marriage from those who intend to claim the advantages of the scheme. But it would be a mistake to hamper the scheme at the outset with restrictive provisions of a contentious character.

Another proposal, which has found some favour with the Labour Party, is that—at least as a first step towards child endowment—there should be a considerable extension of communal services and assistance in kind. This is put forward in a report[1] issued recently by a Committee of men and women appointed by the Executive Committee of the Labour Party.

The report shews the indecision and confusion of thought existing on the subject even in a party nominally committed to the principle of " distribution according to need". Its definite proposals, when disinterred from a considerable mass of descriptive matter and restatement of familiar Labour Party principles, amount only to the suggestion that the party shall work for the following services:

1. Universal free education from the nursery school to the University ; with " maintenance grants according to the existing policy of the Labour Party " (elsewhere explained to mean " when needed").

2. Universal free medical, nursing and health services.

3. Adequate maintenance of mothers for 6 weeks before and 6 weeks after childbirth.

4. Pure milk for expectant and nursing mothers and for infants up to five years of age at cost price, " or, when desirable, free".

5. At least one meal a day during school terms for " all children". (Presumably this means all school-going children.)

6. School clothes and boots "for all the children " (presumably, again, those attending school).

But the report does not say whether these meals and clothes and boots are to be provided free or at cost price and Dr. Marion Phillips, who acted as secretary to the Committee, admitted when questioned that this " had not been decided. It was a matter for discussion". But the point is vital. If the meals, etc., were not to be given free, this set of proposals is not even a first step towards family maintenance. It does nothing at all for the maintenance of the normal healthy child, except help the mother to bring it into the world. If they were to be given free, I venture to say bluntly that the scheme is so imperfectly thought out as to be quite indefensible. It is a step towards child endowment, but the sort of step which does not take one from the bank of the less desirable territory into the more desirable, but plunges one into mid-stream. Why give free food and clothes to the school-child and deny them (except on a poverty qualification) to infants, whose

---

[1] *Motherhood and Child Endowment*, published by the Labour Party, 1923, 6d.

mothers are more in need of supplementary resources and less able to earn them ? Why give the mid-day dinner in school terms and leave the parents to provide it on Sundays and holidays ? What is this but to make holidays into days of penance ?

It is plain that this partial scheme is only intended as a beginning ; that the idea is gradually to extend the existing beginnings of communal services into a complete system covering the whole of a child's existence from the cradle to adolescence—food, clothing, recreation, holidays. The promoters lay much stress on the greater economy of such a system as compared with individual provision through individual homes. But in the first place, is it so certain that such a scheme would prove cheaper ? Those who rely on the general principle of the economy of large-scale production forget that in this case it means a duplication not a substitution. The home and the mother are there anyhow, not to be eliminated except by communalizing the whole existence of adults as well as children. To provide for feeding the whole school population would mean reconstructing, or making costly additions to, the existing school buildings, and paying trained staffs to prepare the meals and supervise the children throughout the day.

Again, would this barrack existence be good for all children of all ages ? Its promoters assume that children are like Ford cars, best and most cheaply produced by standardizing all the elements of their well-being, instead of infinitely various and individualized human beings. Communal life might suit the healthy child of average ability. But would it suit the backward and repressed child, the delicate and nervous, the able and imaginative ? Would it encourage development of the qualities of initiative, resource, personality that have given this nation its present position in the world ? Let any man or woman of brains cast his mind back to his own childhood and ask which hours he reckons to have been most profitable, those spent in class-rooms and " organized play", or those given to reading books in corners or roaming about streets or fields wrapped in his own thoughts, observations, make-believes ? Direct provision through money allowances would not exclude an extension of the school services to cover meals and uniforms at cost price. But it should be free to the parents to make use of such facilities or not as their knowledge of their children's needs dictated. It would also make possible that

most necessary of all improvements in working-class conditions
—a direct relation, instead of as now an inverted relation,
between the size of a family and the size of house they can
afford to pay for.[1]

Reading between the lines of this Report, it is clear that
the reluctance of the able men and women responsible for
it to commit themselves to the principle of family allowances
is due to motives which, for obvious reasons, they are not
willing to expound quite plainly. First, they have a certain
distrust of the working-class mother and itch to supersede
her by " experts".   Secondly (and far more strongly) they
share the fears and prejudices discussed in Chapter VI, Sections
c, d, e. The Report and the discussion on it are peppered with
hints that any scheme of providing for children " must be
examined very carefully in its relation to the present financial
system and in its effect on Trade Union methods of negotiation
and wage regulation". "What would be the effect on the whole
system of Trade Union bargaining and negotiation of such
a separation of wages from family responsibility ?"   It is
urged that allowances in kind—free medical treatment, free
education, etc.—have not so far reduced wages, but that money
allowances might do so.

In plain words, the writers are clinging to the hope of win-
ning " from behind the skirts of the women and children "
the family wage for bachelors and everyone else, and at the
same time transferring little by little the cost of maintaining
a family on to the community. And they think the employing
class are less likely to notice this manœuvre if the transfer
is made gradually and in kind rather than in cash. But surely
this is to reason from a false analogy and to underrate the
intelligence of the employing class. There is no real analogy
between services such as education and medical inspection
of schools and the provision of food and clothing. Before
education and medical inspection were supplied free, the working
class did not supply them out of wages ; broadly speaking,
they went without. And whatever other faults the employing
class may have, they are not stupid when their own pockets
are concerned. But they have (some of them) consciences as

---

[1] *See* p. 193.   The report suggests "a policy which will accept the right
of every family to a house sufficiently large for all its members, with a regulation
of rents which will give the big families a chance ". Does this remark mean that
the house owner—municipality, guild, or private owner—is to ask the same rent
for a big house as for a little one ? Or what does it mean ?

well as pockets, and I suggest that nothing acts more effectively as soothing syrup on those consciences than partial, half-hearted measures for dealing with the welfare of children. Further, such measures act as soothing syrup on the wage-earners themselves, individually and in the mass. By relieving on a poverty qualification (for that is what the euphemistic "when needed " of the report evidently means) they take the sting out of poverty for the easy-going individuals whose misfortunes are half their own fault; while the pick of the working-class mothers, proud, sensitive, and self-reliant, are left to struggle on with their impossible task of making bricks without clay, and the injustice and cruelty of the disinheritance of the family are veiled from men's eyes.

(*f*) **Should the Children of Unmarried Parents be included ?**

This, as the French have found, is a *question délicate*, about which there are certain to be diverse opinions. It is so much of a side issue that I should not think it necessary to discuss it at all here, if it were not so often raised by critics who regard the scheme from the point of view of eugenics. These fear that if family allowances were freely granted to the mothers of illegitimate children, they would tend to raise the illegitimate birth-rate. I confess at once that I share this view. While it is true that society's treatment of the unmarried mother and her child has hitherto been harsh and unjust, there are surely more suitable and effective ways of remedying the injustice than through a scheme expressly devised to improve the quality of the nation's " child supply " by giving to the family a fuller recognition and a more assured and honourable status. It seems inconsistent with such a purpose to allow any parent or couple of parents to claim the benefits of the scheme, merely because they have chosen to bring a child into the world, regardless of whether they have fulfilled the conditions generally recognized as essential to secure its well-being. Most people would agree that these conditions include a stable home and two parents—a father as well as a mother.

Here it is necessary to draw a distinction between the children of permanent though unlegalized unions, and those who spring from a casual connection, the result of a passing sexual impulse. The war shewed that the former kind of unions were much more numerous than had been before suspected, many being between couples debarred from marriage by a previous unhappy marriage. It was thought necessary for social reasons then to reckon these *de facto* marriages by the granting of separation allowances, and probably it will be thought necessary for similar reasons to include them in a scheme of family allowances. Even here, however, there are drawbacks which the experience of the war revealed. Strict investigation is necessary to prevent fraudulent claims and in many cases close supervision to ensure the welfare of the children, who under the present law may be and often are repudiated and deserted by the father as soon as he has got tired of their mother. But, as these elaborate precautions are unnecessary in the case of ordinary family allowances and should be alien to the spirit of the body administering them, it might be better to leave provision for the children of irregular unions as well as for the "chance child" to the Poor Law, or whatever body, after its promised " break up", has inherited those of its functions which are concerned with the care of children. Or, to prevent hardship in exceptional cases, such children might be admitted to the benefits of the scheme only when both parents were willing to stabilize their union as far as possible by a formal and enforceable recognition of their responsibility for their children and for each other.

(g) The Financial Aspects of Direct Provision

We saw in Chapter V that in the existing voluntary schemes of family allowances, the necessary fund is usually raised by a levy on employers, based either on their wages bill or, more rarely, on the number of workers employed or hours worked. Another possible method applicable to some occupational schemes would be a levy on output, such as the penny per ton of coal handled which forms the miners' welfare fund. This is a technical matter which could only be settled by experts in the industries concerned. Similarly, in considering a national scheme, the question of how the necessary taxation could best be raised is one we may leave to the fiscal expert.

But as bearing on the merits of the rival systems—occupational or national—it may be pointed out that, as French experience shews, a practical difficulty in the way of the former lies in the conflicting interests of industries employing chiefly male labour and those making a large use of women and young persons. Under the present system, the latter group of industries (not on the whole nationally the more valuable) are able to shift on to the former nearly the whole cost of rearing future generations.[1] In order to secure their adhesion to the scheme of family allowances, it has been found necessary in France to invent devices for enabling them to retain this questionably just privilege.[2] Under a national scheme of provision, it would disappear automatically.

But there is a much larger sense in which the " financial aspect " of direct provision must be considered, before the statement of our case is complete. Apart altogether from the question of how the money would be found and from whose pockets, directly or indirectly, it would come, what would family allowances cost ? What portion of the national dividend, the divisible heap, would they swallow up ?

The answer so obviously depends on two indeterminable factors—the scale of the allowances and the size of the heap, that I might make this the excuse for evading a troublesome question. But to do so would be to lose an opportunity of illustrating the superior economy of the direct method of providing for children, not over the cost actually expended on their maintenance—no one knows or will ever know what that is ; we only know from its fruits that it is too little— but over the estimated cost of adequate provision under the present uniform wage system. In making the comparison I shall be obliged to move in the region of large and speculative figures and thus run the risk that opponents of the scheme will seize on them and treat them as though the whole scheme depended on them.

In Chapter II we saw that, in the opinion of the statisticians best qualified to form an opinion, the conception of a minimum " living wage " based for men on the needs of the five-member family and for women on their individual needs, has neither been realized nor is realizable out of the nation's present resources. How would the problem be affected by the introduction of family allowances ?

In order to give an answer which allows of comparison with the earlier discussions, we must of course take the same standard of " human needs", viz. that adopted by Mr. Rowntree in his famous book, and use as he has done pre-war figures, which I will afterwards translate as far as possible into present-day values. Let us take then his estimate of

35s. 3d. as covering the maintenance of the standard family at a modest level of comfort. He allows :—

		Man		Wife		Each child (of three)			Total	
		s.	d.	s.	d.	s.	d.		s.	d.
For food	.	4	4	3	6	2	5	.	. 15	1
„ clothing	.	1	9	1	0	0	9	.	. 5	0
„ rent	.	.		.		.		.	. 6	0
„ fuel	.	.		.		.		.	. 2	6
„ household sundries		.		.		.		.	. 1	8
„ personal sundries	.	.		.		.		.	. 5	0
									35	3

Equivalent at the present cost of living (Nov. 1923 [1]) to 61s. 8¼d.

In deciding how much of this should be provided through family allowances, let us for the moment consider only the children, assuming that the wife is provided for by strengthening her claim on the man's wages, which should at least be enough for the support of two persons. [2]   Let us further estimate the child's share as low as possible, both because this is in accordance with existing facts, [3] and because for obvious reasons it is wise for the propagandist of family allowances to leave the man as large a share as possible of the divisible heap. [4] I assume therefore that the cost of a child is merely the cost of its food and clothing plus, say fourpence a week for sundries. That gives 3s. 6d. per child, or 10s. 6d. for the three children, leaving 24s. 9d. as the minimum wage for a man (at present values 6s. 1½d. per child and a minimum wage of 43s. 3¾d.)

How does this revised estimate affect the possibility of securing for every wage-earner's household at least a " human needs " standard ? Further, what would be the effect of the new system on the distribution of the wage-bill or of national resources ?

We must revert to Mr. Sidney Webb's table of pre-war wages, [5] not only to facilitate comparison with previous figures, but because there are not, so far as I know, any present-day figures available of a similar character. Taking then his estimate

[1] The cost of living index number for November 1923 was 75 per cent. higher than that for July 1914, the date of Mr. Rowntree's calculations.

[2] See pp. 15, 129.   [3] See p. 44.

[4] But I would remind the reader that if the man's share were estimated on his individual needs ; if " real wives " were provided for through allowances and " phantom wives " eliminated ; and if the children's share were taken to include a portion of the rent and a more generous allowance for " sundries", the economy of the system over that of the uniform family wage would be considerably greater than that shewn in the figures which follow.

[5] See p. 20.

of 8,000,000 " men in situations " and allowing them an average of 1·19 children each[1], we have 9,520,000 children under fourteen to be provided for. At 3s. 6d. a head, this would cost £86,630,000 per annum, or 4s. 7d. per wage-earner per working week.[2]   Assuming that the group of wage-earners already receiving over 24s. 9d. (say 25s. to fit the classification in Mr. Webb's table) paid for their children's allowances as far as possible out of wages, the amount that would have to be contributed by the State or by employers to bring those receiving less than " human needs " level (as above defined) up to that level would be:—

Addition to wages of 2,560,000 men receiving below 25s. . .	£27 million
Allowances for children of ditto	£27½ ,,
Addition to allowances for children of 1,680,000 men receiving between 25s. and 30s. at 1s. 10d. per man.[3] . . .	£7¼ ,,
Total . . .	£61¾ million

instead of the £130,000,000 estimated by Dr Bowley as necessary to secure the same standard on the basis of the uniform family wage.

In translating these figures into present-day values we shall assume that wages have risen, broadly speaking, in proportion to the cost of living, and that the proportion of men below "human needs" level is the same as before.   This is probably near enough the truth to make the figures of use as a very rough guide to the cost of achieving a national minimum. On this assumption then, and allowing for an increase in the numbers concerned proportionate to the increase in the general population,[4] the cost would be, under the uniform wage system, £237½ million per annum, under the system of family allowances, £112¾ million.[5]

[1] See p. 15.

[2] The year being taken at forty-seven working weeks, to allow for unemployment, sickness, etc. The children's allowances would, it is assumed, be paid for the whole fifty-two weeks.

[3] In this group, in which the average wage is 27s. 6d., i.e., 2s. 9d. above the minimum, the men could not contribute more than this sum per head per (working) week towards the children's allowances ; the balance of 1s. 10d. would therefore have to be met by the State.

[4] From 45 million in 1911 to 47 million in 1921.

[5] Applying the same calculations to women:—to raise the wages of the 3,000,000 women wage-earners to the " human needs " level (20s. a week) would cost at least £56 million per annum (see above, p. 25 n.), or at the present day £102¼ million. But if the claim of " equal pay " were conceded, the cost of raising women's wages to the same minimum as the men's would be at least £89½ million if the minimum was based on the needs of two persons (24s. 9d.), or £163½ million if it was based on the needs of the uniform family (35s. 3d.)—or, at present day values and allowing for increase of population, £163¼ and £299 million respectively.

These figures have been given to vindicate the superior economy and effectiveness in producing family well-being of direct provision as against the theory that has held the field so long. But it should not be necessary to remind the reader that, first, direct provision is not necessarily bound up with the theory of a national minimum excepting so far as children are concerned ; secondly, the problem of securing the latter would not in fact be solved merely by raising the lower paid workers to an agreed or legalized minimum. Unless this process were accompanied by or led to a proportionate raising of the wages of all workers, it would in effect result in depriving those now at or close above the minimum of the " rent " of their presumably superior efficiency. This is open to objections which would be felt both by the workers themselves and by those who already regard with apprehension the tendency towards the approximation of the wages of unskilled and skilled labour.

Leaving the question of a national minimum out of account, we have seen that allowances for children of wage-earners would cost at 3s. 6d. per child (6s. 1½d. at present values) a sum equivalent to 4s. 7d. per wage-earner per working week (8s. 0¼d. at present values).

This could be raised either wholly out of the existent wage-bill, or partly out of employers' profits, or partly or wholly at the expense of the general taxpayer—as the resources of the nation and the bargaining strength of the various parties to the negotiation might determine. If it came out of the wage-bill and were met by a cut on wages of 4s. 7d. per man, the result would be to leave the share of the divisible heap received by the group of workers at each wage-level exactly the same as before, but redistributed in the form of wages plus family allowances. It would be in fact a strict scheme of horizontal redistribution according to family needs, leaving the slope of vertical distribution unchanged.

Obviously such a cut on wages would be felt keenly by the childless men, especially by those at the lower wage-levels. In other forms of social insurance—health, unemployment, old age—it has been recognized that schemes which demand a sacrifice, on the part of those who are not benefiting and perhaps will never benefit, for the sake of the general welfare, should receive at least a contribution from the community. When the scheme has specially concerned the wage-earner,

the employers have been called on for an additional contribution.

In this case it is clear that if a levy is made on the community as a whole, the case weakens for confining the scheme
to the wage-earning classes. The casual workers—whom it
would be difficult to bring into any occupational scheme—
the salaried workers, the small employers, and the rest of
the not-too-prosperous part of the community, might well
protest at being taxed to provide benefits which their own
children do not share.

But postponing for the moment our final summary of the
merits of occupational versus national provision, let us consider the cost of the latter. Here we are on safe ground in
taking present-day figures.

The total population of children under fourteen in Great
Britain may be estimated from the 1921 Census as roughly
11¼ million.[1] To provide for these at 6s. 1½d. per week
(i.e., 3s. 6d. plus 75 per cent. increase on pre-war cost) would cost
about £179 million per annum. In addition, another £13¾
million would be required to provide allowances for the
widowed mothers[2] of dependent children—their children
being of course included in the general scheme. Against this
may be set the saving of the sums spent in poor relief, free
meals and charities of all kinds.

The following additions would seem necessary to a reasonably adequate scheme:—

To raise the age of dependency to fifteen would add roughly
another million children.

To raise the scale by, say, 1s. 6d. per week per child as its
contribution towards rent, fuel, insurances, recreation and
domestic assistance for the mother of a large family, would
bring the cost roughly to £223 million or £243 million (according to the age of dependency).

These are vast sums. But the reader who has followed
our argument so far will not quail before them, for he will
not need reminding that they would not, if realized, represent
a new charge on the community, but an old concealed charge
made visible and compelled for the first time to yield full
value. Or, if they did involve an additional charge, it would

[1] i.e., Scotland, 1,343,452 (actual figures); England and Wales, 9,890,200
(estimated from county returns already published).

[2] See p. 87.

only be because, and to the extent that, the share of the divisible heap hitherto enjoyed by the children of the nation has been inadequate for their proper maintenance. Yet if, just because he realizes that this is so and that the deficiency is probably a large one, doubts do assail our reader as to whether, after all, the community can afford to spend so much, let him reassure himself by the contemplation of other large figures quoted in this volume. Let him consider the national expenditure on drink, tobacco and amusements and ask himself whether a nation which manages to foot a bill of well over £260 million[1] for only three of its little luxuries could not manage to set aside nearly as much to provide the elementary necessities of life for its entire child population. At least should such a scheme ever become " practical politics" and the eight million women voters have time to absorb these facts and figures and ponder them in their hearts, it will, I think, be hard to convince them that the argument "we cannot afford it" is a valid impediment.

(h) Conclusion

The reader should now be in a position to judge for himself as to the relative merits of direct provision for families through occupational pools or through State endowment.

To sum them up briefly : the advantages of the pool system are chiefly psychological, in the sense that they are concerned with the reaction to the scheme of those it affects. Because it can be adopted piecemeal and experimentally, it is more likely to commend itself, at least as a first step, to a conservative-minded, cautious nation. It will be easier to get it going because it is a smaller matter to convince a group of people, experienced in the difficulties of providing for families through the present wage-system and conscious of their own direct responsibility as employers or leaders of working-class opinion, than to convince a Parliament or a Government. The grading of allowances to suit the different standards of life and eugenic needs of different sections of the population, which is essential if the full advantages of direct provision are to be reaped, will come about much more easily and naturally through occupational pools than under a State system, though it is technically quite possible under the latter. For the same reason, the pool

---

[1] *See* above, p. 41. This is a conservative estimate of the net sum, after deducting taxation. The gross sum is over £500 million.

scheme is better suited to allay the more rational of the fears
discussed in Chapter VI—the fear of stimulating population
in the wrong places and the fear of diminishing the incentive
to industry—since it is plain that if either of these results did
happen, those who are responsible for the pool covering the
occupations adversely affected could check it by varying the
amount and conditions of the allowance.

On the other hand, the State system has many material
and a few psychological advantages. It would be a far more
complete treatment of the whole difficulty. It could be made
to cover, by a single Act of Parliament, all classes and occupations, including some which it will be very difficult, for
technical or psychological reasons or both, to bring under
occupational schemes. It could be more economically administered, since the State has already nearly all the necessary
machinery of administration—the post office, the educational
and public health services. It would rectify the very serious
anomaly by which the industries employing little adult male
labour are enabled to escape their fair share of what should
be a national burden by shifting it on to other trades. This
again could technically be done under the occupational
system, but it would practically be difficult to enforce it.

On the psychological side, the advantages of a State system
are that it implies a more complete act of restitution to the
family, by acknowledging that its claim on the nation rests
on its own value and not on the occupational services of the
father. For the same reason it would do more to raise the
status of motherhood. But the opportunist who values a
bird in the hand more than two in the bush, might perhaps
rather deem these two points a disadvantage, since they are
a direct challenge to the hidden Turk.

Lastly—and I leave it to the reader to determine whether
the point tells in favour of an occupational scheme or a State
system—under the former the question of whether family
allowances should constitute an addition to the existing wage
bill, or a redistribution, or a mixture of both, would be fought
out within the industry and decided according to its circumstances and the bargaining strength of the parties concerned ;
under a State system, the incidence of the cost on the various
classes of the community would depend in the first instance
on the Government which happened to be in power when the
system was introduced. What its ultimate reaction might

be on wages is a question I will not discuss, but will content myself with the surely safe generalization that, in the long run, the share which each class in the community secures for itself of the nation's wealth will depend, not on whether the share comes to it in the shape of profits only, or wages only, or profits and wages plus family allowances, but first, on the size of the divisible heap ; secondly, on the value of the contribution made by the class to the heap ; thirdly, on the skill with which it uses its economic and political bargaining power to secure the equivalent of its contribution.

As a security, however, against extravagant demands on the one hand and unfair attacks on wages on the other, the solution proposed by the New South Wales Labour Party might some day provide a satisfactory basis for a compromise between the two sections of opinion. At their Conference in 1921[1] they proposed

(a) The fixation of a basic wage for a man and wife, based on the stabilized cost of living.

(b) The maintenance of all children of the nation by a direct charge on the whole community by means of a graduated tax on all incomes.

Such a solution would imply a definite abandonment by Labour of the attempt " to eat their cake and have it " by drawing maintenance for their children from the nation and simultaneously including it in the wage bill. On the other hand it would prevent employers from using family allowances as an excuse for forcing the lower grades of workers below a reasonable standard of life.

All these questions of method and tactics lie in the future ; perhaps in a not so very remote future. The British public has yet to be converted to the need for direct provision and no propagandist who knows his countrymen and has measured the strength of some of the prejudices he has to combat, is likely to underrate the difficulty of his task. But facts are the best of all allies and the propagandist who looks out, like Sister Anne, from the lonely watch-tower of the mind, to see if from any direction help is coming, will find it easy to keep a stout heart. There are several figures in the distance that may bring the needed reinforcements. There is Foreign Competition, which may force the British manufacturer to realize that, if the high standard of life of the British workman does handicap him, there is no need to double the handicap

[1] *See The Next Step*, p. 11.

by continuing the present wasteful method of satisfying this standard.[1]   There is the Falling Birth-Rate, which has not yet fallen low enough to satisfy Mr. Keynes, but is falling with a steadiness and a perversity of misdirection which alarm most people and may startle them, as it has done the French, into a new respect for the family.   There is Dr. Marie Stopes, as hard to silence as a mosquito, shrilling out her message and plunging her barbed truth into the minds of many hitherto docile matrons.   There is the Woman's Vote, that new force, not quite certain what it wants, but strong enough to bend the politicians to its will, when it knows it.   Finally, there are the Disinherited themselves—millions of them—a little Holy Family enshrined in every man's heart, and likely to prove itself in the long run, as its prototype has been in history, too much for the Turk.

[1] For example, at the time of writing (October 1923), the papers are full of gloomy reports from the textile industries; their difficulties being attributed by the British manufacturers to the competition of France, especially of Roubaix-Tourcoing, with its lower cost of production.   It will be remembered that this is the district where the system of family allowances is most widely adopted and fully developed.

CHAPTER VIII

SUPPLEMENTARY

DEVELOPMENTS AT HOME AND ABROAD
1924-1927

Since this book was first published in March 1924, the movement it records has undergone considerable developments.

In Great Britain, the progress made has been mainly one of opinion, which has not yet taken shape in concrete achievement. Three years ago, the subject in this country was practically unknown and undiscussed outside two groups, viz., the score or so of men and women, chiefly professed students of economics or sociology, who formed the Family Endowment Council (*see* p. 132, Notes 1, 2), and secondly, the women belonging to the vanguard of the feminist movement. Naturally enough, it is still within these two sections of opinion—economists and feminists—that interest is keenest, but the subject is rapidly working its way to the front as an accepted topic of discussion among those interested in social reform, whatever their political colour.

Among economists, Sir William Beveridge has given practical evidence of his belief in family allowances by securing the adoption of the system for the teaching staff of the London School of Economics of which he is Director. In the spring of 1926 it was decided, we believe with the consent of all concerned, that certain funds available for additional emoluments should be used not in raising salaries, but in supplementing them by substantial allowances for children throughout the whole period of their education up to leaving the University. It is significant that this step should have been taken by the only teaching body in this country devoted entirely to the study of economics and sociology. This, however, is not the first working scheme in this country. It was anticipated nearly a century ago by the system of children's allowances still existent in the Methodist Connexion. The present scale provides at least £8 per annum from birth for each child of a minister, supplemented by £12 educational allowance. The interest taken in the subject at Cambridge is shown by the fact that questions upon it figured in both Parts of the Economic Tripos and in the May examinations of 1924.

Among women's organizations, the National Union for Equal Citizenship and the International Women's Suffrage Alliance (representing feminist opinion in practically all civilized countries in the world) have included Family Allowances among the reforms for which they work. The National Council of Women here has signified adhesion to the principle. The Liberal Women's Federation has appointed a committee of investigation which has produced a favourable report. The Women's Co-operative Guild, which attracts to itself the cream of the married working women, and the Women's Unionist Organization are collectively studying the subject.

Within the political parties, the Independent Labour Party is the first to have placed Family Endowment upon its programme. At its annual Conference in April 1926, a scheme was brought forward prepared by a committee including Mr. H. N. Brailsford and Mr. J. A. Hobson. It proposed a legal minimum wage supplemented by family allowances at the rate of 5s. for each child up to 14, the benefits to be limited to those covered by the National Health Insurance Act, or of equivalent economic status, the funds to be provided by taxation of the wealthy. This proposal was adopted by the I.L.P. and laid on its behalf before the Annual Conference of the Labour Party. This proposal, after a perfunctory discussion, was referred to a committee for consideration. The able group of young Liberals connected with the Summer School Movement have paid some attention to the subject, which was included among several recommended to the Party for study guided by questionnaires.

The most significant symptom of the growth of favourable opinion in this country has, however, been the recommendation contained in the Report of the Royal Commission on the Coal Industry. The Commission devoted part of the Chapter on wages to the subject of family allowances. They point out that

"Logically a minimum wage based in any way on a reasoned estimate of requirements for any given standard of frugal comfort, involves and should be accompanied by a system of family allowances."

The Report quoted the evidence submitted by the Family Endowment Society showing that

" family allowances are practically universal throughout the mining industry of those countries which compete most actively with our own, including Germany, France, Belgium, Holland, Austria, Czechoslovakia and Poland. Mr. Frank Hodges, coming before us as General Secretary of the International Miners' Federation, gave similar evidence, both as to the practically universal character of the system in the mining industry on the Continent, and as to the growing disposition of the miners, who had had experience of it, to approve it."

The section concludes with the following recommendation :

" Fifth, irrespective of the level of wages, we regard the introduction of a system of children's allowances—to be paid for out of a single pool, either for the whole industry or for each district that adopts it—as one of the most valuable measures that can be adopted for adding to the well-being and contentment of the mining population. If the total sum available for workers' remuneration can be kept at the present level, the allocation of a small part of this to children's allowances will raise materially the general level of comfort; if the full remuneration cannot be maintained the harmful effects of any reasonable reduction can be largely mitigated."

Unfortunately this recommendation, with the rest of the Commission's Report, has been submerged in the welter of the seven months' dispute. The Government's offer to appoint a Committee to consider the recommendations relating to family allowances and profit-sharing was ignored by both miners and owners, and in view of the embittered relation between them, no further action seems likely at present. An active propaganda carried on by the Family Endowment Society during the dispute has, however, resulted in awakening a new interest in the subject among many of the leading miners in the districts reached, and that may bear fruit in the future.

To set against this growth of favourable opinion, it has become clear that there are a few people irreconcilably opposed to our proposed reform, and a large number who vaguely dislike it ; the majority in all classes as yet know nothing of it or too little to have formed any judgment.

The declared opponents have pursued precisely the course indicated on page 31. They have made no attempt to deny or refute the facts and figures which show the impossibility of securing a reasonable standard of comfort among the workers without the aid of family allowances. They have simply ignored these facts and contented themselves with urging certain objections. Even these objections are precisely those anticipated and discussed in Chapter VI. The past three years have not added a single weapon to the armoury of our opponents, except the fact that in certain European countries where family allowances were adopted as a post-war measure on a partial and temporary basis, without the security of equalization funds, the system has wholly or partly faded away.

Remarkable testimony as to this lack of reasoned opposition has been given by Mr. Lloyd Roberts, who spent three weeks studying the family allowance system on behalf of the Chemical Employers' Federation in France, Belgium and Germany. He records that he had received specific instructions to search for objections, but so far as the principle was concerned, had entirely failed to find any. The sole opponent met with in the course of his tour was the Director of the German Federation of Employers. But his " was a personal opinion, not based on any difficulties experienced in connection with the scheme nor supported by any evidence of harmful results from its operation."

Three reforms which became law during 1925 have substantially alleviated, without completely removing, the harsh conditions described in pages 69-89 as affecting unhappy wives, widows, and orphans. The Guardianship and Custody of Infants Act has abolished the monstrous legal fiction that the husband has " a primary right to the sole control of his children " (p. 73). It lays down the principle that " it is expedient that equality between the sexes should obtain with regard to the guardianship of infants and the rights and responsibilities conferred thereby" and requires the Court to observe this principle in all cases brought before it. The Separation and Maintenance (Married Women) Act removes some of the worst impediments which have prevented an ill-treated wife from obtaining a separation, especially by permitting her to apply for and obtain the order before she has actually left her husband. It is, however, a meagre little Act, which still leaves several serious hardships unremoved. The Widows', Orphans', and Old Age Contributory Pensions Act makes provision for the great majority of working-class widows and orphans on the modest scale of 10s. for the widow, 5s. for the first child, and 3s. for each subsequent child under 14 (or 16 if in full-time school attendance). The contributory basis of this Act has doubtless many practical advantages, especially at a time when the finances of the nation are straitened. But in view of the proved inadequacy of wages in most occupations to meet the actual existing needs of families with young children (see pp. 17-23), or of self-dependent women earners, there is something anomalous in requiring men and women to provide out of their wages simultaneously for the present and future needs of themselves and their dependents.

All these three Acts were the result of constructive suggestion and persistent agitation by women's organizations. They are an evidence of the growing desire of women to use their new instrument of the vote to remould those parts of the social structure which press heavily on their own lives.

The figures showing child dependency in the wage-earning classes given in Chapter II, pages 12-15, were estimates based on Dr. Bowley's material. The 1921 Census results—not then available—now furnish us with actual figures applying to the whole population of England and Wales and also for certain typical occupations which have been separately reckoned :—

	Of men over 20 years of age.					
	General Popula-tion	Agri-cultural Workers	Chemical Workers	Miners	Railway Workers	Teachers
Single . .	26·6	34·7	19·3	25·4	32·1	25·7
Married or widow-ers with no child-ren or children " not stated "	34	30·3	30·2	23	27·6	37
Married or widow-ers with one child	16	12·6	18·1	17	17·2	19·6
With 2 children	10·5	8·6	13·4	13	11·1	11
,, 3 ,,	6·2	5·7	8·6	9	6·1	4·2
,, 4 or more	6·7	8·1	10·4	12·6	5·9	2·3
Children per man	·88	·9	1·2	1·3	·85	·6
Percentage of child-ren in families of 4 or more .	37%	45%	41·2%	46·7%	32·69%	16·7%

" Children " denotes those under 16 years of age, including step-children.

It will be noted that the table on page 13 estimated children *under 14* ; this table shows children *under 16*. It is not possible to put both tables on the same basis. But the 1921 Census shows the total number of men of and over 20 in England and Wales to have been 11,053,842, and the children under 14, residing in households with male heads, to have been 8,553,069, or about 77 children per 100 men. The Census officials consider that the number of children returned in the dependency tables was probably too low by 4 to 5 per cent. But allowing for this and for the fact that the proportion of children in the wage-

earning classes is slightly higher than that of the whole population, it is clear that my former estimate of 119 children per
100 wage-earning men is too high.   For the occupations
separately ascertained the Census figures are :—

Per 100	agricultural labourers	.	.	.	.	.	80	children.
„ „	workers in manufacturing chemical industry		.	.	106	„
„ „	coal miners	.	.	.	.	.	.	110	„
„ „	railway workers	.	.	.	.	.	.	83	„
„ „	teachers	.	.	.	.	.	.	59	„

It appears, therefore, that the failure to fit the facts of a
wage based on the " normal family " of five persons would
be even greater than before estimated.

We saw that, before the War, the greatest cause of " primary"
poverty in the households surveyed by Mr. Rowntree and
Dr. Bowley was the inadequacy of the wage to meet the
needs of the number actually dependent on it.   Dr. Bowley
now points[1] out that owing to the fall in the birth-rate, coupled
with the rise in wages of unskilled labour, the proportion
of households in poverty from this cause has considerably
diminished.   It should, however, be remembered that the
income-level he adopts as exempting from poverty is one
postulating the inhumanly austere life described on pages 17-18.

But if in this respect the falling birth-rate may be held to
have weakened the case for family allowances by mitigating
one of the evils of the present system, yet in another it has
strengthened it by reducing the risk of over-population.   Dr.
Bowley sums up the statistical position as follows :—

" To summarize ; at most there will be 180,000 additional applicants for work
(male and female) annually from 1921-1931, unless the age of retirement is raised,
or the relative number of women occupied is increased, and this is at present being
reduced to about 120,000 by emigration.   From 1931-1941 the most to be expected
is 47,000, which will also be reduced by emigration.   So far from there being an
excessive working population, the annual rate of growth after 1931 will be only
0·2 per cent.   The growth after 1941 depends on the birthrate after 1926, as to
which no judgment can be formed."[2]

Since this was written the birth-rate has continued to decline.

The passionate interest of working women in the subject
of birth-control (see p. 66) has become more articulate and
has manifested itself for example in the remarkable uprising
of the Labour women which forced the Executive of the Party
at its Annual Conference of 1926 to take back their resolve
to shelve the question.   The motives which have led to the
reaction against large families are partly, but only partly,

[1] *Has Poverty Diminished ?* P. S. King & Son, 10s. 6d., 1926.
[2] *Is Unemployment Inevitable ?* Macmillan & Co., 1924, 8s. 6d.

economic[1] and would be affected but certainly not wholly removed by family allowances.

The literature dealing with our subject has been enriched during the three years by four valuable books, as well as by a steady flow of pamphlets and articles issued by the Family Endowment Society. The most recent of these books, by Mr. H. R. Vibart,[2] contains as well as an interesting and impartial general statement of the case, a much fuller treatment of the foreign system, especially French and Belgian, than I have had space for here. The same may be said of the Report issued by the International Labour Office,[3] of which a 1927 edition is promised. Professor Paul Douglas's book[4] covering much the same ground contributes a remarkable new fact, viz., his demonstration that even in the wealthy U.S.A., where every wage-earner is popularly supposed to own a Ford car and to breakfast on beefsteak, the payment of wages on a " normal family " basis would be practically impossible. His figures are briefly as follows :—

He calculates the cost of man, wife and 3 children at the American standard of working-class comfort at \$1,700 a year (equivalent roughly to £410). He reckons that if every man earned this sum and every woman, boy and girl enough for self-dependence, the cost would swallow up 82 per cent. of the entire income of the U.S.A. The remaining 18 per cent. would be insufficient to pay other necessary charges, including wages and salaries above the minimum, rent, interest, savings for industrial development, cost of government, even if all these were cut down to the minimum. He further calculates that the proposed basis would result in providing for forty-five million fictitious wives and children. These figures should be compared with those corresponding for Great Britain (pp. 13-16 and 23-29) and Australia (pp. 133-147). They may perhaps suggest that standards of living are relative, and that whatever the standard thought reasonable by the public opinion of a given community, there will always tend to be a sense of grievance so long as men during their prime, when their families are dependent on them, are in a markedly inferior economic position to that enjoyed by their juniors and seniors without such responsibilities.

[1] See Chap. III (d) and VI (a).
[2] *Family Allowances in Practice* (P. S. King & Son, 10s. 6d.) 1926.
[3] *Family Allowances* (I.L.O.), 1924.
[4] *Wages and the Family* Chicago, (University Press, 15s.) 1925.

Mr. Cohen's book, on a smaller scale than the other three,[1] is devoted to an exposition of the method of providing for family allowances through the system of compulsory contributory insurance. This forms a valuable alternative to the two methods discussed earlier in this book, viz., State Endowment paid for wholly by taxation, or a voluntary system paid for by employers through *Caisses* or equalization funds. It divides the cost of the allowances between the three parties who are in fact concerned in the well-being of children—the State, of which they are future citizens; industry, of which they are the future workers; and actual and potential parents. The burden upon the Exchequer would in the first instance be much lighter than in an all-State scheme and could be subsequently increased or diminished as after experience of the system public opinion might demand. By using, with the necessary extensions, the already existing and well-understood machinery of unemployment insurance, the system could be made to cover the whole wage-earning population with a minimum of administrative expense, delay and fuss. We should avoid the danger, which may occur under the Equalization Fund system, of creating vested interests in the shape of piecemeal schemes which may fail to cover the whole country, yet (as in the case of the Approved Societies under Health Insurance) prove an obstacle in the way of a national scheme. Those who prefer one of the alternative methods usually close their eyes to the fact that, on the one hand, the process of covering the whole country with voluntary schemes is likely to prove infinitely slow; on the other, it is most unlikely that any Chancellor of the Exchequer of any political party will be bold enough to plump the whole cost of an all-State scheme on to the Exchequer at once, unless the scheme is so meagre that its results may discredit the principle.

At the same time it may be conceded that the insurance method brings difficulties of its own. As outlined by Mr. Cohen, it covers neither " workers on own account," such as hawkers, crofters, lawyers, doctors, nor the higher salaried workers. This difficulty could be met by supplementary schemes, adapted to the needs of each group and entitled to the same measure of State aid as the insurance scheme. A more serious objection is that contributory insurance is already felt as a burden by all three parties and the recent

[1] *Family Income Insurance, by* J. L. Cohen (P. S. King & Son, 1s.,) 1926.

addition made by the Widows', Orphans', and Old Age Pensions Act makes it difficult to suggest a further addition, at least for some years to come. But in any case it will be some years before public opinion will be ripe for Family Income Insurance. Every kind of new taxation or compulsory contribution excites a considerable amount of grumbling among those whose pockets are affected. But this is not incompatible with a deep-lying appreciation of the benefits insured. There is evidence of this in the Report of the recent Royal Commission on National Health Insurance, which notes that in spite of the fierce opposition against the scheme at its inception, the Commission received " very little evidence directed against the scheme as a whole, nor have we reason to think that there exists any considerable body of opinion adverse to the principle of National Health Insurance". On the other hand, they had " received from many different quarters a large volume of evidence in its favour".[1]

Further, the benefits of Family Income Insurance would be enjoyed by a far larger proportion of the population for much longer consecutive periods than any of the existing forms of social insurance. It would quickly be realized— or so one may reasonably anticipate—that these benefits extending through the years of family dependency are well worth the sacrifice they involve during the preceding and following years of comparative affluence.

Lastly, it is urged that the insurance method would involve a rigid uniformity and leave no room for the freedom to experiment, the adjusting of contributions and benefits to suit the varying capacity to pay and standard of comfort, which mark the continental voluntary system. There is much truth in this and it is, perhaps, the most serious objection to any form of State scheme likely to be adopted in this country. But first, there will be room left for experiment in the supplementary schemes for the workers not covered by the insurance scheme. Secondly, even as regards the latter it should be remembered that it is only British custom that makes a flat rate of contribution and benefits seem an inevitable part of State insurance. In some other existing European schemes, contributions and benefits do vary with wages, and hence with the standard of life of the contributors. Thirdly, there is nothing to prevent our studying the experiments of

[1] Chap. III, Cmd. 2596. 6s.6d. 1926.

other countries and thus reaping some of the advantages, while leaving to others the disadvantages, of a voluntary system.

The history of the movement in other countries during the past three years may be briefly recorded.

The IRISH FREE STATE has decided to introduce marriage and children's allowances into the Civil Service, for the majority of those employed excepting post-office officials. The scheme, which introduces equal pay for men and women, applies to new entrants only, and as marriage is not recognized until the age of 25, the allowances will not be payable for some time. The scale is not yet definitely fixed. It is to cover children under 16, or 21 if invalids or continuing their education.

In AUSTRALIA, the subject of child endowment has occupied an increasingly prominent place in the election promises of politicians and in party conferences, but nothing substantial has yet resulted. The two Bills introduced into the Parliament of New South Wales by successive Governments in 1919 and 1921 (see pp. 148-152) found no successors until 1925, when a Bill brought forward in the Parliament of Queensland was abandoned owing to change of Government. In the same year an equally abortive measure was introduced in South Australia, but abandoned owing to the insistence of the railway workers on an increase in the basic wage rate which absorbed all the surplus revenue. Mr. Bruce, the Premier of the Australian Commonwealth, announced on taking office that:—

" The question of child endowment is one of vital importance. It could not, under the constitution, be dealt with by the Commonwealth alone, nor can it be dealt with by the States without dislocating the basis of inter-State trade. It can only be dealt with nationally. It is proposed to refer the question to the Commonwealth and State Arbitration judges, with a view to their recommendations being considered at a Conference of Commonwealth and State Governments."

In New South Wales, the State Industrial Commission in December 1926, refused to recommend a rise in the existing basic wage for men of four guineas, pointing out that the wage, if adequate to the needs of a family of five, would require to be 106s. weekly, and that a wage so based involved provision for 973,000 non-existent children, while 288,000 children belonging to larger families would remain unprovided for. The actual number of dependent children of male wage-earners was only 452,000. In February 1927, the Government introduced a Child Endowment Bill, under which 5s. weekly would be paid for each child under 14 of an employee whose family income, including the allowance, did not exceed £364 annually, the cost to be met by employers' contributions at the rate of 6 per cent. of the wage bill, if under Federal awards, or 6½ per cent., if under State awards.

In NEW ZEALAND, after two stillborn Bills fathered by the Labour Party, the Conservative Government in the summer of 1926 introduced and passed into law rapidly and with very little opposition a Family Allowance Act. This confers a State allowance of 2s. for each child from the third to the ninth of a family, from birth to 15 years old (or over if incapable of earning), provided that the family income from all sources, including the allowances, does not exceed £4. The allowances are payable to the mother. As the basic wage for industries covered by Arbitration Courts Awards is £4, assumed to meet the needs of a four-member family, this measure is plainly of the nature of statutory poor relief. The cost is estimated at about £250,000 a year.

In FRANCE the progress has been steady and apparently without drawback. It may be measured by the following figures:—

	June, 1923.	May, 1926.
Caisses	120	195
„ in agriculture	3	27
Firms covered by *Caisses*	7,600	14,000
Workers covered by *Caisses* . . .	880,000	1,300,000
Workers covered including firms not belonging to a *Caisse,* railways, mines, State and Municipal employees . .	2,500,000	3,600,000
Year's expenditure on family allowances .	763 million frs.	1,152 million frs.

Owing to the fluctuating value of money and the general tendency to increase the scale of allowances in real as well as nominal value, figures showing the amounts paid have a very temporary validity. The following table shows the *average* of the rates paid by 30 of the principal *Caisses* in May 1926, with their purchasing power at about the same date expressed in English money. The calculation has been worked out by Mr. J. H. Richardson, of the International Labour Office, on the basis of the cost of a basket of food commodities in London and Paris at the date in question. The commodities chosen were those principally used in workers' households, the quantity of each being based on the average consumption of British and French workers.

	Amount of Allowances.		Approximate British Equivalent based on rates of exchange.		Approximate British Equivalent based on relative purchasing power.	
	francs.		s.	d.	s.	d.
1 child . .	25		3	6	5	0
2 children .	63		8	6	12	6
3 ,, .	109		15	0	22	0
4 ,, .	173		24	0	34	6
5 ,, .	240		33	0	48	0
6 ,, .	318		44	0	63	6

These figures illustrate the unsoundness of the common practice of comparing the cost of living, standard of life, etc., in France and England by simply translating figures relating to one country into their exchange value in the other.

It should be noted that the rates paid by the railways, mines, State and municipal authorities are higher than in any *Caisse* except Roubaix-Tourcoing.

Trade Union opinion in France has become steadily more cordial towards the principle of family allowances, while maintaining its objection to the exclusive control by employers. In March 1924, a letter was sent to a number of the largest bodies by the Family Endowment Society, inviting their opinion on the system, especially with regard to its effect on the industrial position of married and single workers, on the Trade Union movement, on family life, and on the birth-rate. Not one of the replies expressed any hostility or recorded any evil results of any kind, although most expressed the usual opinion in favour of collective control. The following extracts (translations) from these letters and from resolutions recently passed are representative:—

The Secretary of the General Federation of Workers (*Confédération Générale du Travail*) writes:—

"The allowances enable a fairer distribution of the produce of labour and a higher standard of life for the children. They have no real effect on the birth-rate. We could not maintain that the allowances have not reacted on the bachelor's wage. But in actual practice an organism which aims at equity and solidarity justifies certain sacrifices. . . . Trade Union solidarity has not been impaired by the system . . . We in France regard the allowances as purely and simply a redistribution on sounder and more humane lines of the wage bill. The employers have no right to arrogate to themselves the moral credit of a sound social institution."

In announcing the promulgation of the Decrees making family allowances compulsory in Government contracts, the officials of the C.G. de T. declared: "Now that the Decree has been issued, employers will not be able to withhold family allowances on any pretext; the workers' right to them has been admitted, and the trade unions will see that it is respected."

The Secretary of the Federation of Catholic Trade Unions writes:—

" The system of pools avoids preferential employment of single men or reduction of their wages." They urge that the extension of the system should find a place in the election programme receiving their support.

The National Conference of the C.G.T.U. (the Federation of Communist Unions) in 1926 stated that:—

" The majority of the proletariat who benefit from the allowances believe the system to be a good one. We cannot run our heads against this conception, and in approving the principle of family allowances by means of social insurance urge that employers' contributions should be assessed on profits."

Other professional bodies who have approved the principle at their annual Congress or elsewhere include the Federations of Post Office Workers, Agricultural trade unions, the Union of Railway Workers, the Federation of Architects of Northern France. The National Association of Lawyers is drafting an insurance scheme for their own members which includes a family allowance system.

There are beginning to be some slight indications that family allowances, coupled with a vigorous propaganda in favour of large families, are tending to check the decline in the birth-rate. This is reported to have increased among workers covered by the *Caisses* from 36·9 in 1921 to 39·2 per 1,000 workers in 1925. The Michelin Tyre Co., with a specially high scale of allowances, claims a correspondingly high birth-rate. But the great influx of Italian workers into France and the possibility that fathers of families gravitate to firms with family allowance schemes make figures of this kind somewhat unreliable.

In BELGIUM progress has also been steady. The figures for 1926 show 15 *Caisses*, covering 800 firms and 224,173 workers. Including the mines and some other large-scale undertakings which pay allowances directly, including also the State and municipal employees, the total number of workers covered by family allowance schemes is estimated at 630,000. Amounts average 15 francs per month for one child and are usually on an ascending scale for subsequent children.

The opinion of the Trade Unions has become definitely in favour of the principle, but demands collective control. For example:—

The Federation of Belgian Christian Trade Unions writes:—

" The existing system is not satisfactory, but we do not want a State system. We consider that contributions should be levied on the produce of industry, and paid into a National Industrial Pool, administered by a Joint Committee, and subsidized by the State. The Trade Unions can resist any reduction of the single man's wage that might result from the system. Their solidarity has not been impaired by the allowances. A greater stability of employment is reported, but statistics are lacking."

The General Council of the Belgian Socialist Party pronounced in favour of the principle at their Congress in 1923, but hold that the system should be collective.

The Belgian Miners' Federation endorse the principle, and their Secretary writes in 1924:—

" Should you ask whether the allowances have a favourable influence on the private life of the worker, I find the proof in the fact that they are everywhere accepted, and more important still, being paid direct to the mother, they are a valuable aid towards balancing the household budget ; hence less anxiety and as a result a more joyous family life."

In 1925 he writes:—

" The allowances have had no effect on the basic wage. Neither have they in any way affected Trade Union solidarity. On the contrary they have actually to some extent furthered Trade Union influence."

The 1925 Report of the British Department of Overseas Trade says:—

"It is almost generally admitted now that the family bonus system is of real economic value and that by improving the present and future conditions of the workers it is capable of exerting a direct and beneficial influence on the prosperity of the country. Another feature in the economic strength of Belgium is the absence of strikes and the spirit of understanding and common sense which characterizes the settlement of the wages questions which have inevitably arisen. The comprehension of the fact that the interests of employers and employed are ultimately common is being fostered by the system of family allowances which has within two years of its inception made extraordinary progress."

In GERMANY, the system during the past two years has tended to decline. A table giving the percentage of collective agreements which include family allowances from 1922 to 1925, shows in mining agreements a decline from 59·1 to 40·6; in the chemical industry from 83·9 to 41·7; and in the paper industry 72·1 to 29·7.

Competent German authorities attribute this to two causes. The chief of these is the failure to develop the device of equalization funds, which have never exceeded eleven, now fewer. During the increasing unemployment of 1924-1926, the married workers, lacking this safeguard, have to some extent been actually prejudiced in their search for employment, and the fear of this has outstripped the reality. Secondly, the custom of treating family allowances as an integral part of wages instead of as a separate service, has aroused the jealousy of the single men. Hence the system has become unpopular both with married and unmarried, and employers in search of an economy have found it easier to discontinue allowances than to lower wages.

In HOLLAND, there has been little change in the position. Family allowances are still paid in the public services and there are a few equalization funds in certain industries, but the allowances are on a small scale.

In most other European countries the system, when introduced, was regarded as a temporary post-war measure and has to a great extent disappeared. There are, however, signs of revived interest in the subject, especially among public officials, economists, and feminists.

In AUSTRIA, the allowances, though compulsory since 1922, were not adjusted to variations in the cost of living and became of so little value that the expiry of the law in March, 1926 passed almost unnoticed.

In CZECHO-SLOVAKIA, the custom of recognizing family needs by payments in kind, clothing and housing, is still fairly common but money payments have mostly lapsed.

In THE FOUR SCANDINAVIAN COUNTRIES, the system—never widespread—has disappeared, except to a very limited extent in the public services, banks, etc.

In POLAND, allowances are still paid in the public services, the mining industry, some branches of the sugar and metal industries and in agriculture.   Elsewhere they have been discontinued in spite of protests from the workers.

In SWITZERLAND, children's allowances are paid to the employees of the Federal Government, the Lausanne tramways, the Église Libre.   There are a few scattered schemes in industry, including an equalization fund among Bern watch-makers.

In PALESTINE, family allowance schemes have been adopted by the General Federation of Jewish Labour, all Zionist Institutions, and the township of Tel Aviv.

INDEXES

Index to 'Eleanor Rathbone: Spokeswoman for a Movement'

Note references are to the numbers of the endnotes themselves, to be found between pages 97 and 120.

Jarrow march, 63, n.188
Jewish refugees, 11, n.198

Labour Party, 11, 56, 66, 67, 72-3, 93,
    n.203, n.208
Land, Hilary, 92, n.161, ns.301-2, n.311
Last, Nella, n.276
Lewis, Jane, n.301
Liberal Party National Conference (1979),
    13
Liverpool Women's Industrial Council, 10,
    48
London Women's Parliament, 77-8, 82, 83
Luxemburg, Rosa, 29, n.68

marriage, 25, 64-5, ns.54-5
Married Women's Association, 74-6, n.239
Married Women's Property Act (1882), 17
maternal mortality rate, 35, n.87
maternity benefit, 35, 38
Maternity and Child Welfare Act (1919), 58
Matrimonial Causes Act (1923), 58
miners' strikes, 58, 60, n.182
Miners' Union, 67, 70-1, n.182
mother and baby centres, 35, 36
motherhood endowment, *see* endowment
    of motherhood

National Health Service, 69, 86, 87, n.239,
    n.279, n.283, n.287
National Health Service Act (1946), 86
National Insurance, 76, 82, 86, 88, n.12
National Insurance Act (1911), 35
National Insurance Act (1946), 68, 69, 82,
    86
National Union of Societies for Equal
    Citizenship, 49, 52, 56, 59
National Union of Women's Suffrage
    Societies, 9, 49
National Union of Women Workers, 47,
    n.92, n.149
New Feminists, 51, 52, 56, 67, n.162
Nightingale, Florence, 16

Pankhurst, Emmeline, 18, 20
Pankhurst, Sylvia, 28, 36, 50, 60, 68
Poor Law, 18-20
Poor Law Guardians, 18, 19, 20, n.32
professions for women, 16-17, 37, 56, 67

rape in marriage, 32
Rathbone Eleanor, 9-12, 15-18, 48-57
    passim, 70-74 *passim*, 95-6 *passim*; on
    Family Allowance Bill/Act (1945), 89-
    91 *passim*, 95-6; on family endowment,
    40, 55, 56, 67-8; financial independence
    of, 11, n.204; on housing, 59-60; on
    immigration, 11, 96, n.1; maiden speech
    to Commons, 59-60; refugee work,
    n.198; support for Spanish Republicans,
    64, n.198; view of eugenists, 30, 32,

n.163; wartime administrator, 48-9; and
    widows, 20-1
rent strikes, 59, 60
*Report on the Conditions of Widows under
    the Poor Law in Liverpool*, 10, 20, 23
Rowbotham, Sheila, n.163, n.205
Royden, Maude, 50-1
Russell, Dora, 57, 58

Separation Allowances, 44-8 *passim*, 78,
    80-2, 84, n.92, ns.129-30, n.133, n.143
Sex Disqualification Removal Act (1919),
    58
sexual abstinence, 26-7
single mothers, 12, 46, 55, 89, n.139
Spender, Humphrey, 62-3, n.188
Stephens, Jessie, 47-8, n.147
Stocks, Mary, n.167
Stopes, Marie, 26, 65
strikes, 25, 26-9 *passim*, 47, 58-60, n.182;
    see also Children's Strike, General Strike,
    miners' strikes
suffragette movement, 9-10, 15, 18, 28, 47-
    50 *passim*, 66, n.26, n.28, n.32, ns.145-7
Summary Jurisdiction (Separation and
    Maintenance) Act (1925), 58
Summerskill, Dr. Edith, 75, 76, 82, 90
Supplementary Benefit, n.283

tax credit scheme, 93-5, n.304
Third World, women in, 11, 13-14, 32, 54,
    n.40, n.76, n.166
trade unions, 36, 45-7, 67, 72-3, 83, 93,
    n.92, n.108, n.276; *see also* Miners'
    Union
Trades Union Congress, 72-3, 83, 93, n.203
    n.208, n.266

unemployment, 14, 18-19, 60-2 *passim*,
    83-5
Unemployment Act (1921), 61
unemployment benefit, 61-2, 78, 84, 86,
    88-9, n.105, n.184, ns.269-70
Unemployment Insurance Statutory
    Committee, 84
United Nations, 12, 13-14, n.17
United States, 13, 21, n.40, n.72

wages, 52-3, 62, 81, 84, 93, n.9, n.82,
    ns.98-9, n.160, n.259, n.311; for
    mothers, 41-4, 52, 53, n.82; *see also*
    Wages for Housework Campaign,
    endowment of motherhood
Wages for Housework Campaign, 12, 89,
    n.88, n.107, n.115, n.287
Webb, Beatrice, 17
Webb, Sidney, 29
Widows, Orphans and Old Age Contributory
    Pensions Act (1925), 58
widows, State payments to, 10, 18, 20
Wilkinson, Ellen, 65-6

Index to

THE DISINHERITED FAMILY

This index, with slight modifications, is taken from the edition of 1949.

separation allowances, Army, 172-3
Separation and Maintenance (Married Women) Act, 383
separation orders, 201 ff.
settlements, marriage, 325
sex antagonism, industrial, causes, 229
sex prejudice, unconscious, 155
Shaftesbury, Lord, 131
short time, 161
slope of distribution, 153-4
Smith, Adam, 128, 133, 134, 315
Smith, Ellen, 253
South Australia, 389
Spain, 309
Speenhamland system, 136
spending habits, youthful, 160
Stamp, Sir Josiah [Lord], 150 ff.
standard of living, 143-4, 236
Stevenson, Dr., 314, 316
Stocks, Mrs. J.L., 322
Stopes, Dr. Marie, 379
Storey, Mr., 275-6
Stuart, Frank D., 253
subsistence level, and wages, 133-4
Substitution of Women, Home Office pamphlet, 224, 225
substitution of women's for men's labour, difficulties, 224
surplus, bachelor's, 160, 165
surplus, wage, advantages of, 164
Sweden, 309; married person's property, 205-6
Switzerland, 308, 394

Tawney, R.H., 187
Taylor, John, 225
Taylor, W. Cooke, 130
teachers, and family allowances, 348
Teachers, National Union of, 239-40
teaching, women in, 230, 232; and equal pay, 239 ff.
time-table, housewife's, 182-3
tobacco, expenditure on, 166-7
Trade Boards, 248
trade unions, French, and child allowances, 295, 299, 391-2; and unemployment insurance, 351; and women's labour, 219-20, 221-3, 231

training of women workers, 220
Tynan, Miss, 233

unemployment insurance, 209, 351
unemployment relief, 176
uniform wage concept, 137 ff.
university women, and marriage, 246
unmarried mothers, allowances to, 289
unpaid service, undervaluation of, 252; waste of, 188

value of women's labour, estimation of, 249
Vandeputte, M., 297
Vibart, H.R., 386

wage-bill, estimated, of manual workers, 146
wage-earners, number of, 141
wage-earning capacity, full, age of attainment, 158
wage fixing, in Australia, 261-2
wages and the family, relation of, 132-3
war-time conditions, working class and, 173
wartime, employment of women in, 222
Webb, S. & B., 141, 145, 165, 187, 219-20, 251, 258, 318, 322, 351, 372
Wells, H.G., 191, 207, 257
widows, 207 ff.; number of, 212; pensions, 209, 213, 309, 383
Widows', Orphans' and Old Age Contributory Pensions Act, 383
wife, legal rights and disabilities, 199 ff.
wives, amount given by husbands to, 167-8
Women in Industry, Committee on (1918), 223, 231-3, 259
women workers, selection methods, 224
Women's Co-operative Guild, 381
Women's Emancipation Bill (1919), 231
Women's Employment Committee (1916), 222, 226
women's labour, difficulties in introduction of, 221
Women's Unionist Organization, 381
working mothers, family allowances and, 365

young workers, slackness of, 161
Yule, J.G. Udny, 316